RETHINKING SCRIPTURE

RETHINKING SCRIPTURE

ESSAYS FROM A COMPARATIVE PERSPECTIVE

Miriam Levering
Editor

STATE UNIVERSITY OF NEW YORK PRESS

Published by
State University of New York Press, Albany

Printed in the United States of America

For information, address State University of New York Press, State University Plaza, Albany, N.Y., 12246

Library of Congress Cataloging-in-Publication Data

Rethinking scripture.
Includes index.
Contents: Introduction / Miriam Levering — The study of religion and the study of the Bible / Wilfred Cantwell Smith — Scripture as form and concept / Wilfred Cantwell Smith — [etc.].
1. Sacred books—History and criticism
I. Levering, Miriam, 1945-
BL71.R48 1989 291.8'2 87-9919
ISBN 0-88706-613-5
ISBN 0-88706-614-3 (pbk.)

10 9 8 7 6 5 4 3 2 1

To Wilfred Cantwell Smith,
our teacher and example;
and to the memory of
Kendall A. Folkert,
colleague and pioneer.

Contents

Acknowledgments

We are grateful to the editors of the *Journal of the American Academy of Religion* for permission to republish "The Study of Religion and the Study of the Bible," by Wilfred Cantwell Smith, and "'Scripture' in India: Towards a Typology of the Word in Hindu Life," by Thomas B. Coburn.

Miranda Shaw prepared the index; Miranda, Debbie Myers, Joan Riedl and Barbara Hickey spent many hours typing and proofreading the text.

INTRODUCTION

Rethinking Scripture

Miriam Levering

People throughout the world have found words to provide a frame for the sacred, to mediate knowledge of truths and to have moving or transforming power. Some Hindus, for example, have recognized speech as a goddess (Vāc), even as creative divinity itself, while certain sounds/words (*śabda*) are themselves seen by Hindus as channels of the divine energy of creation. Many communities affirm unambiguously that certain words (the Ten Commandments, the Qur'ān) come directly from God. Others understand the Word as the best metaphor for the self-revelation of what is ultimate, even if that Word takes the form not of words but of persons or deeds.

In other communities true speech or true writing is understood to issue from human minds with special clarity. Even in these cases it is commonly an important and treasured insight that true words exercise power, for to hear them, recite them, or study them is to be transformed.

Words that are powerfully true can be occasional. But many communities have found that certain words continue to be effective over and over again in creating and refreshing authentic life. These communities have sought to crystallize and transmit their most important verbal traditions.

It is perhaps in this latter case particularly that one is justified in speaking of 'scripture,' and also of 'classic,' for the concepts of scripture and classic result from the hope that the tradition-valued word can be transmitted just as it has been received.

Much of great interest to the student of human cultural traditions occurs when communities crystallize scriptures and classics. Many have noted that the problem of interpretation arises: how does one relate the timeless truths captured in precept and story to the living experience of a different time?

Another sort of consequence is perhaps less widely noted. Such texts once chosen and fixed can be made to bear different burdens, and offer different treasures, in the lives of communities and individuals than the same text not yet singled out for this special treatment (i.e., in a pre-scriptural or pre-classic state) could do. People do things with, and expect things from, these verbal traditions that they do not from other texts.

Thus to say that a 'scripture' is perceived as true and experienced as powerful, and is the object of an attempt at faithful transmission, still does not capture all that we mean when we say that certain words or texts are 'scripture.' As various authors in this volume suggest, 'scripture' is a relational term. That is, it refers to kinds of relationships that people enter into with these texts. It seems helpful to propose that 'scriptures' are a special class of true and powerful words, a class formed by the ways in which these particular words are received by persons and communities in their common life.

This collection of essays is entitled "Rethinking Scripture: Essays from a Comparative Perspective." In what follows I wish to address briefly the questions: why 'rethinking'? why 'scripture'? and why a 'comparative perspective'?

WHY 'RETHINKING'?

A number of years ago Wilfred Cantwell Smith, in his essay "The Study of Religion and the Study of the Bible" (which is included in this collection of essays), challenged graduate programs in Biblical Studies and the Study of Religion to prepare teachers who could teach courses, not on how the biblical texts came to be what they are, but on what the Bible has been for Jewish and Christian communities since it became scripture. He realized that while we as scholars now know quite a bit about the religion of Israel and of early Christian communities, we have not yet reflected very much on what it is for something to be scripture, or for human communities to 'scripturalize' (produce scripture) and to relate to words as scripture.

Somewhat later, William A. Graham and Kendall Folkert began to discover, as they studied and thought about the Muslim experience of the Qur'ān and the scholarly treatment of the canons of the Jains of India respectively, the great potential interest in opening up the topic of scripture to further reflection within the comparative history of religion.

They in turn inspired Smith to begin a global examination of forms and concepts of scripture in many religious traditions.

Smith's interest, and the seminars he led at Harvard for graduate students and for college teachers (the latter under National Endowment for the Humanities sponsorship in 1982 and 1984), drew Thomas B. Coburn, Barbara Holdrege and myself into the topic. As had been the case for Folkert and Graham, we noticed with amazement that the history of the forms and concepts of sacred texts in the traditions we studied (Hindu, Jewish and Chinese respectively), topics we had thought obvious and fundamental, had been little addressed by previous scholarship in a truly reflective fashion. Likewise, we all found it striking that the phenomenology of religion as practiced by men such as W. Brede Kristensen and Gerardus van der Leeuw, and the history of religion as practiced by Joachim Wach, Mircea Eliade and others, had so far given very little attention to 'sacred text' as a widespread and important phenomenon. It seemed possible that there were important questions that had thus far been neglected.

There have been reasons for this neglect. The study of non-Western religions began with an overemphasis on texts as the best source of information concerning the beliefs and practices of unfamiliar religious traditions. A great interest in discovering, translating, and studying the origins and content of the 'scriptures' or 'sacred books' of other traditions followed. In general during this period, scholars tended to assume unconsciously that each such text occupied a place in the religious life of its community and tradition similar to that occupied by the Bible in some branches of Protestant life: a free-standing source of religious doctrine, authority, and inspiration, whose meaning could be grasped without too much reference to original or later contexts.

The results of this beginning were and continue to be unfortunate. As Wilfred Cantwell Smith writes in his second essay in this volume, "Scripture as Form and Concept: Their Emergence for the Western World": "We have tended to derive our concept of scripture from the Bible." Indeed, as Folkert points out in his essay, Western studies of other historic traditions have been distorted by the implicit assumption that such traditions would have a book, or canon of books, that serve as the locus of authoritative doctrine, and that such books are read, used and thought about in much the way Protestants read, use and think about scripture. Even our understanding of the role of scripture in Christian and other Western religious communities has been marred by these assumptions, since it is clear that our implicit notion of 'scripture' is not derived from a careful consideration of the whole of Jewish and Christian experience and reflection, but only from very small parts of it.

In reaction to the narrowness of this approach, phenomenologists of religion and other later groups proposed that attention should be focused on myths, actions and symbols that expressed religious meanings rather than on texts and beliefs. Much has been gained thereby. An important advance is the realization that the cultures of oral peoples are as profound and sophisticated as the cultures of literate peoples. An emphasis on looking at religious achievements through texts privileges the literate over the oral, and the elite strands of a tradition over the folk or popular strands. Great religious insights and expressions can be transmitted without the benefit of written texts. Insights into all human religiousness have been attained by a sustained reflection on the religious expressions of early or oral cultures.

Yet a consequence of these steps forward in the field seems to have been the neglect of the comparative study of the ways in which words and text in fact have symbolic or mythic power. While members of these scholarly movements have acknowledged that texts could be 'sacred' in ways analogous to those in which spaces, actions, and ritual objects were sacred, little attention was paid to the category called "sacred text." To some it may have seemed that scripture or sacred text—though a commonly found phenomenon in religious traditions within chirographic cultures—was not a form of religious expression the study of which led people into the heart of human religiousness, as life-cycle ritual or pilgrimages might be. Others perhaps concluded that, whereas pilgrimages might be quite comparable across traditions, sacred texts really were not.

Thus while, by developing a generic or comparative category such as sacred text free of the limitations of our Western-formed concept of scripture, phenomenological or morphological scholarship in religion might well have remedied the bias introduced by the unconscious prevalence of the Protestant model, it has not yet done so. The current usage of 'sacred text' or 'normative text' within the field is a step forward. Yet one result of the lack in the writings of Van der Leeuw, Wach, Eliade, Kristensen and their followers of any substantive discussion or cross-cultural exploration of the category of sacred text is that 'sacred text' is in practice often used with much the same assumptions that informed our biased concepts of 'scripture' and 'canon,' with the addition of some insights about 'the holy' or 'the sacred' derived from Eliadian reflections. The category is undeveloped: the contemporary scholar is often aware that the 'sacred texts' of the tradition she or he is describing are not parallel to Western scriptures as commonly understood, but finds that the undeveloped, catch-all category of 'sacred text' has given her or him few analytic tools with which to delineate the differences.

This impasse demonstrates the potential usefulness of a self-conscious pursuit of a generic concept. Thus we seek to inaugurate with these essays the research and reflection needed to develop concepts of scripture, sacred text, canon, and sacred words as categories within the phenomenology of religion so that global, generic, and comparative study of these important phenomena—fruits of the human tendency to 'scripturalize'—can cast light on the experiences and choices faced by religious communities past and present. We seek to reverse the present situation; as Wilfred Cantwell Smith states: "We are now in a position where our understanding of the Bible, and of much else across the world, may begin to be derived from a larger concept of scripture."

I believe that such study will also show that 'scripturalizing,' (the propensity to produce scriptures), and the ongoing reception of scriptures in the context of religious life, are in fact comparable across traditions. I further believe that a study of those human activities does lead to a better understanding of the heart of religious life, not least because it is concerned with the fundamental human and religious experience of shaping and being shaped in one's relation to ultimate and comprehensive value through the medium of words.

WHY 'SCRIPTURE'?

Readers may question why some of us continue to use the word 'scripture' to name the generic concept that we seek. If biases and misleading expectations continue to result from our unconscious assumption of the universal applicability of Western forms and concepts, why not use a neutral term like "sacred text" or "holy book"? Furthermore, scripture is a term freighted with Protestant (and also Catholic and Jewish) pieties, with all the attendant emotions aroused by those in our culture. Why tie ourselves to these?

Some of us do feel forced to abandon the term 'scripture.' Thomas B. Coburn chooses to discuss "the Word" in India because the connotations of writtenness that seem inevitably tied to the term scripture are misleading in the Indian case.

Kendall Folkert advocates abandoning the word scripture for the comparative study of religion as a whole. He proposes substituting "canon," a term which has for him the advantage of preserving the meaning of "regulative" without being heavily freighted with other expectations. For Folkert there are at least two types of "canon," depending on whether it is a "vectored" or "vectoring" phenomenon within the tradition. The implication is that 'scripture,' with all the assumptions we make about it, is appropriate only to Canon I, or vectoring texts. The Western scholarly tendency is to expect vectoring from texts, and apply Canon I expectations to sacred texts that are vectored by other principal carriers of religious life.

The rest of us, for a variety of reasons, are inclined to try to live with the term 'scripture,' which, as the dictionary indicates, has recently acquired a generic meaning.

One reason is that connotation-free neutrality is not really gained with 'holy book' or 'sacred text.' 'The holy' and 'the sacred,' related as they have been to concepts of hierophany, are in their current usage within the field not neutral terms; they are terms that bring with them connotations from a cosmology. Thus, by using 'sacred' or 'holy' one does not entirely avoid the problem.

Another reason is that we are seeking to address people to whom 'scripture' is a live religious term. To use a neutral term is to encourage students and believers to separate study from 'real life.' Such separation occurs too often in the minds of students in the classroom when many traditions are being studied. Students think that "they" have sacred texts, while "we" have scripture. We are not asking them to think about sacred texts, we are asking people to think about scripture—something that is never a neutral object divorced from an engaged subjectivity.

Further, a case could be made that scholars would benefit from using two terms. 'Sacred text' could continue to have the broad, unspecific usage that it now has, able to mark the specially holy status of many kinds of texts, oral and written. 'Scripture' could be used to meet a need for a more limited category than sacred text, referring to the normative, bounded or semi-bounded written traditions that typically occur in the religions of chirographic cultures. For this latter, more limited category, scripture as a historically developed concept in the West has, as Graham points out, some positive virtues. " 'Scripture'," he writes, has "several connotations that offer a solid basis for a meaningful concept of sacred religious text." It implies a "relatively sizeable, usually composite text." It contains "the idea of a collection of material that, whatever its history, is perceived as a unitary whole." It suggests "the implied authority and sacrality of a text with unique claim to transcendence and truth." And it refers to material that at least can be, and usually is, eventually written down.

Finally, my own observation is that the use of 'sacred text' so far, though well meant, has largely served to hide rather than expunge the distorting Western assumptions derived from the biblical analogies. Perhaps it is better to use the term 'scripture' and thereby bring these assumptions out into the open, face them, and work through them. As was demonstrated to all of us who attended Wilfred Cantwell Smith's summer seminars for college teachers in 1982 and 1984, the stretching that results from a broad accumulation of genuine comparative knowledge and reflection does enable one to enjoy an expanded, non-reified use of the term, ever freer from the bias produced by unconscious Western models.

WHY A 'COMPARATIVE PERSPECTIVE'?

This leads us to the question about the fruitfulness of comparative study. There are really two questions here.

The first question is, do comparisons among instances of relations between people and their texts, or between forms and concepts of texts, lead to fruitful generalizations and also illumine each separate term in the comparison? For example, do we learn things about why and how the Bible has been consequential for Westerners by looking at what the Veda has meant to Hindus?

The answer to this question should be apparent from the essays presented here. To take one example, to compare the Bible to the Veda in India is, as Coburn's essay shows, to be shocked out of one's unconscious assumptions about scripture. Westerners tend to believe scripture should offer sacred story or moral instructions—at the very least, content should matter. Yet in the case of the Vedas, the power and truth of the sacred performance of the words is in no way diminished by the fact that no one, neither the reciter nor the hearer, understands them.

Another assumption that Westerners have is that scriptures are always found to be fixed and bounded in canons. Yet some among India's oral 'textual' accumulations that deserve comparison with Western scriptures (e.g., the Purāṇas and, arguably, the Upaniṣads) seem not to be historically or conceptually closed groups. To look at the Hindu practice is to find one's mind opened to see the actual porousness and unsettledness of the boundaries of scripture in the West. One becomes aware of the extent that, even after the canon was closed in Christian and Jewish communities in the West, ways have been found to add to and subtract from the corpus of words treated scripturally, to allow the Word in that way to be dynamically recreated.

Also, to look at the Hindu experience is also to see more clearly the ways in which the scriptural power of the Bible has included its power as symbol as well as the power related to its content.

The second question is, does the category of scripture dissolve as the particulars of the scriptural experience of each tradition come more fully into view? As one looks at more and more cases of the form, concept and reception of texts that seem at first glance to be similar to the Bible, do proposed similarities or family resemblances among them all as a class seem hopelessly vague? Distorting? Forced? Or simply to fail altogether?

Let us consider for a moment the texts that we would all intuitively regard as scriptures and as comparable, texts like the Qur'ān, the Vedas and Upaniṣads, the Jewish and Christian Bibles, the Tripiṭaka of the Buddhists, the Avesta of the Zoroastrians, the Ādi Granth of the Sikhs, and the Taoist canon.

Certainly the fuller and more informed the study of even these texts, the more different they appear to be. They differ of course in their genres and contents. For example, the Protestant Old Testament (as well as the New) contains many historical narratives and reflections on the significance of historical events, as well as commandments. The Vedas taken in the most inclusive sense contain hymns, ritual prescriptions and interpretations, and teachings relating to gnosis; historical narratives do not figure prominently, nor do commandments about social behavior.

Further, these texts differ in their expected and actual roles in relation to institutions, religious specialists, and to individual reciters/readers. The Buddhist Tripiṭaka is intended for and used mainly by persons who renounce household life, practice scrupulous ethical self-restraint, and pursue a rigorous course of mental self-examination. The Ṛg Veda, on the other hand, designed as it is to play a role in maintaining good relations with the gods, is and always has been the province of ritual specialists serving the religious needs of householders. Any generalizations that would hold for even this narrow set of sacred texts would be not terribly illuminating.

A glance at recent efforts to make generalizations about the characteristics of sacred texts reveals not only how little light is shed by generalizations, but also how misleading they may be. Let us take the following list as a sample of the generalizations that seem to suggest themselves to scholars looking for possible parameters for a category of 'sacred text':

1. There are often beliefs that the text is of divine origin, or the product of special insight.
2. Whatever their origin, they are regarded and treated as sacred, that is, powerful and inviolable, to be treated with respect.
3. They are regarded and consulted as normative, authoritative for a community in various aspects of its religious life: for worship, doctrine, and behavior.
4. The texts, whether written or oral, are regarded as closed and fixed, not to be added to or subtracted from. In other words, they are treated as a canon.

5. When the sacred text is in the form of a book, it is regarded as complete. It contains everything of importance, and can be applied to all aspects of human life.

6. The texts are used by members of the community in religious and ritual contexts.

7. Sacred texts testify to that which is ultimate.[1]

These are intuitively appealing generalizations, yet they are curiously misleading. I suspect that these characterizations are so intuitively appealing because all but one of them belong to the widely shared common sense characterization of the Bible. But a fully informed comparative study casts considerable doubt on the universal applicability and fruitfulness of these characterizations. Characterizations that are strongly true and significant about the Bible or the Qur'ān at certain historical moments turn out to be only weakly true, and far less significant (or significant in a different sense), as statements about other scriptural texts.

For example, there clearly are communities (e.g., Hindu, Mahāyāna Buddhist) in which neither the 'fixity' of texts nor the boundedness of canon seem always to be sought after. (See Coburn's essay.)

'Completeness' is another dubious generalization. The Chinese literati beginning in the eleventh century eventually came to see the Chinese Classics as complete in the Western sense. Yet in the cases of other generations and social classes even within China, it is doubtful that they regarded the Classics as complete, or even would regard completeness as desirable. The Vedas are a corpus of sacred texts whose role is in many ways analogous to the "typical" scriptures (the Qur'ān, the Bible, etc.), and yet it is not clear that they were expected to be a source of wisdom, knowledge, or legal and ethical standards for all the important aspects of life. After all, texts like the *Manusmṛti* which gave regulative ideals for Brahmin life, the kind of text we would expect to find in a scriptural corpus, are not found in the Vedas.

Further, what is meant by 'complete' is probably quite different in different kinds of religions. The followers of Nichiren in Japan clearly have a scriptural book: they regard the *Lotus Sūtra* as a complete source of truth and power to change one's life. But it would be misleading to say that they see the *Lotus Sūtra* as providing a complete source from which to derive ethical or legal prescriptions or holy social institutions, as Jews have done with the Torah. In a Western context 'completeness' suggests the 'completeness' of Torah, not the 'completeness' of a text that was never intended or used as a source for the social laws of a community.

To say that what characterizes a text that is regarded as sacred is that it is seen as possessed in its own right of a (usually beneficial) power, and not to be profaned, is again to make a statement far truer of some relationships between scriptures and communities than of others.

For example, many Mahāyāna Buddhists in China have thought texts to possess the power to work miracles, and some of them have thought that important. We are told that Hsüan-tsang, a great 8th century Chinese Buddhist scholar and translator who made a lengthy pilgrimage to India to collect scriptures for translation into Chinese, had many experiences of the miraculous power of the scripture, the *Heart Sūtra*, that he recited on the way. It is said that since by the display of miracles "the ultimate efficacy of this Scripture had been demonstrated, he believed that this was Wisdom . . . that if he did as he was told, he would without fail outpass the limit of enlightened intuition and fulfill the word of [the Buddha]."[2]

But there were other Chinese Mahāyāna Buddhists, for example those of the Ch'an teaching lineages, for whom the *Heart Sūtra* was equally scripture, to whom the idea that the *sūtra* might posses miraculous powers, or indeed any kind of power, was completely unimportant and even dangerous to one's practice. Likewise the idea that the mark of a 'sacred' text is that it is one that one does not profane, while probably present to some degree in most cases (though arguably not in the Ch'an Buddhist case), varies from awe and fear on the one end of the spectrum to respect and courtesy on the other.[3]

Likewise the emphasis on the authoritative status and normative uses of scripture as a defining characteristic may derive in part from a Protestant concern with the sources of the authority of its tradition and the nature of the normative character of its Scripture.[4] Being regarded as authoritative or normative in certain matters perhaps should be a defining characteristic of the category of 'scripture' as distinguished from the larger category of 'sacred text.' Yet the nature and scope of such authority or normativity may be much narrower or much different from what we who are molded by Protestant culture tend to imagine, and the purposes for which authority is sought may be quite different.[5] A mere statement that normativity characterizes sacred texts leaves undislodged many assumptions about the universality of attitudes that are in fact most especially Protestant.

Thus this kind of approach to the world-wide phenomenon of sacred text does not seem to escape the influence of Western models. Additional elements are added, but the influence of Western experience and commitments on the concept, while hidden, still seems to remain subtly formative.

But the more fundamental problem is that the generalizations are so much less illuminating than they at first seem. Almost every one either fails to cover all important cases or misleads in its language or emphasis. Once one introduces all the necessary qualifications the generalizations become almost meaningless. It becomes clear that the number of cases that truly fit is far smaller than the number that do not fit well enough to make the generalizations useful. The very limited success of recent efforts at generalization by sensitive and well informed scholars gives power to the view that, considered as objects of comparison, 'scriptures' or 'sacred texts' do not make a single category.[6]

Clearly there are problems with defining the category by trying to arrive at lists of characterizing features. If we instead attend principally to the dynamics of the relations that people have had with texts, their ways of receiving texts in the context of their religious projects, then the whole matter becomes more hopeful. On the one hand, for the sake of a broader understanding of the significant differences that emerge, one allows the category to dissolve. But as one does so, paradoxically, one finds that dynamic structures and polarities emerge that allow the category to take on new meanings. As a result one does not become impatient with it so quickly.

The essays in this volume attempt this rather different kind of approach. One conclusion one might draw from them is that more is gained by looking for, not static, universal characteristics, but polarities and relationships that recur in the dynamics of human relations to specially sanctioned texts. In our efforts so far the following polarities and other dynamic patterns have come into view.

POLARITIES

Form/Fluidity

The first step is to realize how much we Western scholars (perhaps biblical and church historians are exceptions), have allowed our minds to be dominated by the idea that 'scripture' has a single form and expresses a single concept. The second step is to see how misleading this domination can be. We can do this by becoming aware that what we believe to be the most typical Western form and concept of scripture had historical origins as the product of a historical process. We need, however, also to realize that this dominant form and concept in fact was never a static matter: the forms and concepts of scripture over the West's many centuries of history, though tending in a certain direction, have been continually changing. Smith's essay tracing the interlinking developments in the Near East and Mediterranean worlds shows how the typical pattern of Western thinking and acting came to be, and at the same time liberates the reader from the expectation of encountering, even in the West, a static, unchanging form and concept.

Orality/Writtenness

'Scripture' at first seems necessarily to refer to written texts in their character of being written. But that is not the end of the matter. As Graham's essay shows, it is crucial to understanding the richness of scripture as a part of living religious experience to realize that scriptures worldwide have never been mere books to be read silently but have had their life in oral-aural reception. Thus, scripture, which is most often a creation of the transition in culture and mental experience from oral culture to written culture, nonetheless is a form through which religious communities have continued to recreate the oral-aural experiencing of words. Could it be that such oral experience is essential to religious life?

Boundedness/Openness

It is a fallacy, as Coburn's and Folkert's essays point out in the Hindu and Jain cases—and the same could be said for Buddhists and others—to expect scriptures or canons of scriptures to be neatly bounded. In fact, wherever they appear, scriptures are characterized by being treated as both bounded and open. In the rather rare cases where communities saw value in closing the canon, new scriptural or semi-scriptural forms have been created (e.g., the Talmud) to allow for the ongoing process of insight or revelation.

'Vectoring'/'Being Vectored'

Kendall Folkert suggests in his essay that the category "scripture" does need to be broken into two types, which he calls "Canon I" and "Canon II." Canon I type scriptures occur where, as for example in the Protestant case, the scripture is the principal authority for and carrier of the symbolic activities of the tradition. Canon II sacred texts, though important to their religious traditions, are not the principal vectors, but derive their importance from other vectors (liturgy, for example, or rules and procedures of monastic practice). Whether it is important to have a closed canon, whether it is important to regard the text as an independent, pristine source, of quite a different nature from other texts and commentaries in the tradition, and so on, depend, Folkert argues, on whether the text is principally a vector or whether it is principally "carried" by other vectors in the tradition.

Cosmic Status/Contingency

Another polarity clearly crucial to the concept of scripture is that symbolized by the almost universal phenomenon of attributing to the text a divine or special origin. Talk about texts delivered by divine messengers (e.g., in the Near East), or discovered in rivers inscribed on the backs of turtles (in China), or created first before the world is created (the Jews) clearly points to a special experience one has while seeking truth through studying and living in relation to these texts. Barbara Holdrege's essay calls our attention to the dangers of not taking seriously these metaphors and claims as testifying to an ongoing apprehension of truth and power given to those who cherish these texts. Wherever it is also recognized that these texts are also at the same time contingent, historical manifestations (cf. the discussion in Coburn's and Levering's essays, as well as that of Holdrege), this creative polarity emerges in its richest forms.

Normativity/Selection and Reinterpretation

This polarity has long been recognized as being at the heart of the phenomenon of 'scripture' and 'classic,' and has already captured the attention of many scholars. Illuminating treatments of the relation between authority and reinterpretation that we have discovered include those of James Sanders and David Tracy. An issue here that perhaps deserves more attention globally is that of "actual canons," the selections that religious communities and individuals make of those parts of their scriptures that they truly cherish and relate to scripturally.[7]

MODES OF RECEPTION: INFORMING, SYMBOLIZING, TRANSACTING, AND TRANSFORMING

Scriptures are scriptures because of the ways they are received, and because they can sustain and repay those kinds of reception. Looking at the reception of sacred texts in a concrete context—a convent within the Chinese Buddhist tradition—I found, broadly speaking, four dynamically interrelated ways in which texts were incorporated into the religious life of the *pi-ch'iu-ni* (nuns):

Informative Reception

To be informed is to read and listen in such a way as to allow oneself to be shaped by studying, and taking seriously, the authority and message of a text.

Transformative Reception

Buddhist nuns seek and value a path that brings about a personal transformation toward ultimate well-being, clarity and compassion. Most, if not all, reception of sacred texts within the convent, and within Buddhist tradition generally, expects that one outcome of one's interaction with them will be personal transformation.

Transactive Reception

Certain kinds of texts (e.g., *mantras*, *dhāraṇī*) are understood to have been specifically made available to bring about certain changes in the experience of others, or in the circumstances affecting one's own practice. More generally, the recitation of even those texts not specifically meant for the purpose of taking action also causes things to happen.

Symbolic Reception

Texts that can be received in such vital ways, that have such intimate connections with truth and power, can come to symbolize, even to be an icon of, the truth and power that comes through them.

It is characteristic of scriptures that they are received in many ways at once. Sam D. Gill has recently suggested in an important essay that we attend to two kinds of functions sacred texts have: "the informative function" and "the performative functions."[8] I suggest that in reflecting on the reception of sacred texts in different traditions and contexts, we will find these four modes of reception an even more useful starting place. I believe we will also find that whereas forms and concepts of scripture are highly specific to the tradition and its sociohistorical moment, ways of receiving scripture 'scripturally' are similar enough to be compared fruitfully, so that the experience of one tradition can shed light on that of another.[9]

We hope that readers of these essays will be challenged to rediscover the fruitfulness of the search for a generic concept of scripture or sacred text. We have found that it is the search that is fruitful, quite apart from whether such a generic concept could ever be constructed in a manner satisfying to everyone. The search for such a category has de-reifying, liberating value; yet an approach through the dynamics of relationships, yielding polarities and modes of reception of the kinds just discussed, demonstrates areas in which the search can have constructive value as well, as one moves phenomenologically from particulars to generalizations to a new understanding of the particular.

A NOTE CONCERNING KENDALL FOLKERT'S ESSAY

A painful loss affects the shape of this book. Our beloved colleague Ken Folkert was killed in a motorcycle accident in 1985 while doing field-work among the Jains in India. The essay included here unfortunately was left in some respects unfinished. We are sure that the reader will agree that the ideas expressed are so important and provocative that it would have been a serious omission not to include it. In order to preserve the power of Ken's own expression, I have left the essay largely untouched. Ken would most likely have added more notes had he had a chance to return to this work before final publication. I have made no attempt to supply them, for a great deal of guesswork would have been involved. Fortunately it is Ken's ideas that make this piece valuable, and those are quite clear as they stand.

It is evident from the essay and from many conversations on scripture that Ken felt very deeply that changes of emphasis would improve the work in the field of Biblical Studies, changes that, he noted in later discussions, were already beginning to happen.[10] Initiating a conversation with biblical scholars on the points raised in his essay was something Ken very much hoped to accomplish with its publication. It is most unfortunate that we will not benefit from Ken's own further participation in that conversation.

A NOTE CONCERNING WILFRED CANTWELL SMITH'S ESSAY

At his request, and to preserve his own preferences of usage, Wilfred Cantwell Smith's essays have not been changed to render them consistent with the usage in other essays.

A NOTE ON THE DEDICATION

All of us of the younger generation want to dedicate this book to our inspiring teacher and example, Wilfred Cantwell Smith, and to our late colleague Kendall Folkert, in appreciation of their imaginative, ground-breaking scholarship, and of their special presence in our lives.

NOTES

1. This list is based very loosely on Ninian Smart and Richard D. Hecht's "Introduction" to their *Sacred Texts of the World: A Universal Anthology* (New York: Crossroad, 1982), pp. xii-xv.

2. Anonymous preface to a transcription of Hsüan-tsang's translation of the *Heart Sūtra*, Tun-huang manuscript S. 700, translation modified from that of Leon Hurvitz in "Hsüan-tsang (602–664) and the Heart Scripture," Lewis Lancaster and Luis Gomez, ed., *Prajñāpāramitā and Related Systems* (Berkeley, California: Berkeley Buddhist Studies Series, 1977), p. 110

3. An even more important cause for dissatisfaction with this generalization is the fact that these two hallmarks of 'sacredness' by no means exhaust the range of attitudes manifested by religious persons to the texts that mediate their religious relationships and aspirations. To derive our sense of what it means to say that texts are sacred from what it means to say that stones are sacred restricts our exploration of the affective dimension of the reception of scripture.

4. It is interesting that Max Müller, after rejecting divine origin as the criterion for selecting the *Sacred Books of the East*, settled on the fact that the text had been chosen by the tradition to be the final authority in religious matters as the crucial criterion:

> It was suggested that those books only should be considered sacred which professed to be revealed, or to be directly communicated by the Deity to the great teachers of mankind. But it was soon found that very few, if any, of the books themselves put forward that claim. Such a claim was generally advanced and formulated by a later generation....So we agreed to treat as Sacred Books all those which had been formally recognized by religious communities as constituting the highest authority in matters of religion, which had received a kind of canonical sanction, and might therefore be appealed to for deciding any disputed points of faith, morality or ceremonial.

5. I find helpful here David L. Bartlett's reflection in his *The Shape of Scriptural Authority* (Philadelphia: Fortress Press, 1983), that different kinds of literature in the Hebrew Bible claim and exercise different kinds of authority. Authority is single neither in purview nor in nature.

6. Another example is the even more sensitively constructed chapter on "Scripture" in a new introductory textbook, *Religion: An Introduction* (San Francisco: Harper and Row, 1985) by T. William Hall, Richard B. Pilgrim, and Ronald R. Cavanagh. Here the generalizations are derived from a combination of reflection on "the sacred" and "the holy," for which they acknowledge a debt to Eliade, and reflection on the Western, particularly Protestant, emphasis on scripture as revealing sacred history, moral and legal codes, and right belief. The authors speak of scripture as "revealing what is holy," "giv[ing] evidence of the holy, inspir[ing] experience of the holy"—a virtue of this insight is that it emphasizes experience, including noncontent-based symbolic experience, as well as belief and authority. Yet "the holy" tends to be linked historically with ideas about religion as based in an encounter with a numinous "other"; not all Buddhists or Hindus would be quite as comfortable as would members of some other traditions with heavy reliance on metaphors of "otherness."

7. Cf. Miriam Levering, "Scripture as Icon," unpublished paper given at the American Academy of Religion, Nov. 1983.

8. Sam D. Gill, "Nonliterate Traditions and Holy Books: Toward a New Model," in Frederick M. Denny and Rodney L. Taylor, eds., *The Holy Book in Comparative Perspective* (University of South Carolina Press, 1985), p. 234.

9. The attempt to characterize scriptural reception by starting from Buddhist experience seems a useful complement to existing attempts at a general characterization of "sacred text" that have started from biblical or nonliterate models.

10. Kendall Folkert mentioned specifically several of the chapters in David Noel Freedman and Michael Patrick O'Conner, eds., "The Bible and its Traditions," *Michigan Quarterly Review* 22:3 (1983).

1

The Study of Religion and the Study of the Bible

Wilfred Cantwell Smith

One of the most exciting new developments on college and university campuses in recent times, and also one of the most significant and potentially creative developments on the religious scene, is surely the emergence and flourishing of liberal-arts departments of religion. Perhaps what is happening can be summed up most pithily by saying that the transition has been from the teaching of religion to the study of religion. Where professors used to instruct, they now inquire. They once attempted to impart what they themselves knew, and what they hoped (of late, with decreasing expectation) to make interesting; now, on the contrary, they inquire, into something that both for them and for their students is incontrovertibly interesting, but is something that they do not quite understand.

Part of the excitement and potential significance derives from the fact that, for the first time in many long years, with the setting up of religion departments a number of very bright, very concerned young men and women find themselves enabled to throw themselves with vigor and thoroughness into a serious wrestling with religious issues, intellectually, with no prior commitment as to where they will come out in the end. At one time the Church offered the only full-time employment for an intellectual with religious interests, or a religious person with primarily intellectual interests. This worked well, classically, so long as the concept

God signified, intellectually and emotionally, reality and truth; later, when a commitment to truth began to be felt and seen as different (or perhaps different) from a Christian commitment, fewer and fewer took up (or could take up) the challenge. Now that appointments in religion departments are available, highly promising, highly intelligent, highly serious young people are once again able to devote themselves unreservedly to the task of searching for understanding, knowledge, and integrity in the religio-intellectual field.

The transition from the seminary to the liberal arts department, as the locus of inquiry, has been marked conspicuously by a change, then, in emphasis and form and mood; yet less conspicuously than some would like by a change in content. The traditional seminary divisions of the subject matter or "disciplines," still characterize the religion department more thoroughly than many wish. The salient upsurge of the study of Asian religious life is an obvious exception. One may be allowed to wonder, however, whether both student and faculty eagerness in "History of Religion"—usually signifying the history of religious groups other than one's own—is altogether related to the novel content, or whether it is in substantial part a function rather of the new mood and method, orientation and attitude, that are brought to bear in these new studies and are felt to be missing from the old. Does the popularity of the study of Asia religiously stem, at least in part, from the fact that those who study it are able to approach it with to-day's interest, to-day's questions, to-day's moods and methods? The study of Christian data still seems bound within questions, moods, methods of an earlier era.

Let us take the field of Bible as an illustration. If I were chairman of a religion department, I would certainly wish to have in the curriculum a course on the Bible, and on the faculty a person competent to teach it. What kind of course and what kind of teacher, however, would I be looking for?

The courses actually available, and the training of those actually available to teach them, are on the whole calculated to turn a fundamentalist into a liberal. Often they can do this with great skill, but it is hardly any more a relevant task. The more advanced or sophisticated Biblicists have moved beyond this, to the point where they are competent historians of the religious life of the ancient Near East or of the first-century Eastern Mediterranean world. This is fine, for that small group who happen to be interested in the religious history of those particular sectors of the total religious history of humankind; but these people seem on the whole little equipped to answer a question as to why one should be especially interested in those particular times and places, rather than in, let us say, classical India or medieval China or modern America.

The sort of course and the sort of teacher for whom I would be looking in the field of Bible would be different. Let me attempt to delineate what, as I see it, might fruitfully be attempted.

The course that I envisage would be concerned with the Bible as scripture. It would begin with some consideration of scripture as a generic phenomenon. The questions to which it would address itself would be questions such as these: What is involved in taking a certain body of literature, separating it off from all others, and giving it a sacred status? What is involved psychologically; what, sociologically; and what, historically? How and where did it first come about? How did the Christian Church happen to take up this practice? What attitudes, magical or otherwise, towards writing are involved? And—once this is done—what consequences follow? One would wish a brief but perhaps striking comparativist introduction: the concept and role of scripture in other major communities—Jewish, Hindu, Buddhist, and the like. Salient differences, as well as striking similarities, could be touched briefly. (For example, the thesis could be considered that in the Islamic system the Qur'ān fulfills a function comparable to the role played in the Christian pattern rather by the person of Jesus Christ while a closer counterpart to Christian scriptures are the Islamic Ḥadīth "Traditions.") The role of formalized and sacralized oral tradition in some societies, as distinct from both written scripture on the one hand and ordinary colloquial discourse on the other, might also be broached. The religious significance of the introduction of writing into human history would be touched upon, perhaps. The basic issue would be: scripture as a religious form.

All this, however, would be introductory only. The bulk of the course would be historical: an investigation into the history of the Bible over the past twenty centuries. Before one considers this with any specificity, the prime point is to recognize that in this fashion the Bible would be treated as a living force in the life of the Church. My own field is Islamics; and in that field I devote a fair amount of time and energy to trying to make vivid to my students the fact that the Qur'ān, if it is to be understood in anything remotely approaching its religious significance, must be seen as not merely a seventh-century Arabian document (which has tended to be the way in which Western Orientalists, as distinct from religionists, have treated it) but also as an eighth-, and a twelfth-, and a seventeenth-, and a twentieth-century document, and one intimately intertwined in the life not only of Arabia but also of East Africa and Indonesia. For the Qur'ān has played a role—formative, dominating, liberating, spectacular—in the lives of millions of people, philosophers and peasants, politicians and merchants and housewives, saints and sinners, in Baghdad and Cordoba and Agra, in the Soviet Union since the

Communist revolution, and so on. That role is worth discerning and pondering. The attempt to understand the Qur'ān is to understand how it has fired the imagination, and inspired the poetry, and formulated the inhibitions, and guided the ecstasies, and teased the intellects, and ordered the family relations and the legal chicaneries, and nurtured the piety, of hundreds of millions of people in widely diverse climes and over a series of radically divergent centuries.

To study the Qur'ān, then, is to study much more than its text; and much more of social conditions than those that *preceded* (or accompanied) its first appearance in history and contributed to its formation. The important history for an understanding of this scripture (as scripture) is not only of its background but also, and perhaps especially, of its almost incredible ongoing career since. What produced the Qur'ān is an interesting and legitimate question, but a secondary one. Less minor than it, less antiquarian, religiously much more significant, is the marvelous question, What has the Qur'ān produced? Indeed, any interest that the former question may have is derivative from the power of some at least tacit answer to the latter. It is because of what the Qur'ān has been doing, mightily and continuingly, in human lives for all these centuries *after* it was launched, that anyone takes the trouble to notice its launching at all. For religious life, the story of formative centuries is logically subordinate to that of subsequent ages. (It is possible to overlook this fact only from within faith; that is, only when the significance for the later period is taken as given.)

The Qur'ān is significant not primarily because of what historically went into it but because of what historically has come out of it; what it has done to human lives, and what people have done to it and with it and through it. The Qur'ān is significant because it has shown itself capable of serving a community as a form through which its members have been able (have been enabled) to deal with the problems of their lives, to confront creatively a series of varied contexts. To understand the Qur'ān is to understand both that, and how, this has been happening.

One may go further and ask: What is it about being human, that one can take such a book (one that outsiders often do not even find interesting) and, having made it a scripture for oneself, can go out into the world and in terms of it build a community and a civilization, produce literature and art and law and commercial structures, and in terms of it continue to find meaning and courage in life when the civilization wanes, and nobility in death when life wanes?

He or she is a feeble and sorry historian who underestimates—under-perceives—the power of symbols in human life, or the power of a scripture to function symbolically and as an organized battery of symbols.

To return to the Christian Bible. It has not played in Western or Christian life the central role that the Qur'ān has played in Islamic life; yet the query, what significance *has* it had, is clearly no mean question.

The first point, then, is to see the Bible not merely as a set of ancient documents or even as a first- and second-century product but as a third-century and twelfth-century and nineteenth-century and contemporary agent. Since I myself am an historian, I suppose that my evident predilection is to treat this historically, and to feel that in no other way can its significance be understood. As already suggested, however, I feel that its role (and indeed the role of anything else) in history can be illuminated, and even must be illuminated, by light thrown on human history by psychological, sociological, and comparativist perspectives. The dominant point in this case is to understand the potential and the actual roles of such a scripture in the life of the imagination, its role as an organizer of ideas, images, and emotions, as an activating symbol.

The analytic mode that for some time has dominated Western intellectual life, particularly academic life, tends to take anything that exists and to break it down into parts. Historians too have become victims of this, even at times to the point of failing to recognize that the first business of any historian is to be astonished that any given thing in the historical stream does exist and to try to understand how it came together and what its coming together subsequently meant. If something has been important, we must analyse not only it but also its importance; its history, almost, is the history of its importance. The analysis of a thing is interesting and can be highly significant, but only subsidiarily; strictly, the history of that thing *begins* once its parts are synthesized. The historian's task is to study the process of synthesis, plus the subsequent process of that synthesis as it moves through later history.

There has developed a tendency, one might almost say, to "orient history backwards," as though the task of the historian vis-à-vis any phenomenon in the course of the human story were to observe it and bit by bit to analyse its component parts and causes and antecedents, and to trace them farther and farther back into more and more remote antiquity. Does the historian need reminding that time's arrow is pointed the other way? That the history of a thing is rather its ongoing life, its ramifying results, its development and growth and change, eventually perhaps its disappearance or disintegration (forwards) into parts or its transmutation into something else? By all means let us, with regard to anything, know how it became; but let us study further how and what it went on becoming. The study of history must be in large part the study of creativity.

The first imperative for the student of the Bible, accordingly, in the modern world, is not to take the Bible for granted and then to see what it says or what constituent elements went into it, or anything of that kind; but rather to explain how it came about as a *scripture*, how it came to be that the various elements that comprise it were put together, and how it came about that Christians continued, century after century, to find reason to go on prizing and sacralizing it and responding to it—and with what results.

One minor illustration. Marcion used to be regarded as a "heretic," and he has been studied as a person who wished to "leave out" the Old Testament from the Bible. This pre-supposes a two-Testament Bible, instead of being astounded by it. It is possible to take Marcion, rather, as an illustration of the fact that we cannot take for granted that the Christian Bible should be in two parts (let alone exist at all), that it should subsume the Jewish Bible by a device that simultaneously incorporates and supersedes it, and so on. Involved here is the subtle question of the relation between two religious systems or communities. One could touch briefly here on the somewhat comparable, somewhat different, Islamic handling of both Christian and Jewish positions, as things once valid but now superseded, and on the general issue of how a religious *Weltanschauung* can cope with another community that is historically prior to it in time, but may prove incapable of coping with one that arises subsequently. It would be going too far afield to explore this issue at any length, but any treatment of the Christian Bible that failed to deal with it at least seriously, if briefly, could hardly be considered adequate. The fact that the Jewish Bible is called (and not merely called; rather, is perceived as) the "Old Testament" in Christendom (and still in the Harvard Ph.D. program!) has had profound consequences both in Christian history and Jewish history (through Christian-Jewish relations).

(A comparativist aside. The history of the Jewish Bible, despite the similarity of text, would constitute a different course—or a separate sector of the Bible as scripture. The fact that the same material has functioned, of course differently, in the lives of two different communities over the centuries could itself be educative, and exciting. How differently, it would be the business of such a study to unfold. That the story of the Exodus served—mightily—as a symbol [activating, salvific?] of liberation for Jews in a way perhaps comparable to that of the Resurrection for Christians could be explored. And so on. But here I leave all this aside.)

The fact having been considered, then, that the Christian Church decided (consciously or unconsciously) to have a scripture, and constructively determined that it should have this particular one, the story just begins. The history of scriptural interpretation has been a traditional study (it is even a sub-rubric, or optional extra, in the general examinations of some present Bible doctorates); but this is only a small part of the issue that is now raised. The interpretation ("hermeneutics") of the Bible, and even a study of that interpretation, *presupposes* that a Bible exists and even presupposes that it is (or has been thought) worth interpreting—presupposes without comment the very things that are most fascinating and have been most decisive.

The question is not merely, given a scripture, how did the Church exegete it at various stages; but also, what roles did that scripture play, what difference did the fact that the Church had one, make in the life of the Catacombists, in the intellectualizing of the Fathers, in the reactions of Christians at Rome in the time of the barbarian devastations, and so on. What was the significance of a Bible in the Dark Ages, for scholastic theology and for Gothic cathedrals and the religious orders? In the life of the imagination in medieval times, did the vignettes of incidents from the life of Jesus impinge on the consciousness of Europe through biblical passages, directly, or through stained-glass windows? Later, how did the Bible function in shaping the mystical imagination and the poetry of St. John of the Cross?

For a study of the Bible and its role in the religious life of humankind, the Reformation obviously signifies a massive new development. (Most Biblical studies for the past hundred years in our seminaries and academic institutions have been studies from within that transition, rather than studies about it. They have assumed that the Bible has the status and the importance that the Reformation gave to it, rather than scrutinizing and interpreting to us that status and importance. It is from this assumption, for instance, that current Biblical scholarship and its doctoral programs arise and therein fail to see, even to-day, that for the subsequent West, it is the Bible that has made ancient Palestine significant, not vice versa.) What the new post-Reformation role for the Bible did to people, to their imaginations, to their perception of the world, to their sexual life, to their domination of a new continent in America, are such matters that, if one does not understand them, surely one does not understand the Bible.

Along with the Reformation as—of course—a major factor of historical change in the role of the Bible in Chistendom, and along with a wide range of other large and small factors operative at about the same time, another clearly major factor was the invention and widespread use of printing. Our envisaged course would examine what happened to the role of the Bible in personal and social life when it was not only translated into the vernaculars but was also multiplied mechanically by type-print. (The relation of printing to scripture is not straightforward, however. In Christendom, the Bible was virtually the first thing to be printed, and was foremost in Western humanity's response to the medium; in the Islamic world, on the other hand, when printing was introduced it was agreed that secular books might be printed but the Qur'ān deliberately was not.)

Closely linked with the question of printing, whose historical impact on the Bible has, of course, been complex, the spread of literacy has also been of major impingement. We may take one colorful example of this matter from life on this American continent, where among some of us tales from the pioneering days of homesteaders are part of the living lore with which we grew up. In some families the time is not altogether remote when the Bible was perhaps the *only book* in a given home. It was treasured and reverenced in a way to which the fact that it was the only book in the home is surely hardly irrelevant. Clearly that situation is radically different from a modern home where the number of books is overwhelming. Our culture has gone through an intermediate phase in which a good library was a matter of pride and dignity, even of prestige; a library which certainly included the Bible, probably as an outstanding item. Nowadays, in contrast, the number of books pouring off our presses is inundatingly vast; a collection of books is a burden for which the apartment-dweller hardly knows how to find space; and in this situation the role of a scripture—no matter what its content might be, nor what one's faith—can hardly be the same as it was in that pioneering homestead context.

One need not agree with McLuhan that the age of the printed book, the Gutenberg era, is over, to recognize that with the astronomic number of new books being published every year the age of a very special book, treated differently from all others psychologically, metaphysically, sociologically, is changed.

The more standardly recognized change in the West's and the Church's understanding of the Bible over the past century has been that effected by the rise of historical criticism. Again, most recent Biblical study has been produced from within that movement. The undergraduate course that we are envisaging here would, rather, look at that movement from the outside: would describe it, analyse it, assess it. The movement, effectively, is over. It can no longer dominate, nor even serve, our understanding of the Bible. Rather, almost vice-versa, it becomes instead part of the nineteenth- and early-twentieth-century history of Christian handling of scripture. Clearly a great motif in any modern study of the Bible as scripture would be an inquiry into what happened to it as scripture with the rise, struggle, triumph, of historical criticism, and what happened to the local congregation, to the individual Christian, to personal piety, to the Sunday service.

One of the questions that an historical study of the development of the Bible in religious life would profitably tackle, I have long felt, is its role in the bifurcation in Western cultural and intellectual life between myth and history. We are beginning now to apprehend the historical as one form of human consciousness, and to see that form arising historically, recently. Now that we are beginning also, and still more recently, to have a deep and potentially authentic, although still incipient, understanding of the role of myth in human life and society, we can apprehend much more significantly what was happening when the Bible functioned mythically. We have not yet had much serious study of the historical process by which this function has become disintegrated in modern times. To carry it out would require rigorous scholarship and brilliant sensitivity; but it would be enormously rewarding.

With the relatively recent rise in Western consciousness, culminating in the nineteenth and early twentieth centuries, of the new sense of history, and the (consequent?) careful and rigorous distinction between history and myth, something major happened. One might put the matter this way. Previously—certainly all through the Middle Ages, the early Reformation stage, and among pious Christians right up until the twentieth century—the Biblical stories functioned simultaneously as both myth and history. When a sharp discrimination between these two was pressed in Western intellectual life, what happened by and large was that the West opted for history and rejected myth. This was true even of the Church, which when it had to choose decided to treat the Bible historically. (An heroic choice? And a fateful one. It speaks well for the integrity and courage of the Church's leaders that they chose relentlessly to pursue what they thought to be truth, in this dilemma; but it speaks for their lack of creative discernment, that they, like their contemporaries, thought that historiography had to do with truth but myth did not.)

Might one almost make symbolic of this development, the moment (eighteenth century) when Bishop Ussher's date 4004 B.C. was bestowed on the first chapter of Genesis? Later, the Church agonized over the fact that that date for creation was wrong. We may recognize now that the problem was not that particular date, but any date at all, the giving of a date; the notion that one is dealing here with historical time, rather than mythical time. (More exactly: this *became* a problem. For there was an earlier time when it was not so, a time before Europe had discovered that myths do not have dates.) If instead Bishop Ussher had used, and editions of the Bible had put in the margins or at the top of the page, the phrase *in illo tempore*, would our history over the past while have been different?

Probably not, because only now are we beginning to apprehend intellectually or self-consciously what kind of realm it is, what dimension of our life, to which that phrase, or "once upon a time," refers. When a medieval peasant went to church and saw in a stained-glass window or heard in a sermon an incident from the life of Jesus, he or she did not apprehend that incident as something that happened historically in *our* modern sense of history. Rather, their apprehension was a complex one, in which the counterpart factors to what we today would regard as the mythical were, I should guess, at least as substantial as those counterpart to our modern sense of literal chronological history. Through the sacraments and much else, but also because he or she lived before the separation between myth and history, Christ was a present reality in their life—in a way that has ceased to be the case for most moderns, at the end of a process of demythologization the course of which a modern student of the Bible ought to be able to trace for us. The impetus to demythologize, and the price that our culture has paid for this and for its inability to remythologize, are matters that it is the business of a religion department to study and to elucidate. (Bultmann is to be studied in relation not to the first century so much as to the twentieth; just as Wellhausen was once interesting for an interpretation of the second and first millenia B.C., but now for the nineteenth century A.D.)

Myth and history can be re-integrated by the modern intellect, perhaps, by pondering the role of myth in human history. The course that we propose would be no less rigorously historical than the most austere of historiographies; but it would be the history of myth that would be illuminated, or better, the historical functioning of myth, the history of humanity with myth (and more recently—aberrantly?—without it). An historical study of the Bible, to be done well, would inherently have to be an attempt (typical, some would contend, of a religion department's task in general) to understand human history as the drama of our living our life in history while being conscious of living it in a context transcending history. The mythical, far from contrasting any longer with the historical, can nowadays be seen as what had made human history human. Even those who do not see this, must recognize that the mythical has in substantial part made human history what it has in fact been. Certainly the history of the West is in significant degree a history of the role of the Bible. Our task, important and exhilarating, is to elucidate this.

Most illuminating of all to elucidate, would be how the Bible has served, and for many still serves, spiritually: What is the meaning of the (historical) fact that through it persons and groups have found commitment, liberation, transcendence? In it over the centuries have come into focus for its readers human destiny and all our ultimate concerns. At certain historical moments it has given both shape and power to humankind's drive—or call—to social justice; at other moments, to their capacity—or gift—to endure tyranny and terror. It is a scripture in that it deals, has dealt, so far as the actual lives of persons and groups is concerned, only secondarily with finite things and primarily with infinite; here has been given form the human sense of living—in terror, fascination, mystery, and grace—in relation to what is more than mundane, in oneself and beyond. Through the Bible people have found not merely ancient history but present salvation, not merely Jesus but Christ, not merely literature but God, millions attest. Those who do not use or understand these terms must wrestle with the fact that multitudes of persons have through the Bible been involved with that to which they give such names. To study the Bible must be to strive to understand it as a channel, which it has observably been, between humankind and transcendence. The Bible has not itself transformed lives, but has introduced persons and societies to that which transforms, its committed readers affirm, the historical observer reports, and the department of religion must note and interpret.

The final sector of our course would deal with the question, What does the Church, what do moderns, do with the Bible now? Now that we know and understand that the material that constitutes the Bible is what the historical critics tell us, what next? Now that we have some sophisticated awareness of the role of scriptures in various kinds of culture, of the role of symbols in various kinds of psychology and society, of the role of myth in human consciousness, what next? Now that we have seen what the Bible has been in human life in the past, what shall it be now? This part of the course could be descriptive and analytic, a study of the process of what has recently been and is now happening. It could also, in the case of some scholars and teachers of a possibly creative quality, be constructive.

The role of the Bible in contemporary Christian life—in personal piety, in liturgy, in theological normativeness, in much else—would be an inquiry continuous with a study of the dynamic role of the Bible in the life of the Church, and of Western society, over the past many centuries, as well as instructive in itself.

What the Bible has been, has done, what role it has played in human life; and what it is doing in modern life, what role it is playing; and in a few cases where imaginative extrapolation is allowed, what it may become, what role it may or might or should yet play in our lives—these are significant questions, which a religion department might surely tackle, both legitimately and rewardingly. The relation of the Bible to Palestine, one is almost tempted to say, we might leave to the orientalist departments. From religion departments we look for some study, I would hope historical, of the relation of the Bible to us.

If I were chairman of such a department, I would very deeply desire to have a course among the departmental offerings on the History of the Bible as Scripture. Yet where could I find a scholar with doctoral training equipping him or her in this field?

2

Scripture as Form and Concept: Their Emergence for the Western World

Wilfred Cantwell Smith

Taken for granted for some while now in the West has been that of course many religions have scriptures. Of course these differ in what they have to say; yet there has been little hesitation in applying the term "scripture" to them all, generically. The word is itself Western, and earlier had been applied specifically, and only, to the Bible, as revered by Christians and—rather differently—by Jews.

Everything that exists on earth, however, has come into existence historically; and it is rewarding, as one considers the history of human affairs, to take nothing for granted, inquiring rather into the process by which things that exist have emerged. This turns out especially so of matters so massively important in human life as Scripture has widely proven itself to be. It is rewarding, further, to note how things with which we are familiar and that we take for granted, partly because they have been with us for a long time, have in fact changed (evolved, degenerated) over time: have differed from century to century. It is rewarding also, in comparativist vein, to come to recognize how differing cultures and civilizations and religious orientations have perceived things that to hasty view appear similar. Similarities no doubt there are, both from century to century and from community to community. Yet differences can be no less important, especially when they turn out to be stark. Differences of content among the diverse scriptures of the various religious groups have of course been recognized, as already remarked. Differences of form, of concept, of the role of Scripture in human life, in piety or politics, of what it means to regard a text as scriptural, have been less studied—either over time or over space.

As our sub-title intimates, this present inquiry is into the historical process by which the notion of scripturalizing arose, a couple of thousand years ago in the Near East. That process can be seen as coming to a head, as it were, in the Qur'ān. It can be seen as constituted, gradually, of many strands, some of which go back very far, others of which were later than is often sensed. Our suggestion is that an understanding of our human situation, of matters in which we have been and are involved, can be furthered by our becoming more conscious of that process.

It is illuminating, I suggest, to begin with the seventh century A.D. as the virtually culminating stage of the process, and to trace it then backwards in time.

"Islam . . . is pre-eminently a . . . religion of the book," says the phenomenologist van der Leeuw;[1] and any of us who study Muslim history or any facet of Muslim life can document that characterization richly. Many years ago I advanced the view that the notion of a parallel between the Muslim Qur'ān and the Christian Bible, as two instances of the genus scripture, is of course a first approximation, but only that; closer to the truth of the two situations is an analogy between the role of the Qur'ān in Islamic life and thought, and the role in Christian life and thought of the figure of Christ. For Christians, God's central revelation is in the person of Christ, with the Bible as record of that revelation. The counterpart to the latter, in the Islamic scheme of things—the record of revelation—is the Muslim so-called "Tradition," *hadīth*, a secondary group of writings in the Islamic complex—decisive, yet secondary.[2] This thesis has been fairly widely accepted of late, even among sophisticated Muslim thinkers, let alone among comparativist Western scholars. Qur'ān is to Muslims what Christ is to Christians. It is difficult to exaggerate the centrality, and the transcendence, of the Muslim scripture for Muslim faith.

Other communities have produced sacred books, as we know; in the Islamic case it was the sacred book, rather, that produced the community. Muslims, from the beginning until now, are that group of people that has coalesced around the Qur'ān. Muhammad is important in the Islamic worldview because he brought the Qur'ān; he derives his significance from that fact. The Muslim world protested when, in the 19th century, the West called their religious movement "Mohammedanism," as though he were primary. (Similarly, Christians protest when Muslims honour Christ "because he brought the New Testament," as though it were primary.) For Muslims, God is primary; their relation to Him (*islām*) is mediated through the Qur'ān. For them, it stands uncreated, pre-existent. The Word of God is eternal, is an attribute of God Himself; and like other attributes, "it is not He nor is it other than He." Apart from these theoretical considerations, the practical role of the Qur'ān in Islamic life has throughout been central: not only morality, piety, liturgy, and what the West calls law, but in art—especially calligraphy—, in grammar, and so on.

Muslims pay Jews and Christians the compliment of calling them also "People of the Book," by which they mean that these groups have what approximates, whether closely or in partially distorted fashion, to religion in its true and proper form—as distinct from pagans and idolaters who, without divine revelation in this form, are lost.

I have begun with these remarks not in order to speak about Islam, but in order to speak about Scripture. The Islamic instance represents the notion par excellence of Scripture as a religious phenomenon; and my thesis is that it does so as the culmination of an historical process to be discerned in the Near East, gradually solidifying over the centuries. Scripture as a form and as a concept gradually emerged and developed in the Near East, I am suggesting, in a process of slow crystallization whose virtually complete stage comes with the Qur'ān.

Many have of late been reconstructing the story of this matter, internally as it were, for the Bible; first the Old Testament, and then the New. Here we are endeavoring to see the emergence of the Bible's (one could say, the two Bibles', Christian and Jewish) context. For the process in which it was, or they were, involved—the process in which, one might better say, their coalescences were in due course involved—seems to have transcended their particular formation. I am already suggesting that it transcended it in time at this end by showing up in a more developed form in the 7th century A.D. in the Islamic movement. It transcended it in time at the other end by having got launched, scholars have begun to recognize, in Babylonia and pre-Israelite Canaan in the second millenium B.C., as we shall remark later. It transcended it religiously, I think that we can see, if we note (moving backwards now from the Qur'ān) the later Zarathushtrian and the Manichee and the Mandaean and the Babylonian and the Ancient Egyptian.

It transcended it also culturally, if one takes into account, as I think we must, the Alexandrian grammarians' canonizing of what we in their wake still call the classics of Greek literature, at roughly the same time as, or a little before, the emergence (in the same town) of the Septuagint. One could readily argue that these, including the Greek Septuagint, had an influence on the development of a Jewish notion of scripture and then later a Christian one—or vice-versa: influences, if one is to use that word, were active in both, or let us say all, directions. Yet rather than arguing that, at least here, I shall suggest rather that all the variegated parts of these several developments can best be understood as various details within one over-all process—which I am calling the emergence of scripture as form and concept for the Western world.

When I say that the Qur'ān culminates this process, I do not mean to suggest that the process altogether stops at that point. A thousand years later the Granth Ṣāḥib, the scripture of the then emergent Sikh community in India, the form of it and the concept of it and its place in the personal piety and corporate polity of the Sikh community for the last three or so centuries, were manifestly influenced in turn by the Qur'ān: by Scripture as a form and a concept in the religious life of the Muslims with which the Sikh movement emerged as continuous. (It was continuous also, in another way and I think less closely, with the Hindu.) Even closer to our own day, Joseph Smith in the United States with his Book of Mormon, for example, illustrates that the notion was still generative as recently as the 19th century, even though in the 20th it has become rather problematic even for older traditions.

Yet none of these instances carries our development any further. Qur'ān and Bible have served as models for subsequent instances, but there has been no *development* since the Qur'ān. In, probably, the 9th century A.D., or in any case substantially after the Muslim conquest of Iran, a Zarathushtrian book states that Zarathushtra "brought the religion" and engraved the 1200 chapters of it on tablets of gold.[3] Indeed, for a time modern scholars thought that the writing down of the Avesta in the form of a book occurred after the rise and dominance of Islam: partly in imitation; partly under Muslim pressure, as a Zarathushtrian response to explicit Islamic recognition of the higher status, political and economic as well as spiritual, of communities with a scripture.[4] More recently, it has been recognized that that process in the Zarathushtrian case had in fact begun somewhat before the rise of Islam: yet not very long before. In any case, it came to fruition only after the arrival of the Muslims and under their influence. A rendering of the Avesta into some sort of written form can nowadays be discerned as attested incipiently at least in the sixth century A.D. Yet its consolidation into a recognized holy book seems definitely to have followed upon the establishment in Iran of the Islamic outlook.[5]

The Zarathushtrian case is illuminating for two reasons. One is its instancing a bilateral or intertwining relationship of two scriptural developments. Indeed, not only did certain steps in the long-drawn-out Iranian process occur under the influence and stimulus of the Qur'ān, but also vice-versa. The Qur'ān can be seen not only as continuous with the Biblical tradition of a written sacred book, which is explicit within it, but also as continuous with the more distinctively oral/aural tradition that for long had characterized the Zarathushtrian case. This raises the second of these points, concerning the concept "scripture" itself, and especially the word.

When a century ago through Oxford University Press Max Müller published—and this was an important event in Western culture—his 50-volume series of world Scriptures, he entitled it "Sacred Books of the East". He did not hesitate to call them "books," I imagine. The word "Bible" designated books, and the word "Scripture" designates what is written. The word *Qur'ān*, on the other hand, signifies not what is written but what is recited. Those who know Hebrew will recognize the Semitic root *qara'a* occurring in, for instance, Isaiah 40: "A voice *crying* in the wilderness"—or "proclaiming", one might say. The Qur'ān is the sacred book par excellence, no doubt; yet equally, it represents (as do other scriptures also, but some less strikingly) divine revelation as spoken and heard. Until to-day, reciting of the Qur'ān is a high art, of religious moment. The Qur'ān is the first book in the Arabic language; and the notion of writing is decisively included, proudly, in its own text. Nonetheless, alongside reading the Qur'ān and the merit and art of writing it, the hearing of the Qur'ān and the at times highly technical art and the deep devotion of reciting it aloud have from the earliest times and until today played a salient role in the life of Muslim culture and personal piety.[6]

The word "Scripture" signifies what is written down; as do all its cognates and counterparts in Western languages: *l'Écriture* ; *Scrittura* ; *die Schrift* ; plus *hē graphē*, *hai graphai* in the preceding Greek, for instance in the New Testament; and the Hebrew *K^etûbîm*—this last regularly for the later components of the Tanakh, or Old Testament, used much less often to include its earlier, more basic, elements. We shall see the importance of this point presently. Similarly the word "Bible", the Greek *biblia*, the Hebrew *seper*, signify "book" (a word that has itself changed its meaning virtually every century over the last twenty-five). Nonetheless the Bible, over much of its life, and not only for those many who held it sacred and were illiterate, has been heard, as well as—and until recent centuries no doubt much more than—received through the eyes, off the page. It has been said that the Protestant Reformation, in stressing the Preaching of the Word, and in rejecting what it called the idolatry of the mediæval Church's images, constituted a shift from the visual to the aural for at least Northern Europe's primary apprehension of the Divine. Its emphasis on the Bible was part of this. When the 1611 King James Version of the English Bible certified on its title-page that it was "Appointed to be Read in Churches", this did not mean that anyone who had a private copy should repair to the local church building whenever he or she wished to peruse its pages. Rather: in the Christian case also, the oral recitation—or proclamation—of God's Word, in the hearing of the people—but also more quietly, from memory, in the privacy of one's personal life—means that the word "scripture" in its etymological sense is not a fully accurate, fully adequate, term for our phenomenon.[7] Might one say that no Christian service, from baptism to burial, let alone the weekly gathering on Sunday, is formally authentic—could one say, none is official?—without a public reading, aloud, from Scripture?

In the early Christian Church, by the way, the Syriac word for what in the service we call "lesson" (French, *leçon*, recitation), or for "reading the lesson"—to use that tautology—is *qeryāna*: whence, evidently, "Qur'ān".[8]

This double involvement, then, written and oral/aural, book and recitation—although something in which the Bible has participated, in both the Christian and the Jewish case (the Jewish term *miqra'* is from the same root)—is once again displayed most fully by the Qur'ān. In this matter, the Qur'ān culminates a Near Eastern process of which the written strand may be more characteristic of the Semitic background, the recitation aspect more characteristic of the Iranian. For a thousand years, what we with some uncouthness call Zarathushtrian "scriptures" were primarily recited, chanted, incanted; "murmured", as the outsiders' reports of Persian matters in this connection regularly put it.[9] The Persian terms themselves[10] are rather: to learn by heart, to memorize; but apparently this memorizing was regularly done out loud (as is still true among Bombay Pārsīs, as I personally have had occasion to observe).

In the world-wide prevalence and usage of sacred texts as a generic human (or divine?) matter, one finds two broad types into which we may classify the various instances: those where reciting, or reading out loud, is primary; and those where the written form is. In several cases the alternative form is then secondary. In several cases an historical shift can be traced from the one to the other, slowly over the centuries, or more rapidly. In some cases (but most strikingly only with the Qur'ān?) the two are quite conjoined. Yet they may certainly be distinguished.

The Hindu instance (especially with *śruti*) was primarily and emphatically oral for millennia—indeed, at least until the European Max Müller's printed edition of the Rig-veda from 1854. Turning the Hindu *Veda* into a written book is an entrancing instance of nineteenth-century

Western cultural imperialism, here quietly imposing the Western sense of "scripture". The pre-Islamic Zarathushtrian instance is oral like the Hindu; yet coming into belated but eventually fairly close contact with the Semitic written form and concept, it serves as a kind of link. I have not yet investigated the degree to which a post-Persian-contact phase in the Qur'ān's orality can be discerned.

Although the Avesta was probably written down, at least in part, by 550 A.D.—that is, in still pre-Islamic times—it seems not to have been thought of as a *book* until post-Islamic, a couple of centuries later.[11] As has been true also elsewhere at times, at first writing was perceived as simply a mnemonic device, to facilitate or to ensure that the oral rendering be accurate. The oral form was clearly primary; and for many centuries it had been unsupplemented.

The world, then, into which Islam and the Qur'ān emerged was one in which already religious communities had each its scripture, in some form. This was the situation in the Near East in the early seventh century A.D.; and indeed it was so also already in the sixth, though one must not imagine that situation to have been static. In the middle of the sixth, as we have noted, the Avesta—in a language then no longer spoken—was written down, in a script invented for the purpose; and a Pahlavi (that is, a vernacular) translation of (some parts of) it also appeared in written form. Also by the opening of the sixth century the Babylonian Talmud, many scholars feel, was (or was virtually) completed; others speak of the end of that century.[12] To put this last point in another way: *Tôrāh she be-'al peh*, the divine instruction to humankind in the form that had been oral among Jews, reputedly since Sinai, was around 500 or 600 A.D. crystallized in authoritative form. This process had closed in a century or two earlier for the Jewish community of Jerusalem: its Talmud was "brought to closure" by the beginning of the fifth century.[13] In these two cases also, it is interesting to note, the authoritative or "canonical" form of the Talmud, as a consolidated text, was the oral version. For several centuries the written form remained peripheral, secondary.[14]

In the fourth century much was going on, throughout the area. This was the century during which the Christian community made substantial (although not yet quite final) progress in coalescing a new, supplementary, scripture for itself, in the form of what it came to call a New Testament.[15] (It was in Greek, as were also its previous Scriptures, which thereupon became its Old Testament: the Septuagint.) Also in the fourth century the vigorous Manichee movement formalized its seven books of scripture, paralleling, it seems consciously, its explicit rival contenders for a following.[16] The Manichee movement was up-to-date in these and other formal matters from the start. Its founder Mani already in the third century (though the text may be apocryphal, perhaps from the fourth) is presented as saying that other founders of new religious movements wrote no books, but rather left that to their disciples, citing Zarathushtra, the Buddha, and Jesus.[17] He himself will make no such mistake: he sees to it that his message he himself will commit to writing.

This is an extremely interesting observation: it seems to suggest that already in the third or fourth century the idea had got around, at least to perceptive minds, that religious movements have each a book, that a new religious movement must have a new written book. On more careful scrutiny, however, the stage reached at that point is not so clearly advanced. To have the message of one's group's original leader preserved intact in written form and thus available is not yet to indicate necessarily how formally scriptural, how sacred, that writing is perceived as being (as, for instance, Wittgenstein's followers, keen to publish posthumously their master's words, of course know[18]). Even to revere what someone says, and then to have it written down, is not yet necessarily to have a holy book. And as we have said, it seems to have been the fourth century, rather than the third, that a crystallized Manichee canon is fairly well congealed, though doubtless in the third the process may have got underway.

In both centuries, what interests me here is the wider context in which this was so. In that wider context the Manichee emergence and development are not merely a symptom, though they surely are that, but also an active and activating participant. They influenced the others, as well as vice-versa. It is from the fourth century also that we have our earliest documentation of the Mandaean thesis, important later, that their own and other communities' scriptures were affirmed to be pre-existent.[19] They expressed this idea in a form that the Qur'ān later echoes, and still later and more elaborately, Muslim theology and folklore; a form of which the second-millenium-B.C. Babylonian and Canaanite motifs at which we shall be looking presently are a forerunner: namely, in the idea that there are books in heaven from before creation with humanity's destinies inscribed in them; and that the Saviour had had privileged access to these books, bringing their contents (later, it was said, bringing the books themselves) down to earth to share with his fellow humans. There is some question, however, whether it be apt to call these notions "Mandaean" this early. Perhaps. The community that cherished them and that goes by that Aramaic term for "Gnostic" coalesces in the next century (the fifth) or so[20] as a distinct identifiable and self-conscious group—perhaps in part as a result of these Gnostic scriptural writings (these traditions that became written, became scriptures)?

At the end of that same fourth century a centralizing Christian

Pope in Rome decided that a coherent unified Latin version of the scriptures (it would hardly yet be correct to say, "of the Bible") would be helpful; and he asked Jerome to work on it. This laid the basis[21] for what crystallized in the sixth century or later[22] as the Vulgate—which then for a thousand years (half again that much for Roman Catholics) *was* the Christian Scripture for the Western Church. This version had no predecessors in Latin as a unified, boundaried, authoritative entity, a Scriptural book; even though various parts of it had predecessors: this and that discrete writing, in this and that divergent wording—especially scattered in North Africa. Nor did the new version itself yet constitute such an entity, although it did much to further the process.[23] (In Rome itself, the use of Greek for a Biblical text had continued well into the third century.) Gradually the Greek word *biblia*, a plural, became during the Middle Ages in Latin a singular.[24]

Before the fourth century, as we have noted, the Scripture of the Christian movement was in effect the Septuagint,[25] a product of Greek Alexandria of the third to first centuries B.C. and beyond; of which, more below. For like the Manichee, but with a much narrower, much less pluralist, awareness, the Christian movement too emerged into a world where the religious milieu of which it was aware, the Jewish, already possessed a scripture (or we should better say, "Scriptures"), as we can see in action from the numerous references to what is written, in the pages of the Gospels, and, to a less extent, in the Epistles. Yet the Old Testament as one knows it to-day was only partially in mind, had only partially coalesced; as the re-iterated phrase "The Law and the Prophets" illuminates (naming two out of the three groups of writings presently constituting the canon) —occasionally, The Law and the Prophets and the Psalms (Luke 24:44)—and often more simply a reference to what is written by Moses (Jesus seems to have envisaged Moses as literally writing out the Pentateuch, by hand). The crystallizing process was in Jesus's day unmistakably under way, yet had progressed by then only to a certain stage. It had gone far enough, however, that the idea of a religious community's having scriptures was adopted, appropriated, absorbed, almost unwittingly.

Of course we have scripture from the past, the early Christians felt. The only significant person seriously to question the idea was Marcion, in the second century, who saw the new Christian movement as substantially different from the one out of which it otherwise felt that it had come, yet from which by now (second century) it was sharply alienated. It is sufficiently different, he suggested, that it need not conform to previous dispensations in the matter of Scripture; just as it need not in other matters, such as law, or even in monotheism. Even he does not seem to have suggested no scripture at all, however; his idea was, rather, the striking one that rather than continuing to have the Jewish scriptures the Church should generate a new scripture of its own. It is an anachronism, however, to think of him as advocating simply "the New Testament," as we used to be told. He proposed a set of writings in some ways comparable to, yet sharply distinct from, that as yet quite uncrystallized corpus (one might say: non-existent as a corpus[26]). It comprised two parts: an *Instrumentum*, and *Antitheses*: the former constituted of an abbreviated Lucan gospel and selected letters of Paul, drastically amended; the latter, of his own composition, a kind of commentary on the former.[27]

His movement was not without result. It became indeed a movement, especially in the third century but enduring in Syria into the tenth; it was more than idiosyncratic. The result was not what he had in mind; yet one may see his movement as playing a significant role in the process that concerns us. The Church did not drop the Jewish scripture idea, but adapted it rather, with a *tour de force*, some might say: one accomplished over the next couple of centuries. There are partial parallels later in partial theory though not in practice in the Qur'ān; and 1000 years later the Sikh scriptures emulated this again in a minor fashion.[28] Yet in the end it could be contended that Christian scripture is the only instance in world history where one movement explicitly incorporates the scripture of another as such within its own, adding things new but making the old part and parcel—even if, in ways never fully clarified,[29] a somewhat subordinate part and parcel. It accomplished this during the fourth to sixth centuries, as we have said. It was moving gradually towards it already in the third, of course.

That was the century also in which the Jews culminated a two-hundred-year process in their first crystallizing of what had been somewhat diffuse oral legal traditions into the systematized and later written Mishnah.[30] This was the century, too, in which the Corpus Hermeticum was completed.[31] Also, and relatedly, in process at this time was a certain coalescing, though yet incomplete, of texts for a movement that is still alive and well in modern America, India, and elsewhere: astrology. The world history of astrology is complex but not unmanageable: until I began this present inquiry I had not realized how interconnected has been its elaborate and widespread development around the world, what a coherent historical process it has constituted, from Egypt in Hellenistic times[32] into Western Civilization generally, also eastward to India, and thence, along with the Buddhist missionary movement, to China and on.[33] The chief Sanskrit translations and popularizing texts appear from the second and especially third centuries A.D.;[34] the important Hellenistic work *Tetrabiblos* of the second century A.D..[35] and the fifth-century compendium of Hephaestos of Thebes,[36] are among texts that helped to give this movement partially systematized coherence in the West. Yet neither the movement, nor these or others of its writings, ever attained a status of the same order as the scripturalizing communities that we call religious. Maybe I should not have introduced this item into our discussion here; I thought it perhaps legitimate to note that things were going on some of which did, and some did not, attain a degree of crystallized specialness for which words such as "sacred" serve. Although I know in fact relatively little about it, it seems clear that the astrology movement, although incorporating materials from earlier Babylon, emerged basically in the area and period that here concern us and developed then into a world-wide affair with enormous influence in the history of humankind since, as a more or less coherent system of ideas—and yet, never became a community, and never generated scriptures, two facts whose possible interrelation would perhaps be worth exploring; and it may remind us too that, *pace* nineteenth-century Western interpreters' tendencies, religious movements are substantially more than systems of ideas.

The second to the seventh centuries A.D. in the Near East, then, show us the Scripture movement in process of crystallizing. The various new religious movements of that time and place each participated in that over-all process, in ways—and this focuses my thesis—that varied at least as much, I get the impression, with the century concerned as with the particular movement under consideration: the Christian, the various Gnostic and later Mandaean, the Zarathushtrian (not exactly a new movement), the Manichee, various minor groupings, and finally the Islamic. This phase begins with the Jewish movement already to some degree possessed of a scripture, its crystallization reputedly or symbolically culminating in the so-called Council of Javneh (Greek, Jamnia) about 90 A.D., but actually somewhat later,[37] and having developed to that point very gradually over many preceding centuries. The story of that long gradual development is nowadays being studied and told with increasing care and emphasis,[38] and I leave the telling to others, contenting myself with calling attention to one or two highlights, and chiefly suggesting once again the context within which it seems to have been embedded—or better, to have been dynamically involved.

In that context, I note specifically three matters: the Greek classical tradition; the tradition from Babylon and early Canaan of a celestial-tablets idea or divine books; and the general tradition of writing. One ought to include the Iranian developments[39] and those from Ancient Egypt also,[40] but I leave them aside, with due apology (awaiting further study). (I leave aside also the ceremonial reciting of ancient epics in neo-Babylonian festivals, and other Mesopotamian matters.[41])

The Greek tradition is fairly perspicuous. Crucial for us is the emergence, in what we therefore have come to call post-Classical times, of a formal concept of classics. Hereaclides Ponticus already in the middle or more probably late fourth century B.C. adjudged Aeschylus, Euripides, and Sophocles to be the Athenian tragedians of salient worth; and presently those three, and they alone, were not merely read but cherished. The others, and I gather that there had been several, were forgotten, their texts are lost, and these three were launched on the career of elevated status with which they have been honoured ever since, until to-day.[42] On the whole the process occurred a little later than this, especially in the third century B.C., and especially in Alexandria, where the *grammatikoi*—the word itself is illuminating: "those concerned with what is written"—carefully edited accurate texts, carefully adjudicated which writings should be included in their canon (I do not find it reasonable to call it otherwise than that), and established a corpus of what we now recognize as "the Greek Classics."[43]

There is a complication here: for those classics were the product not only of the so-called classical Greek age; they included Homer (and Hesiod). Already in what we to-day call classical Athens the Iliad and Odyssey were a privileged tradition: semi-scripture, if you like, of the oral type.[44] Alexandria in the third century turned them carefully into scripture of the written type, thus enabling them to serve like the writings (*sic*) of Plato, Aristotle, and the dramatists, as ideal literature also for the non-Greek-speaking phases of Western civilization since that time.

The Alexandria milieu is context for our concern here also in another sense. At virtually the same time, Greek-speaking Jews there and in upper Egypt were involved in important connected developments. In the early third century B.C. in their Egyptian synagogues the Pentateuch was being read in Hebrew followed by a rendering in Greek; later that century a separate Greek version appeared, as in effect almost a book, a formal entity. By the end of the next century the view was promulgated that that translation, the so-called Septuagint, had itself been miraculous:[45] a scripturalizing step, strikingly. By the end of that third century (by which time Hebrew was no longer current even in Palestine, let alone in Egypt), the second batch of Hebrew writings, the Prophets, was perhaps more or less canonized in Palestine,[46] and gradually the Septuagint was enlarged by such new additions (but not exactly the same ones as its Hebrew counterpart). By the year 1 A.D. almost the whole of what Christians later called the Old Testament, except Qoheleth, was in the Septuagint. (Qoheleth was added perhaps a century later.[47]) I mention all this partly because it strikes me that a canonizing process, especially if one thinks of it as in part an integrating of former disparate or at least independent components into one reified entity, is unavoidably hastened by the translation matter. Before a notion of canon has been formalized or finalized one in fact must decide what to translate; what to incorporate into the in this case Greek repository; into one's liturgically functional as well as revered and normative ("sacred") book.

In this double sense, Alexandria played a highly significant role in the scripturalizing process. The Septuagint was not merely a translation, however; in due course it incorporated within itself additional writings composed originally in Greek. That is, it not only participated in the scripturalizing process, but carried it forward. Another way of putting this point is to say that the Greek-speaking Jews continued the process begun by and now inherited from their Semitic-speaking ancestors.

Yet there is more: a triple or even fourth sense. For Alexandria, and its classical tradition, provided still another element without which scripture is not a viable operating concept and form—or at least, not for material previously unscripturalized. For this Greek city developed the pattern of interpreting allegorically ancient texts whose literal meaning is out of tune with newer conceptions. That pattern too it inherited from "classical" Athens; Hellenistic thinkers developed it carefully and acutely, the philosophic interpretation of Homer and Hesiod specifically.[48] Jews in this environment appropriated, absorbed, this; with the result that by the end of the B.C. era Greek-speaking (*lege* Greek-thinking) Jews introduced this immensely consequential orientation into also Biblical interpretation; or we may say, into interpretations that made a Bible continuingly possible. Specifically, Philo of Alexandria was the first to do so; we all know that he was not the last. In this he was simply following up tendencies well established among his fellow Hellenistic Jews; and among his fellow Alexandrians, pagan as well. Put another way, he was inserting the on-going development of Biblical interpretation into the larger transcending context of the process of the development of classicized or canonized ancient texts.[49]

My second consideration for the B.C. period is the concept of heavenly tablets. The Swedish historian of religion Geo Widengren noticed some years ago a parallel between the Babylonian Tablets of Destiny idea, attested in cuneiform from before or about 1000 B.C., and the notion, even the phrasing, of revelation serving in the Qur'ān; and he set to tracing the outworking of the idea and found it running as a continuous thread repeatedly showing itself here and there through the almost two thousand years of intervening religious history in the region.[50] Not every one of the details in his argument carries conviction; yet in general it is evident that he is on to something major. The Semitic gods Samas and Adad are depicted in the ancient texts as giving inscribed tablets in a bag to the mythical king En-me-du-ran-ki. Hammurabi (the late third or early second millenium B.C.) is presented as having been given the law code by that god Samas;[51] and in a land where, unlike Egypt, there is virtually no stone, that law was copied in the usual manner of clay tablets but the original was cut in diorite, and set in the temple of Marduk: representing as it did the cosmic order, not merely a mundane. And I remember the excitement with which only rather recently I noted that not merely the notion but indeed the actual word, *lawḥ/lūaḥ*, in its Arabic and Hebrew forms respectively, is the same for the celestial tablets on which the Qur'ān is eternally inscribed[52] and for the tablets of revelation given to Moses on Sinai.[53] Widengren elaborates the revelation idea, to which also to-day we are in our own way heirs; he does so by delineating the ancient Mesopotamian Assembly of the Gods notion, where on New Year's Day in a book (*sic*) the events of the coming year on Earth are written (*sic*). Outstanding individuals become decisively important to their fellow human beings if they can somehow ascend to heaven and become privy to what is in that celestial book; an alternative is that one of the gods, preferably their chief, may take the initiative and show or give the book or parts of it to such a person. A recently published Harvard doctoral dissertation shows that such an idea of Divine Council, with a special human person somehow having privileged access to its records, obtained also in pre-Hebrew Canaanite lore, and argues that it may have been with that source rather than directly with Babylon that later Hebrew ideas were continuous.[54] If we speculate as to the situation in Israel in, say, 1000 B.C., we may suppose that in a given village there was no book and perhaps nobody was literate but that around the campfires at night tales were told and vividly received of Moses and his divine tablets received at Sinai, written by the finger of God.

The Qur'ān as divine revelation is a late yet fairly exact crystallization of the process that begins with this divine knowledge cut in stone and made available to humankind. Less fully yet not negligibly the Bible as we know it, considered as a revealed book, is a development from this campfire imagery. Later on, Moses came to be thought of as having received at Sinai not only "the ten words" cut in stone, but five whole books known to-day as the Pentateuch; and still later, as having received these latter in writing and as well an oral instruction (Hebrew: *tôrāh*) "finally" cast in book form by Judah ha-Nasi by ca. 200 A.D. as the Mishnah, and eventually in more ample form as the Jerusalem Talmud by 400 or still more amply as the Babylonian Talmud by 500 or 600. This latter date is that by which the other stream from this tradition, the Christian, had almost closed in on its channel of a similar development from the same source, by giving to its scripture, by then fairly well consolidated, a status that recaptures in many respects these notions of divine book vouchsafed to earth. I myself growing up in the early years of this century on this continent in a more or less fundamentalist home inherited some such view of the Bible as a divine writing sent down among us.[55] We have already noted this with the Gnostic-Mandaean material; to some extent the Manichee; and by the ninth century A.D. the Zarathushtrian.

Hindu, Buddhist, Chinese counterparts, teasingly similar in other ways, have little or none of this particular notion.

Our brief survey is virtually done, but one may close with just a word about writing as such. A study of scripture should begin, perhaps, rather with language, that distinctively and profoundly human characteristic. Modern linguists have studied its prose dimension, not much its poetry; I am coming to think that a true understanding of the human must wrestle with three major modes of language: prose, poetry, and scripture. That, however, I leave aside until another occasion; here, just a word about writing. To-day we are all so literate, have become so familiar with writing and with books, that we have forgotten the aura that once surrounded this mysterious contrivance; the counterpart in our day has I suppose been recently rather the computer, awesome to some. And regarding published books, which to-day inundate us, one may recall the story apparently going the rounds in the Soviet Union of the enthusiast who busied himself typing out *War and Peace* by hand and giving copies to the young, on the grounds that nobody these days of course takes printed books seriously. It was not always so.

Writing emerged in the Near East about 3000 B.C., in Egypt (hieroglyphic) and in Mesopotamia (cuneiform).[56] For long it was the prerogative of a circumscribed elite, of temple and palace bureaucracies. Somewhere about 1500 to 1200 B.C., the alphabet was invented [57]—a step in the direction of democratization: from then on, what the bureaucracy thought important could be preserved, as before, but smaller and unofficial groups could now do the same if they were serious about it. A significant step was taken, or anyway is illustrated, in 621 B.C.: the Josiah reform[58], triggered by the discovery of a book in the Jerusalem temple. Whether the work was composed and surreptitiously lodged in the temple in order to be discovered so, as was contended for a time, or was rather, as some modern scholarship[59] tends to prefer, found there perhaps inadvertently, does not affect my argument; since in any case the book was in fact composed, and in fact set forth innovating ideas. Illustrated here is a transition from writing as a way of fixing the status quo to writing as the manifesto of a dissident group; from writing as recording to writing as creative.

Prior to this, writing served to make permanent what was already established, authoritative. Here, by contrast, the idea was to establish what was newly written. This begins the process to which we have all become heir: writers who write (*sic*) new ideas to change the course of history.

The revolutionary nature of this was masked. The new ideas could prove revolutionary only insofar as they seemed traditional; and the work that was discovered was ascribed to Moses (who had died some six centuries earlier) as a so-called "prophet" figure. What a brilliant, what a consequential, forgery or misunderstanding!—consolidating the outlook of the eighth- and seventh-century-B.C. prophets in a written document. Instead of something being written down because it was important, this message was considered important because it had been written down.

Probably this was not simply a hoax. The book, though novelly forward-looking in the sense of proposing innovations, was also traditionally backward-looking not only in that its programme for reform was couched in terms of ancient authority, specifically Moses, but also in that the author or authors did genuinely feel, it seems, that their programme was reviving or re-forming (in the literal sense of forming once again) inherited traditions from of old. (There is some evidence that this appeal to a reconstructed picture of a community's earlier age being presented anew as a model for the present, for inspiration and aspiration, reflects in an innovative fashion a new mood of attention to the past that was emerging at that particular period—around the seventh century B.C.—not only in Palestine but rather widely in the Near East, from Egypt to Assyria and Babylonia.[60]) Reformers, as the word itself affirms, have ever since regularly presented themselves as re-establishing a pristine past while actually proposing a novel future. Apart from that more general consideration, at this historical stage writing as such was not yet conceived as an instrument for introducing newness.

I said that I would omit from this hastening survey of the B.C. period the Persian development. Let me just remark, however, in the matter of written language, on the massive Behistūn or Bîsitūn inscription in Iran,[61] about 500 B.C.: that decisively imposing statement incised on the vast rock-face whereby the Emperor Darius proudly asserts his accomplishments, desiring all to remember them and to be impressed. May Ahura Mazda, he proclaims, protect and reward him who preserves, punish and curse him who destroys, this[62]—a sentiment echoed often by scripturalists later.[63] On a much smaller scale, this strand in our process is continued in the Safaitic inscriptions in the Arabian desert half a millenium or so later.[64]

In fine, my suggestion is that the emergence for the Western World of scripture as a form and as a concept—a form and concept playing a prodigiously important role in human lives and societies throughout our history until to-day—is a rich and complex process, deserving more attention than I, certainly, have yet been able to give it, a process fascinating and rewarding to study. We have tended to derive our concept of scripture from the Bible; I am suggesting that we are now in a position where our understanding of the Bible, and of much else across the world, may begin to be derived from a larger concept of scripture.

I close without developing that larger concept, but would wish to stress its importance. An historian of religion, entranced to find scripture of one or another varied sort—but how varied!—virtually across the civilized world, and entranced to find human beings virtually throughout the world evincing apparently some almost common human propensity to scripturalize, is inclined to feel that the *content* of this or that scripture, however interesting and however diverse, needs supplementing in scholarly study by this other inquiry into the *concept* of scripture; generically, and in particular cases. It has been an amazing idea, an astonishing form. Moreover, this is no antiquarian inquiry: both our Church and our civil society to-day need an improved understanding of scripture.

Readers will have noticed my remarking above that the concept of scripture has not developed since the Qur'ān in the seventh century—an astonishing fact; needing nuancing, yet a grave fact for at least the West. It constitutes a luxury that we can no longer afford. Our world needs a new concept of scripture. The movement that began with Spinoza with his new orientation to the Bible texts, and that has grown into the massive and important enterprise calling itself historical criticism, has hardly provided that new concept. The result of its immensely illuminating work has been to dismantle for us our inherited notion of scripture, leaving us with a focus on content but without form; or at best, given the new concern with canon, with a form but without a concept.

Brevard Childs[65] and others[66] chide the discipline for traditionally ignoring the problem: studying the Bible as if it were not scripture. My way of putting this matter is to observe that modern Biblical scholarship, practising what is dubbed historical criticism, has studied the texts of the Bible in what I call their pre-scriptural phase. A more recent development now emerging, grown restless with that, concerns itself with the Bible in terms rather of literary criticism, treating those same texts not now "like any other historical document", to use the Spinozian phrase, but rather "like any other piece of literature", to use the recent one. This, in my view, is to consider the Bible in its post-scriptural phase. The long intervening era is omitted. All the texts that make up the Bible existed for a time before they became scripture; and as such they can constitute the subject-matter, at that level, of one type of inquiry. They continue to exist as texts for certain people to-day for whom they no longer serve as transcendent luminosity, as a heavenly word; and at that level, can become the focus for another type. A still more significant concern, I make bold to suggest, especially of course for those of us in the study of religion but indeed for an understanding in general of the human condition, and my own primary interest in the matter of late, lies, one might say, between these two, at least chronologically, yet beyond and above them, perhaps, in other senses: lies in the study of the Bible as scripture. My suggestion is that this may become a next great development in our studies.

The question, however, is difficult; and the reason for that is also a reason that it is both exciting and important: namely, that we scholars do not in fact understand what scripture is. We do not know how to treat a text as scripture. We do not know what it means to say that for nigh on two thousand years the Bible was scripture for a large sector of humankind. Yet we must of course say it, with force; and say, too, that the Bible is significant at all because of this enigmatic fact. Also the Qur'ān, the Gita, the Chinese classics.

To the small question, how did a concept of scripture arise, I hope that I may perhaps have contributed here if not a preliminary partial answer, at least a provocative suggestion that the query is significant. More important is the question, which I proffer as an issue worth widespread pursuing over the next say twenty-five years: how are we to understand what scripture has been over the centuries, in its various instances, once it arose, playing its monumental role in human history, sociological and personal. Still more important is the next challenge, to both academia and Church: to forge a new concept that will serve our understanding of the world-wide phenomenon in the past, and will serve also our living with our own and our fellows' scriptures (or, for the sceptics, at the very least with our fellows' scriptures) now—and in coming centuries.

NOTES

1. "Islam . . . Vor allem . . . ist eine rechte Buchreligion." G. Van der Leeuw, *Phänomenologie der Religion* (Tübingen: J.C.B. Mohr [Paul Siebeck], 1933), p. 415. I have cited from the English translation: G. Van der Leeuw, *Religion in Essence & Manifestation: a study in phenomenology*, trans. by J.E. Turner (London: Allen & Unwin, 1938), p. 438.

2. Wilfred Cantwell Smith, "Some Similarities and Some Differences Between Christianity and Islam: an essay in comparative religion," first published in: James Kritzeck and R. Bayly Winder, edd., *The World of Islam: studies in honour of Philip K. Hitti* (London: Macmillan, and New York: St. Martin's Press, 1959), pp. 47–59 (esp. p. 52), and several times reprinted (most recently in Wilfred Cantwell Smith, *On Understanding Islam* (Berlin & New York: de Gruyter, [1981], 1984), pp. 233–246); also in Urdu translation. (As this work is going to press, it

has been brought to my attention that this theme was set forth earlier in Continental scholarship by Nathan Söderblom. See Annemarie Schimmel, "The Muslim Tradition," in Frank Whaling, ed., *The World's Religious Traditions: current perspectives in religious studies* (Edinburgh: T. & T. Clark, 1984), p. 133. I am much indebted for, and delighted by, this information.]

3. *A Catalogue of the Provincial Capitals of Ērānshahr (Pahlavi text, version and commentary)* by J. Markwart; ed. by G. Messina (Roma: Pontificio Istituto Biblico, 1931 - Analecta Orientalia 3), p. 9, § 4; see also the remarks to this section on pp. 28–29, where *inter alia* the alternative is mentioned of his having written rather on 12,000 cowhides, another widespread view. The word used in classical Sanskrit for "book" (*pustaka*) is not of Sanskrit origin but is a loan-word from the Persian term for "hide".

4. This position was set forth influentially by François Nau, "La dernière rédaction de l'Avesta," being chapter iii (pp. 192–199) of his article "La transmission de l'Avesta et l'époque probable de sa dernière rédaction", *Revue de l'histoire des religions*, 95 (1926-27): 149–199.

5. The "some form" of book emerged apparently during the reign of Khosrow Anoshīravān (A.D. 531–579), probably as a court initiative. The consolidating of a canon (oral) is probably somewhat earlier than this; and there is some evidence for a scattered writing down of passages from that still predominantly oral-recitation tradition also from before Khosrow's time. Yet the elevating of such writings into a form that may reasonably be called a book may be even later: it is on this point that my word "incipiently" is based. Widengren, who pushes an early writing of texts at least as strongly as do other scholars, nonetheless says explicitly that this next step occurred after the Islamic movement had arrived: "When the Arabs conquered Iran . . . it was only then that they [the Zoroastrians] started thinking of Avesta as a *Book*," containing a divine revelation received by Zarathustra (p.52 of his op. cit. infra within this note). On this whole matter for Iran the most recent summary is "The Written Avesta" in Mary Boyce, *Zoroastrians: their religious beliefs and practices* (London, Boston, &c: Routledge & Kegan Paul, 1979), pp.134–135. For earlier statements, see Geo Widengren, "Holy Book and Holy Tradition in Iran: the problem of the Sassanid Avesta," in F.F. Bruce and E.G. Rupp, edd., *Holy Book and Holy Tradition* (Manchester University Press, and Grand Rapids: Eerdmans, 1968), pp. 36–53; Richard Frye, *The Heritage of Persia* (Cleveland and New York: World Publishing Company, 1963), p. 213; R.W. Bailey, *Zoroastrian Problems in the Ninth-Century Books: Ratanbai Katrack Lectures* (Oxford: Clarendon, 1943, reprinted 1971), pp. 169–170. It is clear to all concerned that the oral tradition took precedence over the written throughout this period and beyond; also it is widely recognized that when the Muslims conquered Iran, they did not forthwith perceive the Zarathushtrians as a community possessing a holy book. This aspect of the matter is taken up again later in our text.

6. See, for instance, Labib al-Said, *The Recited Koran: a history of the first recorded version*, translated and adapted by Bernard Weiss, M.A. Rauf, and Morroe Berger (Princeton: Darwin Press, 1975). This is an abridgement and adaptation

of an Arabic work: Labīb al-Sa'īd, *al-Jam' al ṣawtī al-awwal li-l-Qur'ān al-karīm, aw al-muṣḥaf al-murattal* (Cairo: Dār al Kātib al-'Arabī, 1967). Further: F.M. Denny, "The *Adab* on Recitation: Text and Context," in *International Congress for the Study of the Qur'an... Canberra... 1980* (Canberra: Australian National University, n.d. [sc. 1983], second edition), pp.143–160; also, Fredrick M. Denny, "Exegesis and Recitation: their development as classical forms of Qur'anic piety," in: Frank E. Reynolds and Theodore M. Ludwig, edd., *Transitions and Transformations in the History of Religions: essays in honor of Joseph M. Kitagawa* (Leiden: Brill, 1980) pp.[91]–123. For a striking elaboration of the point that originally the word *qur'ān* served to designate a reciting of a scriptural passage, see William A. Graham, "Qur'ān as Spoken Word: an Islamic contribution to the understanding of scripture," in Richard C. Martin, ed., *Islam and the History of Religions* (Tucson: University of Arizona Press, 1984) and his "The Earliest Meaning of 'Qur'ān'," *Die Welt des Islams* (vol. 64, 1984), both forthcoming. Cf. also our next note.

7. My colleague William A. Graham, Jr., is currently at work on a major study of the oral/aural use of "scripture" around the world, including at some length the Christian case over the centuries. An initial fruit of his study in this realm appears as his contribution to this present volume. Cf. also our preceding note.

8. Arthur Jeffery, *The Foreign Vocabulary of the Qur'ān* (Baroda: Oriental Institute, 1938), pp. 233–234; with the references there cited. More recently and fully: John Bowman, "Holy Scriptures, Lectionaries and the Qur'an," in A.H. Johns, ed., *International Congress* (op. cit., our note 6 above), pp. 29–37.

9. An example: the use of the Syriac term *reṭnā*, sometimes accompanied with disparaging adjectives. See, for a Christian instance, *Histoire de Mar Jabalaha, de trois autres patriarches, d'un prêtre et de deux laïques, nestoriens*, ed. Paul Bedjan (Leipzig: Harrassowitz, 1895), p.240, line 5. The same word was used in Zarathushtrian references in Jewish Aramaic: e.g., *TB Sotah* 22a, cited in Saul Lieberman, *Hellenism in Jewish Palestine: studies in the literary transmission, beliefs and manners of Palestine in the I Century B.C.E.—IV century C.E.* (New York: Jewish Theological Seminary, 5722-1962—Stroock Publication Fund), p. 88, where this author translates "The magician mumbles and understands not what he says".

10. Widengren, "Holy Book..." (above, our note 5), pp. 45–47.

11. See our note 5 above.

12. E.g., Haim Zalman Dimitrovsky, summarizing modern scholarship in general, in his article "Talmud and Midrash" in the New Encyclopaedia Britannica, 15th edn. (1974), Macropaedia, 17: 1006-1014; on the 6th-century date, see p. 1008. The reservation implied in my adverb "virtually" in the sentence in my text is based on Hermann L. Strack, *Introduction to the Talmud and Midrash* (New York: Atheneum—a Temple Book, 1980), chap. 9, "History of the Talmud Text", pp. 76ff., and the recent writing of Jacob Neusner, the most thorough investigator and an advocate of the 600 A.D. date.

13. Dimitrovsky (our preceding note just above), loc. cit., p. 1008; and Neusner.

14. In the academies, discussion was always based on oral texts. If there was a problem regarding a particular passage, the Rabbis called on the *tannā'*, a professional memorizer who functioned the way published books do for us to-day. His memorized version was authoritative; written texts, in contrast, were but notes to aid beginners, and were quite private and without authority. See Lieberman, op. cit. (above, our note 9), "The Publication of the Mishnah", pp. 83 ff., esp. p. 88. See also Binger Gerhardsson, *Memory and Manuscript: oral tradition and written transmission in Rabbinic Judaism and early Christianity* (Uppsala, Lund: C. W. K. Gleerup; Copenhagen: Ejnar Munksgaard, 1961–trans. (from the [unpublished?] Swedish) by Eric J. Sharpe, esp. "The transmission of the Oral Torah", pp. 71 ff.; and H.L. Strack, op. cit. (our note 12 above), p. 77. (It may be noted, in passing, that while Gerhardsson's book has been criticized for its interpretations on the Christian side, now superseded, evidently it remains recognized as excellent on Judaic matters.) For long, the written Torah was what is to-day the Pentateuch; the oral Torah was oral. In my observations earlier in this present article regarding an "Iranian" predilection for oral/aural "Scripture," Semitic for written, as possible influence on or continuity with later Islamic, I admitted unclarity as to historical connections in this matter; and I admit further unclarity as to possible continuities between Jewish "oral Torah" and Muslim oral Qur'ān, and indeed as to possible comparable continuity between Iranian (Mesopotamian?) practice and Jewish developments. More historical work is requisite here.

15. The Greek so translated (῾η καινη διαθηκη) designated originally a new divine dispensation: "This cup is the new testament in my blood . . .", Luke 22:20, King James version (cf. the Revised Standard version, ". . . new covenant . . ."). For a discussion of the historical process by which the phrase changed its meaning to become the name of a collecion of texts, see W.C. Van Unnik, "῾Η καινη διαθηκη—a problem in the early history of the canon" [*Studia Patristica*, 1 (1961): 221-227] in *Sparsa Collecta: the collected essays of W.C. Van Unnik* (3 voll., Leiden: E.J. Brill, 1973-[in process]—Supplements to Novum Testamentum, 29–31), 2(1980): [157]–171. For the general process of a canonizing of a New Testament as a scripture (in significant part, of course, as *the* scripture) of the Church, see, for instance, chapters 5-6-7 of Hans Freiherr von Campenhausen, *Die Entstehung der christlichen Bibel* (Tübingen: J.C.B. Mohr [Paul Siebeck], 1968—Gerhard Ebeling, ed., Beiträge zur historischen Theologie, 39); Hans von Campenhausen, *The Formation of the Christian Bible*, trans. J.A. Baker (Philadelphia: Fortress, 1972); and Werner Georg Kümmel, "Die Entstehung des Kanons des Neuen Testaments," in his *Einleitung in das Neue Testament* (Heidelberg: Quelle & Meyer, 1973—which is formally a revised 17th edn. of a 19th-century Feine-Behm work of the same title), esp. pp. 420–444; in the English translation, by Howard Clark Kee: Kümmel, *Introduction to the New Testament* (Nashville and New York: Abingdon, 1975), see pp. 475–503. And see below: e.g., at our notes 27 ff.

16. See G. Haloun and W. B. Henning, "The Manichaean Canon," being part ii, pp. 204–212, of their "The Compendium of the Doctrines and Styles of the Teaching of Mani, The Buddha of Light," in *Asia Major*, (1953), pp. [180]–212.

17. The remarks are quoted in translation from an unpublished manuscript in the Berlin State Museum, in Johannes Leipoldt und Siegfried Morenz, *Heilige Schriften: Betrachtungen zur Religionsgeschichte der antiken Mittelmeerwelt* (Leipzig: Harrassowitz, 1953), p. 7. The suggestion that the passage is aprocryphal comes in Haloun and Henning, op. cit. (our preceding note, just above), p. 211.

18. See L. Wittgenstein, *Lectures and Conversations on Aesthetics, Psychology and Religious Belief*, Cyril Barrett, ed. (Oxford: Basil Blackwell [1966], 1970), noting especially the Preface, pp. [vii]–[viii]. The opening paragraph of that Preface, displaying our modern sense of a book as not merely composed by but carefully proof-read by its author, reads: "The first thing to be said about this book is that nothing contained herein was written by Wittgenstein himself. The notes published here are not Wittgenstein's own lecture notes but notes taken down by students, which he neither saw nor checked. It is even doubtful that he would have approved of their publication, at least in their present form. Since, however, they deal with topics only briefly touched upon in his other published writings, and since for some time they have been circulating privately, it was thought best to publish them in a form approved by their authors." These "authors" of the notes are dutifully listed on the title-page, in a sub-title: "compiled from notes taken by Yorick Smythies, Rush Rhees and James Taylor." (All of Wittgenstein's now available works were published after his death by his disciples, except only the *Tractatus*, 1921; the posthumous *Investigations* he had vacillatingly intended, on and off, to publish; yet not, it would seem, in just the form in which the work eventually appeared. See Ludwig Wittgenstein, *Philosophische Untersuchungen/Philosophical Investigations*, translated by G. E. M. Anscombe, (Anscombe and R. Rhees, edd.), Oxford: Basil Blackwell, 1953; note especially the Vorwort/Preface-Foreword, pp.ix–x[e].)

19. This statement is based on the Mandaean texts the *Book of John* and the *Ginza*, as interpreted by Widengren. See *Das Johannesbuch der Mandäer: Einleitung, Übersetzung, Kommentar*, Mark Lidzbarski (Giessen: Töpelmann, 1915), texts, pp. 137 lines 6–8, 242 lines 7–8; trans., pp. 134, 222; and *Ginzā: der Schatz, oder das Grosse Buch der Mandäer*, Mark Lidzbarski (Göttingen: Vandenhoeck & Ruprecht, and Leipzig: J.C. Hinrichs, 1925), Book III, line 1—p. 65; Geo Widengren, *The Ascension of the Apostle and the Holy Book (King and Saviour III)*, (Uppsala: Lundequistska, and Leipzig: Harrassowitz, 1950—Uppsala Universitets Årsskrift, 1950:7), p. 74 in particular, though see also his chapter 4, "Mandaean Literature" (pp. 59–76) in general. (Note his negative statement on p. 71.)

20. See my *Meaning and End of Religion*, ([New York: Macmillan, 1963] London: SPCK, and San Francisco: Harper & Row, 1976), pp. 283–284, 285–286.

21. So far as the resulting New Testament is concerned, Jerome's work provided only the four Gospels, as his revisions of extant Latin translations—revisions done in the light of the Greek. Probably no other New Testament books are from his hand. In the case of the Old Testament, Jerome, who lived part of his life in Palestine and knew Hebrew, adopted for those Christian Scriptures the then inno-

vative discrimination between the books in the Greek Septuagint—the Christian Bible—that were also in the Hebrew canon and the several others that were original in Greek, or had been canonized only in the Greek. He coined the word "apocrypha" for these latter. The distinction hardly took hold, however, until the Reformation. Most editions of the Vulgate do not evince it. Only its Old Testament books from the Hebrew, however, were from his hand in the Latin; the Latin versions of the others that became included (except of the Greek parts of Daniel and Esther, and of the Aramaic of Tobit and Judith) were by other translators.

22. "The first unambiguous reference to a collection of Biblical books within one cover occurs in the work of Cassiodorus (*Institutes*, I. xii. 3)", who died ca. 580; "the oldest known MS. containing the whole Vulgate is the Codex Amiatinus", at about the turn of the seventh-eighth century. (These quotations are from the article "Vulgate" in the *Oxford Dictionary of the Christian Church*, ed. F.L. Cross, 2nd edn. edd. F.L. Cross and T.A. Livingstone, London &c: Oxford, 1974.) It was the early thirteenth century, however, before one-volume Vulgates became common, according to the careful scholars Richard H. Rouse and Mary A. Rouse: "*Statim Invenire* : schools, preachers, and new attitudes to the page," in *Renaissance and Renewal in the Twelfth Century*, Robert L. Benson and Giles Constable, edd., Cambridge, Mass.: Harvard, 1982, p. 221: they even state that "The Bible . . . in the twelfth century had invariably been in multiple volumes" (ibid).

23. Mediæval manuscripts of the Vulgate differ not only in text. (It was within a week of the ninth century when Alcuin finally produced a standardized text and offered it to Charles the Great at his coronation, who then pushed its acceptance; even so, "corrupt" copies, and mixed copies with partly old-Latin and partly Vulgate readings, remained current.) They differ also to some degree as to what books, especially of the New Testament, are included or excluded. See, for instance, Kümmel (op cit. above, our note 15), who nevertheless seems to hold that, despite these admitted variations, "really" the extent of the New Testament was fixed "from the beginning of the fifth century on" for the Latin Church (p. 501), while noting that for the Greek Church and the Oriental Churches the situation for the New Testament was different.

The Gelasian Decree, variously attributed to Pope Damasus in the late fourth century, to Pope Gelasius at the end of the fifth, and to an unknown sixth-century hand, is relevant to the whole development but not as authoritatively as once it seemed. Similarly the Muratorian "Canon," a modernly unearthed relatively early list, was not authoritative perhaps at all.

24. Nonetheless, it was only after the advent of printing and the emergence thereby of a rather new conception of what is a 'book,' that the various Christian Churches in the sixteenth and seventeenth centuries formally defined, gave explicit shape to, their Bible—saw it as a unit with demarcated boundaries, and formalized what specific "books" (*sic*) make up its contents: made it a scripture, one might almost say, in the Qur'ān sense. Had this been previously attained, they would presumably not have diverged among themselves in their then series of first formal canonizations. The Roman Catholic Council of Trent decreed that

most of the now challenged "apocrypha" were indeed fully canonical, even the few exceptions being published in the Vulgate since that time as an Appendix. Luther had excluded the Apocrypha, though included them—with still fewer exceptions—in his German translation of the Bible, but also as an appendix, discriminating them as good but not authoritative, not "Holy Scripture"; the King James Version (1611) in English did much the same until the nineteenth century, following one of the Thirty-Nine Articles (1562). The Eastern Church, in the latter part of the seventeenth century at the Senate of Jerusalem, determined that four of the Greek Old Testament books were canonical, but no others; in the matter of the New Testament, for them the Book of Revelation was not included.

25. See, for instance, Hans Freiherr von Campenhausen, "Das Alte Testament als Bibel der Kirche, vom Ausgang des Urchristentums bis zur Entstehung des Neuen Testaments," in his *Aus der Frühzeit des Christentums: Studien zur Kirchensgeschichte des ersten and zweiten Jahrhunderts* (Tübingen: J.C.B. Mohr [Paul Siebeck], 1963), pp. [152]–196. Also: Albert C. Sundberg, Jr., *The Old Testament of the Early Church*, Cambridge: Harvard University Press, and London: Oxford University Press, 1964 (Harvard Theological Studies, xx).

26. Speaking of what stands to-day as our New Testament, a recent scholar writes that at that time "such a thing did not exist, even as an idea" (*war ein solches nicht einmal als Vorstellung vorhanden*)—Campenhausen, *Entstehung . . .*, op. cit. (above, our note 15), German p. 165, Eng. p. 193.

27. Modern study begins with Harnack. The fullest recent study is John Knox, *Marcion and the New Testament: an essay in the early history of the canon* (Chicago: University of Chicago Press, 1942). For a more recent informative delineation of the matter, see Chapter 5, "The Emergence of the New Testament", of Campenhausen, *Entstehung . . .*, op. cit. (above, our note 15), German pp. 173–201, Eng. pp. 147–164. This sets forth the thesis, now widely accepted among scholars, that the emergence of a canonized New Testament was the Church's response to Marcion's initiative in proffering a Christian Scripture. [Later: After this present article was submitted for publication, the following appeared: R. Joseph Hoffman, *Marcion: On the restitution of Christianity...*, Chico, California: Scholars Press, 1984. It does not seem to alter my argument.]

28. The Sri Guru Granth Sahib includes primarily the hymns and sayings of the Sikh Gurus, but also a relatively small percentage of other passages by "the Bhagats" (Panjabi; cf. Sanskrit *bhakta*) of a slightly earlier time or not formally members of what has coalesced into the Sikh community.

29. The relative force of the two Testaments, for Christian faith, is an exceedingly subtle and involuted matter. The Old began as solely, and remained for centuries as more, authoritative; the two were in principle equal for many centuries; the extent to which the New supplements, interprets, re-interprets, or supersedes the Old defies neat formulation.

30. See, for instance, the Lieberman chapter "Publication . . ." mentioned in our note 14 above.

31. *Corpus Hermeticum*, A. D. Nock, ed., trans. A.-J. Festugière (Paris: Société d'édition, 2 vol., 1945; second edn., 1960; volume 3, *Fragments: extraits de Stobée*, ed. & trans. Festugière, 1954—Collection des Universités de France: Association Guillaume Budé). A good introduction is Festugière, *Hermétisme et mystique païenne* (Paris: Aubier-Montaigne, 1967).

32. An excellent recent summary for Greek developments, with full bibliography, is Zeph Stewart: "Astrologia," pp. [588]-605, in his "Astrologia e magia," being §5 of his chap. VII, "La Religione" in tome 2, *Economia, diritto, religione* (1977) of vol. 4, *La società ellenistica* of Ranuccio Bandinelli, dir., Luigi Moretti et al., redd., *Storia e Civiltà dei Greci* (Milan: Bompiani, 5 voll. in 10 tomes, 1977–1979).

33. For the entire movement, an excellent survey, with good bibliography, from the pen of the Indologist and widely erudite historian of science Pingree (cf. next note), is available in the article "Astrology" in The New Encyclopaedia Britannica, 1974, Marcropaedia, 2: 219–233.

34. The most consequential of these in the second century that is known was made ca. 150 A.D. at Ujjain by a certain Yavaneśvara from an Alexandrian text, but it has since been lost although a widely influential third-century verse-rendering of its material, by one Sphujidhvaja, the *Yavanajātaka*, has recently been published with English translation and extensive commentary (D. Pingree, ed. and trans., *The Yavanajātaka of Sphujidhvaja* [Cambridge, Massachusetts: Harvard University Press, 2 voll., 1978; Harvard Oriental Series, Daniel H. H. Ingalls, ed., vol. 48]). The opening pages of the introduction to this work (I: 3–6) and pointedly the "Index of Authorities cited: I. Greek and Latin" (II: 466–471) tell the story. For a somewhat earlier and more general account, see the same writer's article "Astronomy and Astrology in India and Iran," *Isis* 54 (1963): 229–246.

35. Known also as the *Apotelesmatika*. The text has been critically edited as volume III:1 of *Claudii Ptolemaei Opera quae exstant omnia*, F. Boll and Ae. Boer, edd. ([1940], revised edn., Leipzig: Teubner, 1957). An earlier edition of the text, with English translation on facing pages, is available as *Ptolemy: Tetrabiblos*, F. E. Robbins ed. and trans. (Loeb Classical Library—London: Heinemann, and Cambridge, Mass.: Harvard University Press [1940], fourth impr., 1964).

36. *Hephaestionis Thebani apotelesmaticorum: Libri Tres, Epitomae Quattuor*, David Pingree, ed. (Leipzig: Teubner, 2 voll., 1973-1974—Bibliotheca Scriptorum Graecorum et Romanorum Teubneriana: Akademie der Wissenschaften der DDR, Zentralinstitut für alte Geschichte und Archäologie).

37. See, for example, Sid Z. Leiman, *The Canonization of Hebrew Scripture: the Talmudic and Midrashic Evidence* (Hamden: Argon, 1976—Transaction of the Connecticut Academy of Arts & Sciences, vol. 47); specifically on the question of Javneh see pp. 120–124; and Jack Lewis, "What Do We Mean By Javneh?" in Sid Z. Leiman, ed., *The Canon and Masorah of the Hebrew Bible: an introductory reader* (New York: Ktav, 1974—the Library of Biblical Studies, Harry M. Orlin-

sky, ed.). These two agree that Javneh decided nothing. Other scholars are coming to doubt that there ever was a Javneh affair at all.

38. For a sampling of the very large and growing literature on this matter, in addition to the two Leiman works referenced in our preceding note just above, see Brevard S. Childs, "The Problem of the Canon", being chapter 2 of his *Introduction to the Old Testament as Scripture* (Philadelphia: Fortress, 1979), p. [46]- 68, and its extensive bibliography. (Cf. also his chapp. 3,4, pp. [69]–106.) In the Leiman-edited collection, note esp. the articles of Zeitlin and Freedman; over against the latter, on "The Law and Prophets," which argues for an early date for a canonizing of these two classes of texts, see the unpublished Swanson dissertation noted in Childs, p. 49, and the Sundberg item in our note 25 above. Further, see the important studies of James A. Sanders, *Torah and Canon*, Philadelphia: Fortress, 1972, and *Canon and Community: a guide to canonical criticism*, ibid., 1984.

39. Cf. the bibliography listed in our note 5 above, where we touched on some of the later phases of these. I have not much investigated the pre-written phases.

40. This area I have not much explored. Relevant would be the following: Johannes Leipoldt und Siegfried Morenz, op. cit. (our note 17 above). Cf. also Johannes Leipoldt, "Zur Geschichte der Auslegung," and Siegfried Morenz, "Entstehung und Wesen der Buchreligion"; both in *Theologische Literaturzeitung*, 75 (1950): 229–234 and 709–716. Further, C. J. Bleeker, "Religious Tradition and Sacred Books in Ancient Egypt," in Bruce & Rupp, op. cit. (our note 5 above), pp. 20–35.

41. It has been suggested that one should investigate classicizing tendencies in Ashurbanipal's library; and the translation process from Sumerian into Akkadian, with its of course inescapable selectivity, might be compared to the later Alexandrian classicizing of Greek Texts? One scholar speaks of a "long process of canonization" of Sumerian literature: William W. Hallo, "Toward a History of Sumerian Literature," in *Sumerological Studies in Honor of Thorkild Jacobsen* (Chicago: University of Chicago Press, 1974 [The Oriental Institute of the University of Chicago: Assyriological Studies - no. 20]), pp.181–203; see esp. 194–201 for this author's explicit though somewhat guarded use of the terms "canon" and "canonization." Further, note the section on "Belles Lettres . . ." in William W. Hallo and William Kelley Simpson, *The Ancient Near East: a history*, John Morton Blum, gen. ed. (New York, etc: Harcourt Brace Jovanovich, 1971), pp. 163–167. See especially the reference to the cultic reciting of the *Emūma elish*, the "epic of creation," in the neo-Babylonian New Year's festival, p. 166.

42. What is more, a large number of plays by these very poets had been extant but was not included in the corpus as preserved, and consequently those have been totally lost; they are not part of what have become in the West the Greek Classics.

43. On this general matter see, among other sources, the following. Albin

Lesky, "Die Überlieferung der griechischen Literatur," being Chapter I of his *Geschichte der griechischen Literatur* (Bern, München: Francke, [1957-1958] rev. edn. 1963), pp. [15]–20—cf. the English translation of the revised edition: "The transmission of Greek literature," in his *The History of Greek Literature*, trans. James Willis and Cornelis de Heer (London: Methuen, 1966), pp. 1–6. Rudolf Pfeiffer, *History of Classical Scholarship* (Oxford: Clarendon Press, 2 voll., 1968-1976)—see especially vol. I: *From the Beginnings, to the End of the Hellenistic Age*, chiefly Part Two, "The Hellenistic Age," pp. 85ff.; particularly its chap. 5, "Alexandrian Scholarship at its Height", pp. [171]-209, esp. p. 203 to the end. (See also, in his vol. II: *From 1300 to 1850*, p. 84, a discussion of the first use, at the Renascence, of the terms *classicus, classici.*) "G.P.G." (sc. Georges Paul Gusdorf), "The Hellenistic Period" in his article "Humanistic Scholarship, History of" in the New Encyclopaedia Britannica, 1974, Macropaedia, 2: 1172–1173. Ernst Robert Curtius, "Klassik," being chapter 14 of his *Europäische Literatur und lateinisches Mittelalter* (Bern: A. Francke, 1948), pp. 251–274 (cf. also chap. 16: "Das Buch als Symbol," pp. 304–351), and in English translation: Curtius, *European Literature and the Latin Middle Ages*, trans. Willard R. Trask (New York: Pantheon, 1953—Bollingen Series, xxxvi), pp. 247-272 (cf. also "The Book as Symbol," pp. 302–347).

44. A good deal has been written on this matter, without necessarily using the concept "scripture": including an interesting brief passage in the first lecture of James Adam's 1904-1906 Gifford Lectures, posthumously published as his *The Religious Teachers of Greece* (Edinburgh: T. & T. Clark, 1908), pp. 7–15.

45. The notion of the miracle was subsequently embellished, but is based on a work known as the "Letter of Aristeas to Philocrates." This has been published, with a careful Introduction, as Moses Hadas, ed. & trans., *Aristeas to Philocrates (letter of Aristeas)* (New York: Harper & Brothers, 1951, for the Dropsie College—Solomon Zeitlin, ed.-in-chief, Jewish Apocryphal Literature). The exact date of this letter within the second century is still under discussion; Hadas opts for ca. 130 B.C.

46. On the canonizing process see our note 38 above.

47. See, for example, Robert H. Pfeiffer, *History of New Testament Times: with an introduction to the Apocrypha* (New York: Harpers, 1949), p. 179.

48. See, for instance, Lesky, and vol. 1 of Rudolf Pfeiffer, opp. citt. above, our note 43.

49. On this development see especially Jean Pépin, *Mythe et allégorie: les origines grecques et les contestations judéo-chrétiennes* ([1958?] 2ème édn., Paris: Études augustiniennes, 1976).

50. Geo Widengren, *The Ascension of the Apostle and the Heavenly Book* (King and Saviour III) (Uppsala: Lundequistska, & Leipzig [and Wiesbaden]: Harrassowitz, 1950—Uppsala Universitets Årsskrift 1950: 7); and his *Muḥammad, The Apostle of God, and his Ascension* (King and Saviour V) (ibid., 1955—Uppsala

Universitets Årsskrift 1955: 1). This material brings into focus matters that were adumbrated in some of this author's earlier Swedish work, *Religionens Värld* (Stockholm: Svenska Kyrkans, Diakonistyrels, 1945) and were developed by him later in his revised German translation, 1969, of the second edition of that Swedish work: *Religionsphänomenologie* (Berlin: deGruyter, 1969).

51. So the usual view. Driver and Miles, in a footnote, question that the relationship between the god and the laws is quite so clear, though relationship clearly there is: the diorite stele mentioned in the latter part of our sentence in the presentation here has at its top an engraving of the god, with Hammurabi reverently before him and the text of the laws engraved around the stone below. See G.R. Driver and John C. Miles, edd., *The Babylonian Laws*, edited with translation and commentary, volume 1, "Legal Commentary" (Oxford: Clarendon, 1952), p.28, fn. 4.

52. Qur'an 85:22, etc.

53. Exodus 24:12, etc.

54. E. Theodore Mullen, Jr., *The Divine Council in Canaanite and Early Hebrew Literature* (Chico, California: Scholars Press, 1980—Harvard Semitic Museum: Harvard Semitic Monographs, Frank Moore Cross, Jr., ed. #24).

55. This delineation over-simplifies by telescoping somewhat the eventual transition from book form to written book form, on which we have touched above in passing at our notes 5, 6, 7, 14, 24. The 19th-century view of Scripture with which I grew up was particularly reified, as was typical of Western 19th-century religious thought generally perhaps.

56. See David Diringer, *The Alphabet: a key to the history of mankind* ([London: Hutchinson, 1948], third edn., 2 vol., London: Hutchinson, and New York: Funk & Wagnalls, 1968). Despite the book's title, the first two chapters deal with the non-alphabetic writing of Mesopotamia and Egypt, the cuneiform and the hieroglyphic.

57. Ibid.

58. II Kings 22 and 23.

59. Of modern scholarship I have followed largely E. W. Nicholson, *Deuteronomy and Tradition* (Oxford: Blackwell, and Philadelphia: Fortress, 1967).

60. For a situating of the Josiah-Deuteronomy "reform" in a broader geographic context and a linking of it with the then contemporary situation in Assyria, see William Foxwell Albright, *From the Stone Age to Christianity: monotheism and the historical process* (Baltimore: Johns Hopkins, and London: Oxford, [1941] 2nd edn. 1946), pp. 241–244. On the Assyrian and Mesopotamian role in our matter more generally, cf. also our ref. 41 above.

61. "Behistun" is the traditional Western name; the present-day village near which it stands is in modern Persian Bīsitūn or Bīsutūn or Bīsotūn. See [King,

L. W., and R. C. Thompson, with prefatory remarks by E. A. Wallis Budge and Mr. King], *The Sculptures and Inscription of Darius the Great on the Rock of Behistûn in Persia: a new collation of the Persian, Susian, and Babylonian texts with English translations, etc; with illustrations* (London: The British Museum, 1907). In addition to the texts, this gives a good and illustrated description of the monument. A more recent edition and translation of the Old Persian text are found in Roland G. Kent, *Old Persian: grammar, texts, lexicon*, second edition (New Haven: American Oriental Society, 1953), pp. 116–135. A more accessible brief account is available in, for instance, A.T. Olmstead, *History of the Persian Empire (Achaemenid period)* (Chicago: University of Chicago Press, 1948), pp. 116–118; or in the article s.v. "Bīsitūn" in The New Encyclopaedia Britannica, 1974, Micropaedia, 2: 45.

62. The blessing and curse are to be found on lines 72–80 of the fourth column; in the Kent translation, p. 132 §§66–67.

63. Cf. Revelation 22:18, 19. Coming as this does at the end not only of the Book of Revelation, but of the Western Christian Bible, this passage has often been read as applying to the Bible generally. A similar motif is common among inscriptions of the Graeco-Roman world, especially of tombstones; though here the curse is often on those who disturb the tomb, rather than those who disturb the writing as such; nor am I clear as to the relative dating of such inscriptions and the Behistun one. I do note that this type of curse is evidently considerably more common among Greek tombstones in Asia Minor than on the mainland. See Richmond Lattimore, *Themes in Greek and Latin Epitaphs* (Urbana: University of Illinois Press, 1942—Illinois Studies in Language and Literature, vol. XXVIII, nos. 1-2), pp. 106–127 (compare on Christian inscriptions, pp. 306–309).

At a more general level, not referring specifically to a written text, and without the curse, cf. also such passages as Deuteronomy 4:2 and 12:32. Further, note also W. C. van Unnik, "De la règle Μήτε προσθειναι μήτε 'αφελειν dans l'histoire du canon," [*Vigiliae Christianae*, 3 (1949): 1–36] *Sparsa collecta*, op. cit (above, our note 15), 2:[123]–156.

64. See Willard Gurdon Oxtoby, *Some Inscriptions of the Safaitic Beduin* (New Haven: American Oriental Society, 1968—American Oriental Series, vol. 50); esp. p. 17.

65. Brevard Childs, *Biblical Theology in Crisis* (Philadelphia: Westminster, 1970). See also Part I ("Introduction") of the Childs work mentioned above in our note 38.

66. One example among several that might be offered: Walter Wink, *The Bible in Human Transformation: toward a new paradigm for Biblical study* (Philadelphia: Fortress, 1973). See especially his first two brief chapters: "The Bankruptcy of the Biblical Critical Paradigm" and "Is Biblical Study Undergoing a Paradigm Shift?". In the lengthy remaining, third, section the author proffers his own Jungian alternative. See also his poignant "Conclusion," pp. 81– 83.

3

Scripture and Its Reception: A Buddhist Case

Miriam Levering

INTRODUCTION

In many of the religious traditions of the world certain words and texts, whether preserved and transmitted orally or in written form, are regarded in ways somewhat similar to the ways Westerners regard their scriptures. Westerners tend to call these words and texts "scriptures" or "sacred texts," but a concept of scripture that can illuminate these phenomena in many cultures, and that directs attention to the essential or distinguishing features of these texts as opposed to others, has so far proved elusive.

In discussing what these words and texts have in common, and what distinguishes them from other words and texts in the same tradition or culture, three approaches predominate. The first points to allegations about the genesis of these texts, or to claims about their ontological status. In this view, what distinguishes scriptures or sacred texts from others is that they are believed to be revealed by transhuman powers, to convey eternal truths, or to replicate the speech of the gods.

The second is a functional approach: one often hears that what distinguishes scriptural texts from others is that they are used as normative or authoritative bases for communal life in its relations to the sacred.

The third pursues the significance of an observation about the reception of such texts: they are treated as "sacred," that is, powerful and inviolable.

Clearly all of these approaches bring into view essential features of what makes scripture distinctive. Yet there remain other aspects of scripture and its role in human communities which these approaches do not bring fully into view. Including these aspects in our search for a generic concept would permit us to see how multidimensional an experience the human experience of words and texts as scripture is.

These other features come into view with yet another approach that includes but goes beyond the approaches mentioned above. This approach involves seeking what essentially characterizes scripture by examining all of the ways in which individuals and communities *receive* these words and texts: the ways people respond to the texts, the uses they make of them, the contexts in which they turn to them, their understandings of what it is to read them, or to understand them, and the roles they find such words and texts can have in their religious projects.

Such an approach reflects a conviction that however the "scripturality" of scripture may originate in a community, what characterizes its scripturality for persons and communities is that the words or texts in question are understood to be able to play special roles in religious life. Being able to play these special roles, scriptures come to be read and used differently from other texts. They remain scriptural as long as they are found to sustain those different ways of being read and used (which I will call "modes of reception") in the context of a religious life.

Modes of Reception: The Need for Comparative Study

To achieve a generic concept of scripture that includes what modes of reception can tell us, a comparative study of modes of reception of words and texts in many different traditions is needed.

Modes of reception are of course tradition-specific. They are shaped by the concepts of the sacred or ultimate held by a given community, and by its understanding of relationship with the sacred and/or of ultimate self-transformation.

Yet it is nonetheless true that comparative study of these modes of reception, and the drawing of general concepts from the concrete specificity of the historically found traditions, should allow what we learn of each tradition to enhance our understanding of the others. This is particularly necessary because while in any given tradition many modes are present, in any tradition at a given socio-historical moment only certain modes are fully conscious and thematized. It is not too much to hope that knowledge of more than one tradition's modes of reception, and more than one way of interpreting the meaning of such reception, will expand our awareness of the possibilities of relation to ultimacy mediated through scriptural texts, even in the traditions we know best.

A preliminary survey indicates that four fundamental modes of reception are found wherever words and texts are scriptural. These are:

1. the informative mode: allowing texts to shape one's understanding of the world. (An exploration of the informative mode should also include exploration of the views of many subtraditions that word, text and tradition are of limited value as midwives to wisdom.)
2. the transactive mode: "doing things with words"—the text is scripture because reciting or reading it enables one to act in the power of the ultimate.
3. the transformative mode: finding words a gateway to a deeper encounter with an Other or to a transformation of self; exploring the power of the text as symbol to mediate transformation and enhancement of personality.
4. the symbolic mode: finding that word or text can be itself a symbol of the ultimate.[1]

A Chinese Buddhist Example

In what follows I offer a description of the reception of words and texts in a contemporary Buddhist convent in the Chinese cultural tradition of Taiwan. I will also supply some historical background to enable the reader to sense the place of the present practice in the context of the tradition that informs it.

BACKGROUND

I will begin by sketching briefly the development of different attitudes toward words and texts within the Indian and Chinese Buddhist traditions. The attitudes described here should not be confused with the modes of reception themselves. Rather, such an overview should provide a context for understanding the specific forms of those modes within the Chinese Buddhist tradition.

Indian Buddhist Attitudes toward the Tradition-Sanctioned Word

In what seems to historians to be the earliest strata of the teachings in surviving records, Buddhists, probably beginning with the Buddha, take what we might call an anti-authoritarian position with respect to the word. They assert that the words of a tradition, whether it be the Brahmanical Vedic tradition with its revealed texts or their own Buddhist teachings, should not be taken as authoritative because of their source, but should be regarded as true only when proved to be so by the individual practitioner using her own reason and experience.[2]

On the other hand, the tradition never denied the importance of words and texts in transmitting the Buddha's teaching. Properly understood, the words do convey the truths one needs for successful practice toward enlightenment. This understanding of the value of words in the tradition was given greater emphasis following the disappearence of the living teacher at the Buddha's death. The tradition relates, in the *Mahāparinibbāna Sutta*, that when the Buddha was asked on his deathbed who should be his successor as supreme teacher, he told his disciples to take the *Dharma* (teaching) as their refuge and their lamp.[3] The tradition also relates that shortly after the Buddha's death five hundred realized disciples (*arhats*) met to recite the Buddha's teachings in order to agree on a reliable and authoritative body of teachings, since it was these which would now have such importance in guiding present and future practice.[4] Although the teachings of the Buddha were handed down orally exclusively for many centuries after the Buddha's death, yet their importance as teaching was reflected in the stress within the tradition on accurate memorizing and reciting of these texts. Teachings were authenticated by the fact that one could demonstrate that the teachings were credible, that they had been heard by a specific hearer, that he had heard the Buddha teach them at a particular time and place, under a particular sponsorship, and to a particular assembly of listeners.[5] This emphasis on the importance of the Buddha's words as teaching, and of clarifications and extensions of them by later disciples, we might call the kataphatic or informative reception of the word as authoritative teaching.

We find this informative, pedagogical dimension extended in early Mahāyāna *sūtras* such as the *Perfection of Wisdom in Eight Thousand Lines* and the *Lotus Sūtra*, where there is an extraordinary emphasis on the importance and status of the *sūtra*, tending toward an orientation toward the text that can be termed "iconic" or "presentational."[6] *Sūtras* now are seen as embodying, and providing a direct means of access to, all of the Buddha's knowledge, wisdom, and supernatural powers. Thus in the *Lotus Sūtra*, for example, the Buddha Śākyamuni says:

> . . . All the *Dharmas* possessed by the Thus Come One [i.e., the Buddha], all the Thus Come One's supernatural powers of self-mastery, the treasure house of all the Thus Come One's secrets, all the Thus Come One's profound affairs are entirely proclaimed, demonstrated, revealed and preached in this scripture.[7]

In the *Perfection of Wisdom in Eight Thousand Lines*, a *sūtra* whose message is that everything, including *sūtras* and teachings, is "empty" of substantial existence, and which thus offers an authoritative teaching that teaches detachment from authoritative teaching, Śākyamuni Buddha says to Ānanda:

> Therefore then, Ānanda, again and again I entrust and transmit to you this perfection of wisdom, laid out in letters, so that it may be available for learning, for bearing in mind, preaching, studying and spreading wide.... For the Tathāgata has said that "the perfection of wisdom is the mother, the creator, the genetrix, of the past, future, and present Tathāgatas, their nurse in all-knowledge." ... You should attend well to this perfection of wisdom, bear it well in mind, study it well, and spread it well. And when one learns it, one should carefully analyze it grammatically, letter by letter, syllable by syllable, word by word. For as the *Dharma*-body of the past, future and present Tathāgatas is this *Dharma*-text authoritative. In the same way in which you, Ānanda, behave towards Me who at present reside as a Tathāgata—with solicitude, affection, respect and helpfulness—just so, with the same solicitude, affection and respect, and in the same virtuous spirit, should you learn this perfection of wisdom, bear it in mind, study, repeat, write and develop it, respect, revere and worship it. That is the way for you to worship Me, that is the way to show affection, serene faith, and respect for the past, future and present Buddhas and Lords.... [I]n the same way in which I am your teacher, so is the perfection of wisdom.[8]

Lay Buddhists at first, and then all Buddhists (as the distinction between monastic and lay decreased in importance in the new Mahāyāna movements) had developed the practice of showing reverence and making offerings to the relics of the Buddha enshrined in large reliquary mounds called "*stūpas*." In the Pali texts this practice is specifically sanctioned by the Buddha; in the *Dīgha Nīkaya* the Buddha specifically recommends this practice to laypersons, saying that it will bring them peaceful minds.[9] The *stūpa* with its relics became the place where the continuing life of the Buddha was most powerfully felt.[10] In Mahāyāna texts such as the *Lotus Sūtra* the text symbolically becomes assimilated to the relic of the Buddha as the locus of the Buddha's presence and power,[11] and the object of offerings and reverence. In Mahāyāna *sūtras* such as the *Lotus Sūtra* and the Perfection of Wisdom *sūtras* the reader is told that *sūtras* are more worthy of offerings and reverence than the relics of Buddhas, because the truth (*Dharma*) that *sūtras* contain and the training that they prescribe is the source from which Buddhas come.[12]

The Mahāyāna *sūtras* emphasize that there is an all-important practical reason why *sūtras* must be memorized, copied, recited, and expounded: without this transmission, no future Buddhas would arise.[13] *Sūtras* are to be the teachers of future generations in the same sense that Śākyamuni was the teacher of his contemporaries. Yet beyond this, it is clear that to the authors of the Mahāyāna *sūtras*, *sūtras* themselves manifest and embody the activity, wisdom, and power of the transcendent *Dharma*. *Sūtras* as words that can be recited and copied are neither clearly distinguished from the teaching that the words convey, from the transcendent wisdom to be realized through their study and practice, from the Buddha whose words they are, nor from his supernatural powers. All four of these are treated in the texts as dimensions of the same reality. A person who is reciting or copying the words or making offerings to the text or its preachers is worshipping and giving joyful attention to the *Dharma* they convey, and through doing so is in the presence of, has direct access to, and will definitely come to realize, transcendent wisdom and all-knowledge. In this understanding, words do not merely express truth, they are the living presence of true and powerful reality.

In contrast, another attitude that appears from the early days of the tradition and in the earliest texts is the suggestion that the real essence of the Buddha and the *Dharma*, namely, the ultimate truth to which the Buddha was enlightened, is beyond the grasp of words, particularly metaphysical categories, and its apprehension requires leaving words behind. In this aniconic or apophatic attitude, words are useful only in so far as they mediate immediate perception of truth, which is discovered to be inexpressible in words. This apophatic attitude becomes quite marked in later Indian and Central Asian strands of Mahāyāna, where it was explicitly taught that the word of the Buddha, as word, is not fully adequate to the communication of the experience of the Buddha's enlightenment.[14] That truth transcends words and that words are 'empty' as vehicles for the transmission of truth is shown, the tradition suggests, by the Buddha's silence when asked metaphysical questions, by Vimalakīrti's "thunderous silence" when asked to express his understanding of the meaning of non-duality[15] and by the oft-repeated statement that the Buddha taught for forty-nine years and never said a thing.[16] In this view the words of the Buddhas are medicines to cure specific mental diseases; one who is well not only does not need them, but might be made ill by grasping onto them. These apophatic understandings of the relation between words and truth were never eclipsed; indeed, the attitude toward words within the Mahāyāna in particular may be described as a polarity between apophasis and kataphasis, with one sometimes stressed more than the other, but with both continually present and in creative tension and relationship.

Finally, within Indian and Central Asian Mahāyāna, in both its exoteric and esoteric traditions, we find the view that certain words (*mantra*, *dhāraṇī*) are given to adherents by Buddhas and Bodhisattvas to supply empowerment (*adhiṣṭhāna*) and protection in the course of their practice and preaching, support for wholesome mental states, and certain powers for mundane and transmundane purposes.[17] In some conceptualizations these words are powerful because they are the very speech of cosmic Buddhas, reproduced by the adherent in its very sounds (often unintelligible to human listeners). Here the transhistorical Buddhas and Bodhisattvas are not only teachers of *Dharma*, but sustainers of practice by their empowerment (*adhiṣṭhāna*) and protection through *mantra*s and *dhāraṇī*s. It is significant that here also they offer their powers and protection through the gift of words. In this essentialist view, it is understood that in the case of these words, there is an ineradicable correspondence between the specific words as mediators of ritual agency and the cosmically grounded powers they communicate.

Chinese Transformations of Indian Models

From the early days of Buddhist missionary activity in China, Chinese Buddhists drew upon a native model in order to understand how to receive the *sūtra* literature to which they were being introduced. The Buddha, they concluded, was, like Confucius, a great sage (*sheng-jen*), whose infinite wisdom led him to create a teaching (*chiao*) through which to benefit and transform the human world. To transmit this teaching he created "*ching*," a word used to translate the Sanskrit term "*sūtra*," but which was already in use as a term referring to the normative texts of the Confucian sages. Thus, *ching*, texts which are reliable in that they are the word of the Buddha, are the precious teaching of the Buddha and the means by which he transforms the world through transforming the minds of sentient beings. Were there no texts, there could be no authentic teaching, and the transformation could not take place.[18]

The Chinese also needed no encouragement from their Indian Buddhist counterparts to revere the faithfully transmitted written text. In India the teachings of the Buddha had at first been passed down orally; it was only much later, approximately at the time of the rise of the Mahāyāna, that the teachings were written down and that we find, as we do in early Mahāyāna *sūtra*s, adherents being urged to copy and preserve written texts as well as to memorize and recite them accurately. But the Chinese received most of the Buddhist teachings in written form at a time when they already had an established tradition of placing great value upon and preserving the written classics (*ching*).[19]

As knowledge of differences among the teachings in Indian Mahāyāna *sūtras* and commentaries grew in China, Chinese Buddhist scholars sought ways to grasp their teachings systematically and to see their interrelationships. These scholars created hermeneutical systems that classified the various teachings, and the *sūtras* which contained them, into categories such as provisional and ultimate, abrupt and complete.[20] Each school within which a hermeneutical system was developed identified a *sūtra* or a group of *sūtras* as conveying the highest, complete and perfect teaching of the Buddha, while others contained teachings suited to students at lower stages of understanding. These schools, such as T'ien-t'ai and Hua-yen, seem to have taught that devotion to and study of the *sūtra* containing the perfect teaching could bring one to the highest enlightenment, not simply because that *sūtra* contained the truest doctrine, but also because it embodied the full expression of the Buddha's mind. These schools combined the informative with the iconic views of *sūtras* as the words of the Buddha.

Other Chinese Buddhists, however, who began with the Indian view that the word of the Buddha is a skillful device by which the Buddha enables the adherent to make progress toward *nirvāṇa*, and from the *śūnyavādin/prajñāpāramitā* paradox that, although the Buddha preached for forty-nine years and his disciples studied his teachings (*Dharma*), the Buddha had never spoken a word and there had never been a teaching to study, arrived at a more aniconic or apophatic understanding. Here the native Chinese tradition also played a part, as Chinese Buddhists such as Seng Chao incorporated the insight of the author of the statement found in the *Chuang-tzu* that the books of the sages contain only the tracks left by their mind; there is much that they cannot communicate directly at all, and much else that contact with their living presence might communicate to later generations that their words cannot. Even with respect to what words can convey, unless the meaning of the words is grasped in everyday experience, the words remain a dead thing. Ultimately the experience of the meaning indicated by the words shows that meaning to transcend all distinctions upon which words depend. Chinese Ch'an (Zen) Buddhists in particular often affirmed that the object of study of the Buddha's words is to "get their point," that is, to discover for oneself the intuitive wisdom of *prajñā*, not to be attached to, or misled by, the study of their words and concepts. The following exchange is illustrative of the encounter between Chinese Buddhists of apophatic and kataphatic persuasions.

> A lecture-master (a monk who devoted himself largely to giving lectures on the Buddhist *sūtras* and treatises) asked: "The Three Vehicles' twelve divisions of teachings (that is, the totality of the Buddhist scriptures) reveal the Buddha-nature, do they not?" "This weed-patch has never been spaded," said [the Ch'an master] Lin-chi.

> "Surely the Buddha would not have deceived men!" said the lecture-master. "Where is Buddha?" asked Lin-chi. The lecture-master had no reply....
>
> ...[To the whole group Lin-chi then said:] "Does anyone else have a question? If so, let him ask it now! But the instant you open your mouth, you are already way off. Why is this so? Don't you know? Venerable Śākyamuni said: '(*Dharma*) is separate from words, because it is neither subject to causation nor dependent upon conditions.'[21] Your faith in this is insufficient, therefore we have bandied words today."[22]

From the lecture-master's pedagogical-iconic point of view, the totality of the Buddhist *sūtra*s, the record of the words spoken by the Buddha himself, were not only the authoritative repositories of doctrinal theory, they also revealed by their very nature the ultimate truths of Buddhism. From the Ch'an point of view, to try to grasp the *Dharma* through stating it in words or trying to say something about it is to make it an object of thought and thereby miss it. The student must ultimately discover that the Buddha and the teaching (*Dharma*) are realities that transcend words, and that they are completely present everywhere.

THE CONVENT

The Convent Community

Briefly, the religious community of the convent from which the following observations are drawn consists of four temples, located in different cities, towns and counties, all under the supervision and administration of one *shih-fu* (roughly equivalent to abbess). Around sixty *pi-ch'iu-ni* (*bhikṣuṇī*, nuns) and a few laypeople live in the four houses taken together. The community is in a Ch'an Buddhist *Dharma*-transmission lineage, but does not emphasize seated meditation or *kung-an* (=*kōan*) practice. Nor does the practice reflect an exclusive commitment to the Pure Land tradition, though Pure Land faith is very strong, and many of the nuns say that rebirth in the Pure Land is their goal. The convent should be thought of as belonging to the catholic Chinese Buddhist community of the present day, where sectarian distinctions and *Dharma* lineages exist but often mean very little. The Chinese monastic order (*saṅgha*) as a whole follows the eclectic, synthetic tradition prevalent at least since the seventeenth century, with each abbess or abbot constrained only by custom in her or his selection of communal practices. As to individual practice, each nun is free to select from among many forms of practice and many guiding texts those upon which she will rely.

The Goals of the Community

There seem to be at the convent two complementary conceptions of what a convent is and what the goals of the community should be. First, a convent is understood to be a community of persons dedicated to cultivation of the Buddha's path as a life-goal: the term the nuns used for this is the Chinese term *hsiu-hsing* (cultivation). When asked about in what *hsiu-hsing* consists, the nuns refer to an early Indian Mahāyāna conception that practice consists of the famous "three studies" (C. *san-hsüeh*): *śīla* (originally the keeping of the precepts, but later, more broadly, eschewing evil actions and doing good actions), *samādhi* (the cultivation of mental concentration) and *prajñā* (the cultivation of wisdom, particularly intuitive, liberating wisdom).

But at least since the time of the *Lotus Sūtra*, the practice of the three studies has been carried out in the devotional wing of the Mahāyāna in the context of the immense assistance and support one can receive, through their supernormal powers and their inconceivable store of merit, from Buddhas and Bodhisattvas who are further along on the path. As the nuns of the contemporary Chinese Buddhist convent understand it, this support is experienced to the extent that one makes sincere efforts and offers sincere reverence to Buddhas and Bodhisattvas, expressing that reverence, as the Indian Mahāyāna *sūtra*s suggest, by offerings of flowers, incense, light, hymns of praise and so forth (C. *pai-fo*). One also may participate directly in the powers of Buddhas and Bodhisattvas by invoking their protection and compassionate powers in support of one's practice and of one's preaching and propagating activities. Finally, of all of the kinds of assistance promised by the Buddhas, Amitābha's power to enable one to be reborn in the Pure Land is perhaps the most fervently sought.

Thus, in a devotional Mahāyāna context such as that found in a Chinese form in the convent, the rubric of the three studies can still be used to describe the dimensions of *hsiu-hsing*, expanding the concept of *śīla* (good actions) to include merit-cultivation, bodhisattva-actions for others, and such highly meritorious devotional actions as worship (C. *pai*), repentance (C. *ch'an-hui*), praise and eulogy (C. *tsan*), the making of vows, the invocation of empowerment through *dhāraṇī*s and *mantra*s, and the recollection of Buddhas and Bodhisattvas through visualization or name-recitation as a way of establishing a powerful connection with those Buddhas and Bodhisattvas and their powers.[23]

In addition to providing a context for *hsiu-hsing* for nuns, the convent's existence had also a second meaning, also frequently mentioned. A convent is a *tao-ch'ang*, a place of practice of "the Way" and a place for offerings to the Buddhas, and as such it is maintained for the sake of the world beyond its walls.[24] It must offer lay people a place where they can pay reverence to the Buddhas and Bodhisattvas; where by offerings to the nuns and to the Buddhas and Bodhisattvas they can cultivate merit to be transferred to their relatives and ancestors;[25] and where by the power of the good karma and cultivation of the nuns, lay people will feel an attraction to the Buddha's way out of suffering.

RECEPTION OF TEXTS IN THE CONVENT

In relation to both of these meanings of the convent's existence, the study and recitation of tradition-sanctioned texts, particularly "*sūtra*s," "*mantra*s" and "*dhāraṇī*s," play a very large part. Nuns recite *sūtra*s, *mantra*s and *dhāraṇī*s daily or continually, mentally or aloud. They copy *sūtra*s, expound *sūtra*s, listen to recitations and expositions of *sūtra*s, meditate by visualizing personages and scenes described in *sūtra*s, and read *sūtra*s. Laypeople recite *sūtra*s, *mantra*s and *dhāraṇī*s at home silently or aloud, and go to monasteries to listen to monks and nuns expound *sūtra*s. They copy *sūtra*s, and sponsor the publication and distribution of *sūtra*s. They form lay societies to recite *sūtra*s together at the convent biweekly or monthly. If the convent and its lay associates are typical, holding these words of the tradition present in the mind, ear and mouth may be considered a central and pervasive form of practice chosen by nuns and laypeople in contemporary Chinese Buddhist communities. For these communities the tradition-sanctioned word supports, undergirds, and symbolizes their religious aspirations as much or more than the Bible supports religious life in Protestant Christian churches.

The Informative Mode: Individual Study and Attending Sūtra *Lectures*

The Goals of Study. One nun told me that there is a central reason why there must be monks and nuns: the *sūtra* literature is so vast that, for it to be passed down with understanding, there must be those who devote their whole lives to its study. Since there are so few monks [in Taiwan], the burden of this task now rests on nuns.

But why should this massive task be undertaken? Why is it so important to the society that there should be persons who devote their whole lives to it?

The answer was that it is by following the Buddha's teachings as they were preached by the Buddha himself that one can cross the sea of suffering and attain *nirvāṇa*.

The Hermit and the Study of Sūtras. Several of the nuns regularly read *sūtras* on their own. But the most revealing conversation that I had about this was with a man who after various enlightenment experiences had taken up the life of a hermit in a cottage adjoining the property of the convent. He planted a garden, and placed in the cottage a complete copy of the Ta-tsang-ching, the authoritative text collection (often somewhat misleadingly called "canon") of the Chinese Buddhist tradition.[26] His daily routine consisted of meditating, cooking, gardening, and reading the *sūtras* and other texts in the Ta-tsang-ching, all fifty-odd volumes, massive and difficult to read, from cover to cover. When asked why he was doing this, his answer had several parts.

First, he said, for progress on the path to Buddhahood one must have both *chien-ti* and *ching-chieh*. *Chien-ti* is a matter of having correct ideas on which to base one's practice. If the ideas are wrong, the practice will go wrong. The study of *sūtras* and their commentaries, as well as the recorded sayings of Ch'an masters, leads to correct *chien-ti*. But one must also do meditation, since correct *chien-ti* alone is nothing without *ching-chieh*, advancement to a higher stage in one's mental training and concentration.[27]

But surely one could attain a correct understanding without reading through the entire Ta-tsang-ching? He replied that his teacher had read through the entire Ta-tsang-ching after his initial enlightenment experience. His teacher had commented that it would be boring and stupid to read it through prior to an enlightenment experience, but that after such an experience, it was very helpful. He himself had had an enlightenment experience that had enabled him to enter the path, and thus was ready for the same project.

The hermit's attitude provides insight into the problems and opportunities of receiving *sūtras* in the informative mode on one's own. On the one hand, it must be done. But even with the help of commentaries, it is likely to be difficult, to the point of futility. *Sūtras* are technical, repetitive, and refer to phenomena occurring only to meditators in higher states of concentration. Above all, there are too many of them. For most people, it is appropriate to confine study and recitation to a selection only. To set out to read them all, as the hermit and his teacher have done, is unusual and admirable because of the aspiration it symbolizes.

Attending Sūtra *Lectures.* Given the difficulties of individual study, the most popular approach to becoming informed by the words of the Buddha is attending lectures offered by eminent monks and nuns.

In the Indian Mahāyāna, preaching the *Dharma* on the basis of *sūtras* seems to have been an early and important institutional development. Early Mahāyāna *sūtras*, such as the *Perfection of Wisdom in Eight Thousand Lines* and the *Lotus Sūtra*, urge the practice of preaching the *Dharma* based on the *sūtra* upon all "bodhisattvas," that is, adherents of Mahāyāna. If the picture described in these *sūtras* can be taken to reflect in some measure the reality of early Mahāyāna communities in India and Central Asia, then preaching on the basis of *sūtras* must have been one of the basic activities by which communities were built and the teaching spread.[28] The writing of commentaries on *sūtras* was also a principal expression of the study and the teaching of the *Dharma* within the Mahāyāna.

In China this tradition of preaching and writing commentaries on *sūtras* continued to develop. Early biographical collections called *The Lives of Eminent Monks* and the *Continued Lives of Eminent Monks* included a classification of monks as "exegetes" (*i-chieh*), indicating that from early times explanation of the meaning of *sūtras* was an important activity at which certain monks and nuns excelled. Similarly the great scholars and systematizers of Chinese Mahāyāna frequently expressed their ideas as commentaries on *sūtras*. More broadly, since early times the Chinese Buddhist tradition has institutionalized the office of "*Dharma*-master" (*fa-shih*). This title and function are given to the scholarly monk or nun who is qualified to expound *sūtras* orally—usually only certain *sūtras* in which he or she has specialized.[29] Although today in Taiwan most monks and nuns are called by the courtesy title "*Dharma*-master," the tradition of regarding this as a specialized office continues, as seen in the fact that only certain learned monks and nuns are regarded as truly qualified to expound *sūtras*. As in the past, such monks or nuns continue the practice of offering periodically a series of lectures on a given *sūtra*.[30]

In the convent that is the subject of this study, no one has yet become qualified to be a lecturer or expounder of *sūtras* or of any of the Chinese Buddhist scholastic traditions. Several, however, do regularly attend lectures given at one of the larger monasteries by a monk whose learning in the field of the *Hua-yen (Avataṃsaka) Sūtra* and its commentarial tradition is widely recognized. Others attend lectures on the *Lotus Sūtra* offered by a nun who heads a Buddhist academy and specializes in the T'ien-t'ai scholastic tradition. These lectures usually take a commentarial form: the nun or monk recites and comments on each passage in the *sūtra* in turn, starting at the beginning; the entire exposition may take years if the *sūtra* is a long one.

The Transformative Mode in Lecturing and Listening to Lectures

Clearly the informative mode is not an unimportant mode of receiving texts in the religious lives of these practitioners. Yet the testimony of my informants was that transformative mode of reception—listening to exposition and reading for the sake of attainment of insight and the resulting formation of character—is an equally important dimension of the reading and study of texts.

For example, it was pointed out to me that the reading and expounding of *sūtras* is preceded by reciting the following verse to establish the right frame of mind:

> The unsurpassed, profoundly deep, fine, wonderful *Dharma*,
> Difficult to meet with in hundreds of thousands of *kalpas*,
> Now I can see and hear, accept and hold it;
> My only hope is to grasp the real intention of the *Tathāgata*.

Another profound comment on the experience of listening to *sūtra* lectures was made by an intelligent and devout young lay woman, a teacher of English at a Buddhist high school. She said that as a young student she had attended *sūtra* lectures "to get something out of it." She had noticed many old ladies just sitting back and doing their recitation of Amitābha's name on their strings of beads as they listened, not taking notes or even appearing to listen too closely.[32] She had come to see that these ladies had the right attitude: not to listen with the intent to gain something, but to let the mind become calm (the name recitation would help), and let what struck you strike you. That was the only way that what was living in the text and in the spirit of the expositor would call forth what was living in you.

She also said that in the old days a teacher would expound a passage from a given *sūtra* in the morning, and in the evening the students would be called upon to expound the same passage again. If they just spouted what they had heard the teacher say that morning, they were scolded, for the ultimate result of such rote learning would be that with each generation the life of the teaching would be further lost.

She also said that in *sūtra* lecturing, as in preaching, the authority of the exposition comes both from the fact that the text is the Buddha's word and from the perceived degree of inner understanding and attainment of the *sūtra* lecturer. Merely clever or learned expositions of the *sūtras*, and even rhetorically moving ones, are not ones to which people listen day after day or week after week. This is because the listener listens both to the text and to the heart/mind of the expounder, and the aim is both deeper knowledge of the teaching and personal transformation of the hearer.[33]

Thus there is continuity between contemporary attitudes and those of the earlier Indian and Chinese Buddhist traditions. The pedagogical, kataphatic approach to the sanctioned word vital in both the Indian and Chinese traditions still remains important. Study of the Buddha's words is seen as essential to the correct understanding on which sound practice is based. One chooses to read them, lectures on them carefully, treats them with reverence as one seeks instruction from them, immerses oneself in them with a mind open to insight.

Yet at the same time, contemporary nuns and their lay friends emphasize the transformational dimension of study and listening to lectures. All of the persons I talked with told me, in one way or another, that words are meaningless or useless without insight, and that study should not be carried out in such a way as to block the insight, causing the teaching and the learner to become more nearly dead rather than more fully alive. In this sense, truth is transmitted not through words or intelligence or cognitive understanding alone, but from an enlightened mind to a mind capable of insight. I would suggest that this kind of reflection on the transformative dimension of informative reception is typical of persons who are receiving texts as scriptures, and that only texts that can sustain such dual reception continue to be scriptures.

The Transactive Mode

From one point of view, this essay in its entirety could have been entitled "The Reception of Scriptures as Ritual Action." To read, listen to, recite, study, copy, and meditate upon scriptures in religious traditions is in every case an action, and one that takes place in a ritual context.

In discussing the transactional mode, however, we are concerned with reception of texts specifically *for the purpose of* taking some kind of action or establishing some kind of relationship. We will speak here of the transactional mode where scriptural words are received as given to be used in ritual action, not principally with an eye to one's own transformation but in order to obtain protection or powers; to create merit; to bring benefits to others; to enact confession or repentance; to make vows; to offer devotion and praise; and to express and bring into effect relationships between members of the community living and dead, and between those members and transhuman agents.

Action as Understood within Mahāyāna Buddhist Traditions. In the Buddhist tradition all of human existence is understood on one level as consisting of actions (Sk. *karma*) (of body, speech, or mind) and the fruits (Sk. *phala*) of actions. Thus, any interaction with a text is seen as a meaningful action that bears fruit (has consequences) for the attainment of one's highest aspirations to Buddhahood and for one's life in this world (the realm of *saṃsāra*). In Indian Mahāyāna Buddhist *sūtra*s the concept of merit (Sk. *puṇya*) is invoked to refer to the capacity of good actions to bear good worldly fruits for the actor.[34] Likewise merits incurred by one person that would ordinarily produce one kind of fruit may be transformed so that they bear fruits of another kind for that same person, or transferred to another person.

In addition to the notion that actions in general are marked by being meritorious, harmful or neutral, there is the idea that specific actions of body, speech and mind are appropriate to those who seek Buddhahood. This is the case not only because they are highly meritorious, but also because they are 'skillful,' that is, directly instrumental in the pursuit of the religious goal. These include among others: repentance; feeding hungry ghosts; giving; practicing concentration (*dhyāna*); and reciting names of Buddhas, *mantra*s and *dhāraṇīs* as a way of establishing connection and receiving empowerment offered by Buddhas and Bodhisattvas.

These specific actions must, however, be supplemented by the deliberate creation of merit through all kinds of good actions. The need for this kind of merit creation is presented within the rhetoric of contemporary Chinese Buddhist practice as a function of the vast store of negative habit energies that our past actions have brought about through countless aeons. Due to the power of delusion, every thought, word and deed of each sentient being during countless lifetimes has been tinged with ignorance and selfish desire, and thus has created negative fruits. This is a tremendous force working against enlightenment, as well as against ordinary, mundane well-being. To have any hope at all, a practitioner has to act to create enormous positive merit and eliminate past negative accumulations.

Reciting and Copying Sūtras *as a Generalized Meritorious Action.* Reciting, reading and copying *sūtra*s are among the vastly meritorious actions that can eliminate past negative accumulations.[36] Most Mahāyāna *sūtra*s teach that their own propagation through memorizing, reciting, and copying is an act of immense merit. In China as in other Mahāyāna countries, monks and nuns have taken up *sūtra* recitation as a form of practice. This is encouraged, for example, by the *Sūtra of Brahma's Net*, a rule book for monks and nuns probably written in China. This text, which from earliest times has served as a fundamental guide to monastic practice, is studied today by every nun and monk at the time of ordination. It gives ten major commandments and forty-eight minor commandments for monks and nuns, and including the following, the 44th minor commandment:

> As a child of the Buddha, one must always with singleness of heart accept, observe, read and recite the *sūtra*s and *vinaya* of the Mahāyāna.[37]

Not only was reciting *sūtra*s always enjoined on practitioners, but it also was specifically selected by some monks and nuns as a practice on which to concentrate their efforts. In China from early times monks and nuns took the continual recitation of a particular *sūtra* as a special practice.[38] Many believed that chanting a given *sūtra* continually was also an especially effective means for generating supernormal powers.[39]

Monks and nuns were by no means the only practitioners to devote themselves to merit creation and devotion through *sūtra* recitation. Since earliest times in China, as in other Mahāyāna countries, laypeople have participated indirectly by making offerings to monks and nuns as "fields of merit" for the recitation of *sūtras*; the merit that grows as a fruit of this planting is transferred to the ancestors or relatives of the lay donors or devoted to the fulfillment of other desires. Indeed, the chanting of *sūtra*s is the most common form of merit cultivation and transferrence by monks and nuns that occurs as a result of lay sponsorship. The Buddhist publishing industry also is largely supported by lay donors planting merit by sponsoring the copying and publication of *sūtra*s and other Buddhist texts.

More directly, lay people also formed societies that met regularly to recite *sūtra*s. The one founded in Hang-chou in A.D. 822 by the monk Nan-ts'ao illustrates the fully developed form that these *sūtra*-recitation societies were to take. In A.D. 826 the famous poet Po Chü-i (722-846) wrote an account of the society:

> Monk Nan-ts'ao . . . invited monk Tao-feng of the Ling-yin Monastery to lecture on the *Hua-yen Sūtra*. When he heard about [the Buddha] Vairoçana in the section of the Lotus-womb World, [Nan]-ts'ao became so elated that he uttered an earnest wish, hoping that he could urge a group of one hundred thousand people, monks and laymen, to recite the *Hua-yen Sūtra*. Each of the one hundred thousand people would in turn urge a thousand others to recite one chapter of the same *sūtra*. The entire assemblage would meet together quarterly. [Nan]-ts'ao also carried out his earnest wish and organized the group into a society, and regulated the proceedings through quarterly vegetarian feasts. From the summer of 822 to the present autumn, fourteen such vegetarian feasts have been held. At each feast, [Nan]-ts'ao offered incense respectfully and knelt before the image of the Buddha, making the following supplication, "May I and every member of the society be reborn before Vairoçana in his paradise within the Golden Wheel of the Precious Lotus, floating on the Great Ocean of Fragrant Waters in the Lotus-womb World. Then I will be satisfied." [Nan]-ts'ao solicited enough funds from the members to purchase an estate of ten *ch'ing* of land, the income from which was used to defray the expenses of the vegetarian feasts . . . .[40]

Po Chü-i's own comments on this lay society give an indication of how such practices were conventionally regarded:

> I have heard that the merit of donating one strand of hair or one grain of rice will never be lost; how much greater is the merit gained in preparing with ceaseless energy the boundless offering of four vegetarian feasts annually, supplied by the income of a thousand *mou*? I have heard that the power of one earnest wish and the merit of [reciting] one verse will never be lost; how much greater then is the merit accruing from a thousand mouths uttering the twelve divisions of the canon? Moreover, how much greater also when hundreds of thousands of ears are listening to myriads of *sūtras*?[41]

In the convent these traditions of recitation of *sūtras* for the sake of the creation and transfer of generalized merit continue, most notably in four forms:

First, at the death of relatives of lay members (*hsin-t'u*), or on memorial days and anniversaries of their deaths, a certain number of nuns are invited to the homes of lay members to recite *sūtras*. The merit is transferred to the dead relatives. This practice is conducted chiefly in the homes of families marking a day in the funeral cycle of forty-nine and then one-hundred days following the death, and then marking yearly anniversaries of the death of a relative.[42]

Second, *sūtras* are recited intensively during the special *Dharma* assemblies (C. *fa-hui*) held several times a year (see the discussion of *Dharma* assemblies below).

Third, the *Sūtra of the Past Vows of the Earth Store (Kṣitigarbha) Bodhisattva*[43] is recited daily by the nuns throughout the seventh month, with the merit transferred to the ancestors of the lay members of the convent.[44] The context is provided by Kṣitigarbha's "birthday" on the twenty-fourth day of the seventh month, and by the fact that the whole month is devoted to expressing compassion and filial piety through assistance to those reborn as hungry ghosts and in the hells. Lay people come to join in those daily recitations, taking their places at long tables at which the *sūtra* texts are set before them. During that month also, a special hymn to Kṣitigarbha is read as part of the daily office. The *sūtra* itself describes the hells and their punishments in vivid detail, as well as the sins to which they correspond. It then describes the vows and acts of the Bodhisattva Kṣitigarbha to free those reborn in the hells. Kṣitigarbha vowed to devote all his merit to that purpose until all were freed.

Fourth, on lay initiative a lay society similar to the ones mentioned above meets regularly twice a month throughout the year at one house of the convent to recite the *Lotus Sūtra* together and sponsor a vegetarian meal. The members of the society, called the "Lotus Association," are all women. From ten to twelve o'clock in the morning on the first and fifteenth of the lunar month, the women recite as many chapters as they can in the time allotted. The nuns lead them in this recitation on their rhythm instruments, and then at noon perform with them an extended service of offerings to the Buddha. This service includes requests for the transfer of the merit that has accrued from the recitation to the members' relatives and to all sentient beings. After a short sermon by the abbess, the twice-monthly event ends in the convent refectory with a vegetarian lunch prepared by the nuns. The activities of this Lotus Association constitute one of the main organized ways in which this house of the convent interacts with lay people.

Reciting Texts as Action for Specific Purposes: The Daily Office and the Dharma *Assemblies.* More important to the nuns than the practice of simply reciting *sūtra*s in order to create and transfer generalized merit is the practice of reciting certain words and texts to bring about specific effects. To recite these texts sincerely and single-mindedly is to take the action of creating those specific fruits. Examples include texts that bring the practitioner powers for specific uses; texts that transfer merit toward a specific fruit (e.g., rebirth in the Pure Land); texts that enable one to take actions to help others, such as those that release the denizens of the hells and bring them to the convent to receive food and preaching; texts that invoke the names of many Buddhas for the purpose of repentance to wipe out past transgressions; and texts that consist of vows to set the direction for the future.

Often specific modes of receiving these words are mandated in the canonically preserved versions of the text. That is to say, not only are the words to be spoken prescribed, but also what she is to do as she recites the text, what she is to imagine and think about as she is saying the prescribed words and carrying out the prescribed actions, and what effects she should expect. Often a narrative is included, to provide the reason and context for the Buddha's original gift of the word or text, as well as a model of the way it should be received. These texts exist so that actions can be carried out in a ritual context.

In addition, one can distinguish still another kind of text whose recitation constitutes a kind of action: the "expressive text." An example would be the hymns included in the morning and evening recitation services that express gratitude and praise.

Ritual Action and Texts in the Daily Offices. One important context for this kind of reception of texts is the "daily office" carried out in most convents and monasteries morning and evening.[45]

Commentaries tell us that one purpose of these morning and evening recitations is to guide and sustain the practice of monks and nuns by providing them with a "daily work." Performing this daily work will assure that they are doing enough toward enlightenment (and making enough merit) to justify their continuing to receive offerings from the laity. It also will guarantee that beginners have the right understanding of practice.[46]

Still other goals of these recitations, however, are evident from the content and purposes of the text chosen. The daily offices consist primarily of transactive texts (including *dhāraṇīs*) found in the Ta-tsang-ching. The actions that are taken by reciting these texts include:

i. Protecting the practice of the nuns from disturbing forces such as demons and sexual desires, and invoking, through *mantra*s and *dhāraṇīs*, various special conditions and powers to promote successful practice, and to protect the monastery and the nation.

The morning daily office begins with a recitation of the *Śūraṅgama Mantra*, which has the specific purpose of dispelling sexual temptations, and thus facilitating single-minded practice the rest of the day. Its effectiveness in defeating sexual imaginings was mentioned to me specifically by more than one nun. For example, one of the nuns told me that sometimes in the night she experiences feelings of sexual longing or imagination. The remedy, she says, is to recite a *mantra* like the *Śūraṅgama Mantra* immediately. If one does this, the feeling will go away.

The *Śūraṅgama Mantra* is followed by ten other *mantra*s and *dhāraṇīs* that protect the practitioners and foster practice in specific ways; for example, one assures that the practitioner will have enough material resources to continue to practice. Another important *dhāraṇī* included in the daily office is the Great Compassion *Dhāraṇī* of the Bodhisattva Avalokiteśvara. This specifically invokes Avalokiteśvara's protection against all kinds of demonic forces.

ii. Feeding hungry ghosts, through a tantric-derived ritual called the "*Meng-shan shih-shih*".

A short form of this ritual is done daily; it makes up a rather large part of the evening office. By the use of *mantra*s, those who suffer as hungry ghosts, unable to eat or drink but perpetually hungry, are enabled to eat and drink; then seven visible grains of rice are multiplied, thanks to another *mantra* that must be said with single-minded concentration, into millions of grains of rice so that the hungry ghosts may be satisfied.

This done, the *Dharma* is preached to them, and the "Three Refuges" are taken on their behalf. The nuns told me stories about the necessity of keeping one's mind on rice while the multiplication *mantra* was being said. One nun had found her mind wandering to the question of where she had left her room key, and thus had created millions of room keys for the hungry ghosts!

iii. Offering praise and gratitude to Buddhas and Bodhisattvas.

This is done by reciting and chanting hymns of Chinese origin. At the very beginning of the morning and evening offices a hymn, called the "incense hymn," invokes the presence of the Buddhas and Bodhisattvas. Later hymns, particularly in the evening office, praise Amitābha Buddha and describe his Pure Land.

iv. Repenting all faults.

This is another rather large sub-ritual of the daily office. Rituals of repentance have a long history in Indian, Central Asian and Chinese Buddhism, and at times have constituted a principal activity of monks.[47] The particular sub-ritual used today in the daily office is not found in this form in a canonical text, and the tradition holds that this particular ritual was compiled in China.[48] This ritual accomplishes repentance through the recitation of the names of eighty-eight Buddhas.

v. Establishing connection with Buddhas and Bodhisattvas by invoking their names.

Within the office, certain names of *sūtras* and names and titles of Buddhas are recited because they serve as a channel of invocation or connection between the individual and powerful Buddhas and Bodhisattvas. The notion here seems akin to the notion of the *mantra*: the name, title, image, *mudrā* or *mantra* of a Buddha is provided for the explicit purpose of providing a means of participating in the reality of that Buddha, with the expectation that a bond will be formed and the worshipper transformed.[49]

vi. Reciting Amitābha Buddha's name and seeking rebirth in Amitābha Buddha's Pure Land.

The evening office includes a rather long passage of repeated recitation of Amitābha's name, done as a chant, while the nuns proceed ceremonially around the Buddha Hall.[50]

vii. Refuges and vows.

Repeatedly within the offices nuns take refuge in the Buddha, chiefly through reciting different versions of the "Three Refuges": "I take refuge in the Buddha, I take refuge in the *Dharma*, I take refuge in the *Saṅgha* (the Assembly of the Buddha's followers)." The nuns also take vows concerning their intention to practice the path and reach Buddhahood. This is done chiefly through reciting the four "Bodhisattva Vows" in various versions.

ix. Transferring merit.

On every occasion that merit is made, it is transferred to the benefit of all sentient beings. This is done by a formulaic verse.

The Yearly Dharma *Assemblies.* A second context for recitation as action was the cycle of *Dharma* assemblies on a regular schedule each year. At each of these a central liturgical and merit-making activity was the recitation of texts. On all of these occasions lay associates of the convent would come to the convent to participate in the services and in the recitation of texts, and would sponsor these occasions, so that the merit derived therefrom would be transferred to their ancestors or living relatives.

The most important of these *Dharma* assemblies is held for several days surrounding the fifteenth day of the seventh month in the lunar calendar. This is the Yü-lan-p'en festival.[51] Its themes are: (a) the compassion of the Buddha in allowing the living to assist the dead with merit and sermons, so that the dead may escape the punishments they have earned, and speedily attain a better birth; and (b) the filial devotion of children who act to free their parents and ancestors. On the fifteenth day of the seventh month, the *Fo-shuo Yü-lan-p'en ching* (a text probably written in China, but sometimes referred to in the West as the *Ullambana Sūtra* on the assumption that it had a Sanskrit prototype of that name) is read.[52] This describes the efforts of the monk Maudgalyāyana to free his mother from intense suffering as a hungry ghost, the compassion of the Buddha who enables him to do so, and the specific method given to him by the Buddha. The prescribed method is to call together all of the monks of the ten directions on the fifteenth day of the seventh month (the end of the rain retreat) and give them a spectacular feast. The monks then transfer merit to the parents and ancestors of seven generations, and Maudgalyāyana's mother is released.

Further, for each of three days during this festival, one part of a three-part sermon is read to those reborn in the realms of suffering (in the hells, as a hungry ghost, or as an animal). Each of the three sections takes two hours to chant, and a large number of lay people participate. This text, named *San-shih hsi-nien fo-shih*, is a basic exposition of Buddhist teaching on the Buddha, the *Dharma* and the *Saṅgha*.[53] It is recited with the intention of inducing, in the hungry ghosts and denizens of the hells, wisdom and the desire to be reborn in the Pure Land.

In the eleventh month another *Dharma* assembly is held, at which the *Diamond Sūtra* is recited, along with the *Water Penance* (*Shui ch'an*), a text attributed to a T'ang dynasty (A.D. 618–907) monk.[54] The *Diamond Sūtra* is a short Mahāyāna Wisdom School (*Prajñāpāramitā*) work teaching that the ultimate truth is that all things are empty of self-existence, and therefore cannot be grasped onto. Again, lay people participate in the recitations, and the merit is transferred to their ancestors and relatives.

Finally in the spring a third *Dharma* assembly is held, this time featuring a reading of the *Penance of Liang Wu-ti*, a sixth century emperor famous for his support of Buddhism.[55] At this *Dharma* assembly, as at all the others, the ritual popularly called "*Fang yen-k'ou*" (Release of the Burning Mouths) is performed. This ritual is performed by reciting an esoteric Yoga ritual text called the "*Yü-chia yen-k'ou*."[56] Lay people bring food offerings. The nuns, through the *dhāraṇī*, *mantras* and *mudrās* prescribed by the text, invite the denizens of the hells and the hungry ghosts into the convent worship hall, opening the gates of the hells to make this possible. Through the ritual *mantras* and *mudrās* the nuns then open the mouths of the hungry ghosts, preach *Dharma* to them, feed them, and send them away from the convent. This is a more extended version of the "*Meng-shan shih-shih*" that is part of every evening liturgy.

A Theoretical Note. We will return below to a somewhat more extended note on the general theory that underlies the modes of reception found in the convent. I wish here only to mention that on several occasions the nuns explained to me how they think transactional reception is effective. Their explanations show that they entertain simultaneously two metaphors, one of external transaction and one of transaction taking place within Mind, with the latter metaphor considered to be the more true one. An example from my field notes:

> I was talking today with Ch'en-ta shih about my family situation. She said that I should seek the help of Kuan-yin (Avalokiteśvara), that Kuan-yin is compassion, is very powerful, and meets every need. I said that another teacher had advised me to practice the visualization of Kuan-yin. She replied that that was an excellent idea, but that I could also profit from walking around my room reciting Kuan-yin's name. This was also a good way of practicing *ting* (Sk. *samādhi*), since one's mind quieted down as one did so. She showed me how to walk, reciting the name on a four-beat pattern. I asked whether she herself had ever sought help from Kuan-yin. Yes, over this matter of her brother's military service, about which she had told me. She had made a vow to recite the "Universal Gate" chapter of the *Lotus Sūtra* every morning as part of her petition to Kuan-yin to help her brother. It is important, she said, that one is sincere, single-minded, in one's petition, and that one keep on seeking Kuan-yin's help until the problem is resolved. It is sincerity that makes the response (C. *kan-ying*) by Kuan-yin possible. It is like electricity—both the electric cord and the light bulb are necessary

to produce light. The Bodhisattva is in your mind, and it is your mind that is disturbed and is seeking, and it is the sincerity in your seeking mind that makes the connection possible.

Almost all of the world's sacred texts contain material which is, like many of the texts mentioned above, explicitly understood to be of a ritual nature, that is, useful in bringing about an action or a transaction of some kind. What is striking in the Buddhist case is the degree to which all interactions with all texts, all receptions, are understood to be actions and transactions. Any contact with a tradition-sanctioned text is meritorious, and is urged on practitioners as such.

I have chosen the word "transactional" rather than, for example, the word "performative" to name this category, to call attention to the importance of the fact that in any transactional reception, actions are being taken, and transactions occurring, on many different levels. In the cases we have looked at, transactions take place on the level of *karma*, and also between persons and Buddhas and Bodhisattvas. They also occur symbolically, economically and socially between lay people and nuns, and lay people and their families. Acting in the power of the ultimate is clearly a very important dimension of the reception of texts in this tradition. I would suggest that important parallels exist in other traditions as well, though perhaps not always so explicitly underlined by the theoretical dimension of the tradition.

The Transformative Mode

Texts would not become and remain scriptural unless in and through their reception people experienced transforming power. While the informative and transactional dimensions of the reception of texts as "scripture" are universal and important, religious communities regularly point to the transforming power experienced in and through texts as the special mark of their sacredness. In accordance with the importance that they place on this dimension, religious people often receive texts with attitudes and in contexts that invite experiences of transformation through them.

I have noted above that as Chinese Buddhists read, listen to, study and comment on *sūtra*s in order to become informed by their account of reality, they also seek at the same time to be transformed in their personal capacity to experience wisdom and compassion.

Looking at other areas of their religious practice, an interesting pattern emerges. As we have seen above, certain *sūtra*s, *mantra*s, *dhāraṇī*s, tantric rituals, essays and sermons are specifically intended for transactive purposes, or are recited with transactive intentions. Other texts (e.g., repentance rituals, hymns of invocation and praise, certain *dhāraṇīs* and *mantras*) are intended to aid the practice of the practitioner herself rather than some other person. These texts and their ritual contexts intend and expect transformative effects. The nuns and lay people say little about transformation experienced in connection with the communal transactive *sūtra* and *dhāraṇī* recitations of the daily office or the *Dharma* assemblies. They also seem to take for granted the transforming power of the recitations of transformative texts included in their communal practice, though if questioned they attest to their transformative power. In contrast, they speak voluntarily and enthusiastically about the transforming power experienced through reciting, reading or copying *sūtras* and *dhāraṇīs* in their individual elective practice, whether that practice was principally transactive or transformative in intent.

Sūtra *Recitation.* In connection with the practice of *sūtra* recitation, for example, I was told a good deal about the changes the nuns had observed in an elderly lay woman.

There were living in the convent community several older women who, although retaining lay status, intended to end their days there. When I asked them why they were there, they replied that they had chosen to live there so that they would be able to spend their time reciting *sūtras* and worshiping the Buddha, while enjoying the merit of a vegetarian diet. One of these women indeed did spend the whole day every day in the large Buddha Hall, sitting by a window where the light streamed in, silently or softly reading aloud the words of *sūtra* texts that she held in her lap.

I saw this woman at the convent at intervals over a ten year period. When I first knew her, she was clearly a difficult person. Her face had a habitually sour expression, and she seemed constantly to be finding fault with the nuns. When I returned to the convent several years after our first meeting, she appeared to be a different person. She smiled often and seemed to have only kind things to say. She expressed affection for the younger nuns, who were clearly quite fond of her. On one of my last visits to the convent I learned that she had died the previous day. The younger nuns were most moved and impressed by the manner of her death. Despite the fact that she was not ill, she had seemed to know that she would die very soon, and had made a special trip to the city to see a young nun with whom she was close. When the nun, busy at the time, had suggested that she come the following week, the elderly woman had insisted that the visit must take place immediately. The day following the visit she had died suddenly and peacefully. The nuns saw in this sequence of events a pattern familiar from the tradition: the person whose practice is advanced can foretell her death, and dies peacefully, usually in a state of mental composure (*samādhi*) and without suffering. The nuns attributed this evidence of the lay woman's progress on the path to her years of reading *sūtra*s in the Buddha Hall.

Copying Sūtras. The following excerpt from my field notes contains a telling account of the transformative effects of copying *sūtra*s as a way of concentrating the mind:

> T'an Lao-shih (a lay woman) has gradually admitted to me her interest in Buddhist understandings of the world. She says sometimes that she is not a scholar like me, but rather "just a superstitious worshiper of Bodhisattvas" (an altogether too modest disclaimer). She reads *sūtra*s like the *Heart Sūtra* and the *Diamond Sūtra* over and over, not worrying as a scholar would about whether she understands the occasional transliterated Sanskrit words, but just reading. She is also a painter, and showed me one day at her home her paintings of Buddhas and Bodhisattvas. She is a wonderful painter of eyes—all of the beings in her paintings seem alive because their eyes have real spirit.
>
> She says that she has learned to let things go, not to get upset about things. To see that the things of this world are like smoke, soon over. One day at lunch, T'an Lao-shih told the story of how she had come to Buddhist faith. She had arrived in Taiwan with a child and no husband, herself only seventeen. (I gather that her husband had fought on the communist side and died in the civil war.) She was very shy and had led a sheltered life, and finding herself having to confront all kinds of problems, was overwhelmed. The government read her mail and searched her drawers on suspicion that she might be keeping in touch with her husband's friends. She worked in a factory by day and went to school at night, eventually earning a graduate degree at a highly respected university. No one understood why she did not remarry immediately. She said that she began to discipline her mind to see everything as not worth worrying about. It took a long while, but gradually this discipline began to take effect. She trained herself not to care what others thought or said, not to get involved in the conversations of her colleagues at the school where she taught, conversations about what this colleague had said or that colleague had done. Having been trained as a child in calligraphy, she began to copy *sūtra*s as a mental discipline, not worrying about whether she understood all the words. She also practiced Buddha-name recitation, and began the practice of thanking the Bodhisattvas for their protection. Gradually these practices began to have an effect, and her mind was able to become very still.

> She continues the practice of copying *sūtras*, copying in the morning before work, and painting in the evening.

T'an Lao-shih's practice has several dimensions; for our purposes I wish to call attention particularly to her practice of copying *sūtras* as a mental discipline. T'an Lao-shih says that she reads and copies the *sūtras* not so much to understand their content but to drive unworthy distractions from her mind. Yet, the fact that she copies *sūtras*, and not the daily newspaper, shows that they have meaning for her as symbols and expressions of *Dharma*. The inner intention here is to let go of all deluded thoughts, of all mental objects other than those symbolized by these texts. The act of copying is an aid to concentration for the purpose of realizing within the mind the infinite wisdom and stillness symbolized by the text.

Sūtra *and* Dhāraṇī *Recitation.* One popular focus of such practice is two texts provided within the canon that serve as a special channel between the practitioner and the Bodhisattva Avalokiteśvara (C. Kuan-yin), the Bodhisattva who promises to rescue all who call upon her/him from difficulties and dangers in the present life.

In the following instance it is clear that the nun Ch'en-chih shih, who has taken a vow to recite a chapter of a *sūtra* every morning, does not understand herself to be doing this solely because she wants to impress her memory with its content, or even to have ever fresh acquaintance with it. She is doing it in the context of establishing a link or resonance between her own mind and that of Avalokiteśvara, and text is the preferred symbolic means of doing this, a means provided by Avalokiteśvara her/himself:

> Ch'en-chih shih said that she has an image of Kuan-yin (Avalokiteśvara) in her room, and every morning gets up and goes through a book that contains the "Universal Gate" chapter of the *Lotus Sūtra*[57] and the "Great Compassion *Dhāraṇī*."[58] The latter is divided into eighty-four phrases; each phrase is illustrated by a picture of Kuan-yin that represents the form of compassionate activity invoked by the phrase. She prostrates herself from a standing position after reciting each phrase and looking at each picture—that makes eighty-four prostrations. In the winter, she says, the result is that her whole body is wonderfully warm.

Here Ch'en-chih shih tells of the transforming effect on her body of this practice that links her mind and the mind of Avalokiteśvara. (Within this tradition the warming effect of bowing is not attributed solely to the heat normally generated in any physical exercise.)

These morning recitations and prostrations are only the beginning, however. Ch'en-chih shih told me that throughout the day, as she does her work in the kitchen or sweeps the front garden, she is mentally reciting the Great Compassion *Dhāraṇī*. When someone speaks to her and she finds herself interrupted, she starts over. In addition to this constant recitation, she also makes sure that she does it with full concentration twenty-one times a day. She says that as a result her mind is very quiet and accepting.[59] Ch'en-chih shih also says that another reason for reciting the Great Compassion *Dhāraṇī* is that it provides protection from ghosts and other misfortunes. "When you recite it as far as the syllable '*ang*,'" she said, "the ghosts bow down in homage."

In the above examples, we have seen a number of ways in which interactions with words—*sūtras*, *mantras*, *dhāraṇīs*—have been understood to be related to transformation in the practitioner herself. What is valued is a transformation in one's experience of daily life; the experienced transformation is valuable for its own sake, but perhaps more valuable for being understood to be a step forward along a path toward the total transformation symbolized as 'enlightenment' or *nirvāṇa*.

In some cases the transformation is thought to come about through the greater concentration of mind (*samādhi*, the second of the "three studies") that recitation or copying makes possible. In other cases (e.g., that of the formerly sour old lady), it is the transforming power of attending to the Buddha's word (*Buddhavacana*) as *Dharma* that is given the credit.

In still other cases the effects are understood to result from the specially constituted power of the *mantra* or *dhāraṇī*, or from the power of the compassion of the Bodhisattva invoked by that *mantra* or *dhāraṇī*. Avalokiteśvara gave practitioners the Great Compassion *Dhāraṇī* in order (among other things) to protect them from demonic disturbance in their practice, an effect that is noticeable in a transformation of one's own experience.[60]

The Symbolic Mode

One of the intriguing features of the history of the Buddhist tradition is the appearance of "the cult of the book" in the early Mahāyāna. As mentioned above, there is evidence that *sūtras* at times replaced relics as the supreme symbol of the presence of the living power of the Buddha. It is no longer common practice for *sūtras* to be enshrined as the central object of worship in a monastery or convent. Yet enough remains of this idea—that *sūtra* is the most appropriate symbol to stand for Buddha or *Dharma*—to make it unsurprising that a study of the role of words in a Chinese convent would lead one to attend to a fourth mode of reception, the reception of words as symbols of ultimate truth and power.

In this mode, words and texts are received as symbols that stand for and convey a sense of the ultimate truth and its power. Here texts are read and recited, or alluded to in representation, not so much with their content in mind, nor even with an eye to their transformative and transactional powers, but rather as symbols of the powerful truth in which they are grounded.

Two kinds of symbolic meaning can be distinguished, even though a given symbol usually carries both. The first kind is social meaning. For example, a text serves as a symbol that carries social meanings when it symbolizes the sources and bearers of the authority of the tradition, and even when it symbolizes the nature of the tradition and of the world it imagines.

The second kind is ultimate meaning. Religious symbols have the power of pointing to that which transcends even traditions, that which is ontologically and ethically ultimate. As Wilfred Cantwell Smith says in an article on "Religion as Symbol":

> There is more to human life than meets the eye. More to oneself; more to one's neighbor; more to the world that surrounds us. There is more to the past out of which we come; and especially, it would seem, more to the present moment, maybe even infinitely more. There is more to the interrelationships that bind us together as persons. And the further we probe, men have always found, the deeper the mystery, or the reward, or the involvement. It is this "more," perhaps, that provides at least one of the bases for human religion. We men have seldom been content to be "superficial," to remain on the surface, to imagine that reality does not transcend our finite grasp; and throughout most of our history on this planet we have ordered our lives, both personal and cultural, in terms of that transcendence.
>
> Yet how is one to point to what one does not visually see? How to resort to a milieu beyond all space? How to talk or to think about what transcends not only words but the reach of the mind? How even to feel about what one does not touch? Man's inherent and characteristic capacity to do these things finds expression through his special relation to symbols. These have proven over the centuries sometimes more, sometimes less, adequate to such a task, but in any case indispensible, and ubiquitous.[61]

A text in a religious tradition carries this kind of meaning when it is a symbol of the true nature of things and of the locus of true power for good.

Both are important dimensions of the symbolic reception of scripture, which like other religious symbols, is polysemic. But the most important dimension to the continued reception of scripture as scripture is undoubtedly the second.

It is important to remember that symbols do more than "express" or "represent" ultimate truth or meaning. As Smith continues:

> Such symbols, it turns out, have the power not merely to express men's otherwise inchoate awareness of the richness of what lies under the surface, but also to nurture and to communicate and to elicit it. They have an activating as well as a representational quality, and an ability to organize the emotions and the unconscious as well as the conscious mind, so that into them men may pour the deepest range of their humanity and from them derive an enhancement of the personality. Without the use of symbols, including religious symbols, man would be radically less than human. . . .[62]

To point out that symbols have this activating power is to draw attention to the deep connection between the symbolic mode of reception and the modes discussed above—particularly, of course, the transformative mode. Indeed, the burden of my argument is that scripture is what it is because of the ways it is read and used, and because it can sustain being read and used in such ways: informative, transactional, transformative. In turn, the fact that scripture can be read and used in such ways enables it to become a symbol of the transcendent, a sacralizing agent, even at times an icon of the sacred, within a religious community. Thus symbolic reception depends upon the other modes of reception, and vice versa.

The Symbolic Reception of Words in the Buddhist Tradition. In the Buddhist tradition, words become symbols not only of social relationships, that is, of the authority and power of the tradition, but also of that which transcends. One way of stating this is to say that they not only are, but also symbolize, *Dharma*.

At the outset it is useful to distinguish two different degrees of symbolizing that words and texts are understood to be able to do. Words and texts can be symbols in a weak sense and in a strong sense.

In the weak sense, words can stand for the truth of the tradition, or make it present symbolically in ritual action without in themselves being understood as agents of power in any strong sense.

Words can also be symbols in a stronger sense, one that might be called "magical." In this understanding, powers are given to the human mind and to human agency through words, due to a cosmically instituted link between the words as essential mediators of ritual agency and the cosmic powers they invoke. The ways in which *mantras* and *dhāraṇī* are understood in Chinese Mahāyāna Buddhist communities often exemplifies this mode. They are interpreted as representation-in-sound of cosmic powers (or, since the cosmos is often understood to be also the mind, of mental powers); they elicit those; but beyond this, they give those powers a real presence, understood in a way partly analogous to the way the presence of the divine is understood in Western Christian sacraments or in Eastern Orthodox Christian icons.[63]

It is on the weaker of these senses, the ways in which *sūtras* symbolize *Dharma*, that I wish to focus, for this is the sense that illustrates the symbolic mode of reception at the point of its widest comparative applications. What is the basis for saying that *sūtras*, which are *Dharma*, also at the same time symbolize *Dharma*?

In Buddhism the authority and power of *Dharma* and the authority, mystery and power of Buddha are closely linked. The Buddha did not vest authority and transforming agency in a lineage of gurus; he did not even appoint a successor as supreme teacher. The tradition records that he instead told his disciples to take refuge in the *Dharma* that he had taught. The implication seemed to be that it is *Dharma*, correctly understood and diligently followed, that has the power of transforming the life of the disciple. The *Dharma* at the same time is the supreme truth, full knowledge of which is equivalent to liberation. Later in the tradition, in accord with what seems to be a general Indian assumption that in the realm of gnosis one becomes the Truth that one knows, it is stated that he who sees *Dharma* sees the Buddha, and, beyond that, in the Mahāyāna, that the fundamental 'body' of Buddhahood, transcending time, space and all apprehension by the discriminating mind, is the 'body of *Dharma*' (*Dharmākaya*). Similarly, the true nature of things as they really are comes, among other names, to be called "*Dharma*ness" (*Dharmatā*).

Thus *Dharma* on one level is expressed in words; on that level, *sūtras* not only symbolize *Dharma*, they are *Dharma*, teachings. They are *Buddhavacana*, the Buddha-word, a chief medium through which the Buddha chose to make Truth present in the world of thought and perception.[64]

Yet the teaching in words also provides the bridge to a gnosis, a perception of *Dharmatā* (the true nature of things), and *Dharmakāya* (the true nature of Buddhahood). Both of these are beyond form and inexpressible in words. Thus *Dharma* stands not only for the words, the bridge, within the temporal, conditioned realm, but also that ultimate, unconditioned to which the bridge leads and on which it depends. Most

Mahāyāna schools maintain that *Dharma*, as the true nature of things, also transcends words; words and thought cannot grasp it. It is intriguing that the recitations of words can serve as symbols, indeed in the convent the most important symbols, of the ineffable Truth that grounds them. The accessible to mentation and imagination stands for the inaccessible ground of that mentation and imagination.[65]

The Symbolic Reception of Words in the Convent. Indeed, where the convent is concerned, the recitation of *sūtras* and the making of offerings are its most important acts symbolizing: 1) its intentions and role; 2) the nature of the transforming process that it fosters; and 3) the tradition that it continues. The very large role that preaching, explication and recitation of the tradition-sanctioned words plays in the Chinese convent conveys the message that the Buddhist monastic order is that body that "turns the wheel of the *Dharma*," continuously re-presenting and offering the words of the Buddha to the minds of sentient beings.

The convent's library continues this theme, while at the same time conveying a social message about the nature and authority of the tradition. Convents and monasteries that can afford them want to have a complete copy of a Chinese Ta-tsang-ching, and the four houses of this convent community were not exceptions. Each one had a complete Ta-tsang-ching, kept as a precious possession in a locked but transparent bookcase, and virtually never opened. Although it was certainly intended to be available to any scholarly nun who might need it, its importance was at least partly symbolic. This Ta-tsang-ching symbolizes, as does the monastic library in larger monasteries, the extent of the Buddha's teaching and the tradition's claim to be a part of the high culture, as nothing else can do.[66]

Furthermore, it is significant that in the convent's public practice the sacredness (*Dharma* nature) of many sacred acts is expressed by symbolic reference to the *sūtra* as symbol of *Dharma*. To take an example from rites of passage, in funerals and all ceremonies of merit-making and transference for the dead the reading/reciting of a *sūtra* is the central, even defining, practice, and therefore the central symbol of what is being done for the dead. On one level this can be explained away by saying that *sūtra*-recitation is one of the more convenient forms of merit-making. But why is this particular meritorious activity chosen? Perhaps to recite *sūtras*, rather than to perform some other merit making act, invokes the mystery and power of *Dharma*, and asserts (makes present) the whole authority of the tradition, at the moment of crisis, in a way other forms of merit-making could not do.[67]

A number of other examples that include a significant symbolic dimension have already been mentioned. Two in which the symbolic dimension is most striking are the case of the hermit who has vowed to read through the entire Ta-tsang-ching, and the case of T'an Lao-shih's copying of *sūtras* as a meditative discipline. In both of these instances it is clear that there is a central informative or transformative purpose: encountering useful reflection on experience, concentrating the mind. Yet in both cases it seems that there is an important symbolic dimension. T'an Lao-shih in choosing *sūtras* to copy, even ones she does not understand, expresses her rededication to *Dharma* in all of its senses. The hermit gives himself through its symbol to the entirety of *Dharma*, even the vast amount of it which he may never in this lifetime understand.

A CHINESE THEORETICAL FRAMEWORK

A sixth century Chinese or Central Asian text attributed to Aśvaghoṣa provides an ontology *cum* psychology that may be helpful in understanding Chinese Buddhist reflection on the power and activity of sacred words. According to this text, called the "*Awakening of Faith in the Mahāyāna*," there is only one reality, which can be pointed to by the term 'Suchness' and by the term 'One Mind.'[68] About this reality in its absolute self-nature nothing can be said, except by analogy—thus the ultimate inadequacy of all words in conveying ultimate truth referentially. But this one reality manifests itself as the phenomenal world. In individuals, it is manifest in two dimensions. In its true nature as reality, it is manifest as the originally enlightened mind which all possess, and which is one with Suchness or the One Mind itself. This mind knows no distinctions, sees things as they are, and in its freedom is infinitely creative of wise and compassionate acts.

Due to beginningless ignorance, however, this originally enlightened mind is covered over by deluded mind. Deluded mind arises because of its fundamental ignorance of its oneness with Suchness or the One Mind of enlightenment. Hope lies in the fact that although deluded mind is continually contaminating and obscuring enlightened mind, within us, enlightened mind is also, and more powerfully, influencing deluded mind so that within deluded mind will arise those thoughts and motives that will lead to its destruction.[69] Within the world of distinctions—that is, the world created by deluded mind—the appearance of Buddhas, Bodhisattvas, teachings, *sūtras*, and other forms of sacred word such as *mantras* and *dhāraṇīs* that have powerful effects on the mind are on the deepest level to be understood as beneficial forces which are created by our deluded mind under the influence of, and due to the activity of, our originally enlightened mind. This latter, since it is universal, is also the mind of the Buddha. Those who are on the lower stages of the path will perceive these Buddhas, Bodhisattvas, *sūtras*, *mantras*, and so forth as encountering us, or being given to us, from outside ourselves. Their origin is indeed outside deluded mind, in a sense, yet even they are skillful creations of deluded mind under the influence of enlightened mind within us.

Modern Chinese Buddhists would add to this, as we have seen, that faith and sincerity provide the connective, the electric cord, by which deluded mind allows enlightened mind to penetrate its delusion and make its influence felt. Similarly it is that same enlightened mind in Buddhas and Bodhisattvas (to use the external metaphor) that is capable of creating *sūtras*, *mantras*, *dhāraṇīs* and other forms of sacred word, of iconic symbol, which are perfectly suited to the condition of deluded mind within their hearers and reciters, so that they produce beneficial effects. To express this in the internal metaphor of the *Awakening of Faith*, one might say that enlightened mind creates within deluded mind the perception of apparently external Buddhas and Bodhisattvas, who offer *sūtras*, *mantras*, and other forms of symbols as devices (Sk. *upāya*, C. *fa-men*) suited to the condition of deluded mind.

Thus, if words as symbols of *Dharmakāya* were not in some sense revelation—that is, did not come to us in some sense from beyond deluded mind—we could not rely on them to bring our minds further toward enlightenment. Yet, being words (or images) they fit the condition of deluded mind, and can in a sense occur within it as its creations, bridging the 'other' of 'enlightened mind' and the immediately experienced 'self' of deluded mind to bring about an ultimate transformation.

THE MODES OF RECEPTION AND SCRIPTURE

I hope that the above examples have supported my suggestion that texts are scripture for their readers when they can sustain a variety of ways of being received, including in some manner the four that I have tried to illustrate here. Texts in the Buddhist tradition worthy of the name "scriptures" are texts in which communities and individuals find authoritative information and guidance, texts through the reception of which they are enabled to act in the power of the ultimate, texts that come to symbolize that ultimate, and texts that can be approached in the confident expectation of personal transformation. I would suggest that comparative study would disclose, not a uniform pattern of similarity in the form or content of scriptures, but the presence of at least these four fundamental *modes of reception*.

NOTES

1. A book that became available to us after these essays were in press is Frederick M. Denny and Rodney L. Taylor, eds., *The Holy Book in Comparative Perspective* (Columbia University of South Carolina Press, 1985). This excellent book contains an essay by Sam D. Gill suggesting a two-fold way of looking at how sacred texts are used: "informative" and "performative". As best I can tell from the brief essay, his "performative" category would include my "symbolic" mode as well. Likewise, what I call the "transactive" and "transformative" modes would perhaps both be intended within his discussion of the "performative" dimension of sacred texts. Reflection on the Buddhist case, in which "transactive" and "transformative" dimensions are clearly conceptually distinct, as well as reflection on other examples leads me to believe that a four-fold characterization has distinct advantages. It allows one to give due weight to the transformative and symbolic modes of receiving scripture, without which scripture would not continue to be scripture on the level of personal piety. Further, I believe there are benefits from clearly distinguishing the performative (which I call the transactional) and the symbolic, the power of text to serve as an icon of the sacred; certainly this is true in the Buddhist case, where such a separation is necessarily made.

2. The classic reference here is *Majjima Nikāya* I, p. 265 (Pali Text Society edition). Etienne Lamotte translates from the Chinese translation of this text, *Chung a-han ta-p'in ch'a-t'i ching*, as follows: "[The Buddha] addressed his monks in these terms: 'Now, monks, that you understand and think thus, should you say: We honor the Master, and out of respect for the Master, we say this or that?'—'We would not do that, Lord.'—'What you shall affirm, O monks, is it not that which you have yourselves well recognized, seen and grasped?'—'The same, Lord.' Lamotte, "La Critique d'authenticité dans le Bouddhisme," *India Antiqua* (Leyden: E. J. Brill, 1947), pp. 220–21; my translation from the French. The text is contained in the *Taishō Shinshu Daizōkyō* (J. Takakusu and K. Watanabe, eds; Tokyo: Taishō Issai-kyō Kankō Kai, 1924), no. 26, vol. 1, p. 769b., lines 14–19 (Hereafter cited in the standard Buddhological form of T.26.1.769b.14–19.) A translation is also found in I.B. Horner, *Middle Length Sayings* I (Pali Text Society Translation Series, no. 29; London: Luzac and Co., Ltd., 1954, reprinted, 1967), p. 321. The best translation of this passage seems to be by Rune E.A. Johansson in his *Pali Buddhist Texts* (Stockholm: Studentlitteratur), pp. 19–22. On the topic of Indian Buddhist attitudes toward the verbal tradition of the Buddha, cf. James P. McDermott, "Scripture as the Word of the Buddha," *Numen* 31:22–39.

3. Cf. T. W. Rhys Davids, trans., *Buddhist Suttas*, Sacred Books of the East, vol. 11 (reprinted in Delhi India by Motilal Banarsidass, 1968), pp. 37–8. (Also in T.W. Rhys-Davids and C.A.F. Rhys-Davids, *Dialogues of the Buddha*, Part II, Sacred Books of the Buddhists, vol. 3, 4th ed. [London: Luzac and Co. Ltd. vol. 3, 1959], p. 108.) *Sutta* is the Pali word for the Sanskrit *sūtra*. As a rule, the Sanskrit form of the Buddhist term is used in this book, but here the Pali word is used to distinguish it from a later Mahāyāna text, the *Mahāparinirvāṇa Sūtra*.

4. This meeting is usually called the "First Council," but the term translated "council", *sāmgiti*, means "reciting together"; the notion of reciting for the sake of arriving at a "canon" is included in the term. On this council, cf. J. Przyluski, *Le Concile de Rājagṛha* (Paris, 1926), especially Ch. V, and André Bareau, *Les Premiers Conciles Bouddhiques* (Paris: Presses Universitaires de France, 1955), pp. 21–30.

5. Cf. Kōgen Mizuno, *Buddhist Sūtras: Origin, Development, Transmission* (Tokyo: Kosei Publishing Co., English edition 1982). On the "canonizing" of the Tripiṭaka, see Andre Bareau *et al.*, *Die Religionen Indiens III: Buddhismus – Jinismus – Primitivvölker* (Stuttgart: W. Kohlhammer, 1964), pp. 23–32. Concerning later criteria for inclusion of newly reported teachings in the "canon" of authentic *Dharma*, see E. Lamotte, "La critique d'authenticité," where criteria, articulated in the Pali and Sanskrit versions of the *Mahopadeśa* and in certain other later texts (such as the *Mahāyānasūtrālaṁkāra*, the *Bodhicaryāvatārapañjikā*, and the *Abhidharmakośa*) are discussed.

6. The term "presentational" is used here in the special sense of "making present," as an icon or a sacrament makes the sacred present to Eastern Orthodox Christians, or an image makes the sacred present to many Hindus. My usage of this derives from Roger Schmidt, *Exploring Religion* (Belmong, California: Wadsworth, 1980), pp. 89–92.

7. Leon Hurvitz, trans. from the Chinese of Kumārajīva, *Scripture of the Lotus Blossom of the Fine Dharma* (New York: Columbia University Press, 1976), p. 288. (Hereafter cited as "*Lotus*.")

8. *Aṣṭasāhasrikā Prajñāpāramitā*, translated by Edward Conze as *The Perfection of Wisdom in Eight Thousand Lines and its Verse Summary* (Bolinas: Four Seasons Foundation, 1973), p. 266–67. Hereafter cited as "*Perfection*."

9. "And on account of what circumstance, Ānanda, is a *Tathāgata*, an Able Awakened One, worthy of a cairn? At the thought, Ānanda, 'This is the cairn of that Exalted One, of that Able Awakened One,' the hearts of many shall be made calm and happy; and since they there had calmed and satisfied their hearts they will be reborn after death, when the body has dissolved, in the happy realms of heaven. It is on account of this circumstance, Ānanda, that a *Tathāgata*, an Able Awakened One, is worthy of a cairn." (Trans. by T.W. Rhys Davids in *Dialogues of the Buddha*, Part II, p. 156.

10. On this topic, see especially Akira Hirakawa, "The Rise of Mahāyāna Buddhism and its Relationship to the Worship of *Stūpas*," *Memoirs of the Research Department of the Tōyō Bunkō* 22 (1963), pp. 57–106, and B.C. Bagchi, "The Eight Great *Caityas* and Their Cult," *Indian Historical Quarterly*, 17 (1941): 223–235.

11. Cf. Gregory Schopen, "The Phrase '*sa pṛthivīpradeśaś caityabhūto bhavet*' in the *Vajracchedikā*: Notes on the Cult of the Book in the Mahāyāna," *Indo-Iranian Journal* 17, (Nov.-Dec. 1975): 147–87. Cf. Lama Govinda, *Psycho-Cosmic Symbolism of the Buddhist Stupa* (London: Luzac and Co. Ltd., 1976

and Berkeley: Dharma Publishing, 1976); and Sukumar Dutt, *The Buddha and Five After Centuries* (London: Luzac and Co. Ltd, 1957).

12. Cf. *Perfection*, pp. 105–108.

13. Cf. *Lotus*, p. 178–79

14. For a general discussion of this, see Daisetz Teitaro Suzuki, *Studies in the Lankavatara Sutra* (London: Routledge & Kegan Paul Ltd., 1930), pp. 105–10. (Hereafter cited as "*Studies*.")

15. This forms the climax of chapter 9 of Kumārajīva's translation of the *Vimalakīrti-nirdeśa Sūtra*, T.14.551c.23–24.

16. See, e.g,, Daisetz Teitaro Suzuki's reference to this statement in the *Laṅkāvatāra Sūtra* in his *Studies*, p. 17. For very radical statements of its pole of the tradition, see the two excerpts from the *Viśesha-cinta Brahma-paripṛcchā* translated in Edward Conze, *Buddhist Texts Through the Ages* (New York: Harper and Row Torchbooks, 1964), pp. 278–280.

17. On *adhiṣṭhāna* (the spiritual power of the Buddha which is added to a Bodhisattva and sustains him through his course of discipline), *prabhāva* (sovereign power) and *anubhāva* (the power of the Buddha moving the devotees from within, and enabling them to act in this way or that way), see Daisetz Teitaro Suzuki, *Studies*, pp. 202–205 and p. 356, and glossary.

18. Cf. Shih Tao-an, *Jih-chiao lun*, T. 52. 136b–143c; and Shih Fa-lin, *Pien–cheng lun*, "San-chiao chih-tao p'ien," T. 52. 449a. Cf. Kobayashi Masami, "Sankyō kōshō ni okeru kyō no kannen," in Yoshioka Yoshitoyo hakase kanreki kinen ronshu kangyokai, eds., *Dōkyō kenkyū ronshu* (Yoshioka Hakase kanreki kinen) (Tokyo: Kokushō kangyokai, 1977), pp. 249–69.

19. Cf. J.W. De Jong, *Buddha's Word in China* (Canberra: Australian National University, 1968), for a discussion of this process.

20. Indian and Central Asian Buddhists had distinguished between authoritative texts whose meaning was expressed directly, and texts, no less authoritative, whose meaning required interpretation. In the case of the latter, the Buddha was assumed to have had some motive for not expressing the plain truth fully, or for saying something at variance with the fundamental principles of his teaching. (Cf. E. Lamotte, "La Critique d'interprétation dans le bouddhisme," *Annuaire de l'institut de philologie et d'histoire orientales et slaves*, Université Libre de Bruxelles, IX [1949], pp. 341–61.) The Chinese classification schemes built upon these distinctions and insights, but went somewhat beyond the earlier models in their sweep and creativity. A factor that probably affected the creation of this more sweeping, more radical hermeneutical form was a difference between the ways in which Indian and Central Asian Buddhists had understood their relation to the tradition and the way the Chinese Buddhists understood it. Indians and Central Asians appear to have felt free to preserve their fresh discoveries of the meaning of *Dharma* by creating new *sūtras*. Some Chinese also created new *sūtras*; but many

Chinese, perhaps feeling themselves to be heirs of the Buddha at one remove, introduced fresh meanings of *Dharma* through these hermeneutical strategies instead.

21. Lin-chi quotes scripture back to the scripturalist! The quotation seems to be made up of phrases from two *sūtras*, the *Laṅkāvatāra Sūtra* and the *Vimalakīrti-nirdeśa Sūtra*.

22. T. 47. 496b-c. The translation is that of Ruth F. Sasaki in her *The Record of Lin-chi*, (Kyoto: The Institute for Zen Studies, 1975), pp. 1–2.

23. On the "three studies," cf. Andrew Rawlinson, "The Ambiguity of the Buddha-nature Concept in India and China," in Lewis Lancaster and Whalen Lai, eds., *Early Chan in China and Tibet*, (Berkeley: Asian Humanities Press, 1983), pp. 259–279. Another useful threefold division of the path is that into 'view' (*darśana*), practice (*caryā*) and action (*karma*). Cf. Reginald A. Ray, "Buddhism: Sacred Text Written and Realized," in Denny and Taylor, eds., *Holy Book*, p. 166.

24. Leon Hurvitz writes that "'*tao ch'ang*,' the standard equivalent of the Sanskrit *Bodhimaṇḍa*, is, in purely Chinese terms, the name for the meditation hall in a monastery." ("Hsüan-tsang [602–664] and the *Heart Scripture*," in Lewis Lancaster, ed., *Prajñāpāramitā and Related Systems: Studies in Honor of Edward Conze* [Berkeley: Regents of the University of California, 1977], p. 121, no. 58.) This may be true of an earlier period. Now, however, the term seems to refer to a place for religious offerings, to a place where the Way is cultivated, and by extension to the temple or monastery as a whole, and thus to have a meaning more similar to the original meaning of *bodhimaṇḍa*. Cf. Ting Fu-pao, *Fo-hsüeh ta-tz'u-tien*, (1921; reprint ed. Taipei: Hsin-wen- feng ch'u-pan kung-ssu, 1978) p. 2368a–b.

25. The concept is that the lay people cultivate merit in their gifts to the nuns, with the nuns serving through their practice as particularly fertile "fields" in which to grow merit.

26. The Ta-tsang-ching includes all of the text classes included in the Buddhist Tripiṭakas of the various Mahāyāna and non-Mahāyāna Buddhist schools, that is, *sūtra*, *vinaya*, *abhidharma* and *śastra*. In addition, it includes: ritual texts, tantric texts (*mantra* and *dhāraṇī*), treatises, essays and commentaries written by Chinese Buddhists, collected sayings of Ch'an (Zen) masters, and histories of Buddhism written in China. One might consider it a rather inclusive archival canon. Decisions about what texts were worthy of inclusion in the Ta-tsang-ching were often made at the Chinese imperial court.

27. Although the Chinese terms are different, I take this to be parallel to the view set out in the following passage of the *Laṅkāvatāra Sūtra*, an important Mahāyāna text of the Yogācāra school:

> Twofold are the aspects of personal realization (siddhānta) . . . the personal realization itself (siddhānta) and the external teaching (deśanā) about

> it. . . . The "personal realization" itself indicates the incomparability of personal experience, and is characterized by having nothing to do with words, discriminations and letters. . . . What is meant by the external teaching (deśanā)? It is variously given in the nine divisions of the doctrinal works; it keeps one away from the dualistic notions of being and non-being, of oneness and otherness; first making use of skillful means and expedients, it induces all beings to have a perception (of this teaching) so that whoever is inclined towards it, may be instructed in it. (D.T. Suzuki, trans., *The Lankavatara Sutra*, [London: Routledge & Kegan Paul, Ltd. 1932] pp. 128–29.)

On this topic see also D. T. Suzuki, *Studies*, pp. 348–50.

28. Cf. Schopen "Cult," and Graeme MacQueen, "Inspired Speech in Early Mahāyāna Buddhism I," *Religion* 11, (1981): 303–19. Cf. also J. Leroy Davidson, "Traces of Buddhist Evangelism in Early Chinese Art," *Artibus Asiae*, 11 (1948): 251–65.

29. Cf. J. J. M. DeGroot, *Le Code du Mahāyāna en Chine: son influence sur la vie monacale et sur le monde laique* (Amsterdam: Johannes Muller, 1893), pp. 133–43.

30. For a description of *sūtra*-lecturing and study in monasteries in China prior to 1949, cf. Holmes Welch, *The Practice of Chinese Buddhism. 1900–1950* (Cambridge: Harvard University Press, 1967), pp. 310–14. (Hereafter cited as "*Practice*.") Holmes Welch comments:

> Lectures have played an important role in Chinese Buddhism from the earliest days. Probably one of the reasons why Buddhism succeeded in China was that it included the very Chinese institution of having disciples study a canonical text under the guidance of a master who used it to shape their character. There was a certain parallel to Confucius and Mencius in the monks who even in this century traveled from place to place, a few followers at their side, lecturing on the *sūtra*s.

31. Cf. the translation in Seikan Hasegawa, *The Cave of Poison Grass* (Arlington, Virginia: Great Ocean Publishers, 1975), p. 3; cf. also his comments in footnote 1, p. 167.

32. A popular practice in the Pure Land tradition is recollection of a Buddha called Amitābha by reciting his name over and over, aiming for perfect concentration on the name.

33. This attitude toward the teaching and hearing that take place in *sūtra* lecturing doubtless has a long history in the Mahāyāna. The attitude of the preacher or expositor has long been regarded as important to the goal of transformation. For example, the "Preachers of *Dharma*" chapter of the *Lotus Sūtra* contains the following passage:

> O Medicine King! If a good man or good woman after the extinction of the Thus Come One [i.e., the Tathāgata, a title for the Buddha] wishes to preach this Scripture . . . , how is he or she to preach it? This good man or good woman is to enter the room of the Thus Come One, don the cloak of the Thus Come One, sit on the throne of the Thus Come One, and only then preach this scripture broadly to the fourfold assembly [i.e., the assembly of Buddha's followers that includes monks, nuns, laymen and laywomen]. The room of the Thus Come One is the thought of great compassion toward all living beings. The cloak of the Thus Come One is the thought of tender forbearance and the bearing of insult with equanimity. The throne of the Thus Come One is the emptiness of all dharmas. It is only by dwelling securely among these that he or she can with unabating thought broadly preach this Scripture of the *Dharma* Blossom.... (*Lotus*, p. 179–80.)

Furthermore, the notion that the hearer is to be transformed by listening is an idea that informs the very form of Mahāyāna and non-Mahāyāna *sūtras*. After the Buddha's sermon, there is regularly an account of the transformation undergone by the hearers in response.

34. For a useful brief discussion, see Daigan and Alicia Matsunaga, *The Buddhist Concept of Hell* (New York: Philosophical library, 1972), pp. 23–39. They note that in early Buddhism wholesome acts (Pali *kusala kamma*, Sk. *kuśala karma*) were

> further divided into two different spheres: the first relating to worldly actions (*sava*), which largely pertained to the laity; and the second, to religious or non-worldly actions (*asava*). It was on the level of wholesome *worldly* actions that *punna* was considered to be merit. . . . Although *punna* signified a form of good conduct, it was believed to be confined mainly to the sphere of worldly morality since its goal was deemed to be birth in a happy heaven. . . . (A)s one advanced to the level of religious spiritual awareness, the aim of attaining *punna* for happy rebirth had to be renounced in favor of the nonworldly *Brahmacariya* conduct. (p. 25)

35. Cf. Yuichi Kajiyama, "Transfer and Transformation of Merits," unpublished paper delivered at the Kuroda Institute Conference on Buddhist Hermeneutics, June, 1984. See also section on the question of whether lay people can transfer merits in Helen Hardacre, *Lay Buddhism in Contemporary Japan: Reiyukai Kyodan*, (Princeton: Princeton University Press, 1984), pp. 128– 31.

36. Cf. the *Yü-lin Kuo-shih yin k'o-sung shih-chung*, attached as a preface to the *Fo-men pi-pei k'o-sung pen*, one of the two daily office texts used in the convent. On the connection between reciting a *sūtra* and merit, even when one does not understand the meaning of the *sūtra*, cf. the following passage from the *Saṃdhinirmocana Sūtra*, a proto-Yogācārin work:

> There are beings who do not understand the true meaning (of this text), nevertheless they adhere to (the text) and have faith in it. They adhere to it saying, "This *sūtra* preached by the Blessed One is profound, and (its

meaning) is difficult to see, difficult to know, beyond (verbal) discussion, alien to (verbal) discussion, subtle and known by the wise ones.... The knowledge and the view of the Tathāgata are infinite; our own knowledge and view are like the plodding of a cow." In this spirit, they revere this *sūtra*, they copy it out, they transmit it, spread it abroad, venerate it, teach it and read and study it. All the while, they do not understand my true intention, they are incapable of carrying out the meditation. In this way, their accumulation of merit and wisdom grows and finally, those who had not ripened their beings, do ripen their beings.

[Etienne Lamotte, ed. and trans., *Saṃdhinirmocana Sūtra: l'Explication des Mystères* (Université de Louvain, Receuil de travaux, 2e series, 34e fasc. Paris: Maisonneuve, 1935), pp. 199–200; quoted in Ray, "Buddhism: Sacred Text Written and Realized," p. 166.]

37. *Fan-wang-ching*, T.24. 1009a.20. Tradition held that this was a translation from Sanskrit into Chinese, and attributed it to Kumārajīva, but it was probably written in China ca. A.D. 431–481. Translated into French by J. J. M. de Groot in *Le Code de Mahayana en Chine.*

38. On this subject, see Jan Yun-hua, "The Power of Recitation," in *Studi Storico Religiosi*, vol. 1, no. 2 (1977).

39. Cf. Peter N. Gregory, "The Teaching of Men and Gods: The Doctrinal and Social Basis of Lay Buddhist Practice in the Hua-yen Tradition," in Robert M. Gimello and Peter N. Gregory, eds., *Studies in Ch'an and Hua-yen* (Honolulu: University of Hawaii Press, 1984), pp. 283–93 for some examples of this expectation from reciting the *Avataṃsaka (Hua-yen) Sūtra.*

40. *Po-shih ch'ang-ch'ing-chi, Ssu-pu ts'ung-k'an* edition, p. 59.7a–8b. My translation is modified from that of Peter N. Gregory, "Teaching," pp. 292–93. Also translated in Kenneth Chen, *The Chinese Transformation of Buddhism* (Princeton: Princeton U. Press, 1973), pp. 210–11.

41. *Ibid.*

42. For more on this, see Welch, *Practice*, pp. 179–202.

43. *Ti-tsang-p'u-sa-pen-yüan-ching*, T.442.13.777c–790a; could be reconstructed in Sanskrit as *Kṣitigarbha Bodhisattva praṇidhāna sūtra*, but no Sanskrit original has been found. The "*Sūtra of the Original Vow*" has been translated into English by Tripitaka Master Hsuan Hua and the Buddhist Text Translation Society as *Sutra of the Past Vows of Earth Store Bodhisattva* (San Francisco, 1974). On Kṣitigarbha, Marinus Willem de Visser, *The Bodhisattva Ti-tsang (Jizo) in China and Japan* (Berlin, 1914), though not informed by more recent research, remains the best reference in English.

44. The recitation thus takes place in a context of special invocation of this Bodhisattva and the special remembrance of ancestors. Still, the chief stated purpose of reciting the *sūtra* is to create merit to be transferred to ancestors. That is,

the *sūtra* is recited primarily for the merit of the act, which is not connected to its content, but to its status as a *sūtra*.

45. Two daily office texts frequently used today in Hong Kong and Taiwan are the *Fo-men pi-pei k'o-sung pen* and the *Fo-chiao ch'ao-mu k'o-sung*. The Buddhist Association of the People's Republic of China under Chao P'u-ch'u has recently (between the summer of 1985 and the summer of 1986) published a version entitled *Fo-chiao nien-sung chi* for use in monasteries and convents throughout the country. (I am grateful to Raoul Birnbaum for showing me a copy.) All contemporary daily office texts are quite similar, and owe a great debt to Yün-ch'i Chu-hung's compilation of 1600 entitled *Chu-ching jih-sung*, found in *Yün-ch'i fa-hui* (Collected Works of Master Yün-ch'i, hereafter abbreviated *YCFH*), *chüan* 12. For a fuller description of the meaning of the texts in the daily office, though from a particular sectarian point of view, see Huang Ch'ing-lan, *Ch'ao-mu k'o-sung pai-hua chieh-shih*, reprinted in Taiwan in 1978 by the Fo-chiao Ch'u-pan she. A short description appears in Welch, *Practice*, pp. 53–58 and 71. I am currently working on a book-length study of these offices.

46. Cf. the *Yü-lin Kuo-shih yin k'o-sung shih-chung*.

47. Cf. N. Dutt, *Early Buddhist Monachism* (London: Kegan Paul, Trench, Trubner & Co, 1924), pp. 90–106; for a brief discussion, see Helen Hardacre, *Lay Buddhism*, pp. 132–33.

48. Actually, by a monk who lived in the non-Chinese Tangut kingdom of Hsi-hsia, in what is now Chinese territory. Cf. Huang Ch'ing-lan, *Ch'ao-mu, chüan* b, p. 12.

49. The notion seems related to the idea of selecting to focus on establishing a connection with the "*pen-tsun*" (J. *go-honzon*), that Buddha or Bodhisattva with which it is suitable for persons in a current world or circumstance to have a special connection.

50. This of course reflects a Pure Land Buddhist influence on the daily office dating back at least as far as Chu-hung in 1601.

51. A Sanskrit version of this name is sometimes reconstructed as "Ullambana."

52. T. 16.779a-c. For a recent and comprehensive study of the festival of Yü-lan-p'en, which includes a summary of much previous scholarship on both the festival and the *Yü-lan-p'en ching*, see Stephen F. Teiser's doctoral dissertation, "The Yü-lan-p'en Festival in Medieval Chinese Religion" (Princeton University, February, 1986) and his forthcoming book, *The Ghost Festival in Medieval China*. See also his article "Ghosts and Ancestors in Medieval Chinese Religion: The Yü-lan-p'en Festival as Mortuary Ritual," *History of Religions* 26, (August, 1986): 47–67. There is so much speculation involved in positing an original Sanskrit word for which "yü-lan-p'en" is a translation that it seems wiser to do as Teiser and others have done and leave the word in Chinese.

53. Text can be found in Kamata Shigeo, *Chūgoku no Bukkyō girei* (Tokyo: Tōkyō Daigaku Tōyō Bunka Kenkyūjō, 1986), pp. 873–87.

54. For a description of this text, see Welch, *Practice*, p. 188.

55. *Liang-huang ch'an-fa*; Cf. text entitled *Liang-huang pao-chuan ch'uan-chi* in Kamata Shigeo, *Girei* pp. 888–912.

56. Cf. Welch, *Practice*, pp. 185–87; cf. also Kamata Shigeo, *Ginei*, pp. 117–22 and 214–21; text is included, pp. 826– 872.

57. *Lotus*, pp. 311–319.

58. Found in *Ch'ien-shou ch'ien-yen kuan-shih-yin p'u-sa kuang-ta yüan-man wu-ai ta-pei-hsin to-lo-ni ching*, T. 20.106a–111c; the *dhāraṇî* is on p. 107c.

59. I frequently worked with Ch'en-chih shih in the kitchen, and found this to be true. She is an admirable person: warm, simple, clear, completely genuine, and at peace with herself and others.

60. Even in instances in which the metaphors used place the source of transformation outside the mind (in the Bodhisattva, in the externally given *mantra*, in the *Buddhavacana* of the *sūtra*, in the merit earned from recitation), the transforming powers (the Bodhisattva, *mantra* and so forth) are at the same time understood to be aspects of one's own true mind (e.g., the compassion of the Bodhisattva is not other than the compassion of one's own true mind or buddha-nature). The nuns and lay people with whom I spoke almost always used both internal and external metaphors in describing how and why practices that take true words as mental objects lead to transformations. The words become not merely references to *Dharma*, representational symbols, referential use of language, but constitute the activity of *Dharmakāya* acting within the mind at some level other than that of rational content.

61. Wilfred Cantwell Smith, "Introduction to Part Eight: Religion as Symbolism," in the Introduction to "Propaedia," *Encylopedia Britannica*, 15th ed. (Chicago, 1974), Vol. I, p. 498.

62. *Ibid.*

63. An illuminating comparison is possible between the understanding of *mantra* in the yogic tradition and the understanding of icon as hypostasis in the Eastern Orthodox tradition.

64. There are of course others: it might be argued that silence is another, and visible form (image) and gesture (*mudrā*) a third.

65. In our calling the words and structures of the *sūtras*, *mantras*, and *dhāraṇi* that constitute the teaching, "*Dharma*," they become like metaphors through which we speak of and partially understand the nature of eternal Truth. We establish the metaphor, "*Dharma* is, among other things, transforming, powerful word." This in turn goes along with, even implies, a second metaphor, "Buddha

and sentient beings are (at least) mind." *Dharma* is, at least, an address in words to that which is capable of consenting inwardly to them, of seeing things anew in their light. And sentient beings are, at least, those whom words transform, those who find enlightenment through listening to, reciting, understanding, and embracing the meanings of words.

66. It would be interesting to trace the development of the iconographic representation of Mañjuśrī, the Bodhisattva particularly associated with Wisdom, with a *sūtra* scroll in his hand.

67. It is both interesting and significant that this practice of reciting *sūtras* (C. *ching*) at funerals and rites of intervention on behalf of the dead (including "all souls" festivals) appears also in Taiwan in ceremonies where the officiants are Taoists and specialists in "folk" religious traditions. It seems to be a general concept that one thing one does for the dead is recite texts for them.

68. T. 32.575b–583a; translated into English by Yoshito S. Hakeda as *The Awakening of Faith* (New York: Columbia U. Press, 1967).

69. The metaphor used is "perfuming," in the sense of permeating with an invisible odor.

4

"Scripture" in India: Towards a Typology of the Word in Hindu Life

Thomas B. Coburn

I

At first glance, it appears obvious that the religious traditions of the world have scriptures.[1] Virtually all of the major traditions, and many of the minor, have produced written documents, and the mere fact of their 'writtenness' invites comparison between one tradition and another. The logic behind F. Max Müller's massive editorial undertaking some one hundred years ago—the publication in English translation of the fifty volumes of the Sacred Books of the East—is a compelling one. And a similar logic runs through much of what we do today in the scholarly study of religion. When we do research, a major focus of our attention is upon the literary remains of the world's religious movements. When we teach, a fair portion of what we ask of our students is that they become familiar, in some measure, with the written documents of whatever tradition they may be studying. At one level, the association of religions with scriptures is so obvious as scarcely to merit comment.

At another level, however, this easy association calls for closer examination. We now know, for instance, in a way that was less obvious in Müller's day, that while the Avesta, the *Lotus Sūtra*, and some of the Upaniṣads may clamor for inclusion in any roster of "Sacred Books of the East," there are important differences in the ways these documents have been regarded, and in the roles they have played in the Zoroastrian, Buddhist, and Hindu traditions respectively. Such differences become even more pronounced, we now know, as one begins to consider the literature that, for one reason or another, was denied inclusion in Max Müller's canon. It is, of course, the detailed examination of particular documents in particular traditions that has been one of the chief glories of modern scholarship. The sheer massiveness of what we now know about individual scriptures, particularly those of the Judeo-Christian tradition, is overwhelming. And yet in the teeth of this erudition, there persists a suspicion that we have not been asking the most salient questions of our documents, that, for all of our methodological sophistication, we remain bound by certain preconceptions as to what scripture is, and how its study ought to proceed. It was Wilfred Cantwell Smith who raised these questions most pointedly for biblical scholarship over a decade ago.[2] Subsequently, similar questions, and similarly novel solutions, have been posed by Gerald Larson for our understanding of the *Bhagavad Gītā*,[3] and by Smith[4] and William Graham[5] for our understanding of the Qur'ān. The first half of Graham's essay is an effort to cast these discussions—and, in fact, the whole of scholarship on scriptural matters—in a mold that will facilitate scholarly considerations of "scripture" as a generic phenomenon.[6] As Graham is aware, the utility of such a concept will be determined gradually, as specialists from across the spectrum of religious studies examine the data in their respective fields in light of generic considerations. It is to this exploration that the present essay seeks to contribute, through reflection upon various features, "scriptural" and otherwise, of the Hindu religious tradition.

Having admitted an aspiration to explore the notion of scripture in India, however, one finds oneself immediately in that familiar position in comparative studies, where the terms in which the original question is asked turn out to be ill-suited for understanding the data at hand. Three considerations may indicate why it is necessary to conceptualize our venture here as a typology of the 'Word,' rather than one of scripture, in Hindu life.

The first pertains to the connotations of the English word "scripture." Although the *Oxford English Dictionary* reports that the specifically Jewish and Christian sense of scripture (and allied terms such as holy writ, canon, and bible) has been supplemented over the course of the past century or so by a generic use of the term, what has remained constant is the assumption that we have here to do primarily with a *written* phenomenon, with something that has been inscribed on a page.[7] Indeed, one suspects that the Latin *scrîpturā*, "writing," and *scrîbere*, "to write," are never far from awareness in much discussion of scriptural matters. And yet it is precisely the thrust of Graham's article, and of his ongoing work, as evidenced by his contribution to the present volume, to show how this expectation of writtenness may mask certain important features of how holy words have been operative in human history: They have been oral/aural realities at least as much as they have been written ones, and the way that they have found their way into human lives is not through the eye, but through the ear. To argue the contrary is but to admit that we are heirs of Gutenberg, for the very notion of silent, individualized reading is scarcely known prior to the advent of the printing press.[8] Consequently, in an effort to appreciate the spoken and heard quality of scripture, we here embark upon a study of the Word in India, some embodiments of which have been reduced to writing, but most of which have retained the oral/aural quality as primary.

Our second consideration pertains to a distinctive feature of Indian culture. If one leaves aside the cryptic evidence from the Indus Valley, writing seems to have been known in the subcontinent from perhaps 600 B.C.E.[9] This is at least half a millenium after the earliest strata of the Vedic corpus were composed, and there has never been a happy marriage between the holy words of India, composed, and transmitted orally, and the writing process. Particularly in contrast with, say, China, scribes in India have been of low social standing, and the very act of writing was held to be ritually polluting.[10] A late Vedic text, the *Aitareya Āraṇyaka* (5.5.3), states that "a pupil should not recite the Veda after he has eaten meat, seen blood or a dead body, had intercourse or engaged in writing."[11] The profoundly spoken character of India's holy words is a matter on which we shall reflect below, but for the moment it will suffice to note that we should not be misled by the fact that most of these words have eventually found their way onto the written or printed page. This is not their primary home, and J.F. Staal is not simply being mischievous in discerning a symbolic significance to the fact that Indian books "still tend to fall apart."[12]

If our first two considerations address the fact that scripture in India is not necessarily something written, then the third raises the possibility that the very notion of scripture as a reified, boundaried entity fails to do justice to the Hindu situation.[13] As suggested earlier, such assertions as —". . . . the fixed and established books of God . . . form the core of world religions"[14]—are not, on the face of it, absurd. One can clearly observe what might be called a "process of crystallization of scripture," and the "coherence of tradition around scripture," in a great variety of settings.

In some, such as the Jewish or Christian, the crystallization process may be drawn out, while in others, such as the Muslim, it may be quite abrupt. Following our earlier argument, it is possible to conceive of the scripture thus crystallized as constituting a fundamentally oral/aural presence in the lives of the faithful, but we must go still further in refining our expectations, I think, if we are not to misconstrue the Hindu scene. India has, in fact, known verbal material that is highly 'crystallized,' that is, quite specific, boundaried, and even written. Such items as the principal Upaniṣads, or Tulsī Dās's *Rāmāyaṇa*, appear to be roughly comparable to Western notions of scripture in this regard. For reasons that will become clear in the sequel, however, I would propose that we understand such compact and circumscribable phenomena as a subset of how Hindus have dealt with holy verbal phenomena in general, that is, with what might be designated the Word, some of whose manifestations are dynamic, open-ended, and nonrevertible, rather than boundaried and reified.

As a starting point, let me propose that the most useful unit, the atom or lowest common denominator, if you will, for discussing the Hindu situation is simply the verbal utterance of a particular individual at a particular point in time. He or she may, of course, be reading the words from a written document, or reciting a fixed pattern of words from memory, but he or she may also be telling a familiar story in an engaging new way. I would urge that all of these possibilities have a bearing on scriptural matters in India, and, in particular, I would urge that we not be obsessed with either the 'writtenness' or the verbal fixity of sacred utterances as we approach the Hindu situation.

The specific utility of this apparently oblique way of discussing 'scripture' in India will become apparent after reviewing the traditional ways of conceptualizing Hindu religious literature—ways that we have inherited both from our scholarly predecessors in the West and, in a different fashion, from Hindus living in various times and places—and then indicating some difficulties that arise when these concepts are brought face-to-face with the facts of religious history. Part II of this essay will therefore rehearse common views about the scriptural life in India. Part III will isolate and comment upon some unresolved difficulties and often unarticulated implications of our inherited views. Part IV will then broach a typology of holy verbal utterance in Hindu life. By approaching the matter in this way, we will not simply be testing a Western notion against Hindu data, but we may also, through fidelity to Hindu views, glimpse new dimensions to the phenomenon of scripture when it is generically conceived.

II

Virtually all discussions of the religious literature of India that see fit to take cognizance of Hindu categories also see fit to begin with a discussion of *śruti* and *smṛti*.[15] We may take J.A.B. van Buitenen's opening remarks on "The concept of a sacred book in Hinduism" as representative:

> Orthodox Hindu authors commonly divide their sacred literature into two classes, *Śruti* and *Smṛti*: *Śruti* (literally "learning by hearing") is the primary revelation, which stands revealed at the beginning of the creation. This revelation was "seen" by the primeval seers (*ṛṣi*) who set in motion an oral transmission that has continued from generation to generation until today. The seers were the founders of the lineages of Brahmins (Hindu priestly elite) through which the texts have been, and continue to be, transmitted. From this heritage the Brahmins derive their function as sacred specialists and teachers. *Smṛti* (literally "recollection") is the collective term for all other sacred literature, principally in Sanskrit, which is considered to be secondary to *Śruti*, bringing out the hidden meanings of the revelation, restating it for a wider audience, providing more precise instructions concerning moral conduct, and complementing *Śruti* in matters of religion. While the distinction between *Śruti* and *Smṛti* is a useful one, in practice the Hindu acquires his knowledge of religion almost exclusively through *Smṛti*.[16]

This awareness of two levels of sanctity in Hindu sacred literature has prompted some simply to declare that "to the expression 'Holy Scripture' there corresponds in the case of the Indians the expression 'Sruti'," but even in such cases it is recognized that *śruti* admits of various subdivisions.[17] Of these, it is "the Vedic San-hitas [that] occupy pride of place in Shruti literature,"[18] and, of the Saṃhitās, it is the *Ṛg Veda*, dating perhaps from 1200 B.C.E., that is foremost in both antiquity and sanctity. The four Saṃhitās—*Ṛg, Yajur, Sāma, Atharva*—are understood as corresponding to the four kinds of ritual specialist, and all four Saṃhitās are seen to have gathered other subdivisions of sacred literature around them during the subsequent millenium:[19] the Brāhmaṇas or ritual discussions, the Āraṇyakas or forest books, the Upaniṣads or esoteric mystic teachings, and the Śrauta, Gṛhya, and Dharma Sūtras or manuals of ritual and ethics. It is possible to schematize this growth of *śruti*, known as the Vedic corpus, in terms of a chart that indicates how individual texts are associated with the particular categories and schools of the Vedic tradition.[20]

There are several ways of indicating the relationship between this Vedic corpus, which appears to be reasonably well defined, and the much more heterogeneous *smṛti* literature. Louis Renou has offered the intriguing suggestion that "the division between Śruti and *Smṛti* also marks the frontier between orality and editing,"[21] which, if borne out by further research, has major implications for the idea of scripture in India.[22] More fully developed at present is the idea broached earlier by van Buitenen, that *śruti* is of divine or transcendent origin, and that it has received subsequent elaboration and interpretation at human hands in the form of *smṛti*. Mackenzie Brown, in discussing the Purāṇas, puts it this way:

> Truth was fully revealed ("heard", as *śruti*) in the past. . . . The Vedas are revealed truth, and even the perfect expression of that truth. But . . . they are reserved for the twice-born classes (upper three castes) and are not to be recited in public. Śūdras and women are prohibited from even hearing the Vedas. The Purāṇas, on the other hand, may be heard by all, especially in the *kali yuga* when *Dharma* is in universal decline. The Purāṇas are an "easier" form of truth, adapted to the conditions of class and world age. . . . It is assumed that the [Purāṇic] revisions are made in complete harmony with the truth contained in *śruti*. The Purāṇas represent, then, an interpretation or clarification of the *śruti*, revealing the eternal, immutable truth in a comprehensible form to all mankind in his changing, historical situation. The process of revealing truth by its very nature is never ending. The truth, once revealed in *śruti*, must ever by newly interpreted or explained in *smṛti*.[23]

In addition to the Purāṇas, *smṛti* seems clearly to include the Dharma Śastras, the two epics, the *Rāmāyaṇa* and the *Mahābhārata*, the Tantras, and assorted other items. The full scope of that assortment cannot be specified, however, for the concept of *smṛti* is necessarily open-ended. What validation as *smṛti* consists of is "acceptance among the same class in society who were the source of the knowledge of *śruti*, the Brahmin class."[24] Since the materials that have received such validation have varied enormously both through the centuries and by region, it is senseless even to attempt to circumscribe the material that Hindus have designated as *smṛti*.

Recently, however, it has proven popular, and illuminating, to schematize the growth of the Hindu tradition and its literature through a diagram arranged on chronological principles.[25] In these two diagrams, it is *śruti* that occupies the left-hand third of the chart and that comes to an end, in the sense of both *telos* and *terminus*, with the Upaniṣads, the "Vedānta" or "end of the Veda." The balance of the chart is comprised of *smṛti* material. An alternative way of making this same basic point is in terms of the distinction between Brahmanism, the religion of the Indo-Europeans, revolving around the sacrifice (*yajña*), and the post-Buddhist congeries of movements collectively referred to as "Hinduism," revolving around devotion to a personal deity (*bhakti*), especially in image form (*pūjā*).[26]

Finally, we may note that while virtually all discussions of Hindu religious literature make mention of the categories of *śruti* and *smṛti*, these categories are not usually employed as organizing principles in discussing the specific contents of the literature. Instead, the tendency has been to present summaries of particular documents, which are grouped together according to label (Saṃhitā, Purāṇa, etc.), according to their apparent sectarian preference (Śaiva, Vaiṣṇava, etc.), or, when the discussion ranges beyond the specifically religious literature, according to genre (drama, poetry, etc.) or the language employed.[27] While it is apparent that sometimes the *śruti-smṛti* distinction has been implicitly operative in the determination of salient subdivisions of the material (e.g., Vedic, post-Vedic, etc.), there apparently has been little effort to think systematically about the full range of terms that are employed in the discussion of Hindu religious literature. The prevailing view of that literature, which has been summarized here, is, of course, reasonably apt. It has provided us with a framework for understanding an enormous variety of material, and for orienting the detailed study of particular texts—which in India, as in the West, has been the strong suit of modern scholarship—into the overall pattern of growth of the Hindu tradition. Nonetheless, there are reasons to believe that certain important features of Hindu scripture have been either overlooked or understated by this view. It is to these features that we now turn.

III

Comprehensive inquiry into the terminology and phenomenology of Hindu scripture is clearly beyond the scope of this essay. A highly promising direction for future research, for example, is into the variety of ways that the term "Veda" has been employed, by both Hindus and Western scholars, along with an inquiry into our other inherited terms for Hindu scripture: Upaniṣad, Purāṇa, *śruti*, *smṛti* and the like. Similarly, the nuanced interplay of 'text' and 'context' shows every sign of continuing to be a major focus of monographic studies of Indian phenomena.[28] The salient material, however, is massive and its full analysis must be left for another occasion. What can be done at present is to indicate in a preliminary way why the time is ripe for such a comprehensive inquiry into what might appear to be familiar matters. As a prolegomenon to such an inquiry, we may here focus upon three issues to which insufficient justice appears to have been done in our current ways of thinking about Hindu scripture.

1. The first issue pertains to what might be called the primacy of experience and the ontology of language. The central revision or clarification of our inherited views that it effects is its demonstration that, while it is tempting to say that historically *śruti* precedes *smṛti* (as, for instance, the Thomas J. Hopkins and David R. Kinsley charts indicate), the distinction of the two categories on grounds of relative chronology cannot be sustained.

To appreciate this point, let us return to the basic affirmation that *śruti* is that which has been "'seen' by the primeval seers (*ṛṣi*)."[29] The verbal root of *śruti* is the common verb *śru*, to hear, which suggests that the notion of 'holy hearing' may be an appropriate way to conceptualize the *ṛṣi*'s experience. The root of *ṛṣi* is less certain—it may come from *dṛś*, "to see," or from *ṛṣ*, "to flow," and is perhaps related to *arc* or *ṛc*, "to praise" —but there is no quarrel over the fact that it refers to one who has had the most intimate apprehension of cosmic truth.[30] The fact that the metaphors of *hearing* and *seeing* are applied to the *ṛṣi* in relation to this truth is significant. This identification of two senses as mediators of the *ṛṣi*'s experience is no mixing of metaphor, but an effort to convey the holistic and supremely compelling nature of that experience. It engages one through, and yet transcends, the senses. It seizes one with a unique and irresistible immediacy. It is in such experiences that the human becomes contiguous, even identical, with the divine. In discussing a word often allied with *ṛṣi*, *kavi*, poet, J. Gonda notes that this "is one of those words which show that there was in principle no difference between mental and other qualities attributed to divine and human persons."[31] Elsewhere, he observes:

> The Indian aestheticians . . . were . . . of the opinion that the experiences of the poet, representing the hero of his work and that of the listener, reader, or, in general employer of the word are identical. . . . This consciousness of the presence of truth, of the divine, the eternal or ultimate reality in a work of art which has been created by a truly inspired artist, together with the almost universal belief that words, especially duly formulated and rhythmically pro-

> nounced words, are bearers of power, has given rise to the traditional Indian conviction that "formulas" are a decisive power: that whoever utters a mantra sets power in motion. . . . [*Mantras*] represent the essence of the "gods." They are not made, but "seen" by those men who have had the privilege of direct contact with divinity or the supra-mundane.[32]

Ultimate reality, on this view, may in fact be greater than whatever is predicated of it (*neti, neti*) but it is affirmed at least to have sound-form. By virtue of the extraordinary perspicacity and auditory acuity of certain individuals *in illo tempore*, the rest of us are now able to participate in that ultimate reality. It is *mantra*s that are the sacrament by means of which this participation is effected.

We must, however, go further, for Hindus have not restricted themselves to using the language of the senses to talk about this revelatory experience. The crucial concept here is *pratibhā*, which carries a basic meaning of "a flash of light, a revelation, usually found in . . . the sense of wisdom characterized by immediacy and freshness,"[33] but it is also used in technical discussions of philosophy, *yoga*, and aesthetics to mean "that function of the mind which, while developing without any special cause, is able to lead one to real knowledge, to an insight into the transcendental truth and reality."[34] This notion has a bearing on a wide range of topics, but, for our purposes, one of its features is central: it is not limited to the great seers of the past.[35] It is accessible in the present. *In illo tempore* is (or can be) now. Though the concluding remarks of the illustrious Gopinath Kaviraj have something of a Tantric ring to them, they capture the essential interrelationship of the divine, the human, and the verbal in Hindu life.

> We have seen in the preceding pages that the development of the faculty of omniscience can not be affected unless the mind is purified and freed from the obscuring influence of the dispositions clinging to it from time immemorial. What is known as the "divine eye" is really the mind in its purified condition. . . . It is apparent, therefore, that every man, in so far as he is gifted with a mind, is gifted with the possibility of omniscience. . . . [If we would ask how the impurities of the mind are to be cleared away,] the whole question turns upon the practical issues of mystic culture and we can do no more than briefly touch upon the matter in this place. . . . This help comes from the Guru, a spiritually awake person, in the form of an influx of spiritual energy from him. . . . Concurrently with the opening of this vision to the Yogin he begins to hear the eternal

> and unbroken sound of Nāda (i.e. Oṁkāra), the sweet and all-obliterating Divine Harmony.... When this light and sound are fully realized, but before plunging into the Absolute, the Yogin is elevated into the highest plane of cosmic life.... Being himself saved, he now becomes, if he so desires it, the saviour of humanity. ... He is the Ideal of Perfect Humanity which is Divinity itself in concrete shape and is the source of light and life and joy to the world, deep in darkness and sorrow. It is from him that the "Scriptures" proceed and the world receives guidance and inspiration.[36]

If this kind of ultimately transforming experience continues to be a live option and produces "scriptures" throughout the course of Hindu history, an important qualification must nonetheless be added. As Kaviraj makes clear, it is the *guru*-student relationship that is central to the spiritual perfection of the student. While scriptures may proceed from a perfected individual as by-products of his perfection, they are in no way a substitute for an aspiring *yogi*'s personal relationship with a *guru*. To put it another way, the *guru*-student relationship may well take a written document as its starting point, but so intimate and personal is that relationship, and so essential is it to the correct understanding of the written (or orally preserved) word, that there exists the widespread custom that if a teacher does not find a student worthy of inheriting his manuscripts, he will, in his old age, simply discard them by throwing them into a river—as one would ashes that had been cremated. Written documents, unvivified by personal relationship, are lifeless.

A corollary of the qualification is that, if we would identify the vessels in which the *ṛṣi*'s or *guru*'s transforming experience is, as it were, 'preserved,' we ought not, for reasons already cited, look into written documents. We ought rather, perhaps, to look at other instances where Hindus speak of holistically engaging, sensual, and particularly visual, apprehension of the divine. While I cannot pursue this matter in detail here, the use of the word *dṛś*, "to see," or its derivatives in other contexts is surely not coincidental. *Darśana*, for instance, 'seeing,' is the standard word for 'philosophy,' and one of the reasons that Hindu philosophy is said to be pervasively salvific is because it bears this heritage of 'spiritual apprehension.' The same word is also employed in what appears, to the outsider, to be quite a different context, to label "the single most common and significant element of Hindu worship," namely, what happens "when Hindus go to the temple, (and) their eyes meet the powerful, eternal gaze of the eyes of [the image of] God."[37] One could argue, in fact, that "images are not only visual theologies, they are also visual scriptures."[38] If we spread our net wider, to include other than the sight sense, we may note that *rasa*, taste, looms as a major concept in Indian aesthetics and in various theologies, particularly those of Krishna, to convey the nature of the divine-human encounter.[39] It would appear, therefore, that not only has the kind of experience that Hindus understand to have generated *śruti* been current throughout Hindu history.[40] Beyond this, the holy words that are *śruti* must be seen alongside other transforming, sacramental activities, such as philosophical argumentation, the worship of the divine image form, and the highly nuanced moods (*bhava*s) of Krishna devotees.

When the experiential foundations of *śruti* as an ongoing phenomenon in Hindu life is acknowledged in this fashion, then a number of otherwise puzzling (or, more often, ignored) aspects of the Hindu tradition may be viewed in a new light, with a new clarity. We may glance briefly at one of them.

The traditional Hindu view is that there are 108 Upaniṣads and, of these, a dozen or so are identified as "early," that is, composed in the half-millenium or so after about 700 B.C.E.[41] And yet in the word index of Vedic material that began appearing five decades ago, the *Vaidika--padānukrama-koṣa*,[42] no fewer than 206 Upaniṣads are indexed and some of these "have been written occasionally even in modern times and certainly right up to the Middle Ages."[43] The relatively recent origin of these Upaniṣads, together with the fact that some of them are highly sectarian and that there even exists an "Allah Upaniṣad"—written in praise of Islam at the instance of Darah Shikoh in the seventeenth century—is exceedingly problematical for any view that takes only the early Upaniṣads as normative and that sees *śruti* as historically prior to *smṛti*.[44] The tendency (under Brahmanical and/or Western influence?) has been to dismiss these compositions precisely because of their lateness and their alleged "corrupt" character.[45] The fact remains that some Hindus have called them "Upaniṣads." This fact becomes far less problematical, and is actually highly illuminating, when seen in relationship to our contention that *śruti* must be seen as ongoing and experientially based feature of the Hindu religious tradition.[46]

2. The second issue on which our inherited expectations for scripture in India appear less than fully adequate might be called the "sociology of language" and the "power of holy hearing." While it is tempting to assume that scriptures, either read or heard, serve a didactic role in human lives, the central fact here is that, for many Hindus, the holiness of holy words is not a function of their intelligibility. On the contrary, sanctity often appears to be inversely related to comprehensibility.

To appreciate this point, let us return to Brown's observation that the significance of the Purāṇas is that they "may be heard by all."[47] Notice that he does not tie their significance to the fact that they could be *understood* by all, for they have scarcely been an open book. Nor, for that matter, have most of the items usually considered the scriptures of India. And the reason that these scriptures, even if universally heard, were never widely understood is because they were composed in Sanskrit. Over the past thirty years, the symbolic significance of the Sanskritic language and culture has generated a widespread discussion of 'Sanskritization' which it is not necessary to review here. What we may simply note is that "the name of the language, one of the few not derived from a region or a people, states its own program: *samskṛta bhaṣa* is the ritually perfected and intellectually cultivated language.[48] To be able to speak and understand Sanksrit is a badge of religious and intellectual privilege, for it is the *refined* or "*well-cooked*" language, in contrast to the Prakrits, those uncouth grunts of *hoi polloi*. Sanskrit was therefore always an individual's second language, unintelligible to speakers of the many local vernaculars, but always, for one who knew it, the language of preference.[49] Simply hearing this cultured language bordered on being a numinous experience.

There is an additional dimension, however. It is not just that Sanskrit has an aura of elegance in the present. It also provides linkage to the primal time. Van Buitenen puts it this way:

> Central to Indian thinking through the ages is a concept of knowledge which . . . is foreign to the modern West. Whereas for us, to put it briefly, knowledge is something to be *discovered*, for the Indian knowledge is to be *recovered*. . . . One particular preconception, related to this concept of knowledge concerning the past and its relation to the present, is probably of central significance: that at its very origin the absolute truth stands revealed; that this truth —which is simultaneously a way of life—has been lost, but not irrecoverably; that somehow it is still available through ancient life lines that stretch back to the original revelation; and that the present can be restored only when this original past has been recovered. . . . Sanskrit is felt to be one of the life-lines, and Sanskritization in its literal sense, the rendering into Sanskrit, is one of the prime methods of restating a tradition in relation to a sacral past.[50]

All of this is not to say, of course, that Sanskrit has not been used —by those capable of using it—with every intent to communicate meaning. The case of Rāmānuja—the great theologian of Śrī Vaiṣṇavism who stands at the juncture of the two traditions of Tamil devotionalism and

Sanskrit 'orthodoxy'—is a splendid instance of someone whose piety is deeply indebted to non-Sanskritic sources, but who writes in Sanskrit because of its prestige and symbolic significance, and who does so with great clarity and precision.

Such an instance, however, must not distract us from the basic point, namely, that the sanctity of Hindu scripture—most of which has been composed in Sanskrit—does not necessarily depend upon its intelligibility to one who hears or recites it. Nowhere has this been more clearly demonstrated than in the way the *Ṛg Veda*—apparently the centerpiece of the entire scriptural tradition—has functioned in Hindu life. Like all verbal compositions, the *Ṛg Veda* was produced in an historically particular context, of which the most vivid brief account is Charles R. Lanman's:[51] "To the student of the Veda it is a source of perhaps contemptuous surprise, and to the teacher a source of some little embarrassment, that this venerable document smells so strong of the cow-pen and the byre."[52] Be that as it may, these particularized features of the *Ṛg Veda* have been essentially irrelevant, have passed virtually unnoticed, throughout most of Hindu history because of what Renou calls the "characteristically Indian preoccupation with form rather than meaning."[53] What this has meant is that "at all times, recitation constituted the principal, if not the exclusive, object of Vedic teaching, the same as today... whilst the interpretation of the texts is treated as a poor relation."[54] Such recitation has been undertaken for a variety of ritual purposes, especially as an instrument or intermediary of devotion, and, in this context, matters of verbal signification pale in significance.[55] This has elicited a suggestive comparative remark about the role of the reciter (*śrotriya*, master of *śruti*): "the *śrotriya* who recites without understanding should not be compared with a clergyman preaching from the pulpit, but rather with a medieval monk copying and illuminating manuscripts, and to some extent with all those who are connected with book production in modern society."[56] It may, of course, be that the *Ṛg Veda* and other Vedic materials have been particularly prone to this manner of treatment, because of their composition in the preclassical form of Sanskrit known as Védic: it seems likely that their existence in an arcane, archaic language would have reinforced the prior disinclination to interpret on ritual grounds. However, the propensity to memorize and to recite holy words—perhaps as a manifestation of devotion (*bhakti*), perhaps with the aspiration of having one's consciousness transformed by the *mantras*, as noted earlier—runs very, very deep in Hindu life. There is scarcely a festival in India that is not accompanied by the recitation of some classical text, most often in Sanskrit, in which case, as we have seen, it cannot be intelligible to more than a select few, or in an archaic and therefore, at best, rather opaque form of the vernacular.[57] Whatever else we may conclude about the scriptural life of India, justice must be done to fact that, at least some of the time, Hindus have affirmed that the holiness of the Word is intrinsic, and that one participates in it, not by understanding, but by hearing and reciting it.

3. The third issue on which it appears necessary to rethink some of our familiar patterns of thought might be called the "dialectic between *śruti* and *smṛti*," or the "double desideratum of literally preserving and dynamically recreating the Word." While it is tempting to assume that considerations of content, or genre, or label, or name may enable us to categorize a given text as either *śruti* or *smṛti*, closer examination reveals a subtle and highly suggestive movement between these two kinds of holy Word.

Let us begin with the observation that "scripture," like "cousin," "weed," or "poison" seems necessarily to be a relational concept: it depends for its definition, not upon its intrinsic properties, but upon those properties in relation to people, who value it for better or worse.[58] While the implications of this fact are only gradually coming to be explored, it seems likely that the existence of two central terms for Hindu scripture, *śruti* and *smṛti*, may be a reflection of two different kinds of relationship that can be had with holy verbal material in the Hindu tradition.[59] We have already had grounds to question the sufficiency of understanding *śruti* as chronologically prior to *smṛti* and to observe that *śruti*, in the form of the so-called late Upaniṣads, has *de facto* functioned as an open-ended category in Hindu life. We must now go one step further, however, to observe that, in some cases, there has been an observable shift over time in the way a particular instance of the Word, a particular 'text,' if you must, has been regarded by individuals within the tradition.

Let us begin with the *Bhagavad Gîtā*. The logic for understanding the *Gîtā* as *smṛti* is strong, and the case for such an understanding is regularly made.[60] The text is, after all, situated in the *Mahābhārata*, which is perhaps the premier instance of *smṛti*, and its didactic intent converges magnificently with the traditionally understood role of *smṛti*. Bharati is surely correct in lamenting the recent facile identification of the *Gîtā* as "the Hindu Bible,"[61] but matters are also more complex than he allows. In his last remarks on this text, to which he devoted so much attention throughout his career, van Buitenen concludes that the post-*Gîtā* evidence (the views of various commentators and the author of the *Vedāntasūtras*) "attests to the near-*śruti* prestige of our text at a very early date."[62] There is additional evidence to strengthen such an interpretation. It is a fact, for instance, that the material that has traditionally been understood as *śruti* (the Vedas, Brāhamaṇas, etc.) has shown a much higher degree of textual integrity than *smṛti* material, that is, textual variants are far fewer in *śruti*. It is worth noting then that, in the critical edition of the *Mahābhārata*, the variant readings in the text of the *Bhagavad Gītā* are substantially fewer than in the rest of the epic. Beyond this, the testimony of the colophons is that the *Gītā* is of a piece with the Upaniṣads, for, at the end of the first chapter, out of the fifty-three manuscripts used to constitute the *Gītā* portion of the Bhiṣmaparvan, forty-seven read *bhagavadgītāsu upaniṣatsu*, "in the songs (verses) of the Blessed One, which are Upaniṣads."[63] Finally, in the Vedic word index referred to earlier (VPK), there are no intrinsic grounds for including *Gītā* at all, since, in its origin, it is not Vedic. In the volumes that index the Upaniṣads, however, the *Gītā is* included, based on the rationale that it is "based on or... very intimately related to the Upaniṣads.[64] The *Bhagavad Gītā* may have *originated* as *smṛti*, but it appears to have *functioned* in Hindu life very much as *śruti*.

A similar shift has occurred with regard to the *Devī- Māhātmya*, also known as the *Caṇḍī* or *Durgā-Saptaśatī, 700 (Verses) to Durgā*. This text appears as thirteen chapters in one of the early Purāṇas, where it seems to be a cleverly accomplished insertion in an older text, with the *Saptaśatī* itself probably dating from the sixth century C.E. In terms of content, it is a vivid and utterly appropriate piece of *smṛti*. But in terms of function, (1) it has had an independent liturgical life of its own; (2) in the liturgical context, it "is treated as if it were a Vedic hymn or verse with *ṛṣi*, meters, *pradhānadevatā*, and *viniyoga* (for *japa*)",[65] and (3) it has gathered around itself no fewer than sixty-seven commentaries, the most common concern of which is with how the *mantra*s of the text, and the modest number of variants, should be properly divided so as to arrive at the requisite 700 verses for recitation.[66]

If we enlarge the scope of our discussion here beyond the specific terms *śruti* and *smṛti*, it becomes possible to identify a central dynamic of Hindu treatment of the Word. That dynamic revolves around the tension between (1) the desire to preserve and recite, and not necessarily to understand, a verbally fixed (usually oral) text, and (2) the desire to understand, both for oneself and for others, religious ideas that are presented in verbal form.[67] Since we have just seen that the treatment accorded the *Devī-Māhātmya* seems to be a reflection of the former of these desires, we must note that there is a complementary process that is also at work in the functioning of the text. According to Babb:

> It is important to realize that the *Saptashati*, like all Hindu texts, has two distinct kinds of religious significance. It has, first of all, a kind of intrinsic potency as a collection of sacred utterances. The

> chanting of the *mantras* of which it is composed is a way of pleasing the goddess and tapping her powers. But the *mantras* have meaning of another sort, for together they constitute one of the principal scriptural delineations of the goddess. *The text is to be understood as well as chanted*, and consequently in the editions available in the Raipur bazaar the Sanskrit stanzas are given together with their Hindi translation.[68]

A similar dialectic may be discerned with regard to the Hindi *Rāmāyaṇa (Rāmacaritamānas)* of Tulsī Dās. In origin a sixteenth century "re-creation" or "transcreation" of the Rāma story, which had been told many a time, in many a version, since Vālmīki's original Sanskrit composition a millenium an a half earlier, Tulsī Dās's *Rāmāyaṇa* has been experienced as so powerful and so holy that it is now recited verbatim during Rāmlīlā even though, as noted earlier, its classical Hindi is scarcely transparent to modern Hindi speakers. Held in counterpoint to this recitation, however, are the dialogues between the actors in the festival drama, which occur in modern Hindi and which both translate and elaborate upon the words of Tulsī Dās.[69] As a final nuance in this dialectic, we should note the evidence recently presented in Hawley's *At Play with Krishna*. The story of the cowherd Krishna has, of course, been retold in vital and compelling fashion on innumerable occasions, and a direct line runs from its first appearance in the *Harivaṁśa*, through the *Viṣṇu* and *Bhāgavata Purāṇas*, into the modern vernaculars. On some occasions, such as in the *Bhāgavata*, or in Jayadeva's *Gītā Govinda*, the story has crystallized into a form that might be deemed "canonical"—which in the Hindu case would thus mean "worthy of being recited verbatim." As the Krishna tradition lives in the dramas of contemporary Brindavan, however, there is no 'canon,' because there is no 'text.' There are, of course, familiar songs and plot structures, and lines are remembered from past performances, but "the plays are constantly being recomposed," and the elements of independence and spontaneity are crucial to the vitality of the performances.[70] India, it would appear, wants both the *literal preservation* and the *dynamic recreation* of the Word, and the movement between these two foci —whether or not they be called "*śruti*" and "*smṛti*", respectively—is both subtle and continuous.[71]

IV

We turn now from a consideration of specific issues in the Hindu tradition to a typology that arises out of this consideration, and that aspires to alleviate some of the conceptual difficulties encountered in trying to talk about Hindu scripture. I offer the typology in two different forms, the former, I think, quite defensible and clearly related to what has gone before, the latter more speculative.

The typology is designed to indicate the varied ways that Hindus have related to a range of verbal materials that have originated at different times and places. At the outset, I urged the reader to think of the basic unit for discussing the Hindu situation as the verbal utterance of a particular individual at a particular point in time, and it will now be apparent why we must proceed to such an extreme atomizing of the material. More abstract approaches, based on prevailing conceptualizations, get us into difficulties: the same verbal event—the same utterance—has been variously regarded at different times, and even such familiar categories as *śruti* and 'Upaniṣad' appear to break down when pushed hard enough. In order to keep from being misled by our existing terminology, I am proposing that we let the atomization process go as far as possible, to the level of individual verbal utterance. And then let us see the manner of relationships that Hindus have had with the utterances that are considered sacred. I refer collectively to such utterances as 'the Word.'

There is a further reason why I have called this, not a typology of scripture, but a typology of the Word. We have seen that Hindus have emphasized the oral/aural over the written aspect of words. More than that, however, they have understood that which is mediated through *ṛṣi*s and *guru*s to be verbal-and-yet-more-than-verbal. To convey its nature, they have used a variety of metaphors not just of audition, but of sight. And if we allow the later uses of *darśan(a)* as clues, it smacks also of philosophical truth (*veda*, of course, means "knowledge"), and of reciprocal sight, the experience of knowing and being known. And if it be objected that this sounds more like a typology of revelation than one of scripture, then so be it. It has to be noted immediately, however, that while the Word (*vāc*, Veda, etc.) may be more like 'revelation' than 'scripture,' the closest analogy that we ordinary mortals have for its nature is that it is verbal, has sound-form. Gonda explains its distinctiveness as follows:

> The categories of language are, so to say, a diaphragm, an obstacle which comes between the reality and our consciousness. Whereas in ordinary usage this diaphragm makes its existence and influence felt, poetical language is devoid of these categories and therefore attains to reality before its solidification into discursive thought. Thus poetical language is related to other extraordinary forms of expression, for instance, on the religious plane with mantras.[72]

The Word, therefore, as I am using it here has a deliberate multivalence: It indicates a verbal and humanly articulated reality, but it also has metaphysical overtones and more than a hint of the *mysterium tremendum*.

The first formulation of the typology suggests that Hindus have done five things with these holy verbal events. There is overlap, of course, and few pure 'types' exist. Nonetheless, for the sake of convenience we may think of there being five ways that Hindus have engaged with the Word.

1. They have frozen it, captured it verbatim, treated it as sound eternal, the hum of the universe. While it is primarily the Vedic material, and particularly the *Ṛg Veda*, that belongs here, other material may be treated in this fashion, as we have seen. This is the way, its seems to me, Hindus have treated that which they regard as *śruti*. There are obviously many cases where non-*śruti* material has been committed to memory, but it would appear that the major thing Hindus are saying when they call certain verbal events "*śruti*" is that they are eternal, intrinsically powerful, and supremely authoritative. They are never outmoded. They are worthy of recitation, regardless of whether they are *understood*. Indeed, *mantras* do not "*mean*" anything in the conventional semantic or etymological senses. Rather, they mean *everything*.

   And if we are bewildered by that affirmation, the Hindu response would be for each of us to find an appropriate *guru*, to receive from him (among other things) a *mantra*, to recite it faithfully, and eventually we will come to see the point. This is, in many ways, the most characteristically Hindu view of the Word, and of the various views in India, it appears to be the most radically disjunctive with Western notions of scripture.

2. Hindus have also treated certain stories as salvific and/or normative, and so they have told them over, and over, and over again. Particularly compelling versions of a story may hold people's attention for centuries, and a really powerful version may come to be regarded as if it were *śruti*. Nonetheless, even in those cases, what is important is that the story be *intelligible* to those who hear it. And this may, of course, entail 'transcreation' out of Sanskrit into one of the vernaculars. This is what seems to have been happening through the centuries to the stories of Krishna Gopāla and Rāma, and, perhaps, more broadly in the rich corpus of Hindu mythology.

3. Hindus have composed commentaries as a way of making some embodiments of the Word intelligible in the present. Certain

kinds of the Word, such as the *sūtra* literature, invite or virtually demand commentaries because of their deliberate brevity. (It is said that the author of such a text would sell his grandson to save a syllable.) Other kinds demand commentaries because they are in Sanskrit and therefore require a vernacular commentary in order to make them intelligible: instances of this we have seen in the treatment accorded the *Durgā-Saptaśatī* and the *Rāmāyana* of Tulsī Dās. The pattern of writing commentaries, however, is uneven, clustering around certain texts such as the *sūtra* and *bhakti* literature, and sometimes surprisingly absent, as in the case of most Purāṇas. One suspects that inquiry into the pattern of texts that have attached commentaries is a matter that would repay further investigation.

4. Some embodiments of the Word in India have generated imitations of themselves. The terms of imitation, however, that is, what it is that has been deemed worthy of emulating, have varied. Van Buitenen shows how, for the *Bhāgavata Purāṇa*, it is archaic language, Vedic Sanskrit, that is being reproduced.[73] Parameswara Aiyar, alternatively, indicates the huge variety of texts that have called themselves "*Gītās*" in spite of sometimes departing fantastically from the concerns of the *Bhagavad Gītā* proper.[74] If one were inclined to such terminology, one might say that this response to the Word is a kind of "imitative magic," while our fifth type would be magic of the "sympathetic" variety.

5. Finally, some embodiments of the Word have lived on by receiving additions into themselves. Indeed, a large portion of what Hindus call "*smṛti*," specifically the epics and Purāṇas, seems to welcome additions with open bindings. One might expect this —with its attendant problems for the task of critical editing —where the material is what has traditionally been called "*smṛti*," for the very concept is that of an authoritative, but open-ended Word. Even in what has traditionally been called "*śruti*," however, we have seen that there has been a *de facto* open-endedness. The urge to enfold the new into the old is but one way that Hindus have dealt with the Word, but it appears to cut across the full range of Hindu 'scriptural' material.[75]

The second formulation of the typology is a drastic simplification of the first, and it, in turn, will bring us to a final remark. Might it be possible, one may ask, to reduce this five-fold manner of dealing with the

Word to two basic types? The former might be called "scripture," and the latter "story." Or following Karman's distinction in sacred art, one might call the former "sacramental," and the latter "didactic."[76] One is tempted, perhaps, to suggest a correspondence with the Greek discrimination of *logos* and *mythos*. Regardless of the appropriateness of terms drawn from other contexts, the basic distinction is this. Hindus have shown a propensity to treat certain instances of the Word as eternal and immutable, and they have engaged with some of them (the *Ṛg Veda*) now for about three-and-a-half-millenia: this is type one in our first formulation of the typology. Hindus have treated other instances of the Word as dynamic, as spawning all manner of elaboration, some of it being verbal—and therefore including types two through five above—but much of it being found in festival life, image worship, philosophy, and aesthetics, that is, in *darśan(a)* and *rasa*. The test of whether such elaborations are *authentic* is the simple one of whether or not they receive the sanction of what we might call "Verbal specialists": at times, this means the sanction of Brahmins,[77] but it can also refer to those whose spiritual credentials are experiential, the perfected *yogi*s cited by Gopinath Kaviraj.[78] If I were then to press the case that for Hindus, it is the former of these types that comes closest to 'scripture' as a generic phenomenon—because it is compact, boundaried, and therefore capable of being 'canonized'—then I have enabled myself to observe that, in a Hindu context, the Word has been operative in scripture, but that it is a larger than scriptural phenomenon.[79] And that is an assertion for which I think I would find some theological support in other religious traditions.

In pressing such a case, however, I would then have to note that the distinctively Hindu way of engaging with this compact, boundaried verbal material is to *recite* it, not necessarily to *understand* it. And that is likely to contrast strikingly with the scriptural situation elsewhere in the world.

In anticipation of further efforts to attain clarity on such matters, a final word must be said about the context in which the study of any particular scriptural tradition is undertaken. The thrust of our exploration in this essay has been into the concepts and nature of the Hindu religious tradition. It is well-known, however, that the very concept 'Hindu' is a late one, dating only from the arrival of the Muslims, to say nothing of the more general danger of reification in conceptualizing the religious life.[80] We must be reminded of these facts because there is evidence that the development of the narrowly 'Hindu' phenomenon of scripture has often been intertwined with non-Hindu matters. Staal, for instance, argues that it was the Buddhists who first committed a sacred oral text to writing, in 35–32 B.C.E.[81] While the Buddhist use of holy words is itself far from clear, it would be fruitful to explore Staal's contention here in relation to Renou's suggestion, cited earlier, that the division between *śruti* and *smṛti* also marks the boundary between orality and editing.[82] Similarly, while we know that Sāyaṇa, the great fourteenth century commentator of the *Ṛg Veda*, had his predecessors, it is a fact that he flourished after the Muslim entry into India, and one then wonders whether he might reflect the Islamic tradition that texts are for exegeting, as well as for reciting.[83] Be that as it may, it is now clear that the great significance ascribed to the *Ṛg Veda* in modern India derives in large measure from the labors of an Oxford professor to accomplish the unprecedented task of publishing that text in its entirety. The professor was, of course, Max Müller.[84]

Finally, there are indications that Western notions of critical editing and of an "original text" have represented a sometimes startling intrusion upon Hindu reality, with consequences that are complex and often ill-understood.[85] All of this evidence would suggest that, while we are becoming more alert to the great variety of ways that verbal material has functioned religiously in human lives, both Hindu and other, a fully adequate understanding is not yet upon us.

NOTES

1. A much earlier draft of this essay was written for the National Endowment for the Humanities 1982 Summer Seminar on "Scripture as Form and Concept." I am much indebted to the members of the Seminar, and particularly to the Director, Wilfred Cantwell Smith, for their very helpful comments. This article first appeared in the *Journal of the American Academy of Religion* 52 (1984):435–459, and I am grateful to the editors for permission to reprint it in the present volume.

2. Wilfred Cantwell Smith, "The Study of Religion and the Study of the Bible," *Journal of the American Academy of Religion* 39 (1971):131–140.

3. Gerald James Larson, "The *Bhagavad Gītā* as Cross- Cultural Process: Toward an Analysis of the Social Locations of a Religious Text," *Jounal of the American Academy of Religion* 43 (1975):651–669.

4. Wilfred Cantwell Smith, "The True Meaning of Scripture: An Empirical Historian's Non-reductionist Interpretation of the Qur'ān," *International Journal of Middle East Studies* 11 (1980): 487–505.

5. William A. Graham, "Qur'ān as spoken Word: An Islamic Contribution to the Understanding of Scripture," in Richard C. Martin, ed., *Islam and the History of Religions* (Tucson: University of Arizona Press, 1984).

6. Graham's first twenty-three footnotes provide the basic bibliography for this phenomenology.

7. Graham, p. 207.

8. Jack Goody and Ian Watt, "The Consequences of Literacy," in Jack Goody, ed., *Literacy in Traditional Societies* (Cambridge: The University Press, 1968), p. 42.

9. Kathleen Gough, "Implications of Literacy in Traditional China and India," in Jack Goody, ed., *Literacy in Traditional Societies* (Cambridge: The University Press, 1968), p. 73.

10. Lewis Lancaster, "Buddhist Literature: Its Canons, Scribes, and Editors," in Wendy Doniger O'Flaherty, ed., *The Critical Study of Sacred Texts* (Berkeley: Berkeley Religious Studies Series, 1979), pp. 224–225.

11. J. G. Staal, "The Concept of Scripture in the Indian Tradition," in Mark Juergensmeyer and N. Gerald Barrier, eds., *Sikh Studies: Comparative Perspectives on a Changing Tradition* (Berkeley Religious Studies Series, 1979), pp. 122–123.

12. *Ibid.*, p. 123.

13. In light of both the ease of misunderstanding here, and the importance of the notion of 'oral tradition' in past scriptural studies, it is worth emphasizing that when we speak of the orality/aurality of scripture, we are not indicating an oral supplement to a written tradition. Rather, we are calling attention to the vocal, spoken quality of holy words, which come to life, as it were, only in utterance and hearing. Our remarks below on the *guru*-student relationship are apposite here. The ongoing work of William A. Graham, as evidenced by his essay in the present volume, stands to illuminate greatly the oral/aural quality of scripture in a variety of historical contexts.

14. Goody, *Literacy in Traditional Societies*, p. 16.

15. Günter Lanczkowski, *Sacred Writings: A Guide to the Literature of Religions*, trans. Stanley Goodman (New York: Harper and Row, 1961), p. 82; J. B. Noss, "Sacred Scriptures," *Encyclopedia Britannica III*, Macropaedia 16:126–128; J. A. B. van Buitenen, "Hindu Sacred Literature," *Encyclopedia Britannica III*, Macropaedia 8: 932–940; Benjamin Walker, *Hindu World: An Encyclopedic Survey of Hinduism* (London: George Allen & Unwin, Ltd., 1968), p. 372.

16. J. A. B. van Buitenen, "Hindu Sacred Literature," pp. 932–933.

17. M. Winternitz, *A History of Indian Literature*, trans. Mrs. S. Ketkar (New York: Russell and Russell, 1927), vol. I, p. 55.

18. Lanczkowski, *Sacred Writings*, p. 83.

19. J. N. Farquhar, *An Outline of the Religious Literature of India* (London: Oxford University Press, 1920), pp. 4–23.

20. J. A. B. van Buitenen, "Hindu Sacred Literature," p. 935.

21. Louis Renou, *The Destiny of the Veda in India*, trans. Dev Raj Chandra (Delhi, Patna, Varanasi: Motilal Banarsidass, 1965), p. 84.

22. See also Renou's equally suggestive remark pertaining to the substance, rather than the form, of these two kinds of literature: "The Smṛti introduces a direct formulation, which could be called a rational thought, consisting of erudite texts or (pre-) scientific texts; the Śruti, quite to the contrary is essentially symbolic, basing itself on an indirect and 'second' semantic" (*Destiny*, p. 16).

23. Cheever Mackenzie Brown, *God as Mother: A Feminine Theology in India* (Hartford, Vermont: Claude Stark & Co., 1974), pp. 18–19.

24. Cornelia Dimmitt and J. A. B. van Buitenen, eds. and trans., *Classical Hindu Mythology: A Reader in the Sanskrit Purāṇas*, (Philadelphia: Temple University Press, 1978), p. 4. See Madeleine Biardeau, "Some More Considerations about Textual Criticism," *Purāṇa* 10 (1968): 121.

25. Thomas J. Hopkins, *The Hindu Religious Tradition*, (Encino and Belmont, CA: Dickenson Publishing Co., 1971), p. 142; David R. Kinsley, *Hinduism: A Cultural Perspective* (Englewood Cliffs, NJ: Prentice-Hall, 1982), p. 12.

26. William Theodore deBary, et. al., eds., *Sources of Indian Tradition* (New York: Columbia University Press, 1958), pp. XVII–XXI, 3–6, 205–210.

27. Edward C. Dimock, Jr., et al., *The Literatures of India: An Introduction* (Chicago and London: University of Chicago Press, 1974); Farquhar, *Outline*; Louis Renou, *Indian Literature*, trans. Patrick Evans (New York: Walker and Company, 1964); Louis Renou and Jean Filliozat, *L'Inde Classique: Manuel des études indiennes* (Paris: Payot, 1947), vol. I; Winternitz, *History.*

28. Milton Singer, "Text and Context in the Study of Contemporary Hinduism," *The Adyar Library Bulletin (Madras)* 25 (1961): 274ff.

29. J. A. B. van Buitenen, "Hindu Sacred Literature," p. 933.

30. Monier Monier-Williams, *A Sanskrit-English Dictionary* (Oxford: Clarendon Press, 1899).

31. J. Gonda, *The Vision of the Vedic Poets* (The Hague: Mouton & Co., 1963), p. 45.

32. *Ibid.* pp. 61, 63–64, 66.

33. Gopinath Kaviraj, *Aspects of Indian Thought* (Burdwan: University of Burdwan, 1967), p. 1.

34. Gonda, *Vision*, p. 319.

35. See Kaviraj, *Aspects*, pp. 1–44 and Gonda, *Vision*, pp. 318–348.

36. Kaviraj, *Aspects*, pp. 41, 42, 43, 44; see also Gonda, *Vision*, p. 341.

37. Diana L. Eck, *Darśan: Seeing the Divine Image in India* (Chambersburg: Anima Books, 1981), p. 1.

38. *Ibid.*, p. 32.

39. Edward C. Dimock, Jr., "Doctrine and Practice among the Vaiṣṇavas of Bengal," in Milton Singer, ed., *Krishna: Myths, Rites, and Attitudes* (Honolulu: East-West Center, 1966), pp. 41–63; John S. Hawley and Donna M. Wulff, eds., *Rādhā and the Goddesses of India* (Berkeley: Berkeley Religious Studies Series, 1982).

40. Though T. M. P. Mahadevan shares the common view that *śruti* is virtually synonymous with the Vedas—a view of *śruti* that I am here urging be enlarged—he provides an understanding of the *śruti-smṛti* relation that works well in the larger context: "*Śruti* is primary because it is a form of direct experience, whereas *smṛti* is secondary, since it is a recollection of that experience." (*Outlines of Hinduism* (Bombay: Chetana Limited, 1961), p. 28.) Such a definition would then allow us to reinterpret van Buitenen's remark, cited above, that the Hindu acquires his religious knowledge from *smṛti* as meaning: most Hindus do not have experiences of mystical consummation, but they base their religious lives on records of such experiences.

41. J. A. B. van Buitenen, "Hindu Sacred Literature," p. 935.

42. *Vaidika-padānukrama-koṣa* (Lahore (parts 1–5) and Hoshiarpur (parts 6–16): Visvesvarananda Vedic Research Institute, 1935–1965). The appearance of this word-index is itself a reflection of the novel approach to the Vedas that has emerged over the course of the past century; see our concluding remark on the role of Max Müller.

43. Lanczkowski, *Sacred Writings*, p. 88.

44. Benjamin Walker, *Hindu World*, p. 534.

45. A. C. Bouquet, *Hinduism* (London: Hutchinson's University Library, 1948), p. 47; Walker, *Hindu World*, p. 534.

46. A similar argument, which I here omit in the interest of brevity, could be made with regard to the interpretation of the "supplements" or *khilas* to the *Ṛg Veda*, some of which are virtually modern: see C. G. Kashikar, "Preface" to *Ṛgveda-Sanhitā, with the commentary of Sāyaṇācarya*. N. S. Sontakke and C. G. Kashikar, eds., (Poona: Vaidika Samśdhana Mandala, 1946), vol. IV, esp. p. 907.

47. Brown, *God as Mother*, p. 18.

48. Dimock, et al., *Literatures of India*, p. 10.

49. *Ibid.*, p. 11.

50. J. A. B. van Buitenen, "On The Archaism of the *Bhāgavata Purāṇa*," in

Milton Singer, ed., *Krishna: Myths, Rites, and Attitudes* (Honolulu: East-West Center Press, 1966), pp. 35–36.

51. J. F. Staal, "Sanskrit and Sanskritization," *Journal of Asian Studies* 22 (1963): 261–275.

52. Charles R. Lanman, "Sanskrit Diction as Affected by the Interests of Herdsman, Priest, and Gambler," *Journal of the American Oriental Society* 20 (1899): 12–17.

53. Renou, *Destiny*, p. 25.

54. *Ibid.*, p. 23; see Daniel Ingalls, "The Brahman Tradition," in Milton Singer, ed., *Traditional India: Structure and Change* (Philadelphia: The American Folklore Society), pp. 3–4.

55. Renou, *Destiny*, p. 40.

56. J. F. Staal, *Nambudiri Veda Recitation* ('s-Gravenhage: Mouton and Co., 1961), p. 17.

57. See Richard Schechner and Linda Hess, "The Ramlila of Ramnagar [India]," *The Drama Review* 21 (1977): 79 on the role of Tulsī Dās's Hindi *Rāmāyaṇa* in Rāmlīlā.

58. I am indebted to Wilfred Smith for this comparative way of putting matters.

59. For example, Smith, "True Meaning."

60. Agehananda Bharati, "The Hindu Renaissance and its Apologetic Patterns," *Journal of Asian Studies* 29 (1970): 274; Larson, "The *Bhagavad Gītā* as Cross-Cultural Process," p. 661.

61. Bharati, "Hindu Renaissance," pp. 274–275.

62. J. A. B. van Buitenen, *The Bhagavadgītā in the Mahābhārata* (Chicago and London: University of Chicago Press, 1981), p. 12.

63. V. S. Sukthankar, et al., *The Mahābhārata, For the first time critically edited*, (Poona: Bhandarkar Oriental Research Institute, 1933–1959), 19 vols. The colphons' use of the plural of *upaniṣad* is fascinating, but we cannot pursue the matter here. At a minimum, it substantiates our claim that the terms for various kinds of Hindu scripture stand in need of careful reexamination.

64. *Vaidika-padānukrama-koṣa*, vol. III, part i, Introduction, p. xiv.

65. P. V. Kane, *History of Dharmaśāstra (Ancient and Medieval Religious and Civil Law* [Poona: Bhandarkar Oriental Research Institute, 1958], vol. V. part 1 p. 155n.

66. Harikṛṣṇa Śarma, *Durgāsaptaśatī saptatīkāsamvalitā* ([Bombay]: Venkateśvara [Press], 1916).

67. It may appear banal to say that *words* present *ideas*. However, as we strive for a phenomenology of scripture, it is important to realize that words do not necessarily serve this function, as the Hindu phenomenon of *mantra* demonstrates. Conversely, we need to be reminded that ideas can also be vividly conveyed through such nonverbal media as music and art.

68. Lawrence A. Babb, *The Divine Hierarchy: Popular Hinduism in Central India* (New York and London: Columbia University Press, 1975), p. 218, my italics.

69. Schechner and Hess, "The Ramlila of Ramnagar," p. 79.

70. John S. Hawley, *At Play with Krishna: Pilgrimage Dramas from Brindavan*, In association with Shrivatsa Goswami (Princeton University Press, 1981), pp. xii-xiii.

71. The argument has been made by Harry Buck ("Saving Story and Sacred Book," in J. M. Myers, et al., eds., *Search the Scriptures: New Testament Studies in Honor of Raymond T. Stamm* [Leiden: E. J. Brill, 1969]), drawing on Hindu material, and by Peter Slater (*The Dynamics of Religion* [San Francisco: Harper and Row, 1978]), on a broader scale, that *stories* may fruitfully be understood as living at the heart of the religious life, and of religious traditions. While appreciating that they have presented an important dimension of human religiousness, I find their analyses do not go to the heart of (at least Hindu) matters: as we have seen, India does indeed love to re-create traditional stories, but she also loves to preserve (through recitation) the memorable creations of the past. The typology that I will broach below may be understood as endeavoring to retain the best of the Buck-Slater argument, while seeing it in relation to other crucial features of the Word in Hindu life.

72. Gonda, *Vision*, p. 67; see also p. 346.

73. J. A. B. van Buitenen, "On the Archaism of the *Bhāgavata Puraṇā*."

74. Parameswara Aiyar, "Imitations of the Bhagavad-Gita and Later Gita Literature," in *The Cultural Heritage of India* (Calcutta: Ramakrishna Mission Institute of Culture, 1962), vol. 2, pp. 204–219.

75. It is worth emphasizing that the two epics of India, so often lumped together in discussions of the literature, might, according to this typology, best be understood as representing different ways that Hindus have dealt with the Word: the story of Rāma is comparatively brief and simple and, while any particular version may admit of being memorized (Type 1), it has primarily retained its vitality through being retold in a variety of ways, in a variety of languages (Type 2). The *Mahābhārata*, by contrast, is not a story, but a library or encyclopedia. (See Dimock, et. al., *Literatures of India*, p. 53 for a superb account of what would be involved in conceptualizing a Western equivalent). And it seems to have retained *its* vitality by incorporating diverse local traditions into itself (type 5), a process in which writing appears to have played a significant role (Winternitz, *A History of Indian Literature*, pp. 464–465).

76. James W. Karman, "Art," in T. William Hall, ed., *Introduction to the Study of Religion* (San Francisco: Harper and Row, 1978), p. 119.

77. Dimmitt and van Buitenen, *Classical Hindu Mythology*, p. 4.

78. Kaviraj, *Aspects*, p. 44.

79. Buck, "Saving Story and Sacred Book," p. 93.

80. Wilfred C. Smith, *The Meaning and End of Religion* (New York: Macmillan, 1963).

81. J. F. Staal, "The Concept of Scripture in the Indian Tradition," p. 123.

82. Cp. Dimock, et. al., *The Literatures of India*, p. 11 and K. R. Norman, "Middle Indo-Aryan Studies VIII," *Journal of the Oriental Institute, M.S. University of Baroda* 20 (1971): 329–331.

83. Renou, *Destiny*, p. 23.

84. Ludo Rocher, "Max Müller and the Veda," in A. Destrée, ed., *Mélanges Armand Abel* (Leiden: E. J. Brill, 1978), vol. III, pp. 221–235.

85. Thomas B. Coburn, "The Study of the Purāṇas and the Study of Religion," *Religious Studies* 16 (1980): 341–352.

5

Scripture as Spoken Word

William A. Graham

> For Books are not absolutely dead things, but do contain a potency of life in them to be as active as that soul was whose progeny they are. . . .
>
> John Milton, *Areopagitica*

In the preface to Part II of his German works, Martin Luther at one point characterizes Christian scripture ("*die Biblia*") as "the Holy Spirit's own special book, writ, and word" ("*des Heiligen Geistes eigen, sonderlich Buch, Schrift und Wort*").[1] Luther's use of three terms, "book," "writ(ing)," and "word," to describe Christian scripture may well be more rhetorical than analytical in this instance, but it points to some of the often forgotten or unnoticed complexity of scripture both as a specifically Christian or Jewish phenomenon and as a generic concept in the general history of religion. Specifically, his three terms suggest rubrics for consideration of the

---

This article was written in 1983 as a preliminary study to a longer, now completed book, *Beyond the Written Word: Oral Aspects of Scripture in the History of Religion* (Cambridge University Press, 1987). The bulk of the work on this project was made possible by generous fellowships from the John Simon Guggenheim Foundation and the Alexander von Humboldt Stiftung in 1982–83. Because this article was written at an earlier stage in my work on the problem of scriptural orality, I have made some revisions to it on the basis of my book. However, those who wish to see fuller documentation and development of the ideas presented here are referred to the longer work.

functional diversity of scripture in religious life. This diversity has gone largely unattended, even among scholars, in the common acceptance of a definition of 'scripture' that rarely goes beyond 'sacred book,' in the sense of a written or printed text only. I have argued elsewhere against this kind of objectification in favor of a functional or 'relational' understanding of scripture and tried to show through consideration of the Islamic case how much a scripture can be an oral as well as or even more than a written reality.[2] In what follows, I want to elaborate on these points, particularly that regarding the degree to which a written text, and *a fortiori* a written scriptural text, functions as an oral-aural text in all but the most recent period of modern Western cultural history.

To this end I intend to use Luther's triad of "book," "writ," and "word" as an organizing scheme. The burden of my argument is that scripture is 'sacred book,' but that 'book' must be understood as most peoples in most times and places other than our own have understood it: as both 'writ' and 'word,' as written word and spoken word. This will become clearer as we proceed, considering first the more familiar aspect of scripture as written word, then the specifically oral phenomenon of sacred spoken word, before coming at last to scripture as sacred book in its dual aspect as *both* written and spoken text.

SCRIPTURE AS WRIT

As a writing, a black and white physical entity, scripture is a phenomenon utterly familiar to us. This is the concept of scripture that has come to be primary in the modern Western world, and it is the aspect of scripture upon which modern scholarship has focused virtually all of its attention.[3] Today it is simply taken for granted that 'scripture' means 'holy writ(-ing),' 'sacred book,' or whatever formulation expresses the essentially *written* (or printed) character of holy text as a tangible document.

The reasons for this orientation are not difficult to discover. To begin with, our focus upon the written, documentary aspect of the sacred text is naturally reinforced by the particular historical linguistic associations of the very terms 'scripture,' 'bible,' 'holy writ,' and the like in the Jewish and Christian traditions. We have automatically assumed that the use of these terms (or their cognate equivalents in other European languages)[4] in the Jewish and Christian contexts is applicable to any and all sacred texts around the world. This use turns out to be heavily oriented to the written rather than the oral and aural aspects of the sacred text. Nowhere is this more obvious than in the etymological backgrounds of the words themselves. *'Scripture', 'Schrift,' 'Scrittura,'* and the like are derived from the Latin singular *scriptura*, "a writing," which was a translation of the Greek *graphē*, or its plural *graphai*. Similarly, *'bible,' 'bijbel,' 'bibbia,'* and so forth are forms taken from the late Latin *biblia*, which is a feminine singular formed from a neuter plural. That plural had been used to translate the Greek *biblia* (a collection of writings), the plural of *biblion* (paper or scroll). In form, *biblion* is a diminutive singular of *biblos* (paper or book).[5] These derivational ties have made it seem all the more self-evident when moving beyond the Judaic and Christian worlds to equate 'scripture' (as also, if less often, 'bible') with 'sacred writing(s)' of any kind, and to think thereby of a purely written or printed object that is held to be sacrosanct and authoritative by a given religious community.[6]

Such a conception of scripture as written word is bolstered in our culture by the immense importance that we attach to writing and the written or printed word. There will be occasion below to consider the implications of this for our notion of book, but it is helpful in considering the specifically written aspect of scripture to remind ourselves how important writing is to our own valuation of history and culture.[7] The Egyptologist Alan Gardiner has remarked that "man's successive discoveries, at very great intervals, of the respective techniques of Speech and Writing, have been the two main stages passed by him on his long road to civilization,"[8] and this expresses well our sense of the momentous character of the breakthrough to the written word for the onset of civilization. We commonly use, as Robert Redfield notes, "absence of literacy and literature . . . as a criterion of primitive as contrasted with civilized living,"[9] so strong is the idea that "only phonetic writing has the power to translate man from the tribal to the civilized sphere."[10] We divide "prehistory" from history on the same grounds: absence or presence of writing. It is not that the so-called "preliterate" cultures past or present have no history in the absolute sense of existence over time, but rather that history as narrative investigation of past events, as *historia* (Gr. *historía*, literally, "learning by inquiry"), is ineluctably tied to the critical ordering and evaluation of human affairs in their continuity and change. Such representation of the past in any extensive, critical fashion only becomes possible with the "literate revolution"[11] that alphabetic culture introduces. The written word encourages reflective analysis as well as record-keeping on a new scale.[12] "Study" becomes possible at this point, and with it, the "abstractly sequential, classificatory, explanatory examination of phenomena or of stated truths" that is "impossible without writing and reading."[13]

Although contemporary Western society has placed unusual emphasis on the written, and especially the printed word, written texts have virtually always enjoyed a special status in literate societies. With the notable exceptions of classical Greece and especially India,[14] the writing down of a text, most of all a sacred text, has from ancient times lent it special authority and made it often even the object of overt veneration.[15] Where the written word replaces oral transmission, written fixation of the central religious texts of the society usually follows. This commonly enhances their status as visible heritages of the past and physically present sources of guidance. In many cases it can even affirm or create for the holy text what Karl Kerényi, borrowing from Thomas Mann, has called *Unsterblichkeitscharakter*, or immortality, in the eyes of the faithful.[16] The very permanence and fixity of the written page lends credence to the idea that its sacred word has always existed and always will. Ancient Egypt seems to be a textbook case for the development of such an idea.[17] Once written, the sacred text acquired a visible solidity or even immutability in the eyes of many of the faithful. This process can hardly be reversed, even though the fixing of the holy word in writing is not without corresponding dangers for the spontaneity and living quality of the scriptural text.[18]

There are numerous examples of traditions in which the written fixation and transmission of particularly sacred or otherwise significant and authoritative texts have been crucial to the definition and sustaining of the traditions themselves. After the particularly striking case of Pharaonic Egypt,[19] classical China comes immediately to mind, for the written texts of the five Classics (*ching*) were the basis as well as the overt symbols of all culture from at least the first century A.D., when the Confucian tradition (*ju chiao*) had become dominant.[20] In the Hellenistic world we can follow a cumulative development of the importance of written texts of books that were considered to be 'classics' or 'scriptures' of various kinds. The culmination of this development seems to have come in the Christian movement, with its eventual development of concepts of canon and bible.[21] In traditions as diverse as the Rabbinic Jewish and the Theravada Buddhist, the fixing of a written canon of scriptures is also evidence of how important to a tradition the delineation of 'holy writ' can be, even when great emphasis is placed upon memorizing and reciting aloud the words of the writ.[22]

A corollary of the elevated place of the written word of scripture in many cultures is the notion of a divine prototype for the earthly exemplar. Geo Widengren has devoted a whole series of studies to tracing how the concept of holy writ in the form of a heavenly book emerged and flowered in the traditions of the ancient Near Eastern and Mediterranean world from the earliest stages of civilization in Mesopotamia and Egypt down to the apotheosis of the heavenly-book idea in Islam.[23] As Widengren presents it, the notion of a written heavenly text that is given physically or revealed to a human "bearer of revelation" (*Offenbarungsträger*) for humankind is a leitmotif of religion in this part of the world. He notes that, while the holy writ so revealed is subsequently recited and orally taught, "the written tradition is the normative one, the firm model, for it is scripture (*die Schrift*) as the document of divine revelation, a copy of the sacred book that the bearer of revelation himself received from the divinity."[24]

Although the degree of importance ascribed to this pattern by Widengren is perhaps exaggerated, the peculiar importance of the holy book as written document in the ancient Mediterranean and Near Eastern world is underscored by the widespread occurrence of the heavenly-book motif.[25] Even where this motif does not occur, the idea of the divine origin of holy writ usually does, and this idea is found as easily in East and South Asia as in the West.[26]

The most common explanation of the basis for the special treatment and status of the written word of scripture has been the common perception of writing and the written word as possessing an inherent magical power.[27] (Similarly, of course, scholars have sought to locate the importance of the spoken holy word in the primordial magical power of sound.) Alfred Bertholet maintains that "respect particularly for what is written has penetrated deeply into the human soul . . . ,"[28] and G. van der Leeuw says:

> Writing, then, is magic:—one method of gaining power over the living word. . . . Committing sacred texts to writing therefore was . . . intended . . . to attain power, since with the written word man can do just what he will. . . ."[29]

Certainly the magical or quasi-magical quality of the written word is abundantly visible in the popular use for divination and talismans of copies of sacred books, be they Bibles, Qur'āns, Isma'ili *Ginans*, or Buddhist *sūtras*.[30]

The reverence for the written sacred word goes, however, beyond the purely magical in the recurring veneration and even adoration shown to it around the world. We have today little access to the sense of awe and respect before the physical copy of *any* text that prevailed in ages and (even today prevails) in places in which a book was (is) a rare thing, and a scriptural book often the *only* book. As Ernst Curtius has pointed out, such a sense of awe before a volume of text was still vivid for Shakespeare;[31] how much greater, then, the reverence of wholly illiterate folk (who have been the majority throughout history) in the presence of holy writ? Yet it is not only among the illiterate masses that such holy-writ veneration has flourished. The Sikh veneration of the Granth Sahib is a prime case in point,[32] as is Tibetan Buddhist reverence for the physical copies of the *sūtras*.[33] Recent research by Gregory Schopen has pointed to a "cult of the book" even in early Mahāyāna tradition,[34] and certain forms of Protestant Christian treatment of the Bible can rightly be termed bibliolatry.[35] Nichiren Buddhist reverence for the *Lotus Sūtra*, like Jewish, Muslim, or Mormon reverence for their particular holy writ, is also a well-known fact of religious practice and piety.[36]

The natural and widespread reverence for the physical copies of sacred texts is also, at least in some degree, the result of the desire to set such texts apart from all other forms of written word in definitive, tangible ways.[37] This seems to have been a major motivation for the early Christians' appropriation of the little-used parchment codex, which they made their distinctive vehicle for sacred texts.[38] Similarly, both early and later Bible manuscripts testify to the elaborate care given to the copying and ornamentation of the Bible as a holy object.[39] Such pious copying and illumination or illustration of sacred texts is widely attested. We need think only of Mani's illustrated books of scripture, the staggering variety and artistry of Qur'ān calligraphy and illumination, the massive and elegant block print collection of the Tibetan Buddhist canon, or the reverent artistry and traditionalist zeal with which synagogal copies of the Torah are prepared among Jews to this day.[40]

All of the preceding, then, points us to the central importance of the written character of scripture for an understanding of its function in religious history. This aspect of scripture is, to be sure, the one with which we are most at home in our typographic culture, with its strong print-orientation and book-consciousness. Yet, as already suggested, the very familiarity with which we move among books and handle the ubiquitous printed page has bred in us its own kind of contempt; we have some difficulty empathizing with persons for whom a copy of a text was or is a seldom and wonderful thing, perhaps a magical and awesome thing, before which the proper response is fearful veneration or fervent worship. The power of scripture as holy writ is, however, very much a part of most traditions past and present in which scripture has figured at all prominently. Any comprehension of what scripture is must include awareness of its role and function as written text.

SCRIPTURE AS WORD

If some of the traditional forms of religious piety concerning holy writ seem foreign to modern culture because of our matter-of-factness about the written or printed word, they are nevertheless much easier for us to grasp than are those forms of piety that center on the spoken word. Even if the sense of awe before the written copy of the Bible has waned for many modern Western Christians and for some Jews, it is still probably stronger than is the awareness among these same groups of the power of the biblical text as a memorized and recited word that is 'lived with' orally and aurally, not just in devotional and liturgical practice, but also in everyday life.

This is evident, for example, in the modern Christian, especially the Protestant Christian, emphasis upon scripture as writ. The common habit of referring to Holy Scripture as "the word of God" no longer reflects so much an aural sense of hearing God speak as it does a fixing or reifying of "Word" into a synonym for "Bible" in the sense of "holy writ." Such reification masks in many instances the degree to which the Word is theologically and functionally not a written text but the living, spoken message of the Gospel for Christians. The identity of this vocal message of the Gospel preaching with the vocal word of God that spoke from the pages of scripture was still vivid for Martin Luther. He could speak of "the ears alone" as "the organs of the Christian" and of the ears and tongue as the two things upon which the Kingdom of Christ is based.[41] For all of his and other Reformers' emphasis upon Scripture as *Schrift*, *écriture*, or "writ," the heart of the "book religion" of the Protestant movement was a vivid sense of the living, spoken word of God that is communicated both in Christian preaching and in the reading of Scripture.[42] The Christian was supposed to listen to and to heed this word as the one certain word of truth. *Sola scriptura* was not an idea fixed upon written word, but upon the authority of the word of God. In Luther's words: "It is after all not possible to comfort a soul, unless it hear the word of its God. But where is God's word in all books except Scripture? ... Comfort can no book save Holy Scripture."[43]

In modern, print-dominated culture, as we shall see in the concluding section below, such an oral sense of scripture as word is no longer easy to understand intuitively. Recognition of the importance of oral speech and the oral sacred utterance altogether is today largely limited to scholarship, primarily in anthropology and religion, that focuses upon nonliterate cultures of "extra-civilizational" peoples or the preliterate or semiliterate beginnings of the great civilizations.[44] This is understandable, since, as Gustav Mensching puts it, "the word that is heard precedes (not everywhere, but in many instances) the written word. . . ."[45] Logically and historically the sacred word of holy writ is an extension of the oral sacred word, as we shall demonstrate shortly with a variety of examples.

Yet even this recognition does not suffice to indicate the immense significance of the spoken holy word. Its importance is not only limited to the distant past or to marginal tribal cultures of today; in at least one great world civilization, that of India, the centrality of the oral sacred word has persisted and retained its precedence over the written word as the consummate form for the communication of religious truth. Thus, we shall conclude the following brief look at scripture as word with some consideration of the Hindu case.

In oral or predominantly oral cultures, the transmission of sacred lore as well as the sustenance of ritual life are dependent upon the sacred spoken word. The centrality of the words of myth and ritual has been commonly and persuasively traced to the presence in such cultures of a sense of the spoken word as something alive with magical or transcendent power.[46] Word and act here are not to be separated. There is no cleavage, as there is for most of us, save perhaps in moments of deepest *engagement* in oral acts of worship, between *legomenon* and *drōmenon*, ("what is said" and "what is done"). Speech is action here, never merely Hamlet's "words, words, words."[47]

"The word . . . is a decisive power: whoever utters words sets power in motion."[48] This recognition has led students of both archaic and modern nonliterate cultures to see in the inherent power of the spoken word one of the primal elements in religious faith and practice. The oversimplified extreme in emphasis on the power of the word is the view of Hermann Usener, and after him Ernst Cassirer, in which the identification of the word that names a deity with the deity itself is carried so far as to see in the naming the creation of a "momentary deity"(*Augenblicks-gott*).[49] As a hypothetical model of the "origin" of human personification of the transcendent, this view has at most heuristic value; but as a reminder of the power that words carry, it is instructive. There is much to be said for the perception that especially in the cult-oriented world of oral traditions, and to a lesser degree in any ritual activity, the act of naming makes present, or at least summons the power of, that which is named.[50] What J. F. Staal says of Vedic recitative transmission is probably applicable to the function of the oral sacred word in most cultic contexts, and all the more in nonliterate cultures:

> There is no sharp distinction between word and meaning and between form and contents. In this "archaic" world lie the roots of the efficacy and power of mantra recitation, which is related to "magical" identification as well as to the creative force of the word in poetry, in divine and in human speech.[51]

The sense of word as overt act is especially vivid in the cosmogonic myths of diverse peoples, ancient and modern, in all parts of the globe. Accounts of the origin of the world ascribe the initial creative act again and again to the generative Word. Not only the opening of the Christian Gospel of John or the divine command of Gen. 1:3, "Let there be light," but also the creative word of the god Ptah described in the Memphite cosmogony of ancient Egypt are eloquent testimony to this.[52] Similarly striking is the role of *Vāc*, "Speech," as primordial being or creator-goddess in the *Ṛg Veda*,[53] or the creation story of the South American Witoto tribe and that of the African Dogon tribe.[54] Not surprisingly, the Qur'ān emphasizes God's eternal creative power: on whatever He decides, "He has only to say, 'Be!' and it is (*kun fa-yakun*)" (Sūrah 40:68). The magical, creative power of the spoken word is apparently one of the most basic and widespread of religious themes.

In many of the major, literate traditions of history, the idea of the primordial word of power is linked to the power of scripture itself. This is most explicitly evident in theological formulations such as we find in Rabbinic Judaism and medieval Islam about the preexistence of the divine word of scripture.[55] The idea of the eternality of the Buddha-word or the words of the Veda also reflects the transference of the primal power of the original word of truth to the preserved scriptural texts.[56] Even in the traditions of the heavenly book studied by Geo Widengren, we find more than once that the heavenly writ began before time as the spoken word of God.[57]

It bears repeating that in many senses, speech always precedes writing, cosmically and anthropologically as well as historically. If there is anything that can be called proto-scripture, it is surely the utterances of ecstatics, prophets, and seers in which it is commonly held to be not they but the divinity who speaks through them as their chosen mouthpieces.[58] In societies in which transcendence is not wholly personified nor anthropomorphically conceived, the primal word of truth is also an oral one: in India, it is referred to as *śruti*, "what is heard" by the *ṛṣis*, or seers of ancient times; in classical China, "hearing much" is what constituted "knowledge" for the ancient sages.[59]

The primacy of the oral word and its power are not of course limited to nonliterate or archaic stages of culture and religion. Truth is bound up in significant ways with the spoken word, whether that of a divinity or that of a human teacher or sages.[60] In theocentric traditions, scripture is "the place where God speaks to men."[61] In others, it is in scripture that the primordial wisdom heard and taught by generations of prophets or spiritual teachers is recorded, and in the ongoing tradition of oral teaching, be it of the word of the Buddha or the vedic *mantra*, scripture comes alive as the sacred word of truth spoken, and *only* spoken, by teacher to pupil. Here the role of scripture as oral word takes on central significance within the larger tradition.

Nowhere has this significance been more central, more dominant, than in the Hindu tradition. Here the oral word has remained the only fully acceptable and authoritative form for sacred texts for over two, possibly over two-and-one-half millennia *after* the introduction of writing.[62] The fundamentally oral nature of Indian sacred texts has been noted and commented on by most students of the Hindu tradition, among them scholars of the stature of Georg Bühler, Moriz Winternitz, Louis Renou, J.A.B. van Buitenen, and Jan Gonda.[63] More significant, however, for our interests are the thoughtful and perceptive discussions of the basic orality of Indian texts by J.F. Staal, Walther Eidlitz, and especially Thomas Coburn.[64] These treatments of Hindu scripture offer clear evidence that the pattern in India has been not merely one of prominent oral use of written texts, but one of nearly exclusively oral use and transmission in preference to dealing with written texts at all.

The prototypical sacred texts of the Hindus are called "*Veda*" ("what is known"), in the absolute sense of true knowledge or eternal wisdom that is transcendent (*apauruṣeya*), "not of personal origin."[65] Veda is the knowledge of eternal reality first perceived by the ancient seers, or *ṛṣis* as sound (*śabda*) or speech (*Vāc/Vak*). The *ṛṣis*' apprehension of the sacred sounds of ultimate truth is described variously as "seeing" or "hearing" —metaphorical expressions that, as Coburn aptly characterizes them, together convey "the holistic and supremely compelling nature" of the indescribable revelatory experience.[66] But the abiding and fundamental form of the vedic wisdom is the spoken word—indeed, *vāc* is said in the *Bṛhadāranyaka Upaniṣad* (4.1.2) to be the supreme Brahman, transcendent reality. *Vāc* personified as a goddess is identified in *Śatapata Brāhmaṇa* (2.1.4.10) with Brahman,[67] and described in *Ṛg Veda* (1.164.46) as "the One Real."[68] This association of speech with eternal reality or truth is reflected in the standard traditional categorization of all vedic texts as *śruti* (what is heard), as distinguished from other sacred texts referred to as *smṛti* (what is remembered). *Śruti* as a concept emphasizes both the auditory character of vedic truth and its transcendent, revelatory nature. It is that which was "heard" by those in closest touch with ultimate reality, or Brahman. The aural truth of *śruti* is also linked to Brahman in the formulation *śabda-brahman* (word of Brahman).[69] In the actual sounded syllables of the Veda lie the points of contact with transcendent reality.

The Veda is oral scripture *par excellence*. The many vedic texts that have come down to the present in apparently highly accurate transmission from perhaps as far back as the end of the second millennium B.C., if not earlier, have been viewed as too holy to be committed to writing save in relatively recent times.[70] This is nicely illustrated in the answer that an eighteenth-century European Christian reports he was given when he asked an Indian pundit about "the vedic books." "Veda is that which pertains to religion; books are not Veda" (*Vedam est, quidquid ad religionem pertinet, vedam non sunt libri*).[71] Veda is not a text or texts given by a god and written down as a means of preserving the divine word. It is the word of immemorial truth, and the subsequent oral transmission of it from generation to generation represents the effort to conserve and convey this truth in its exact original vocal form with all its pristine purity and power.

This transmission, and the elaborate cultus that large parts of it accompanied, have been the specialist responsibilities and prerogatives of Brahmin caste groups over the centuries. (Neither a woman nor any man who is not "twice-born"—that is, a *brāhmaṇa, kṣatriya, or vaiśya*—is even supposed to hear the sacred vedic word recited let alone study it.) Both the liturgical texts of the four *Saṃhitā*s ("collections") and their appendages, and the later philosophical vedic texts (primarily the Upaniṣads), have been passed from teacher (*guru*) to pupil (*śiṣya*) down the centuries. This has established the *guru-śiṣya* relationship as the only model for true learning in India. Written texts have been used, certainly, but a text without a teacher to teach it directly and orally to a pupil is only so many useless leaves or pages. The *Aitareya Āraṇyaka*, a late Vedic text, can even speak of writing as a ritually polluting activity, after which the student must purify himself before learning (by reciting) the vedic texts: "He (the *śiṣya*) should not learn when he has eaten flesh, or seen blood, or a dead body, or done what is unlawful, . . . or had intercourse, or written, or obliterated writing."[72]

Such a view of scriptural authority seems to us "strange," as Winternitz puts it, because we cannot grasp "that in India, from most ancient times down to the present day, the spoken word and not writing was authoritative for all literary and scholarly activity."[73] This attitude toward the transmission of sacred texts has extended well beyond the Veda proper. While the *śruti* texts have retained their authority as holy sources for Brahmanic ritual, philosophical speculation, and recitative *mantra*s, the functional scriptures of the masses in India have been other texts, most of which are categorized as *smṛti* rather than *śruti*.[74] The Vedic texts, especially the liturgical books, have been almost a *scriptura abscondita* in Hindu life, but they have nonetheless provided the model for oral treatment of popular scriptural works such as the Purāṇas and Tantras, the *Rāmāyaṇa*, the *Gītā Govinda*, the *Bhagavadgītā*, and other texts of which, as van

Buitenen put it, "it is widely believed or believed by particular religious groups that recitation and listening bestow a special merit."[75] He goes still further and notes that

> for many religious sects, the manner of the Vedic transmission was the prototype of their own transmission. Followers of sects will speak of the "handing down" (*sampradāya*) or of a "succession of gurus or teachers" (*guruparamparā*), and it is well known that written texts contain only part of the doctrines actually handed down in a sect.[76]

It would be possible to go on at length about the oral function and character of scriptural texts in India: *mantra* recitation, public performances of *māhātmyas*, the singing of Bhakti hymns, festival recitations of the *Rāmāyaṇa*—the list would be long. The point, however, remains the same: for Hindus, scripture is, if not exclusively, then overwhelmingly, spoken, oral word *rather than* holy writ. The diverse and numerous sacred texts of Indian history have all been written texts only in the second instance if at all; their authoritative form has always been that of the oral, recited word.[77]

SCRIPTURE AS BOOK

The Hindu case suggests that any functionally adequate concept of scripture as a truly generic term for important sacred texts cannot be tied exclusively to the written word. Given the close connection between 'scripture' and writing treated in the first part of this study, it might seem logical to argue for replacing 'scripture,' at least in scholarly use, with a more neutral term, perhaps simply 'sacred text.' Such an argument would not, however, have a great deal more than theoretical validity to recommend it, even if it had a remote chance of success. 'Scripture' does carry in conventional use several connotations that offer a solid basis for a meaningful concept of sacred religious text.[78] The more important of these are: the notion of a relatively sizeable, usually composite text (as opposed to a single narrative, legal code, discourse, or the like); the idea of a collection of material that, whatever its history, is perceived as a unitary whole;[79] and the implied authority and sacrality of a text with unique claim to transcendence and truth.

Most importantly, the close identification of 'scripture' with the idea of 'book' need not be the limiting factor that one might assume it to be. A proper understanding of 'book' in more than the limited sense of written or printed document will restore to it its legitimate oral dimension as a functionally living text. This in turn makes possible an expanded understanding of scripture as sacred book, one that is both historically and functionally more encompassing than the presently common definition of it as sacred book only in the narrowest sense of holy writ.[80]

Such an understanding demands a clearer idea of the historical role of the book in general and the scriptural, sacred book in particular. In this essay, we can look only at a few salient aspects of this role primarily in the Western world, but these will show clearly how sharply this role contrasts with our usual assumptions in modern Western culture about books in particular as well as the written word more generally. The following examples, drawn from Western religious traditions themselves, indicate how much these assumptions have skewed our understanding of scripture's actual role even in the traditions of faith and practice closest to us. Specifically, in the history of the book-centered spirituality of Christianity, which is the tradition most prone to limit the word of scripture functionally to holy writ, we can see clearly how significantly oral the "Book of books" has actually been for most of its history.

Siegfried Morenz has spoken of "book religion" (*Buchreligion*) as the essential characteristic of the Western monotheistic traditions. He traces its origin to a basic predilection or genius for hearing (*eine Genialität des Hörens*), which was the great gift of the ancient Hebrews, with whom 'book religion' can be said to have begun.[81] His perception of the intimate link between book religion and the auditory rather than the visual sensibility suggests a basic oral and aural dimension of scripture, not merely in the uniquely oral tradition of the Hindus, but specifically in the book-dominated traditions of Jews, Christians, and Muslims. In the Hindu case, the Western treatment of Veda or Purāṇa as holy writ by analogy with the Bible remains an obvious factual error. Much more subtle an error is our common modern assumption that Western scriptural texts—Bible or Qur'ān—can be understood primarily as 'black and white' documents of the written or printed page, and their oral aspects relegated to a minor role at best. (In the Islamic case, certainly, the error should not be subtle to anyone who knows the tradition, but it like the Jewish and Christian cases has commonly been dealt with simply in terms of the visible presence of a centrally important holy writ, even by scholars.)[82]

I want to go beyond the admittedly striking but apparently unique case of Indian sacred texts to argue that scripture in virtually *any* religious context has been, and should be recognized explicitly as having been, a significantly oral phenomenon, whatever its written form and importance. What is at issue here are not the purely oral texts of religious life and history nor the oral origins of written scriptures, but the generally overlooked oral function and quality of sacred texts generally, even those most firmly fixed as written books.

This is not to deny that 'scripture' or 'sacred book' as a concept is linked by far more than its etymology to texts that can be, and at some point virtually always have been, written down. The importance of the writing down of a text has been amply indicated above, and the history of sacred texts almost everywhere shows a tendency towards an elevation of the written word at the expense of the purely oral form of the text. Indeed, it is a tendency visible even in India, and also in the highly oral world of Islam.[83] The significance of the written copies of a scripture or its fixation as holy writ is not in question. Our concern is rather with the degree to which the written text still functions also, and often primarily, as an oral and aural text in religious life.

In our modern Western frame of reference, 'scripture' or 'sacred book' is considered to be identical with 'holy writ' for a number of reasons already noted above. The most important of these is to be found in our more basic identification of book with writing or, more precisely, with 'printed text,' in its most concrete, reified sense. In our minds, a book is a written/printed document of reasonable length to which the basic access is through an individual's private, silent reading and study. To our usual way of thinking, the fixed, visible page of print is the fundamental medium of information (and therefore knowledge: to a degree unknown in any other culture of history, knowledge for us is 'book-learning').[84] More than that, for us writing is the basic form of language: "the speaker or writer can now hardly conceive of language, except in printed or written form; . . . his idea of language is irrevocably modified by his experience of printed matter."[85] We have lost any awareness of the essential orality of language.[86]

In particular, it is "the relentless dominance of textuality in the scholarly mind"[87] that is problematic, for it is modern scholarship that is the bastion of our literate culture and therefore the key to our attitudes toward books. The custodians of learning in our culture have been especially prone to exalt the written or, even more, the printed word as the chief bulwark of learning and progress. The printed page goes hand in hand with the values of modern, "scientific" scholarship, these being (1) suspension of subjective emotions and personal *engagement* in favor of objectivity and visual verification—the values essential to experimental science; (2) observation and analysis of the data of sense perception rather than immersion in them—what George Steiner has summed up tellingly as "the cult of the positive, the exact, and the predictive," or "the mirage of mathematical exactitude and predictability"[88]; and (3) rapid and easy access to "raw data"—the "growing thirst for quantitative information," which John U. Nef describes as a key element in the rise of industrial civilization.[89]

'Objectivity' has been an especially important value in modern Western thought, and increasingly so since the Enlightenment. With scientific detachment have come, however, other kinds of detachment and in general an increased objectification of the world around us. This, too, has been hastened by the printed word of the modern book. Ashley Montagu has observed that "the more literate people become, the more they tend to become detached from the world in which they live,"[90] and certainly our modern print-literacy far exceeds any previous kind of literacy in terms of both facility with and dependence upon alphabet and script. The virtually endless replicability made possible by the printing press adds greatly to the sense of the reliability and objective neutrality of the written word. With print, words and books lose their dynamism and personal quality and become themselves things—that is to say, mass-produced, impersonal objects.[91] As such, they are to be sure well-suited to their roles as neutral bearers of objective content accessible to any literate person who can understand that content. How much more sure, fixed, and unambiguous than the merely spoken or even written word is the printed word, or still more, the technical diagram or mathematical symbol!

Thus, it is no cause for wonder that the whole trend of education in the post-Enlightenment West, especially in this century, has been away from memorization (in essence an oral activity), reading aloud (together with reciting by heart and declamation), and rhetoric (formerly the core discipline of literate education and culture).[92] In their place has come ever greater emphasis upon swifter, more efficient comprehension of printed texts by the silent, scanning reader, and increased reliance upon reference aids and massive information storage of all kinds, from encyclopedias (which came into their own in the West in the eighteenth century) to the computer banks of the present day. The anonymous and impersonal, universally accessible, and "independently verifiable" word of the printed book, which was the first truly mass-produced commodity in history,[93] is the backbone of modern scholarship and of modern, technological society as a whole.

The point of all this is that the decisive emphasis upon the written or printed page at the expense of the memorized, recited, and orally transmitted word is tied closely to the circumstances of the modern technological age—an age that first came to maturity in Western Europe between about 1600 and 1900, and is now beginning to revolutionize for better or worse most other societies in the world in similar if variously configured fashion. Presaged if not inaugurated by the coming of the moveable-type printing press, these circumstances include the growth of literacy rates and spread of mass media, the extension of modern scholarship and education with their mixture of humanistic and scientific assumptions, and the explosion of science and technology in every realm of life.

These circumstances are new in history, and thus have consequences for any effort to understand other societies past or present. The great chasm in forms of communication, religious or secular, is not between literate societies and nonliterate societies, but between our own modern Western, post-Enlightenment world of the printed page and *all* past cultures (including our own predecessors in the West), as well as most contemporary ones.[94] We stand on this side of the epochal transition made in good part by about 1800 in the urban culture of Western Europe, and now still in progress elsewhere, from a scribal or chirographic, still highly oral culture to a print-dominated, primarily visual culture.[95] Our "book culture," like our "book religion," is not even the same as the book culture (or book religion) of sixteenth century Europe, let alone that of classical Antiquity, the medieval West, or the great literary civilizations of Asia past and present.

The considerable gap between our experience and perception as "print-persons" and those of other persons in other places or times has been noted by several scholars, all of whom have something to contribute to an awareness of the eccentricity of our relationship to books and words. H.J. Chaytor's fine study of medieval scribal culture raises clearly the issue of the fundamentally different, because fundamentally oral and aural, character of the mentality of chirographic literacy in the Middle Ages as compared with our modern, visual, typographic literacy. The radical psychological difference of these two orientations has been convincingly elucidated by J. C. Carothers in a study that contrasts oral mentality in contemporary African children with their European counterparts' highly visual and spatially organized ways of dealing with reality. Walter J. Ong and Marshal McLuhan subsequently have dealt at much greater length with what Ong terms the basic "alteration in the ratio of the senses," or "sensorium," of the Western mind that the print revolution has brought about—an alteration that both see as uniquely the consequence of the typographic age (which McLuhan identifies as "the Gutenberg galaxy"). With respect to the impact of Gutenberg's introduction of moveable type printing, Elizabeth L. Eisenstein has provided a massively documented, if also controversial, study of the key role played by the printing press as "an agent of change" in virtually every sector of European-American life since the 1500s.[96] As she would have it, the scientific arena is by no means the least of these, primarily because, "in contrast to scribal culture which had fostered 'hearing the rules of a given science,' print made possible the simultaneous distribution of 'well made figures and charts'."[97]

While some of these studies individually may overstate their case, together they provide a convincing argument for the novel and peculiar nature of modern Western attitudes to the written or printed word vis-à-vis the spoken word. They emphasize that orality does not cease with the advent of writing. It may well be that scribal culture represents a first stage in the demise of the spoken word and its power in the face of an emerging "literate consciousness" (Havelock): in the West, for example, the transition often associated with Aristotle from oral culture to book culture is not an inconsequential one.[98] However, scribal culture itself is still a significantly, even predominantly oral culture, in which reading is still largely vocal and illiteracy widespread. At least until a very late stage in chirographic culture (and perhaps until or even for a while after the advent of printing)[99], there obtains a "dynamic tension" between the oral and the literate, a situation "in which language managed acoustically on echo principles is met with competition from language managed visually on architectural principles."[100] As Havelock, Ruth Finnegan, and earlier scholars such as Moses Hadas and Fredric Kenyon have emphasized, literacy in ancient Greece and Rome was highly oral.[101] Indeed, whatever the expansion of literate consciousness after Aristotle, the fundamental form of publication and dissemination of books remained that of oral reading and recitation from Classical Antiquity right through the European Middle Ages to the coming of printing.[102] What Virgil understood under 'book' and what Dante or Luther understood under the same term, were much closer to one another than either is to what we today conceive a book to be. Similarly, they were much closer to what persons in the other cultures of the world have conceived, and still today in many places conceive, a book to be: something to be read aloud or recited from, an *aide mémoire* and repository of the vocal words of its author.

One of the most vivid examples of the conceptual gap that separates us from nonprint societies is found in an Egyptian New Kingdom papyrus—a relic of a culture that we associate with love for the written word and production of calligraphic and epigraphic inscriptions consciously intended for posterity: "A human being perishes, and his body becomes dirt; all his fellows dissolve to dust. But writings let him live on in the mouth of the reader (lector). . . ."[103] Writing for this author was something that was conceived to be realizable only in the vocal act of reading aloud. Its associations in his mind were aural rather than visual in the first instance—exactly the opposite of our own ingrained response, which would be to think of the fixity of the black and white page, not the sound of the words of the text, as the enduring monument to a writer's memory.

It is ultimately the functional differences between the manuscript book and the printed book that are decisive. These are certainly related to the physical differences in legibility, ease of rapid reproduction, and so forth. But at base, it is the reading process *per se*, both in its psychological and its physical aspects, that is today different from what it was in the West twenty-five hundred, and in large degree even two hundred and fifty years ago—or from what it is in more traditional cultures in the modern world.

Reading for us today is a silent, seemingly wholly mental process: "our implicit model of written literature" is "the mode of communication to a silent reader through the eye alone, from a definitive written text."[104] We assume that reading is simply mental cognition of visual symbols on a page. Our whole training in reading is aimed at ridding us of vocalization and even subvocalization. To 'sound' a text aloud is an exercise for someone learning to read and pronounce a language: it is associated with semiliteracy or reading disabilities. There is, however, much to be said for Ong's contention that "reading" a text means converting it to sound, aloud or in the imagination, syllable-by-syllable in slow reading or sketchily in the rapid reading common to high-technology cultures."[105] Oral speech remains the intrinsic form of human communication,[106] and for most literate peoples of history outside our present society, reading has always been a vocal, physical activity, even for the solitary reader. One mouthed the words of the text and preferably voiced them aloud, not only in reading them but even in composing or copying them into writing.

Classical and late Antiquity knew nothing of silent reading in which the words of the text are not sounded automatically with the lips, as was remarked long ago by Nietzsche, and emphasized by the great philologist Eduard Norden.[107] The classic example of this is the passage in Augustine's *Confessions* in which the young Augustine registers his amazement at seeing the venerable Ambrose reading silently: "His eye glided over the pages, and his heart searched out the sense, but his voice and tongue were at rest."[108] A panoply of further examples from late Antiquity, medieval Europe, and even the Renaissance have been adduced by Josef Balogh in his masterly study of this phenomenon of voiced reading.[109] Chaytor also reminds us that the medieval reader confronted

> a manuscript often crabbed in script and full of contractions, and his instinctive question, when deciphering a text, was not whether he had seen, but whether he had heard this or that word before; he brought not a visual but an auditory memory to his task. Such was the result of his up-bringing: he had learnt to rely on the memory of spoken sounds, not upon the interpretation of written signs. And when he had deciphered a word, he pronounced it audibly.[110]

Balogh points further to the fact that writing was itself oral so long as the values of classical rhetoric held sway; where Christian opposition to these values and the slow copying of the monastic scriptorium held sway, silent writing probably first began to be common.[111] Nevertheless, W. Wattenbach can cite at least one medieval copyist's vivid confirmation of the innately oral nature of his scribal labor: "Three fingers write, two eyes look [at the page]; one tongue speaks, the whole body works. . . ."[112]

Examples of the oral character of reading or writing are, of course, hard to find precisely because it was for so long assumed that only exceptions (such as that of Ambrose) merited anyone's special notice.[113] Like so many of the most basic facts of human existence, this one has been little discussed or remarked so long as it was taken for granted. (The one advantage of distance for the historian writing of earlier ages is that it sometimes enables him or her to see the shape of a forest that could not be compassed from within its own trees and thickets.) And apparently this fact of vocal reading was taken for granted much longer than one might imagine. Balogh cites a few examples that suggest that however much silent reading may have been increasing in the later Middle Ages, the humanists from Petrarch to Erasmus once again turned to "the rhetorical beauty of the literature of antiquity" and consequently emphasized reading with the voice still.[114]

Marshall McLuhan and others look to the coming of printing as the decisive blow that eventually felled the practice of oral, vocalized reading.[115] "As the Gutenberg typography filled the world, the human voice closed down. People began to read silently and passively as consumers."[116] This did not, however, happen overnight. Steven Ozment has remarked that "the first half of the sixteenth century remained very much an oral age" for all the massive upsurge in print distribution.[117] Widespread illiteracy lasted much longer than this period in Western Europe, and even literate readers of the sixteenth and seventeenth centuries worked with a punctuation system designed "for the ear and not the eye."[118]

The triumph of the silent page and reader needs still to be more accurately and precisely documented, but it was probably not complete even among literate classes until at least the eighteenth century, if then.[119] Schiller, as a poet, can still refer to "the speaking page" (*das redende Blatt*), but Adam Müller, in his "Twelve Speeches on Eloquence" of 1812, can only lament the victory of the silent hand, eye, and page of contemporary literacy over the voice, ear, and word of previous times.[120] At least by this time in our Western, post-Enlightenment world, visual, typographic culture seems to have replaced oral, chirographic culture.

The foregoing indicates that it is only in relatively recent history in our modern Western world that the book has become a silent object, the written word a silent symbol, and the reader a silent spectator. If this is true for the book in general, it is arguably true also for scriptural books in particular. Our modern documentary orientation in scriptural studies is a reflection of a wider contemporary conception of scripture as but a particular genre of written or printed word.[121] It is incontestable that the oral word no longer holds the prominent place in the everyday life of our secular culture that it did in pre-modern times, any more than reading aloud or hearing the scriptures remains the primary mode of contact with the Word for the faithful Christian or Jew that it once was. And by comparison with the contemporary Muslim world, not to mention that of the Hindus, the oral and aural presence of sacred texts is truly meager.

Yet where scripture still functions actively in the lives of modern Western Jews or Christians, it more than other kinds of book has retained some oral-aural dimensions because of its ongoing use in devotional life and liturgical practice. The family gathered around the dining room table to listen to the *pater familias* read from the Good Book may seem to many a nineteenth century scene, but it is also one not yet vanished from our contemporary world, any more than Bible-memorizing and recitation of the psalter are only things of the past. Nor is the reading from the Torah in the synagogue any less central to Jewish worship now than it was for the devout in times past.

Thus, we have at least a slender thread of contact with the fundamentally oral character of scripture that was prominent even in our own Western world in the not-so-distant past. Yet we are not well prepared by our own experience and education to recognize, let alone to appreciate, this oral character. I want to conclude this essay on scripture with brief consideration of this once major and natural orality of the scriptural book in the specific context of Western Christianity.[122] In the preponderantly Christian West today, it may seem possible to dismiss even the orality of Jewish scripture, not to mention that of Hindus or Muslims, as something ultimately foreign or unusual. We may even try to project anachronistically our present focus on the written word back into earlier Christian as well as other religious piety. However, once the historical orality of the Christian Bible is recognized, the general oral quality of scripture cannot be so easily dismissed and missed.

Christianity did not begin by being a religion of the sacred book, but true to its Judaic origins it soon became one to a degree unknown in any other tradition in the Hellenistic milieu.[123] It is not unfair to speak even of "an addiction to literacy" in the early Christian movement.[124] Yet this cannot obscure the fact that the public oral reading of the Hebrew scriptures (attested already in the Christian New Covenant itself: cf. 1 Tim. 4:13), as well as the oral character of the Pauline epistles were the mainstays of the early Christian culture.[125] The importance of the position of the early Christian lector in the church order,[126] the development of the liturgy with its readings from Law and Prophets as well as Gospel and "Apostolos,"[127] the chanting or singing of psalms,[128] and the early character of the sermon as either a cento from scripture or exegesis of a scriptural passage testify to the manifold ways in which scripture functioned orally in the early Church.[129] Later development in East and West of collections of scriptural passages specifically arranged for oral recitation in divine service (e.g., the *evangeliarium* and the *epistolarium*, as well as the psalter and breviary) points also to the centrality of the scriptural word in Christian worship.[130]

It has also been noted that even as early as the end of the third century many lay persons, not to mention the early desert monks, knew "the major portions" of scripture by heart.[131] For the Christians of the Patristic age, as Jerome put it, "*Ignoratio scripturarum ignoratio Christi est.*"[132] And Augustine gives us an oblique proof of widespread lay familiarity with the scriptural word when he criticizes the reading of Jonah in Jerome's new Latin translation (later to win recognition as the Vulgate): Augustine complains to Jerome himself that the new version differed from the text which "was rooted in the affection and memories of all the people and repeated in so many succeeding generations."[133] He asserts on another occasion that rather than a sermon, it is better for the Christian congregation to which he was to preach to be put in direct contact with the word of God through his reading scripture instead.[134] The lection, or *lectio*, represented in effect God speaking,[135] a phenomenon by no means limited to formal scriptural reading in worship only.

Historically, one of the most significant sectors of Christian life in which the oral function of scriptural word has been predominant has been the monastic life. In many ways, the monastic traditions were the lifelines of Christendom from the days of the later Roman Empire down to the Reformation and Counter-Reformation in the West, and even to the present in may sectors of the Christian world. These were the conserving traditions as well as the intensifying, concentrating forces of Christian piety and practice through the European Middle Ages.

From the outset, monastic piety centered upon the sacred word of the Old and New Covenants, preeminently the Psalms, Gospels, and Apostolic writings of the still somewhat fluid canon of scripture. The fundamental discipline and spiritual occupation of Christian monks was the oral recitation and contemplation of the divine word, which came to be expressed explicitly in the terms *meditatio* and *lectio divina*.[136] Note the words of Horsiesius (fourth century), the successor of Pachomius, the father of Christian monasticism:

> Consider now the many (scriptural) testimonies, in which the Word of God summons us to meditation on scripture, in order that we make our own in faith that which we constantly repeat by mouth (*ore volvimus*).[137]

John Cassian (d. 435), chronologically the next giant of early monasticism after Pachomius, felt that "as a beginner the monk can only drive out the worldly memories that invade his head by meditation on scripture, prolonged and stable."[138] Such practice of oral meditation became the heart of the Christian monastic enterprise: the *lectio divina* or contemplative, meditative reciting or reading aloud of the divine word of scripture in worship, during work, and in the solitude of one's cell.[139] In the Pachomian Rule's radical stress on the memorization and constant repetition of the Psalms, Gospels and apostolic epistles, we have not an aberrant phenomenon in Christian monasticism that was later abandoned, but a particularly clear example of the degree to which monastic spirituality in both Eastern and Western Christendom has been founded upon constant involvement with the repeating and hearing of Scripture.[140]

We have seen how even the act of copying a manuscript was in medieval times an oral process. Monastic scribes spoke their text as they wrote, and the medieval person thought of the written as something sounded and heard. Gregory the Great can speak, for example, quite unselfconsciously of that "which we heard in the sacred pages" (*quae in sacris paginis audiebamus* . . .).[141] For the great majority of pre-modern Christians—monk, cleric, and lay person alike, the primary contact with scripture was always in the divine service, in liturgy. We need only think of the degree to which the repetition of scripturally-derived prayers, the chanting and singing of psalms, and the preaching of scripturally-based sermons perpetuated the oral and aural presence of the biblical word in everyday life in scribal culture. Then we realize how primary the spoken word of scripture was in the perceptual world of the majority of medieval Christians East and West.

Nor is the basic functional orality of Christian scripture something that ends with the Middle Ages in Europe. The great Reformers themselves evidence a profoundly oral sensibility to the divine word. Their emphasis on bringing that word through vernacular scripture and sermon to the public, literate and illiterate alike, focused upon the divine service of the word (*Wortgottesdienst*) as divine service of scripture (*Schriftgottesdienst*) in which the point of departure was "the reading of the Word of God."[142] Similarly, teaching Scripture became the basis of Protestant education as well. In the new world of German Protestantism, the only books that approached the Bible in influence were the catechism and the hymnal. "The first... was taken in part from Luther's Bible and reflected throughout the same spirit and the same language, [and] the same held true for the hymnal."[143] Memorization of the vernacular Bible also proceeded apace among the Protestant laity and clergy, as anyone who reads the sermons or tracts of these people can recognize. It is remarkable how completely a Martin Bucer, John Calvin, or John Bunyan talks a scripturally saturated language—that is, thinks, speaks, and writes with and out of the vocabulary, stylistic modes, thought world, and imagery of the Bible. Such persons do not so much quote Scripture or use it for proof-texting as they simply "speak Scripture"—a scripture that they can and do recite largely if not wholly by heart.[144]

If one looks at the giant figure of Luther himself and any part of his voluminous works, it is easy to see how vividly the scriptural Word lived for him as God's active speaking to the ears of humankind. He can refer quite simply and naturally to "hearing a letter (*Buchstabe*) from God's Word."[145] Luther himself had the words of Scripture in Greek, Latin, and Hebrew largely by heart—a product of his own Augustinian monastic training, no doubt.[146] The "hearing of the Word of God" (*das Hören des Wortes Gottes*) was the only source of Christian truth, guidance, and joy, according to him. Hearing the Book of God alone suffices: only "the hearing of the word of God" [*das Hören des Wortes Gottes*] can bring true joy such that the heart finds peace in God's presence.[147] And when he speaks of meditation, he says that that means

> always repeat the oral speech and the literal word in the Book and compare them with each other, not only in your heart, but also outwardly, read them and reread them with diligent attentiveness and reflection, [to see] what the Holy Spirit means by them.[148]

Finally, God's Word should of course not only be heard and heeded, but "also learned and retained."[149]

It is true that much of Luther's rhetoric of the Word reflects not only his identification of the Word of God with the revealed text of Scripture, but also his conviction of the possibility of preaching and sharing by witness the Word in the sense of the *evangelium*, the "good news" of the Christ.[150] What he preaches is "the oral Gospel" (*das mündliche*

Euangelion),[151] and this is the *content* still more than the spoken words of the literal text itself: "[The] Gospel is not really that which is in books and composed in letters, but rather an oral preaching and living word, and a voice that resounds through the whole earth and is shouted forth abroad."[152] Still, this preached Word of the Gospel is inseparable from the Word of the Bible. Its special *claritas* comes through the Holy Spirit, which "can be found nowhere more immediately and more alive than precisely in its [the Spirit's] own holy letters, which it wrote."[153]

Many other passages from Luther could be added to these, but the point would remain the same: his language and imagery belong to a world in which the written word is simultaneously the word spoken and heard in full immediacy. This is a world in which the word spoken and heard is primary because the written word is inseparable from it, not, as in our world, an independent, silent notation that may, but need not be read aloud. This is a world in which the book's pages were not so many printed sheets of paper but living pages that "spoke" to the reader. Here holy writ and holy word are one and the same holy book.

We have come, then, back where we began: Luther's dictum on Holy Scripture as "book, writ, and word." We can now surmise how much these three terms must have overlapped and interpenetrated in the conceptual world of sixteenth century Europe. 'Writ' and 'word' are really but changes rung on the theme of 'book,' a paired gloss that amplifies the definition of scripture to its fullness as book—the book that is simultaneously writ and word.

In conclusion, I want to reiterate what has been explicit and implicit throughout: the need to recognize the cultural bias of the commonly assumed limitation of scripture to sacred writing in the narrow sense of a documentary text. A closer look at the role of sacred texts not only in India or Islam, but even in our own Christian West before the present age, reveals the relative narrowness and poverty of a primarily documentary, reified notion of sacred book. 'Scripture' is a relational, not an absolute term. It refers always to a text that is precisely *more* than meets the eye, to one that *lives* in the faith and piety of particular persons. A text is only scripture insofar as it exists in relation to a community of faith—persons who 'hear' it in the fullest sense of the word, who listen to its words, love and cherish them, and live by, with, and for them. Recognition of this basic dimension of scripture is made easier for us in our modern typographic world by an awareness of the orality of the sacred book that is experientially largely closed to most of us. And such recognition is imperative for anyone who seeks to study and to understand the religious faith and practice of other peoples past or present.

NOTES

1. "Vorrede zum zweiten Theil v. 1548," in *D. Martin Luthers Werke. Kritische Gesamtausgabe* (Weimar: Hermann Böhlau, 1883–) [hereafter *WA*], 54:474.

2. William A. Graham, "Qur'ān as Spoken Word: An Islamic Contribution to the Understanding of Scripture," in Richard C. Martin, ed., *Approaches to Islam in Religious Studies* (Tucson: University of Arizona Press, 1985), pp. 23–40, and *idem*, "Scripture", in *The Encyclopedia of Religion* (16 vols. New York: Macmillan, 1986), *s.v.* See also the introduction to my recent book, *Beyond the Written Word: Oral Aspects of Scripture in the History of Religion* (Cambridge and New York: Cambridge University Press, 1987).

3. On the textual orientation of Biblical scholarship, see Wilfred Cantwell Smith, "The Study of Religion and the Study of the Bible," *Journal of the American Academy of Religion* 39 (1971): 131–140, esp. pp. 136ff. Cf. *idem*, "The True Meaning of Scripture: An Empirical Historian's Nonreductionist Interpretation of the Qur'ān," *International Journal of Middle Eastern Studies* 11 (1980), 487–505.

4. For example Ger. *Schrift, Bibel*; Fr. *écriture, bible*; Dutch *schrift, bijbel*; Ital. *scrittura, bibbia.*

5. *Dictionnaire de la Bible* (Paris, 1895–), Supp. vol. 2 (1934): 457a–462b ("Ecriture sainte," part 1: "Le nom"); *Theologisches Begriffslexicon zum Neuen Testament*, 2 vols. in 3, ed. Lothar Coenen *et al.* (Wuppertal, 1967–1971), 1: 151–153 ("Buch"), 2.ii: 1084–1092 ("Schrift"); *Encyclopaedia Judaica* (Jerusalem, 1971–72) [hereafter *EJ*] 4: 816–817, 820–821; *The Catholic Encyclopedia* (New York, 1907–1912) [hereafter *CE*] 2: 543–544 ("Bible"), 13: 635–637 ("Scripture"); James Hastings, ed., *Dictionary of the Bible*, rev. ed. F.C. Grant and H.H. Rowley (New York: Scribner's, 1963) [hereafter *HDB*], *s.v.* "Bible", "Scripture."

6. This tendency was long ago reinforced by F. Max Müller's publication of his famous translation series of non-Western scriptural texts under the title *The Sacred Books of the East* (1879ff.). See also below, pp. 142–147.

7. Cf. Jack Goody and Ian Watt, "The Consequences of Literacy," in Jack Goody, ed., *Literacy in Traditional Societies* (Cambridge: The University Press, 1968), p. 27; I. J. Gelb, *A Study of Writing* (1952; rev. ed., Chicago and London: University of Chicago Press, 1963), pp. 221–223.

8. *Egypt of the Pharaohs: An Introduction* (1961; repr. ed., New York: Oxford University Press, 1966), p. 19.

9. *The Primitive World and Its Transformations* (Ithaca, N.Y.: Cornell University Press, 1953), p. 7. Cf. Hans Jensen, *Die Schrift in Vergangenheit und Gegenwart* (Glückstadt and Hamburg: J. J. Augustin [1935]), p. 2, where the author speaks of "die Bedeutung der Schrift für die kulturelle Aufwärtsbewegung der Menschheit."

10. Marshall McLuhan, *The Gutenberg Galaxy: The Making of Typographic Man* (Toronto: University of Toronto Press, 1962), p. 27; cf. pp. 18, 45, 48. See also J. C. Carothers, "Culture, Psychiatry, and the Written Word," *Psychiatry* 22 (1959): 307–320.

11. This term is Eric Havelock's: see *The Literate Revolution in Greece and Its Cultural Consequences* (Princeton: Princeton University Press, 1982), esp. pp. 23–24. Cf. also Walter J. Ong, *The Presence of the Word: Some Prolegomena for Cultural and Religious History* (1967. 2nd ed. Minneapolis: University of Minnesota Press, 1981), p. 45, on the revolutionary force of alphabetization.

12. Goody and Watt, "Consequences of Literacy," pp. 56–57, 62, 64.

13. Walter J. Ong, *Orality and Literacy: The Technologizing of the Word* (London and New York: Methuen, 1982), pp. 8–9; cf. pp. 14–15.

14. On ancient Greek mistrust of writing and books, see Johannes Leipoldt and Siegfried Morenz, *Heilige Schriften. Betrachtungen zur Religionsgeschichte der antiken Mittelmeerwelt* (Leipzig: Otto Harrassowitz, 1953), pp. 12–14; Frederic G. Kenyon, *Books and Readers in Ancient Greece and Rome* (1932; 2nd rev. ed., Oxford: Clarendon Press, 1951), pp. 24–25; Karl Kerényi, *Apollon, Studien über antike Religion und Humanität* (1937; [3rd?] rev. ed., Düsseldorf: Eugen Diederichs, 1953),p. 166; Carl Schneider, *Kulturgeschichte des Hellenismus*, 2 vols. (Munich: C. H. Beck, 1967–1969) 2: 228. The *locus classicus* for the negative Greek attitude is Socrates' discussion of the harmful effect of writing on the memory in Plato, *Phaedrus* 274–275. On the Indian attitudes, see below, pp. 138–140.

15. Gustav Mensching, *Das heilige Wort. Eine religionsphänomenologische Untersuchung* (Bonn: Ludwig Röhrscheid, 1937), pp. 80–81, 85–87; Leo Koep, *Das Himmlische Buch in Antike und Christentum. Eine religionsgeschichtliche Untersuchung zur altchristlichen Bildersprache* (Bonn: Peter Hanstein, 1952), pp. 4–6; Kurt Goldammer, *Die Formenwelt des Religiösen. Grundriß der systematischen Religionswissenschaft* (Stuttgart: Alfred Kröner, 1960), p. 252; Alfred Bertholet, "Die Macht der Schrift in Glauben und Aberglauben," *Abhandlungen der Deutschen Akademie der Wissenschaften zu Berlin*. Philos.-hist. Klasse. 1948, no. 1, pp. 43–46.

16. *Apollon*, pp. 165-166. Cf. Goldammer, *Formenwelt*, p. 250.

17. Siegried Morenz, *Ägyptische Religion* (Stuttgart: W. Kohlhammer, 1969), pp. 230–233; Leipoldt und Morenz, *Heilige Schriften*, p. 11.

18. On the more negative results of scriptural fixation in writing, see Robert Will, *Le culte. Étude d'histoire et de philosophie religieuses*, 3 vols. (Strasbourg and Paris, 1925–1935) 2: 363; Alfred Bertholet, "Schriften, heilige," *RGG*^{2} 5: 266; Friedrich Heiler, *Erscheinungsformen und Wesen der Religion* (1961; 2nd rev. ed., Stuttgart, etc.: W. Kohlhammer, 1979), pp. 354–357; Gustav Mensching, *Die Religion. Erscheinungsformen, Strukturtypen und Lebensgesetze* (Stuttgart: Curt E. Schwab, 1959), pp. 328–329.

19. See Morenz, *Ägyptische Religion*, pp. 224-243. Cf. Kerényi's observation

(*Apollon*, p. 161): "Ägypten ist ein positives Beispiel dafür, daß das Verhältnis einer Kultur zu ihrer schriftlichen Ausdrucksform für das Wesen der betreffenden Kultur bezeichnend ist."

20. Wm. Theodore de Bary *et al.*, comp., *Sources of Chinese Tradition* (New York: Columbia University Press, 1960), p. 6; Edwin O. Reischauer and John K. Fairbank, *East Asia: The Great Tradition* (Boston: Houghton Mifflin, 1958, 1960), p. 72; Y. Chu Wang, "Ideas and Men in Traditional China," *Monumenta Serica* 19 (1960): 213.

21. Wilfred Cantwell Smith's article in the present volume ("Scripture as Form and Content") makes a convincing argument for this. See also Leipoldt and Morenz, *Heilige Schriften*, pp. 41–52; Ernst Robert Curtius, *Europäische Literatur und Lateinisches Mittelalter* (1948; 2nd rev. ed., Bern: A. Franke, 1954), pp. 254–261.

22. On the fixing of a "canon" of Hebrew scripture, see Gunnar Östborn, *Cult and Canon: A Study in the Canonization of the Old Testament*, Uppsala Universitets Årsskrift, 1950, 10 (Uppsala: A.-B. Lundequistska; Leipzig: Otto Harrossowitz, 1950). On the "canonizing" of the Tripiṭaka, see André Bareau *et al.*, *Die Religionen Indiens III. Buddhismus-Jinismus-Primitivvölker* (Stuttgart: W. Kohlhammer, 1964), pp. 23–32 (further literature: p. 23, n. 1). Cf. A. K. Warder, *Indian Buddhism* (Delhi, Patna, Varanasi: Motilal Banarsidass, 1970), pp. 4–14.

23. *The Ascension of the Apostle and the Heavenly Book*, King and Saviour, 3, Uppsala Universitets Årsskrift, 1950, 7 (Uppsala: A.–B. Lundequistska; Leipzig: Otto Harrossowitz, 1950); *Muhammad, The Apostle of God, and His Ascension*, King and Saviour, 5, Uppsala Universitets Årsskrift, 1955, 1 (Uppsala: A–B. Lundequistska; Wiesbaden: Otto Harrossowitz, 1955); *Religionsphänomenologie* (Berlin: Walter de Gruyter, 1969), pp. 546–573.

24. *Religionsphänomenologie*, p. 566 [translation mine].

25. Koep, *Das himmlische Buch* (esp. pp. 1–2, 127–128); Curtius, *Europäische Literatur*, p. 315, n. 3; Mensching, *Das heilige Wort*, pp. 73–75.

26. Heiler, *Erscheinungsformen*, pp. 350–352; Mensching, *Das heilige Wort*, pp. 72–73; Leipoldt and Morenz, *Heilige Schriften*, pp. 29–36. Cf. the statement about the superhuman nature of the *Lotus Sūtra* by Nichiren cited in Masaharu Anesaki, *Nichiren. the Buddhist Prophet* (1916; repr. ed., Gloucester, Mass.: Peter Smith, 1966), p. 16.

27. Franz Dornseiff, *Das Alphabet in Mystik und Magie* (1922), 2nd ed. (Leipzig and Berlin: B. G. Teubner, 1925), p. 1; *JE* 3: 202–205 (*s.v.* "Bibliomancy"); *Handwörterbuch des deutschen Aberglaubens* 9: 379–381 (*s.v.* "Schreiben").

28. Bertholet, "Schriften," p. 264 [translation mine].

29. Gerardus van der Leeuw, *Religion in Essence and Manifestation*, trans. J.

E. Turner, with Appendices incorporating the Additions of the second German edition by Hans H. Penner (New York and Evanston: Harper & Row, 1963), pp. 435–436 (=p. 495 of German ed.: *Phänomenologie der Religion*, 2nd rev. ed. [Tübingen: J. C. B. Mohr (Paul Siebeck), 1956]).

30. See for example: Bertholet, "Macht der Schrift", pp. 18–32; *Encyclopaedia of Religion and Ethics*, 13 vols., ed. James Hastings. (Edinburgh: T. and T. Clark, 1908–1926) [hereafter *ERE*] 2:615b–618b, *s.v.* "Bibliolatry": (A. Dorner); *JE* 3: 202–205, *s.v.* "Bibliomancy" (M. Grunwald and Kaufmann Kohler).

31. *Europäische Literatur*, p. 307; cf. p. 323.

32. W. Owen Cole, and Piara Singh Sambhi, *The Sikhs: Their Religious Beliefs and Practices* (London, Henley, and Boston: Routledge & Kegan Paul, 1978), pp. 43ff., esp. 54–55; 58–66; 107; 112–135 *passim*. Cf. W. H. McLeod, "The Sikh Scriptures: Some Issues," in Mark Juergensmeyer and N. Gerald Barrier, eds., *Sikh Studies: Comparative Perspectives on a Changing Tradition* (Berkeley, Cal.: Graduate Theological Union, Berkeley Religious Studies Series, 1979), pp. 97–111.

33. Günter Lanczkowski, *Heilige Schriften. Inhalt, Textgestalt und Ueberlieferung* (Stuttgart: W. Kohlhammer, Urban Bücher, 1956), p. 124. A contemporary example of what Lanczkowski calls "ungeheure Verehrung" of the Tibetan canonical collections is the daily circumambulation of the Sūtra library in monastic compounds such as that of the exile community of Dharamsala, India (personal communication, M. David Eckel, November, 1983).

34. "The Phrase *'sa pṛthivīpradeśaś caityabhūto bhavet'* in the *Vajracheddikā*: Notes on the Cult of the Book in Early Mahāyāna," *Indo-Iranian Journal* 17 (1975): 147–181.

35. *ERE* 2:616b–617a ("Bibliolatry").

36. Anesaki, Nichiren, pp. 15ff., 80–86; Y. K. Dykstra, "Miraculous Tales of the Lotus Sūtra; *The Dainihonkoku Hokkegenki*," *Monumenta Nipponica* 32 (1977): 189–198 *passim*.

37. D. Gerhard Ebeling, "Wort Gottes und Hermeneutik," in *Wort und Glaube* (Tübingen: J. C. B. Mohr [Paul Siebeck], 1960), p. 327.

38. T. C. Skeat, "Early Christian Book Production: Papyri and Manuscripts": in *The Cambridge History of the Bible*, 3 vols. (Cambridge: The University Press, 1963–1970) [hereafter, *Camb. Hist. Bib.*] 2: 54–79.

39. Erich Bethe, *Buch und Bild im Altertum*, comp. and ed. posthumously by Ernst Kristen (Leipzig and Vienna: Otto Harrassowitz, 1945), p. 103.

40. On Manichaean books, see Hans-Joachim Klimkeit, "Vom Wesen manichäischer Kunst," *Zeitschrift für Religions- und Geistesgeschichte* 34 (1982): esp. pp. 201–204; *idem, Manichaean Art and Calligraphy*, Iconography of Religions 20 (Leiden: E. J. Brill, 1982), pp. 20–23. For fine examples of the magnificence of

qur'ānic manuscripts, see Martin Lings and Yasin Hamid Safadi, *The Qur'ān: Catalogue of an Exhibition of Qur'ān Manuscripts at the British Library, 3 April–5 August, 1976* (London: World of Islam, 1976). On Tibetan collections, see for example David Snellgrove and Hugh Richardson, *A Cultural History of Tibet* (Boulder, Colo.: Prajña, 1980), pp. 160, 170; Lanczkowski, *Heilige Schriften*, p. 124. For a recent example of the continuing Jewish emphasis on the special preparation of Torah scrolls: "A new Torah . . . an old Tradition, "*The Boston Globe* (May 3, 1982), pp. 13–14.

41. *Luthers Vorlesung über den Hebräerbrief nach der vatikanischen Handschrift*, Latin text ed. Emanuel Hirsch and Hanns Rückert (Berlin and Leipzig: Walter de Gruyter, 1929), p. 250; *Werke: Kritische Gesamtausgabe* (Weimar: Hermann Böhlau, 1883ff.) [hereafter *WA*] 37:512–513.

42. *WA* 10:625–627, *Passim*. Cf. Will, *Le culte* 2: 335, 365; Heinrich Karpp, "Die Function der Bibel in der Kirche,": pt. 4 of art. "Bibel," *Theologische Realenzyklopädie* (1977–) 6: 71, 73. The identity of the gospel "word" that is "heard" with scripture that is "heard" is by no means a straightforward issue in Luther or other reformers' usage. See further Graham, *Beyond the Written Word*, chapter 12.

43. *WA* 10.i.2: 74^{32}–75^{4}. "Es ist yhe nicht muglich eyn seele zu trosten, sie hore denn yhres gottis wortt. Wo is aber gottis wortt ynn allen buchernn außer der heyligen scrifft? . . . trosten mag keyn Buch, denn die heyligen schrifft."

44. For expample, Heiler, *Erscheinungsformen*, pp. 275, 277–279, 283–286; Mensching, *Das heilige Wort*, pp. 71–72; van der Leeuw, *Religion in Essence*, pp. 422–434 (=*Phänomenologie*, pp. 480–494); Robert H. Lowie, *Primitive Religion* (1924; New York: Liveright, 1948), pp. 321–329; Bronislaw Malinowski, "Myth in Primitive Psychology," in *Magic, Science and Religion and Other Essays* (1948; Garden City, N.Y.: Doubleday Anchor, 1954), pp. 93–148.

45. *Das heilige Wort*, p. 71.

46. Van der Leeuw, *Religion in Essence*, pp. 403–412 (=*Phänomenologie*, pp. 457–468); W. Brede Kristensen, *The Meaning of Religion: Lectures in the Phenomenology of Religion*, trans John B. Carman (The Hague: Martinus Nijhoff, 1960), pp. 224–226 (cf. pp. 86–87); Mensching, *Das heilige Wort*, pp. 112–117. Cf. Northrop Frye, *The Great Code: The Bible and Literature* (San Diego, New York, London: Harcourt Brace Jovanovitch, Harvest Books, 1983), p. 6.

47. On the unity of *legomenon* and *drōmenon*: Jane Ellen Harrison, *Themis: A Study of the Social Origins of Greek Religion* (1912; 2nd rev. ed. Repr. ed. London: Merlin Press, 1963), pp. 42–45, 328–331. On speech as act from a philosophical perspective: J. L. Austin, *How to do Things with Words* (Cambridge, Mass.: Harvard University Press, 1962).

48. Van der Leeuw, *Religion in Essence*, p. 405 (=*Phänomenologie*, p. 460).

49. Hermann Usener, *Götternamen. Versuch einer Lehre von der religiösen*

Begriffsbildung (Bonn: Friedrich Cohen, 1896), pp. 279–301; Ernst Cassirer, *Language and Myth*, trans. Susanne K. Langer (1946; New York: Dover, 1953), pp. 33–43.

50. Heiler, *Erscheinungsformen*, p. 276. Cf. Barbara Stoller Miller, ed. and trans., *Love Song of the Dark Lord: Jayadeva's "Gîtagovinda"* (New York: Columbia University Press, 1977), p. 18.

51. *Nambudiri Veda Recitation* (The Hague: Mouton, 1961), p. 16.

52. Morenz, *Ägyptische Religion*, pp. 172–174. The Memphite narrative is translated in John A. Wilson, trans., *The Ancient Near East: An Anthology of Texts and Pictures* (Princeton: Princeton University Press, 1958), pp. 1–2.

53. W. Norman Brown, *Man in the Universe: Some Continuities in Indian Thought* (1966; Berkeley, Los Angeles, London: University of California Press, 1970), p. 28; *idem*, "The Creative Role of the goddess Vāc in the Rig Veda," in *Pratidānam: Indian and Indo-European Studies Presented to Franciscus Bernardus Jacobus Kuiper on His Sixtieth Birthday*, ed. J. C. Heesterman *et al.* (The Hague and Paris: Mouton, 1968), pp. 393–397. See also Louis Renou, "Les pouvoirs de la parole dans le Ṛgveda," *Études védiques et pāṇinéennes* 1 (Paris: de Boccard, 1955): 1–27; Albrecht Weber, "Vâc und lógos," *Indische Studien* (Leipzig) 9 (1865): 473–480.

54. On the Witoto: Konrad Theodor Preuss, *Religion und Mythologie der Uitoto. Textaufnahmen und Beobachtungen bei einem Indianerstamm in Kolumbien, Südamerika* (Göttingen: Vandenhoeck & Ruprecht; Leipzig: J. C. Hinrichs, 1921-23), pp. 633–634. On the Dogon: Marcel Griaule, *Conversations with Ogotemmeli* (Oxford: Oxford University Press, 1975), pp. 16–40 (reprinted in Barbara C. Sproul, ed., *Primal Myths: Creating the World* [San Francisco: Harper & Row, 1979], pp. 49-66).

55. Concerning Torah: Leipoldt and Morenz, *Heilige Schriften*, p. 25; a detailed survey of the idea of Torah as primordial wisdom and the instrument of creation, summed up in the rabbinic dictum, "The Torah is from Heaven" (*Torah min ha-shamayîm*), is given by Barbara A. Holdredge in her article in the present volume, "The Bride of Israel: The Ontological Status of Torah in the Rabbinic and Kabbalistic Traditions" pp. 180ff. Concerning the Qur'ān, see the credal statements of the *Waṣîyat Abî Ḥanîfah* (art. 9) and the *Fiqh Akbar II* (art. 3), trans. in A. J. Wensinck, *The Muslim Creed: Its Genesis and Historical Development* (London: Frank Cass, 1932), pp. 127, 189. Cf. Harry Austryn Wolfson, *The Philosophy of the Kalam* (Cambridge, MA and London: Harvard University Press, 1976), pp. 235–244; cf. pp. 244-303.

56. This can be seen in the Buddhist case in the shift from the more literal understanding of the Buddha-Word (*buddhavacanam*) as transmitted in the Pali "canonical" texts of the Tripiṭaka (but cf. George D. Bond, "Two Theravada Traditions of the Meaning of 'the Word of the Buddha'," *The Maha Bodhi* 83 [1975]: 402-423) to the Mahāyāna notion of the cosmic teaching of the eternal Buddha. Cf. the Buddha's statements in ch. 16 of the *Lotus Sūtra* (*Scripture of the Lotus*

Blossom of the Fine Dharma, trans. from the Chinese of Kumārajīva by Leon Hurvitz [New York: Columbia University Press, 1976], pp. 237-244). See also Sukumar Dutt, *Buddhist Monks and Monasteries of India: Their History and their Contribution to Indian Culture* (London: Allen and Unwin, 1962), pp. 261-264. Concerning the Veda's eternal character, see below, p. 138, and Graham, *Beyond the Written Word*, chapter 6.

57. *Ascension of the Apostle*, pp. 45, 59-62; *Muhammad the Apostle*, p. 129.

58. Heiler, *Erscheinungsformen*, p. 281.

59. On "hearing much," see Arthur Waley, "Introduction" to *The Analects of Confucius*, trans. and annotated by Arthur Waley (1938; New York: Random House, Vinage Books, n.d.), p. 51. Cf. the remarks of William G. Boltz, "The Religious and Philosophical Significance of the 'Hsiang erh' *Lao Tzu* in the Light of the *Ma-wang-tui* Silk Manuscripts," *Bulletin of the School of Oriental and African Studies* (London) 45: 101-102, n. 17.

60. Leipoldt and Morenz, *Heilige Schriften*, pp. 15-17.; Mensching, *Die Religion*, p. 327; Heiler, *Erscheinungsformen*, pp. 298, 351-352; F. Max Müller, ed., *The Sacred Books of the East*, vol. 1 (Oxford: Clarendon Press, 1879), p. xiii. Cf. Ong, *Orality and Literacy*, pp. 96-101 (drawing heavily upon M. T. Clanchy, *From Memory to Written Record: England, 1066–1307* [Cambridge, MA: Harvard University Press, 1979], esp. pp. 230-241).

61. Basil Hall, "Biblical Scholarship: Editions and Commentaries," in *Camb. Hist. Bib.* 3:39.

62. J. F. Staal, *Nambudiri Recitation*, p. 15. This point, and the following discussion of the Indian case is amplified and extended in chapter 6 of W. Graham, *Beyond the Written Word*. Cf. T. W. Rhys-Davids, *Buddhist India* (1903; repr. ed., Calcutta: Susil Gupta, 1957), p. 119, on the possibility that Buddhists were the first to make use of writing in India. Our earliest writen sources in India, other than the undeciphered Indus seals of the second millennium B.C., are the inscriptions of the great Buddhist Mauryan King Aśoka (reg. ca. 269-ca. 232 B.C.): see, for example, Romila Thapar, *A History of India*, vol. 1 (Baltimore: Penguin, 1966), pp. 72–74; A. L. Basham, *The Wonder That Was India: A Study of the History and Culture of the Indian Sub-Continent before the Coming of the Muslims* (1954; 2nd rev. ed., New York: Hawthorn Books, 1963), p. 396. Basham (*ibid.*, pp. 396–398) believes that by Aśoka's time the Brāhmī script had already had years, perhaps centuries of prior development. D. D. Kosambi, *Ancient India: A History of Its Culture and Civilization* (New York: Random House, 1966), p. 88, argues for a date of 700 A.D. as a *terminus post quem* for the introduction of writing from Mesopotamia to India.

63. Georg Bühler, *Indische Palaeographie von circa 350 a. Chr.–circa 1300 p. Chr.*, Gundriß der Indo-Arischen Philologie und Altertumskunde, ed. G. Bühler, vol. 1, no. 2 (Strasbourg: Karl J. Trübner, 1896), pp. 3–4; Moriz Winternitz, *Geschichte der indischen Litteratur*, 2nd ed., 3 vols. (Leipzig: C. F. Amelangs,

1905–1920) 1:31 (=1:33-34 of Eng. trans., *A History of Indian Literature*, trans. "Mrs. S. Ketkar," vols. 1, 2 [1927; New Delhi: Oriental Books Reprint Corp., 1972]); Louis Renou, *Le destin du Veda dans l'lnde*, Études védiques et pāṇinéennes, vol. 6 (Paris; de Boccard, 1960), pp. 37–39; Louis Renou, Jean Filliozat, *et al.*, *L'inde classique. Manuel des études indiennes*, 2 vols. (Paris: Payot, 1947 [vol. 1]; Imprimerie Nationale, 1953 [vol. 2]) 1: 270–271; J. A. B. van Buitenen, "Hindu Sacred Literature," *Encyclopaedia Britannica* (15th ed., 1974) (hereafter, *EB III*), Macropaedia 8: 933b; Jan Gonda, *Die Religionen Indiens*, 2 vols. (Stuttgart: W. Kohlhammer, 1960-63) 1:9, 21-26.

64. J. G. Staal, *Nambudiri Recitation*, pp. 11–17; Walter Eidlitz, *Der Glaube und die heiligen Schriften der Inder* (Olten and Freiburg: Walter, 1957), pp. 7-29; Thomas B. Coburn, "'Scripture' in India: Towards a Typology of the Word in Hindu Life," in the present volume.

65. Jan C. Heestermann, "Die Autorität des Veda," in Gerhard Oberhammer, ed., *Offenbarung. Geistige Realität des Menschen* (Vienna: [Indologisches Institut der Universität Wien], 1974), p. 31; Staal, *Nambudiri Recitation*, p. 11. See also Graham, *Beyond the Written Word*, chapter 6, n. 9.

66. "'Scripture' in India," in the present volume.

67. Cited in Heiler, *Ercheinungsformen*, p. 333. Cf. the statement of the *Aitareya Āraṇyaka*: "'As far as *brahman* extends so far does Vāc,' wherever there is *brahman*, there is Vāc, wherever Vāc, there is *brahman*, is what is meant" (*The Aitareya Āraṇyaka*, ed. and trans Arthur Berridale Keith (1909; repr. ed., Oxford: Clarendon Press, 1969), p. 186. See also p. 163, n. 8, for further references to similar statements in other texts. Cf. Paul Thieme, "Brahman," *ZDMG*, n.s. 102 (1952): 91–129.

68. "*Ékam sát*", cited by Brown, "Creative Role of Vāc," p. 393.

69. Eidlitz, p. 12.

70. Frits [J. F.] Staal, "The Concept of Scripture in the Indian Tradition," in *Sikh Studies: Comparative Perspectives on a Changing Tradition*, ed. Mark Juergensmeyer and N. Gerald Barrier, eds. (Berkeley: Graduate Theological Union, Berkeley Religious Studies, 1979), pp.121–122; Wayne Howard, *Sāmavedic Chant* (New Haven and London: Yale University Press, 1977), pp. 2-8.

71. Theodore Zachariae, review of W. Caland, *De Ontdekkingsgescheidenis van den Veda* (Amsterdam, 1918), in *Göttingische gelehrte Anzeigen* 183 (1921): 148-165. Cf. Leipoldt and Morenz, *Heilige Schriften*, p. 13.

72. 5.5.3 (Keith trans., pp. 301–302).

73. *Geschichte* 1:31 (=Eng. trans. 1:33). Winternitz's term is "merkwürdig."

74. J. A. B. van Buitenen, "Hindu Sacred Scriptures," pp. 933, 940b; *idem.*

"On the Archaism of the Bhāgavata Purāṇa," in *Krishna: Myths, Rites, and Attitudes*. ed. Milton Singer (Chicago and London: University of Chicago Press, 1966), p. 24.

75. J. A. B. van Buitenen, "Hindu Sacred Literature," p. 933b.

76. *Ibid.*

77. See Thomas B. Coburn, "'Scripture' in India."

78. This despite the telling observations of Coburn, *ibid.*, concerning the misleading use of "scripture" (in its usual meaning) to apply to many or most Indian texts.

79. On the unicity of scripture, see Siegfried Morenz, "Schriften, heilige," *RGG*^{3} 5: 1538; Leipoldt and Morenz, pp. 37–52.

80. On this point, see my article, "Qur'ān as Spoken Word" (above, n. 2), esp. part I, "Scripture as a Generic Category."

81. "Entstehung und Wesen der Buchreligion," *Theologische Literaturezeitung* 75 (1950): 709–716. Cf. Morenz, *Ägyptische Religion*, pp. 224–225.

82. On the emphasis upon the written text of the Bible in Jewish and Christian textual scholarship, see, for example, the articles "Bible," *EJ* 4: 814-969; "Bible Canon," *Jewish Encyclopedia* (New York and London, 1901–1906) 3: 140–154; "Bible," *CE* 2: 543–544; "Scripture," *CE* 13:635ff., esp. 635–637; "Canon of the Old Testament," *HDB*, pp. 121–123; "Canon of the New Testament," *HDB*, pp. 123–127; "Bibel" ("IB. "Sammlung und Kanonisierung des AT"; "IIB. "Sammlung und Kanonisierung des NT"), *RGG*^{3} 1:1123–1126, 1131–1138. Much of this focus results from the acute awareness in modern scholarship of the book/tradition dichotomy in Christian thought and the written Torah/oral Torah dichotomy in Judaic thought. Cf. H. Bacht [misspelled on title page as "H. Bracht"], H. Fries, and R. J. Geiselmann, *Die mündliche Überlieferung. Beiträge zum Begriff der Tradition*, edd. Michael Schmaus (Munich: Max Hueber, 1957); Birger Gerhardsson, *Memory and Manuscript: Oral Tradition and Written Transmission in Rabbinic Judaism and Early Christianity* (Uppsala and Lund: C. W. K. Gleerup; Copenhagen: E. Munksgaard, 1961). The almost exclusive focus of modern qur'ānic scholarship on the written text can be seen in virtually any monographic study in the field, with the notable exceptions of Kristina Nelson, *The Art of Reciting the Qur'ān* (Austin: University of Texas Press, 1985), and Angelika Neuwirth, *Studien zur Komposition der mekkanischen Suren* (Berlin and New York: W. de Gruyter, 1981). Cf., for example, the standard English work of Richard Bell, *Introduction to the Qur'ān* (Edinburgh, 1953; rev. ed., *Bell's Introduction to the Qur'ān, Completely Revised and Enlarged by W. Montgomery Watt*. Edinburgh: The University Press, 1970); or the article "Al-Ḳur'ān," by A. T. Welch, in the *Encyclopaedia of Islam. New Edition* (fascicles from 1954) 5:400–428, in which only the final short section on "The Ḳur'ān in Muslim Life and Thought" gives any attention to the oral character of the text. Chapters 7-9 of Graham, *Beyond the Written*

Word, are devoted to rectifying this imbalance of emphasis on the written and recited Qur'ān.

83. In both cases there is considerable emphasis placed upon printed text editions not only of Vedas or Qur'ān, but of countless ancillary works related to these and other sacred texts in the two traditions (e.g., Purāṇas, Ḥadīth). For all the salutary results of such emphasis, it does represent a significant change over only one hundred and fifty years ago in the availability and role of such texts in scholarly as well as everyday contexts, with corresponding effects upon attitudes towards these texts. Cf. Helmuth von Glasenapp, *Religiöse Reformbewegungen im heutigen Indien* (Leipzig: J. C. Hinrichs, 1928), p. V. Cf. also G. Bergsträsser, "Koranlesung in Kairo," *Der Islam* 20 (1932), esp. pp. 2–13 (on the first official printed edition of the Qur'ān text).

84. G. S. Brett, *Psychology Ancient and Modern* (London: Longmans, 1928), pp. 36-37, as cited in McLuhan, *Gutenberg Galaxy*, p. 74.

85. H. J. Chaytor, *From Script to Print: An Introduction to Medieval Vernacular Literature* (Cambridge: W. Heffer, 1945), p. 6.

86. Havelock, *Literate Revolution*, p. 50. Cf. Ong, *Orality and Literacy*, p. 8: "Written texts all have to be related somehow, directly or indirectly, to the world of sound, the natural habitat of language, to yield their meanings. Reading a text means converting it to sound. . . . Writing can never dispense with orality."

87. Ong, *Ibid.*, p. 10.

88. *Language and Silence: Essays on Language, Literature, and the Inhuman* (New York: Atheneum, 1982), pp. 18, 19.

89. *Cultural Foundations of Industrial Civilization*(Cambridge: The University Press, 1958), pp. 6–17.

90. *Man: His First Million Years* (1957; New York: New American Library, Mentor Books, 1958), p. 150. Also cited in McLuhan, *Gutenberg Galaxy*, p. 76.

91. Ong, *Presence of the Word*, p. 114. Cf. his statement in *Orality and Literacy*, p. 118: "Print suggests that words are things far more than writing ever did." Cf. also Carothers, "Culture and the Written Word," p. 311: "When words are written . . . , they become static things and lose, as such, the dynamism which is so characteristic of the auditory world in general, and of the spoken word in particular."

92. Josef Balogh, "'Voces paginarum.' Beiträge zur Geschichte des lauten Lesens und Schreibens," *Philologus* 82 (1926–1927): 237–238; Ong, *Orality and Literacy*, pp. 108–112. On rhetoric, see T. O. Sloan and C[haim] Perelman, "Rhetoric," *EBIII*, Macropaedia, 15: 789b–805b: George A. Kennedy, *Classical Rhetoric and Its Christian and Secular Tradition from Ancient to Modern Times* (Chapel Hill: University of North Carolina Press, 1980), esp. pp. 220–246.

93. David Reisman, "The Oral and Written Traditions," *Explorations: Stud-*

ies in Culture 6 (1956): 25; Walter J. Ong, "Ramist Method and the Commercial Mind," *Studies in the Renaissance* 8 (1961): 167; McLuhan, *Gutenberg Galaxy*, pp. 124–125.

94. This is not to deny the legitimate distinctions that have received so much attention in recent years between oral traditional culture and chirographic culture. Cf. Jack Goody, ed., *Literacy in Traditional Societies* (Cambridge: The University Press, 1968); Jan Vansina, *Oral Tradition: A Study in Historical Methodology*, trans. H. M. Wright [French orig. ed.: *De la tradition orale: Essai de methode historique*, 1961] (Chicago: Aldine, 1965); Ruth Finnegan, *Oral Literature in Africa* (Oxford: Clarendon Press, 1970); *idem*, *Oral Poetry: Its Nature, Significance and Social Context* (Cambridge, London, etc.: Cambridge University Press, 1977).

95. See Ong, *Orality and Literacy*, esp. pp. 117-138, 157-179; Carothers, "Culture and the Written Word," esp. p. 310; Chaytor, *From Script to Print*. esp. pp. 7-8 (including important citation from A. Lloyd James, *Our Spoken Language* [London, 1938], p. 29).

96. Chaytor, *From Script to Print*; Carothers, "Culture, Psychiatry, and the Written Word"; Ong, (esp.) *The Presence of the Word* and *Orality and Literacy*; McLuhan, *The Gutenberg Galaxy*; Eisenstein, *The Printing Press as an Agent of Change: Communications and Cultural Transformations in Early-Modern Europe*, 2 vols. (1979; One-vol. repr., Cambridge, London etc.: Cambridge University Press, 1980); *idem*. "The Advent of Printing and the Protestant Revolt: A New Approach to the Disruption of Western Christendom," in *Transition and Revolution: Problems and Issues of European Renaissance and Reformation History*, ed. Robert M. Kingdon (Minneapolis: Burgess, 1974), pp. 235-270 (offers essentiallly a resume of her book's arguments).

97. Eisenstein, *Printing Press*, p. 698.

98. Kenyon, *Books and Readers*, pp. 24-25; Moses Hadas, *Ancilla to Classical Reading* (1954; New York: Columbia University Press, 1961), pp. 21-22 (quoting the *locus classicus* on the subject, Strabo 13.1.54); Goody and Watt, "Consequences of Literacy," p. 55; Havelock, *Literate Revolution*, p. 11.

99. McLuhan, *Gutenberg Galaxy*, pp. 21, 90.

100. Havelock, *Literate Revolution*, p. 9.

101. *Ibid*., p. 29 (cf. pp. 39–59); Finnegan, *Oral Poetry*, p. 166; Hadas, *Ancilla*, pp. 50-59; Kenyon, *Books and Readers*, pp. 20–21.

102. Ruth Crosby, "Oral Delivery in the Middle Ages," *Speculum* 11 (1936): 88-110. Cf. Chaytor, *From Script to Print*, esp. pp. 10-13.

103. My trans. from the German trans. of the original by Emma Brunner-Traut, in "Die Weisheitslehre des Djedef-Hor,"*Zeitschrift für Ägytische Sprache und Altertumskunde* 76 (1940): 8.

104. Ruth Finnegan, *Oral Poetry*, p. 29. Cf. Balogh, "'Voces paginarum'," pp. 84–87.

105. Ong, *Orality and Literacy*, p. 8.

106. Havelock, *Literate Revolution*, p. 50.

107. Nietzsche, *Werke* (Leipzig: Kröner, 1912) 8: 248, as cited in Balogh, "'Voces paginarum'," p. 231. Nietzsche remarks here "daß die eigentliche Prosa des Altertums durchaus Widerhall der lauten Rede ist und an deren Gesetzen sich gebildet hat; während unsere Prosa immer mehr aus dem Schreiben zu erklären ist . . ."; Norden, *Die antike Kunstprosa vom VI. Jahrhundert v. Chr. bis in die Zeit der Renaissance* (Leipzig, [1898?]; 5th ed., 1 vol. in 2 pts. (continuous pagination), Darmstadt: Wissenschaftliche Buchgesellschaft, 1958), p. 6.

108. *The Confessions of Saint Augustine*, trans. Edward B. Pusey (New York: Random House, Modern Library, 1949), p. 98; Latin orig.: 2nd ed., ed. J. Gibb and W. Montgomery (Cambridge: The University Press, 1927), p. 141[10-11].

109. "'Voces paginarum'," pp. 237–238 (above, n. 92).

110. *From Script to Print*, p. 14.

111. "Voces paginarum", pp. 237-238. Cf. n. 92 above.

112. "Tres digiti scribunt, duo oculi vident. Una lingua loquitur. totum corpus laborat. . . ." W. Wattenbach, *das Schriftwesen im Mittelalter* (1871; 4th ed., Graz: Akademische Druck- und Verlagsanstalt, 1958 [photogr. repr. of 3rd rev. ed., Leipzig: S. Hirzel, 1896]), p. 495. Also cited in Chaytor, *From Script to Print*, p. 14, n. 1.

113. Norden, *Kunstprosa*, p. 6. Balogh's entire study, "'Voces paginarum'," is an attempt to ferret out as many such examples as possible.

114. "'Voces Paginarum'," pp. 234–236. See also Graham, *Beyond the Written Word*, chapter 3.

115. Marshall McLuhan, "The Effect of the Printed Book on Language in the 16th Century," in Edmund Carpenter and Marshall McLuhan, eds., *Explorations in Communication: An Anthology* (Boston: Beacon, 1960), pp. 125–135; Chaytor, *From Script to Print*, esp. pp. 6–8; Balogh, "Voces paginarum," pp. 237–238; Ong, *Orality and Literacy*, p. 118; McLuhan, *Gutenberg Galaxy*, pp. 124–125, 141; Carothers, "Culture and the Written Word," p. 310.

116. McLuhan, *Gutenberg Galaxy*, p. 250.

117. *The Age of Reform 1250–1550: An Intellectual and Religious History of Late Medieval and Reformation Europe* (New Haven and London: Yale University Press, 1980), p. 204.

118. McLuhan, *Gutenberg Galaxy*, p. 84.

119. Ong, *Presence of the Word*, pp. 63, 64, 71–72.

120. Schiller's lines read: "Körper and Stimme leiht die Schrift / dem

stummen Gedanken; / Durch der Jahrhunderte Strom trägt / ihn das redende Blatt" (cited in Jensen, *Die Schrift*, p. 2). Adam Müller has the following to say in his *Zwölf Reden über die Beredsamkeit und deren Verfall in Deutschland* ([1816?]; Frankfort/M.: Insel, 1967), p. 69: "Nachdem die Rede aus dem Gebiet des Ohrs in das Gebiet des lesenden Auges, nachdem sie aus dem Gebiete der Stimme in den Wirkungskreis der schreibenden Hände einmal höchst unnatürlicherweise versetzt worden, so erstirbt sie nun auch, schrumpft zusammen, vertrocknet mehr und mehr: Das Wort schwindet ineinander und wird mehr und mehr zur Zahl."

121. See the references given in n. 82 above. For a history of biblical studies in the modern West, see Hans-Joachim Kraus, *Geschichte der historisch-kritischen Erforschung des Alten Testaments* (2nd ed., Zurich: Neukirchener Verlag, 1969); Werner Georg Kümmel, *Das Neue Testament. Geschichte der Erforschung seiner Probleme* (Freiburg and Munich: Karl Alber, 1958). Shorter summaries are available in the following *RGG*[3] articles: "Bibelkritik: AT" (F. Baumgärtel), 1: 1184–1188; "Bibelkritik: NT" (E. Dinkler), 1: 1188–1190; "Bibelwissenschaft des AT" (C. Kuhl), 1: 1227-1236; "Bibelwissenschaft: NT" (W. G. Kümmel), 1: 1236-1251. A survey of modern scholarship on other scriptural texts of the world is harder to find, but some impression can be gained by referring to Jacques Waardenburg, *Classical Approaches to the Study of Religion: Aims, Methods and Theories of Research*, vol. 1 or 2 (The Hague and Paris: Mouton, 1973); Eric Sharpe, *Comparative Religion: A History* (New York: Scribner's, 1975). Cf. Charles J. Adams, ed., *A Reader's Guide to the Great Religions* (1965; 2nd ed., New York: Macmillan; London: Collier Macmillan, 1977).

122. For a much more extensive consideration of the oral dimensions of the Christian Bible, see Graham, *Beyond the Written Word*, chapters 10–12.

123. Curtius, *Europäische Literatur*, p. 263. Cf. his comment on p. 314 also: "Seine höchste Weihe wurde dem Buch durch das Christentum zuteil. Es war eine Religion des heiligen Buches. Christus ist der einzige Gott, den uns die antike Kunst mit einer Buchrolle darstellt." See also Leipoldt and Morenz, *Heilige Schriften*, p. 118.

124. Ong, *Presence of the Word*, p. 14. For somewhat more sober documentation of Christian zeal for books, see T. C. Skeat, "Early Christian Book Production," *Camb. Hist. Bib.* 2: 512–513. Cf. Adolf von Harnack, *Über den privaten Gebrauch der heiligen Schriften in der alten Kirche* (Leipzig: J. C. Hinrichs, 1912), pp. 33–37; Leipoldt and Morenz, *Heilige Schriften*, pp. 115–122.

125. Norden, *Kunstprosa*, p. 538, speaks of Paul's letters as for the most part nothing but "ein notwendiger Ersatz für die mündliche Rede." On scripture reading in the early Church liturgy, see Leipoldt and Morenz, *Heilige Schriften*, pp. 106–114; W. O. E. Oesterley, *The Jewish Background of the Christian Liturgy* (1925. Repr. ed. Gloucester, Mass.: Peter Smith, 1956), p. 111–112; Paul Glaue, *Die Vorlesung heiliger Schriften im Gottesdienste. I. Teil. Bis zur Entstehung der altkatholischen Kirche* (Berlin: Alexander Duncker, 1907). Note that Glaue's

emphasis on the importance of the lection from the Jewish scriptures in the early Christian community has been contested by Walter Bauer, *Der Wortgottesdienst der ältesten Christen* (Tübingen: J. C. B. Mohr [Paul Siebeck], 1930), pp. 39–48, but Bauer does not deny the importance of these scriptures for the earliest community nor apparently the possible later influence of Torah-reading on Christian worship (after ca. A.D. 100–150).

126. Carl Andresen, *Die Kirchen der alten Christenheit* (Stuttgart: W. Kohlhammer, 1971), p. 209. Adolf von Harnack, *Die Quellen der sogenannten apostolischen Kirchenordnung nebst einer Untersuchung über den Ursprung des Lectorats und der anderen niederen Weihen* (Leipzig: J. C. Hinrichs, 1886), pp. 57–103. Cf. 2 Clement 19.1.

127. E. von Dobschütz, "Bible in the Church," *ERE* 2: 601, citing Justin Martyr (*sc. Apology* 67.3) in about A.D. 150; cf. p. 602 also. See Glaue, *Vorlesung heiliger Schriften*, pp. 62–71. Cf. *2 Clement* 2.4.

128. Egeria, *Diary of a Pilgrimage*, trans. George E. Gingras (New York and Paramus, N. J.: Newman Press, 1970), chapters 24, 25; Eric P. Werner, *The Sacred Bridge: Liturgical Parallels in Synagogue and Early Church* (New York: Schocken, 1970), pp. 129–133; Dobschütz, "Bible in the Church," p. 605; J. A. Lamb, "The Place of the Bible in the Liturgy," *Camb. Hist. Bib.* 1: 568–570; Oesterley, *Jewish Background*, pp. 148–149. This practice was to become most important in Christian monasticism, where the memorizing of the psalms was a prerequisite for participation in the life of the early as well as later orders. See my discussion of the Pachomian monastics in particular in *Beyond the Written Word*, chapter 11.

129. Dobschütz, "Bible in the Church," p. 603; James Stalker, "Preaching (Christian),: *ERE* 10: 215a; Lamb, "Place of the Bible," pp. 568–570, with many primary-source references.

130. Friedrich Heiler, *Die Ostkirchen*, rev. ed. of *Urkirche und Ostkirche* by Anne Marie Heiler, with Hans Hartog (Munich and Basel: Ernst Reinhardt, 1971), pp. 197, 199–204, 213; Andresen, *Kirchen der alten Christenheit*, pp. 237–240 (cf. p. 660); V. Schultze, "Evangelarium," *New Schaff-Herzog Encyclopedia of Religious Knowledge* (Grand Rapids, Mich., 1952) 4: 220–221; J. Pascher, "Brevier," *Lexikon für Theologie und Kirche* (2nd rev. ed.) 2: 679–684.

131. Leipoldt and Morenz, *Heilige Schriften*, p. 120. In an age of low lay literacy, such memorization was a virtual necessity. See M. L. W. Laistner, *Christianity and Pagan Culture in the Later Roman Empire* (Ithaca, N. Y., and London: Cornell University Press, 1951. Repr. ed. 1978), pp. 9, 29.

132. *In Isaiam*, prol. 1 (=*PL* 24: 17).

133. ". . . quam erat omnium sensibus memoriaeque inveteratum, et tot aetatum successionibus decantatum" (Letter 71, in [U]PL 33: 242–243. Cited in W. Schwarz, *Principles and Problems of Biblical Translation: Some Reformation Controversies and Their Background* [Cambridge: The University Press, 1955], p. 38).

134. "Et ego legere volo. Plus enim me delectat hujus verbi esse lectorem, quam verbi mei disputatorem," Sermon 355, 1, in *PL* 39: 1574; cited by Denys Gorce, *La lectio divina des orgines du cénobitisme à Saint Benoit et Cassiodore. I: Saint Jérôme et la lecture sacrée dans le milieu ascétique romain* (Wépion, Belgium: Monastère du Mont-Vierge, and Paris: Auguste Picard, 1925), p. x.

135. Liepoldt and Morenz, *Heilige Schriften*, p. 53, n. 1 (Citing Adolf von Harnack). Ambrose speaks, for example, explicitly of reading scripture as listening to Christ speak (*De officiis ministrorum* 1.20.88 [ed. Georg Krabinger, Tübingen, 1857, p. 62].

136. Jean-Claude Guy, "Le monachisme," subsection of art. "Écriture sainte et vie spirituelle," *Dictionnaire de spiritualité, ascetique et mystique, doctrine et histoire* (Paris, 1932ff.) 4: 163. Guy speaks in another passage (p. 160) of "sacrorum lectionem meditationemque librorum" as one of the basic practices of the first monks, who "se relayaient de jour et de nuit dans le chant des psaumes et la récitation des Écritures." On *meditatio* and its oral character, see Heinrich Bacht, "'Meditatio' in den ältesten Mönchsquellen," *Geist und Leben* 28 (1955): 360–373; Adalbert de Vogüe, "Les deux fonctions de la méditation dans les Régles monastiques anciennes," *Revue d'histoire de la spiritualité* 51 (1975): 3-16. Cf. Jean Leclercq, François Vandenbroucke, and Louis Bouyer, *La spritualité au moyen âge* (Paris: Aubier, 1961), p. 113: "La méditation est l'effort par lequel on fixe dans la memoire, en les répétant, les paroles sacrées." On *lectio divina*, see Gorce, *Lectio divina*. Cf. Corbinian Gindele, "Die Schriftlesung im Pachomiuskloster," *Erbe und Auftrag* 41 (1965): 114–122.

137. Cited by Heinrich Bacht, *Das Vermächtnis des Ursprungs. Studien zum frühen Mönchtum 1* (Würzburg: Echter, 1972), pp. 202–203 [trans. mine].

138. According to Beryl Smalley's description of the goals of Cassian's monastic discipline: *The Study of the Bible in the Middle Ages*, 2nd ed. (Oxford: Basil Blackwell, 1952), p. 28.

139. Jean Leclercq, *L'amour des lettres et le désir de Dieu* (Paris: Éditions du Cerf, 1957), pp. 20–23 (Eng. trans. by Catherine Misrahi, *The Love of Learning and the Desire for God* (New York: New American Library, 1962), pp. 23–26). Gorce, *Lectio divina* Cf. also references in n. 136 above.

140. See, for example, Denys Gorce, *Lectio divina*, pp. xvi–xxix, 63–80. Cf. Jean-Marie Leroux, "Monachisme et communauté d'après Saint Jean Chrysostome," in *Théologie de la vie monastique. Études sur la tradition patristique* (Paris: Aubier, 1961), p. 156; Jean Leclercq, "La lecture divine," *La Maison-Dieu* (1946), no. 1, pp. 21–22; Claude Peifer, "The Biblical Foundations of Monasticism," *Cistercian Studies* 1 (1966): 7--31. See also James McMurray, "The Scriptures and Monastic Prayer," *Cistercian Studies* 2 (1967): 15–37.

141. Cited by J. de Ghellinck, "Pagina et 'Sacra Pagina'. Histoire d'un mot et transformation de l'objet primitivement désigné," in *Mélanges Auguste Pelzer* (Louvain: Bibliothèque de l'Université, 1947), p. 33.

142. Friedrich Heiler, *Katholischer und evangelischer Gottesdienst*, 2nd rev. ed. (Munich: Ernst Reinhardt, 1925), p. 43.

143. My trans. from Wilhelm Walther, *Luthers Deutsche Bibel. Festschrift zur Jahrhundertfeier der Reformation* (Berlin: Ernst Siegried Mittler, 1917), p. 188.

144. Cf. Gerhard Ebeling's Statement: "Unsern Vorvätern war die Bibel Sprachheimat, wenn auch mit wechselnder Intensität und strittigem Verständnis; und deshalb war Gott gewissermassen Sprachzentrum..." (*Gott und Wort* (Tübingen: J. C. B. Mohr [Paul Siebeck], 1966), p. 13).

145. *WA* 16:41$^{18-21}$ "Denn ich hab es zuvor offt gesagt und sag es noch, das es ein theuer und köstlich ding ist, wenn man Gottes Wort höret, Und man solt alle Land durchlauffen, das man wirdig sein möchte, einen buchstaben von Gottes wort zu hören...."

146. Evidenced in such asides as: "Then I ran through the scriptures as I had them in memory" ("Discurrebam diende per scripturas, ut habebat memoria": *WA* 54: 186$^{10-11}$). Luther's Augustinian mentor Staupitz wrote himself concerning the importance of memorizing scripture for the novice monk: "Der Novize soll die Heilige Schriften begierig lesen, ändächtig hören, und eifrig lernen" (cited in K. Thimme, *Luthers Stellung zur Heiligen Schrift* [Gütersloh: Bertelsmann, 1903], p. 7). On Luther's knowledge of Hebrew, Greek, German, and Latin, see Wilhelm Walther, *Luthers deutsche Bibel*, pp. 39–54.

147. *WA* 40.ii: 409$^{23-26}$.

148. *WA* 50: 659$^{22-25}$: Nicht allein im hertzen, sondern auch eusserlich die mündliche redde und buchstabische wort im Buch imer treiben und reiben, lesen und widerlesen, mit vleissigem auffmercken und nachdencken, was der heilige Geist damit meinet." Cf. *WA* 32:64^{24}–65^{6}.

149. *WA* 30.i: 146: "... auch sol gelernet und behalten werden."

150. Cf. the statement of Hans Rückert: "Luther versteht unter dem Wort Gottes immer die viva vox evangelii, das lebendig in der Kirche verkündigte Wort, so daß damit die Geschichte dieser Kirche mit umgriffen ist als das Element, in dem Verkündigung und Weitergabe erfolgen" (as quoted by R. J. Geiselmann, "Das Konzil von Trient über das Verhältnis der Heiligen Schrift und der nicht geschriebenen Traditionen," in Bacht, Fries, and Geiselmann, *Die mündliche Uberlieferung*, p. 126.

151. *WA* 18: 136^{21}.

152. *WA* 12: 259^{10}. "Euangelion ist eygentlich nicht das, das ynn büchern stehet und ynn buchstaben verfasset wirtt, sondern mehr eyn mundliche predig und lebendig wortt, und eyn stym, die da ynn die gantz wellt ereschallet und

offentlich wirt aussgeschryen." Cited by Paul Schempp, *Luthers Stellung zur Heiligen Schrift* (Munich: Chr. Kaiser, 1929), pp. 33–34.

153. *WA* 7: 97[2-3]. "... nusquam praesentius et vivacius quam in ipsis sacris suis, quas scripsit, literis inveniri potest."

6

The 'Canons' of 'Scripture'

Kendall W. Folkert

The purpose of this essay is to introduce a typology of scriptural material that will serve two purposes: (1) the proper framing of such material within the study of different major religious traditions; (2) the illumination of our own scriptural heritage in such a way as to enable serious reflection on the way Christian scripture is studied and taught within the study of religion.

This typology will be illustrated by reference both to a specific non-Christian scriptural case, namely, the Jain tradition, and to several interpretive contexts in the Christian use of the Bible. The basic thesis of the article is that at least two major categories of scripture must be delineated, both in study and in teaching, both in Christian and non-Christian religious history; and that such a delineation can clarify and possibly transform the way in which the study of religion approaches scriptural materials.

THE OVERALL SCOPE OF THE PROBLEM

The study of religion has assumed—to an extraordinary degree—and omitted to reflect upon—to an equally extraordinary degree—the general presence in religious traditions of bodies of scripture, that is, normative, in some sense 'inspired,' in some sense 'sacred' literature. A significant measure of both the breadth of the assumption and the absence of probing analysis can be found by examining a major product of scholarship in this area: the massive *Sacred Books of the East* series, published from the mid-1800s onward, in the heyday of scholarly 'discovery' of non-Christian traditions. The very title of the series (including its reference to the "East") is an index of the problem that wants addressing: the widespread use of a general notion of sacred book, and the unhesitating extension of this notion into the earliest stages of collection, editing, and translating of the literature of major traditions.

At the same time, one can read painstakingly the writings of F. Max Müller and his collaborators in the *Sacred Books of the East* without finding any degree of sustained reflection on either of these two critical points. Müller presents, at various places, a nascent thesis concerning what he calls "book religion"; but neither does his thesis address the question of sacredness as it applies to 'books'; nor does it anywhere fully explore the matter of just how these 'books' were and are actually utilized within the various traditions. The existence of 'sacred books,' in short, seems to have needed no justification.

Given this, it seems proper, and best, to understand the *Sacred Books of the East* not primarily as a failed effort to comprehend the scriptures of religious history, but rather as an accurate reflection of a general mode of thinking about religious traditions and their literature, a mode that persists even now, well over a century after the *Sacred Books of the East* began to appear. The general presence of this mode is indicated, albeit again negatively, by the fact that one can also pore over the somewhat later efforts of phenomenologists and cataloguists (e.g., Gerardus van der Leeuw), and find no systematic treatment of the status of sacred books. The key point seems to be this: that scripture was not and has not been recognized as a religious phenomenon itself, one in need of as much analysis in its own right as any other mode of religious activity or expression.

Two notes need to be added to this opening observation. First, this entire matter clearly is not unrelated to general modes of historiography in Western academic circles. The historian and humanist's unrelenting focus on textual documentation, and the accompanying bifurcation of the study of human communities into history and social science—the latter relentlessly discounting literary evidence—comprises one of the backdrops against which the matter of scripture is played out. Second, as concerns scripture *per se*, the scholarly failure to treat it as a phenomenon itself is intimately tied to the state of Biblical Studies in the same period as that of the *Sacred Books of the East* and other early comparative historical study of religion. The Christian, specifically Protestant, fascination with the Bible as a 'sacred book'—a fascination that is actually a dimension of Christian faith itself—provides another of the background sets for the problem of scripture in general.

To explore fully these two contexts is beyond this essay, but both will be touched upon in what follows. And despite this sketchy treatment, it should emerge that the matter of scripture ramifies broadly into two problem areas in the study of religion that are related to these contexts: the relationship between classical and literary religious forms and day-to-day practice, and the relationship between Biblical Studies and the study of religion as a broader discipline. These problematic scholarly areas are ripe for new approaches, and it is hoped that a new view of scripture can help to break some of the mental logjams that one finds in the field, from curriculum (up and down) to specialized study.

SCRIPTURE AS PHENOMENON

As noted above, the recognition of scripture as an analyzable phenomenon, and the analysis of it, are tasks that have not been done and were not done in the time when the broad notion of 'sacred books' entered the process of organizing and understanding the history of religious traditions. This state of affairs shows itself most clearly in the profusion of names—would-be synonyms?—that litter the field: scripture, holy word, sacred book, sacred literature, Bible, canon, to name only some of the most prominent.

Each of these potential names for the phenomenon bears careful analysis and usage; but the titles of series and anthologies, and the vocabulary of textbook authors, shows little, if any, consistency of usage or care in matching names to specific pieces of literature. (The only relief that occurs is the occasional refusal of authors to translate, and the resultant use of indigenous terms for the material, for example, *siddhānta*, *wu ching*, etc.). This suggests that a more basic force is at work: the assumption of a general, loosely grasped model to which all other apparently similar occurrences are assimilated. That model, quite clearly, is the Protestant image of the Bible. A more important point, however, is that this model has come to dominate the field by default, as it were. This reveals itself if one simply takes the time to consider how the several names of scripture work out when applied with care to the Protestant Bible. To anticipate the results of some subsequent analysis, each name reveals and implies a significantly different dimension of the status of the Bible—or, at least, it should do so.

But the truth is that, much of the time, the names are themselves applied nearly interchangeably to the Bible. The sum of such an observation is that the nature and character of the Bible as a religious phenomenon has not been handled clearly. Or the point can be put another way: the Protestant view of the Bible is significantly restricted to only certain dimensions of the phenomenon represented by the several names applied to it; but the inapplicability of some of the names is not recognized by scholars. Hence, although many terms are in use, the terms are actually subservient to an *a priori* notion of scripture on the Protestant model.

Given this, the first task in dealing with the phenomenon of scripture is to find and fix adequate terminology, and to recognize that such terminology is not equivalent to Bible as the latter is generally viewed. The terminology suggested here is the word canon. The term is in some ways the least of the available evils; but its selection from the cluster of possible names is driven by the way in which its basic meaning—that of law and rule, fundamental axiom, principle or standard—lends itself to the development of a typology of scriptural phenomena within which the other would-be synonyms, and the specific material for which they ought to stand, can be clearly laid out and understood.

The proposed typology is the following: that scripture be understood to occur as a religious phenomenon in two general forms, which can be called "Canon I" and "Canon II." (The obvious paucity of terminological genius is regrettable, but the prosaic choice does have a rationale behind it.) Moreover, each form can and does occur within single religious traditions, the two even existing simultaneously at times. In both cases, the underlying etymologically true sense of canon is active; but the ways in which Canons I and II are actually present in a tradition are significantly different, and the failure to perceive this difference is the major cause of confusion in dealing with scriptures.

What, then, is meant by these terms? Canon I denotes normative texts, oral or written, that are present in a tradition principally by the force of a vector or vectors. Canon II refers to normative texts that are more independently and distinctively present within a tradition, that is, as pieces of literature more or less as such are currently thought of, and which themselves often function as vectors.

Further explanation is clearly in order, though types of material will be explored by example, below. By 'vector' is meant the means or mode by which something is carried; thus Canon I's place in a tradition is largely due to its 'being carried' by some other form of religious activity; and Canon I's significance for a tradition cannot be grasped fully without reference to its carrier and to the relationship between the two. The same meaning applies to vector where Canon II may function as a 'carrier' of religious activity.

The most common vector of Canon I is ritual activity, but other significant carriers are also to be found. Canon II most commonly serves as a vector of religious authority, but it is also to a large degree a carrier of ritual iconolatry and/or individualist piety. By giving careful attention to both the vectors and the activities vectored, one can delineate sub-types under each Canon; and in this fashion, a systematic typology of scripture as a phenomenon can be developed.

A word of caution is in order. The proposed typology does not presume a causal and/or developmental relationship between Canons I and II, nor can it yet be asserted to cover every instance of scripture. Moreover, the preceding paragraphs may strike one as the sort of terminological obfuscation better left to small groups at conventions. Whether the latter is so, the following section should settle. The former concerns are those that accompany any hypothesis, and it must be admitted that the validity of Canons I and II as fundamental categories in ordering our thinking about scripture will require much future testing in many contexts. They are offered as a hypothetical model, but not as one that has no basis as concerns its ability to shed light on some problems in studying scripture.

TWO EXAMPLES OF APPLYING THE MODEL

To show clearly the utility of the typology, it will be used here to explore two blocs of scriptural material. This process will also enable us to see some of the subtypes that can be found within each larger category of Canon. The first example will be the normative texts of the Jain tradition; the second will be the Christian Bible.

From almost the earliest scholarly efforts to portray the Jains up to the most recent, it has been held that the Jains have a specific, clearly delimited body of scripture consisting of some forty-five texts in various fixed categories. It has been assumed that this bloc of scripture dates to the period around 500 C.E., when it was edited into a collection; and it is further assumed that individual parts of this bloc existed as "scripture" throughout some six to eight preceding centuries. It is also widely held that one community of Jains, the Svetambaras, accept this scripture, while another community, the Digambaras, reject it out of hand. Such has been the general portrait of the Jain scriptures since the 1870s; yet there are several nagging problems associated with it that refuse to go away.

The first problem is that texts from the sixth century C.E. (after or contemporary with the editing of the collection) do not, when they describe the Jains' normative literature, list the same texts as are given in the current portrait, nor restrict themselves to forty-five titles, nor use the same categories for the texts. Bedeviled by these inconsistencies, scholars have generally chalked up the variations to loss of texts, alterations, or other accidental causes; but no satisfying accounting for the differences has been put forward.

The second problem is that when one asks contemporary Jains what their scriptures are, one receives widely varying answers, responses that vary not because of ignorance, but because there does not appear to be a wholly accepted body of scripture that is of equal value to the entire community. Moreover, it does not appear true that the Digambaras routinely reject the body of texts ostensibly accepted by the Svetambaras; certainly this proposition must be significantly qualified.

Amid all of this welter, examination of the history of Jain scholarship reveals a signal fact: the forty-five text body of literature was originally put forward as the Jain scriptures by one scholar, Georg Bühler, who was relied upon on this point by all others in the nineteenth and early twentieth centuries. Bühler obtained his information from a single oral source within the Jain community; and while he found it attested to by other oral sources, he also knew that it did not jibe with still other such sources, or with the older literary testimony. Yet he put it forward, and lived to see it perpetuated by other scholars.

Beyond this, a charming anomaly surfaced very early in Jain scholarship. When Hermann Jacobi was asked to make translations of Jain texts for the *Sacred Books of the East*, one of the first two texts so translated and published was the *Kalpa Sūtra*. Yet, as Jacobi had to admit, the *Kalpa Sūtra* that was being published as a sacred book was not in the forty-five text scripture bloc. Despite this, he chose it because of its enormous popularity and value to the community, a fact that is attested by the *Kalpa Sūtra*'s overwhelming presence in manuscript collections and its dominance as a text chosen for illustration by manuscript artists. Ergo, far from being a minor matter associated with obscure texts, the problem of inconsistency in the Jain "scriptures" proved to be an immediate difficulty for scholars. Yet the notion of the forty-five text bloc continued to be put forward.

What were Bühler and the others doing? The simplest answer, and the one that permits the best explanation of the whole range of problems involved, is this: Bühler superimposed a Canon II model of scripture onto a tradition whose literature was of the Canon I variety. This conclusion can be illuminated by reference to two critical points.

First, scriptural material of the Canon I type needs to be understood at all times in terms of its vectors. The Jain tradition exhibits both the ritual-activity-vector mentioned above, and others as well; and the place of scriptures in Jain religious life is only fully intelligible in terms of the vectors to be found in various situations, The problem of the *Kalpa Sūtra* clarifies itself at once in these terms, for the text in question is vectored by a major ritual activity. It is festively read aloud in a communal gathering during Paryuṣana, the penitential and confessional period at the end of the Jain religious year, a ritual time of intense activity for the entire community. Hence the *Kalpa Sūtra* finds its prominence in the Jain community; it is one of the texts most frequently copied and illustrated; Jains speak of it as a normative text, a scripture. That it is not found in the forty-five text bloc of scriptures is not even a matter of moment to the community.

One more example: the older, sixth-century accounts of the Jains' texts that are at variance with the forty-five text model are also vectored by specific religious activities. They are carried largely by a ritually structured monastic course of instruction, one that leaps into view as soon as the commentaries on the texts are drawn into the picture. And so variances between the older accounts and the forty-five text model are not simply the result of happenstance, or, at least, the older model was not merely the prototype of the more recent one, with loss and confusion intervening. But the rationale for the older model will not emerge from the texts alone; its vector finally clarifies its status.

One notes also that this latter vector is discoverable only with the aid of the commentaries on the texts; and this leads to the second critical point concerning Bühler's superimposition of Canon types. Canon II scripture is, among other major features, especially characterized by being viewed as independently valid and powerful, and as such, as being absolutely closed and complete. What is in Canon II is normative, true, and binding; what is outside of it is secondary in all these respects. Therefore, for Bühler and his successors, the existence of different accounts of the range and contents of the Jain scriptures poses a problem, but this problem does not necessarily affect the Jains. In Canon I instances, the vector and its validity are at least as determinative as any limit on the scripture itself. Further, scholars who thought (and think) of scriptures in Canon II modes are likely to do what Jain scholars have done: they ignore or depreciate the commentaries. Some exoneration is called for here; the commentaries were often not fully accessible to scholars. Yet, in their Canon II orientation, the early editors and translators did not wait for or insist on a full commentorial context before pushing ahead with publication and analysis of the scriptures. Nor need one look far in the study of religion to see numerous similar cases in the handling of traditions other than the Jain.

It appears, then, that the Canon I Jain texts have been much obscured, and their role in Jain religious history and life much misunderstood, in virtue of their having been forced into a Canon II mold; it is hoped that this example has shed some light on the working of the Canons I and II typology. Yet this method of treating scripture is not necessarily of full value if it illuminates only one tradition, or if it springs only from a peculiar example of misapplied concepts in comparative religion. A greater test of its value is to turn it onto the tradition that informed the Western scholars, that is, to test it on the Bible itself. And so we turn to our second example.

The basic thesis is simple: that the Protestant Bible is a Canon II phenomenon, and that through much of Christian religious history, and even still at present, the Bible also functions—at times even prominantly functions—as a Canon I text. The startling fact is that scholars have not only imposed Canon II models onto non-Christian traditions; they have also, as Wilfred Cantwell Smith has pointed out, forgotten the rich multidimensionality of the Bible's own role within Christianity. The loosely held, but dominant, Protestant model of the Bible mentioned earlier is also the dominant model for Biblical Studies, and it is an altogether Canon II model.

How, specifically, does the adoption of Canons I and II in viewing the Bible shed light on its status as a phenomenon? To see this quickly, it is possible to look at two areas of material and evidence. The first is the use of the Bible in Christian churches, and the second is the problem of the Christian relationship to the Hebrew scriptures.

It is an interesting exercise to observe the specific status and use of the Bible in various Christian denominations. The available evidence is obvious, and significant. Two basic questions can be asked: (1) how are the Bible's contents used in the church service? (2) what is the Bible's physical status, *qua* book, in the service and church building?

With respect to the first question, one observes a division within Christianity between churches that use a lectionary and those that use the Bible's contents in a more random fashion. In the former case, the contents of the Bible are clearly being vectored. They are carried by the ritual pattern of the Christian year, and are even more specifically vectored by the internal rhythm of the service itself—for example, a Lesson from the Old Testament, a Psalm, a Lesson or Epistle from the New Testament, and finally, hedged by chanting and changing postures, a Gospel portion. In those churches that do not use a lectionary, such clear patterns of vectoring are not prominent; nor even would the theologies of some such churches accept any such limitation on or division within the scripture and its use. It is also clear that significant correspondence exists between churches that use a lectionary and churches whose emphasis in worship in eucharistic, that is, the greater prominence of ritual communion is linked to a structured 'carrying' of the Bible.

With respect to the second question, it is also clear that churches differ markedly in terms of the Bible's physical presence. In some churches, an oversized Bible is prominently displayed, and is usually accompanied by the presence of Bibles in the pews. In others, nary a Bible, oversized or not, is to be found. And again, the correspondence holds: the presence of a ritual vector implies the physical absence of the Bible. Also highly revealing is the link between Bible and clergyman; here one consistently observes a range of phenomena, from no visible link at all, to the presence of the Bible on the lectern before the clergyman, to the physical holding of the Bible by the clergyman. Once more, the correspondence holds: the clergyman whose role is priestly has no Bible; the Protestant evangelist sports his aloft, elevated in his hand.

For all of this material the Canon I and II typology is most apt. The observer would conclude that the liturgical churches' Bible is clearly best understood, if one is seeking its full function in the community, as a Canon I phenomenon; and that the non-liturgical churches' Bible is of a Canon II variety. The typology can be further verified by noting that the Canon II Bible, while not being vectored by the ritual processes of eucharist and sacred calendar, is itself vectoring at least two things: (1) its physical presence as an "icon" of sorts in churches is a clear index of those churches' near-veneration of it as a 'sacred book'; (2) its link with clergymen is a sign of its capacity to vector authority (this latter point may be reduced to an axiom: the less bishops, the more Bibles).

In terms of this essays's general context, the following is clear: the Protestant churches, by and large, are those whose Bible is Canon II. And the specific patterns of use in those churches correspond to basic assumptions that provide the framework for Biblical Studies: (1) that the entire Bible is of equal significance in all its parts, and that the reading and study of all of it is a necessary and even salvific task (the parallel is to the random use of the whole Bible in church services); (2) that the Bible itself is the chief focus of concern, and that, though its contextual setting—rites, commentaries, and other religious acts—may be useful to the scholar, they are distinctly secondary in value (a parallel: the iconization of the Bible as a distinct physical object); (3) that Biblical Studies itself is an absolutely distinctive and separate discipline from the tasks of theology, church history, and liturgics (a parallel: the authority in the church is vectored by the Bible).

These observations concerning the Christian Bible, and the way in which Biblical Studies reflect only a portion of its multiple character, can be related back to the general utility of the Canon I and II typology simply by substituting into the three propositions given above the word *siddhānta* (the most common indigenous Jain term for the forty-five text "scriptures" discussed earlier). The result is three basic misperceptions of the Jains' normative texts, all of which cease to apply when those texts are considered in a Canon I context. Even more revealing is the fact that these misperceptions would come distressingly close to describing the modes of thought that have long governed the study of religious literature in non-Christian traditions; the reader is invited to substitute his or her own choice of non-Christian normative text in order to test the proposition.

To finish off the presentation of examples from the Christian heritage, it will be useful to cite very briefly the problem of the Hebrew scriptures, and to offer a thesis that still requires detailed exploration. It is this: the Old Testament, that is, the Hebrew scriptures as Christians use them, had themselves undergone a process of becoming Canon II materials *within* Judaism prior to their inclusion in Christianity's body of texts. As such, the Law, Prophets, and Writings as they stand are once-removed from many of their original vectors; and the Old Testament does not contain many things that were vectored by activities once prominent in Israelite religion and now gone, for example, liturgical materials.

This Judaic Canon II was then used, as best it could be, in various Canon I modes in Christianity prior to the Protestant Reformation—a reversal, almost, of the squeezing into molds done by scholars of non-Christian scriptures. Finally, with the rise of the Canon II Protestant Bible, those Hebrew texts underwent a second de-vectoring, so to speak, with interpretive consequences whose permutations are truly dazzling.

The foregoing proposals for new looks at both Christian and Jain scriptures in the light of Canon I and II analysis should be—and are meant to be—provocative. But they also constitute a serious typological proposal. Such a venture calls out for at least one more thing, in addition to the detailed working-out of its theses: a "Concluding Anti-Reductionist Postscript." The power, the sacredness, of the word or text is not truly seized by such functional analyses alone. Yet our approaches to the problem of scripture must be pushed outward, and a broader view with systematic force developed, if we are to escape the one-dimensional view of the Bible and of other texts that our unwitting reliance on Canon II models and modes has generated.

7

The Bride of Israel: The Ontological Status of Scripture in the Rabbinic and Kabbalistic Traditions

Barbara A. Holdrege

INTRODUCTION

The term 'scripture,' originally derived from a Judaeo-Christian context, has generally been used by modern scholars to designate the 'sacred texts' that have been canonized or otherwise officially recognized as sacrosanct and authoritative for a particular religious community. The study of scripture since the nineteenth century has been almost exclusively the domain of biblical and orientalist scholars, who have focused on particular religious texts rather than on scripture as a general religious phenomenon. These scholars have used the tools of critical analysis—textual, philological, historical, and literary—in order to determine the cultural, historical, and literary influences that have given rise to individual texts. However, in their focus on historical antecedents, many scholars have tended to treat these texts primarily as historical or literary documents, without placing much emphasis on their sacrosanct status in relation to a religious community.

This prevalent emphasis on the *Entstehungsgeschichte* of a text—the history of the causes and conditions that produced it—has led to a corresponding neglect of *Wirkungsgeschichte*—the history of effects that the text itself has produced in the cumulative tradition of a given community. In the context of scriptural study, *Wirkungsgeschichte* encompasses the ongoing roles that a sacred text has assumed both as a normative source of authority and as a prodigious living force that has inspired, guided, nurtured, and transformed the lives of countless adherents throughout the centuries.[1]

In addition to a lack of emphasis on the effective history of particular scriptural traditions, relatively little attention has been given to the category of scripture as a general religious phenomenon. The study of scripture as a general religious form and concept can be approached from a variety of perspectives. While a number of scholars have been primarily concerned with the functional status of scripture within religious communities, the focus of my investigations is the ontological status of scripture. My study of scripture is concerned not with what people have done with scripture, but rather with what they have conceived scripture to be—its origin and cosmological import, its role as a cosmic reality in creation and revelation. The functional status of scripture within a particular religious community is to a certain extent shaped and informed by the community's conceptions of its ontological status, and yet relatively little attention has been given to this important dimension of scripture.

On the most fundamental level, the sacrosanct status of scripture, which is closely linked with its authority and function within a religious community, is often held to be derived from its ontological status as a divine, cosmic, and/or eternal reality. The sacred power of scripture in a number of the major religious traditions of the world is attributed to its divine or transcendent origin. As such scripture is considered in certain traditions to be a direct revelation or cognition that discloses its divine/transcendent source, reveals the nature of reality, and unfolds its own divine/eternal status as structured in the very nature of the cosmos. Whether conceived as a divine revelation of the Word of God—as in the Judaic conception of Torah and the Islamic conception of Qur'ān—or as a direct cognition of the eternal impulses of knowledge reverberating forth from the Transcendent—as in the Hindu conception of the Vedas—the sacrality of scripture in these cases is derived from its ontological status as a divine/eternal reality. This status is evidenced even in those instances in which scripture is said to have been derived from inspiration rather than direct revelation, as in the Christian conception of the Gospels in which God is believed to have spoken through the inspired minds of the Gospel writers.

The scriptures of certain traditions are ranked according to their level of spiritual authority. In such cases the primary criterion for ranking is generally an ontological distinction in which those scriptures that are held to be a divine revelation or direct cognition of reality are ranked as most sacred and authoritative, above scriptures that were composed by inspired human authors. For example, in the Judaic tradition the Torah (Pentateuch), which is held to be the direct revelation of God's Word, is ranked halakhically above the inspired writings of the Nevi'im (Prophets) and Ketuvim (Writings or Hagiographa).[2] Similarly, in Islam the Qur'ān, as divine revelation, is ranked above the Ḥadīth, which records the sayings and deeds of Muhammad. In the Hindu tradition the Vedas, which are upheld as direct cognitions of reality and thus termed *śruti* (that which is heard), are considered to be more authoritative than all the other sacred texts that are said to have been composed by personal authors and that are therefore comprehensively referred to as *smṛti* (that which is remembered).[3] In the Christian tradition the Gospels, even though not considered direct revelation, are nevertheless ranked above the Epistles and Old Testament as the records of God's central revelation in Christ.

In certain traditions, in particular the Confucian tradition and early Taoist tradition, scripture is viewed as the record of human wisdom in the form of the words and deeds of the sages and as such is not granted a divine or eternal status. However, even in such instances ontological conceptions of scripture may develop over time as the sages themselves —and hence their words—are elevated to divine status. The Buddhist concept of *Buddha-vacana* (word of the Buddha) presents an interesting case. In the Theravāda tradition the words of the Buddha as recorded in the Buddhist *Sūtra*s are granted a special "supradivine" status in that the Buddha's wisdom, as an enlightened human being, is said to transcend the wisdom of the gods. In the later Mahāyāna tradition the Buddha himself is elevated to an eternal, cosmic status, and thus his words and teachings assume a correspondingly cosmic aura. The ontological status of scripture thus constitutes a significant area of investigation that can help to illumine our understanding not only of the sacred status, authority, and function of scripture within particular religious communities, but also of scripture as a general religious phenomenon. In the Judaic and Hindu traditions in particular, which have been the primary focus of my investigations, the ontological conceptions of scripture have a pervasive and enduring significance not only as a recurring motif in the traditional texts, but, perhaps more importantly, as a living force influencing the attitudes and practices of the exponents of the rabbinic tradition and the Brahmanical custodians of the Vedic recitative tradition from ancient times until the present day.[4] The present essay will focus on the ontological conceptions of Torah in the Judaic tradition and will attempt to give a schematic overview of some of the most important themes presented in rabbinic and medieval kabbalistic texts with respect to the status and role of the Torah as a divine reality in creation and revelation.

Ontological Conceptions of Torah

The term "Torah," according to the general consensus of most modern scholars, is connected with the hiphil conjugation of the root *yrh*, "to point out, direct, teach," and thus means "teaching" or "instruction."[5] The term has a variety of meanings in biblical and rabbinic texts. In rabbinic literature Torah is used in at least three different senses: (1) to designate the Pentateuch, as distinct from the other two sections of the Hebrew Bible, Nevi'im and Ketuvim; (2) to refer to the Hebrew Bible as a whole; and (3) to include not only the Pentateuch, Nevi'im, and Ketuvim, which constitute the Written Torah (*Tôrāh še bi-ktāḇ*), but also the Mishnah, Talmud, and Midrash, which contain the halakhic and aggadic teachings that constitute the Oral Torah (*Tôrāh še bᵉ-'al peh*).

In order to clarify what is meant by "ontological conceptions of Torah," we must begin with a consideration of the nature and meaning of revelation in the Judaic tradition. What was the Word of God that is said to have been revealed at Mount Sinai? How is the process of revelation itself described? The revelation of the Torah at Mount Sinai is a favorite theme of rabbinic and kabbalistic literature and is depicted in the Pentateuch itself as occurring in two main phases. In the first phase of the revelation, God himself spoke directly with the people of Israel who stood at the foot of Mount Sinai, declaring to them the "Ten Words" (*'ăśereṯ ha-dîḇrôṯ*) of the Decalogue.[6] In the second phase of the revelation, Moses ascended Mount Sinai and remained there for forty days and nights while God imparted to him the detailed teachings and commandments (*miṣwôṯ*) of the Torah. According to the strictest interpretation the Torah that was revealed by God to Moses constituted the Pentateuch, while according to a more far-reaching interpretation it included not only the Pentateuch but also the Nevi'im, Ketuvim, Mishnah, Talmud, and Midrash.[7] When understood in this broader sense we might conclude that the Torah that Moses received consisted of a concrete written text together with an oral tradition of interpretation that would be capable of clarifying and elaborating the implications of its laws and teachings for subsequent generations. However, if we examine more closely the imagery that is sometimes used to depict the revelation, we can discern yet another dimension of the Torah that is not encompassed by any of the notions discussed thus far.

The revelation of the Torah at Mount Sinai is sometimes depicted in rabbinic literature as a wedding ceremony. In one tradition the wedding celebrates the betrothal of the Lord to his bride Israel. The Lord presents the Torah to Israel as the marriage contract (*kᵉṯûbāh*) binding them in an everlasting covenant.[8] A second tradition portrays the Torah not as a mere legal document but as the bride herself, who is presented in marriage by God, her father, to the bridegroom, Israel.[9] Year after year these different versions of the marriage ceremony are enacted in the two annual festivals dedicated to the Torah. The marriage symbolism is thus not simply a textual phenomenon. It is a part of the living Jewish tradition.

Both versions of the wedding are reflected in the customs of Shavuot, the yearly festival that commemorates the theophany on Mount Sinai. In many Sephardic communities on the first day of Shavuot prior to the Torah reading a *Kᵉṯûbāh lᵉ-Šāḇû'ôṯ* (marriage certificate of Shavuot) is read out, dated the sixth of Sivan—the date traditionally designated for the revelation of the Torah at Mount Sinai—and the eternal covenant is sealed. The most widely used version of the *Kᵉṯûbāh lᵉ-Šāḇû'ôṯ*, composed by the Safed Kabbalist and poet Israel Najara (ca. 1550–1625 C.E.), celebrates the marriage between God himself, who is the bridegroom, and his bride Israel. However, in other versions of the *Kᵉṯûbāh* the Torah is portrayed as the bride who is given away by her father, God, to the bridegroom, Israel.

In the customs of the other yearly festival dedicated to the Torah, Simḥat Torah (Rejoicing of the Torah), the symbolism of Torah as the bride of Israel predominates. On this day, the last day of the festival of Sukkot, the annual cycle of reading of the Torah is completed and a new cycle of reading is immediately begun. The man who is called up to the lectern to read the concluding portion of the Torah is called *Ḥāṯān Tôrāh*, "bridegroom of the Torah," while the man who is asked to begin the new cycle by reading from the first portion of the Torah is called *Ḥāṯān Bᵉrē'šîṯ*, "bridegroom of the beginning, that is, of Genesis."

Implicit in these two versions of the marriage symbolism are two distinct yet interrelated concepts of the Torah. In one version the Torah is presented as a legal contract establishing the conditions of the covenant between God and Israel. This version points to a concept of the Torah with which we are already familiar: the Written Torah together with an oral tradition of interpretation, which specify the laws and teachings that are to be upheld by the people of Israel in fulfillment of their covenant with God. The other version of the marriage symbolism, which portrays the Torah as the bride of Israel, goes beyond these more familiar notions and personifies the Torah as a living, organic entity capable of entering into a dynamic relationship with the people of Israel. In this view the

Torah represents something more than a holy book to be recited, studied, interpreted, and followed. It represents something more than the text inscribed on the Torah scroll and even more than the vast corpus of laws and teachings that constitutes the Oral Torah.

When the Torah is depicted as the bride of Israel it is represented as having a life of its own. It is not simply a body of teachings; it is the embodiment of divine wisdom. It is not simply words inscribed on parchment; it is the living Word of God. The Written Torah was revealed on earth at a particular time and in a particular place within history, but according to certain strands of the Judaic tradition this earthly dimension of the Torah represents only one aspect of its reality. The Torah, as described in certain rabbinic and kabbalistic texts, also has a divine, transhistorical dimension in which it is conceived to be that preexistent, primordial wisdom which has existed in heaven "from the beginning" as a living aspect of God and the immediate source of creation. At the time of the revelation at Mount Sinai the Torah descended from its seat on high in order to make its abode on earth as the bride of the people of Israel. It assumed the finite form of the Written Torah, but the primordial divine wisdom continues to animate the book with secret life, beckoning those who study it to penetrate beyond the outer body to its innermost soul. Those who are capable of fathoming the deepest mysteries of the Torah are called in certain kabbalistic texts true "bridegrooms of the Torah," for they alone have succeeded in entering into divine communion with the bride of Israel in her full glory.[10]

Both of these concepts of the Torah—(1) the Torah as a written document, the meaning of which is unfolded and elaborated through an ongoing oral tradition, and (2) the Torah as a living aspect of God with which one can enter into direct communion—must be taken into account for a complete understanding of the Judaic notion of scripture. If we were to focus on the first concept we would be primarily concerned with the functional status of Torah, with the ways in which it has been studied, interpreted, applied, and reverenced in Jewish education, in law and jurisprudence, in daily observance and practice, and in synagogue worship and personal piety. Each of these areas has been treated in depth by other scholars. The present essay, in contrast, will be concerned with the ontological rather than the functional status of the Torah and will focus on the second concept mentioned above, which presents the Torah as a living, divine reality.

Despite the significance of the ontological conceptions of Torah as a pervasive and persistent motif in rabbinic and kabbalistic literature, few scholars have given serious consideration to these conceptions. Abraham Heschel grapples with some of these conceptions in *Tôrāh min ha-*

Šāmayîm.[11] He suggests that there were at least two essentially distinct approaches to the status and authority of the Torah in rabbinic thought, represented by the school of R. Akiba (ca. 110–135 C.E.), which emphasized the transcendent significance of every jot and tittle of the Torah, and the school of R. Ishmael (2nd c. C.E.), which maintained the more pragmatic stance that the Torah speaks in the language of human beings. Ephraim Urbach has provided some important insights into the rabbinic concept of Written Torah and Oral Torah.[12] Among other significant studies are Gershom Scholem's illuminating essay on the meaning of the Torah in kabbalistic thought and his more recent article on the kabbalistic theory of language.[13] Another landmark study is Mosheh Idel's analysis of the role of Torah in the Hêkalôt literature of Merkabah mysticism.[14]

While these studies focus on particular strands of the Jewish tradition, my study will provide a diachronic analysis of the various layers of interpretation and reinterpretation through which the ontological conceptions of Torah were elaborated and modified in the course of the tradition's formative development, including an examination of major threads of rabbinic and medieval kabbalistic speculation, along with a brief consideration of the antecedents of the concept of primordial wisdom/Torah in pre-rabbinic literature. My primary concern will not be with *Entstehungsgeschichte*, with attempting to determine the historical antecedents and cause-effect relationships in the development of the ontological conceptions of Torah. My concern is rather to trace the broad outlines of the *Wirkungsgeschichte*, the tradition of interpretations of certain seminal notions, with a view to illuminating the lines of continuity as well as divergence between the rabbinic and kabbalistic treatments of these notions. The kabbalistic phase of the analysis will focus primarily on the speculative Kabbalah of thirteenth-century Spain, with particular emphasis on the Zohar. Some attention will also be given to the earlier speculations of the Provençal Kabbalist Isaac the Blind (12th c. C.E.), as well as to the conceptions of Torah found in the writings of sixteenth-century Kabbalists of the Safed school and later Lurianic Kabbalists.

These particular strands of the Judaic tradition have been chosen as the focus of the present study for three reasons: First, they constitute major strands in the tradition's formative development; second, these strands include both exoteric and esoteric orientations; and third, these strands allow us to trace the history of interpretations of the ontological conceptions of Torah from their seed expression to their most fully elaborated manifestations.[15]

The seminal conceptions found in the wisdom literature of the Hebrew Bible and Apocrypha are further developed in rabbinic texts, culminating in the elaborate cosmogonies of the Zohar and other medieval kabbalistic texts.

Although speculations regarding the ontological status of the Torah find their most fully developed expression in kabbalistic literature, many of these speculations are at least adumbrated in rabbinic texts. However, the rabbinic orientation and mode of treatment of these ideas is different from that of the Kabbalists in that they are never systematically developed as part of any consistent cosmology. It is therefore difficult to assess whether such notions reflect a genuine interest in cosmological speculation or whether they are simply homiletical praises of the Torah. It is also difficult to determine to what extent a particular view represents a consensus of opinion, or to what extent it represents the opinion of a single individual or school of rabbinic thought. We have already noted Heschel's suggestion that there were at least two contending schools of rabbinic thought with different conceptions of the Torah's status.

In contrast to the rather fragmentary nature of the rabbinic material, in which aggadic speculations about the nature of the Torah are interspersed throughout the texts, in kabbalistic literature the speculations about the nature of the Torah are generally presented as part of a grand cosmological scheme. The ideas that are found in seed form in rabbinic literature are fully elaborated and cosmologized by the Kabbalists, going beyond metaphorical personification to clear hypostatization. Although we thus recognize a difference in perspective and emphases with respect to the ontological conceptions of Torah found in rabbinic and kabbalistic literature, we also discern sufficient threads of continuity to warrant juxtaposing these two different approaches.

The strands of the rabbinic and kabbalistic traditions that are the focus of the present study do not of course represent the totality of the Judaic tradition, which includes a complex range of diversified and competing perspectives and schools in every historical period. As we have seen, even within the rabbinic tradition there are a number of different perspectives. There are also a variety of schools and orientations within medieval Kabbalah, including not only the "speculative Kabbalah" that is the primary focus of the present study, but also the "ecstatic Kabbalah" or "prophetic Kabbalah" of Abraham Abulafia and his followers and the "practical Kabbalah" of the theurgists. The present study focuses on schools that were particularly concerned with the ontological status of the Torah. The primary aim of the Zohar, for example, in its role as a purported rabbinic Midrash, is to reveal the most profound mysteries of the Torah, and thus its cosmological speculations include a quite highly differentiated treatment of the various levels and stages of manifestion of the Torah in creation and revelation. Another very important approach to questions of the origin and ontology of the Torah can be found in the speculations of medieval Jewish philosophers. However, consideration of these philosophical speculations is beyond the scope of the present essay and must be reserved for a separate study.[16]

The following analysis will examine three major areas of speculation presented in rabbinic and kabbalistic texts with regard to the ontological status of Torah: Torah and creation, Torah and revelation, and Torah and interpretation. The first section will briefly survey the pre-rabbinic antecedents of the concept of primordial wisdom/Torah before moving on to a discussion of rabbinic and kabbalistic speculations concerning the status and role of this primordial Torah in creation. Particular attention will be given to three types of speculation found in rabbinic and kabbalistic texts: the Torah personified or hypostatized as a living, organic entity that is the immediate source of creation; the Torah as the blueprint or plan that the Creator employs in fashioning his creation; and the Torah as the divine language that the Creator speaks in order to bring forth the manifold forms and phenomena of creation. The second section of the essay will briefly review some of the most important rabbinic and kabbalistic traditions concerning the revelation at Mount Sinai, focusing particularly on those traditions that depict the revelation as a recapitulation of creation and that emphasize the unique experiential dimension of the revelation as a direct cognition of the living Word of God. Finally, the last section will briefly consider the extent to which rabbinic and kabbalistic traditions concerning the meaning and interpretation of the Torah point to an underlying conception of its special status as a divine reality.

It is my hope that through illuminating the pervasive and enduring significance of the ontological conceptions of Torah in rabbinic and kabbalistic thought, this essay will challenge us to "rethink scripture," to move beyond our tendency to delimit scripture to the black and white text of 'holy writ' and to embrace a broader conception that can also account for the ongoing role of scripture as a prodigious living force and active, immediate reality in people's lives.

TORAH AND CREATION

Torah and Creation in Pre-Rabbinic Texts

In order to gain an understanding of the rich and complex layers of tradition that underlie and inspire the rabbinic and kabbalistic speculations regarding the preexistence of the Torah and its role in creation, we will briefly survey the stages through which the concept of primordial wisdom emerged in pre-rabbinic literature and became identified with the Torah. After considering the nature of personified wisdom in Proverbs 8.22–31, we will highlight the contributions of the wisdom books of the Apocrypha—the Wisdom of Ben Sira, Baruch 3.9–4.4, and the Wisdom of Solomon—and of the Alexandrian Jewish philosophers Aristobulus and Philo to the development of the concept of primordial wisdom/Torah.[17]

Proverbs 8.22–31: Personified Wisdom as the Artisan of Creation. The nature and origin of Proverbs 8.22–31, in which personified wisdom speaks of her primordial beginnings as the first of God's works, has long been disputed by scholars. The passage is generally considered to be an independent wisdom hymn that forms part of a larger literary unit, Proverbs 1–9, which is distinguished from chapters 10–31 of Proverbs in structure, style, and content. Proverbs 1–9, with its cosmological speculations about wisdom and creation, is generally placed by scholars in the last stage in the development of the Israelite wisdom tradition, as characterized by theological wisdom,[18] and has been variously dated from the Persian period[19] to the early Hellenistic period (between 330 and 250 B.C.E.).[20]

In Proverbs 8.22–31 the figure of personified wisdom declares, "The Lord made me as the beginning (*rē'šîṯ*) of His way, the first of His works of old" (v. 22). In verses 23–26 wisdom elaborates on her unique status as the primal creation of God who was brought forth before the creation of the world, when there were no depths and no springs and before the mountains and hills had been established. Wisdom goes on to proclaim in verses 27–30 that she was already present when God performed the acts of creation. "When He established the heavens I was there, . . . when He marked out the foundations of the earth, then I was beside Him as an artisan (*'āmôn*)."[21]

The exact nature of wisdom's role in creation hinges on the interpretation of the term *'āmôn* in verse 30. This well-known *crux interpretationis* has generally been vocalized in rabbinic and kabbalistic interpretations of verse 30, as well as by modern scholars, as *'ûmān*, "artisan, craftsman"—a term that is thought to have been borrowed from the Akkadian *ummānu* (craftsman). This interpretation is supported by the translations in the Septuagint, *harmozousa*, and in the Vulgate, *componens*.[22] According to this interpretation wisdom is here depicted as God's co-worker in creation.

The other contending interpretation vocalizes *'āmôn* as *'āmûn* (Qal passive participle from *'āman*, "to nurse") or *'ᵉmun* (noun), "nursling, darling." This suggestion is supported by Aquila's translation of *'āmôn* as *tithēnoumenē*, "nursling, foster-child, darling." Alternative interpretations have also been proposed.[23]

It is not possible in the present study to enter into the details of the scholarly debate. However, for the purpose of our analysis the interpretation of *'āmôn* as *ûmān*, "artisan," will be given precedence, since this is the vocalization upon which rabbinic and kabbalistic interpretations of Proverbs 8.30 are based.

A number of theories have been proposed by scholars concerning the nature of the personification of wisdom expressed in Proverbs 8.22–31. These theories can be grouped in three main categories: (1) wisdom as a poetic personification of an attribute of God; (2) wisdom as an objectification of the world order; and (3) wisdom as a mythological figure.[24] The first two theories tend to locate the ultimate source of the figure of personified wisdom in Proverbs 8.22–31 in an indigenous Israelite tradition, while the proponents of the third theory generally look for its derivation in the wisdom traditions and creation mythologies of Egypt, Mesopotamia, and Canaan.[25]

It is not within the scope of the present analysis to enter into the complex range of issues presented by these various theories of the nature and origin of the figure of personified wisdom depicted in Proverbs 8.22–31. However, it does not appear that the Israelite speculations about the nature of wisdom can be reduced to mere poetical praises, nor can they be explained as simply mythological vestiges borrowed from neighboring cultures. One could argue that the notion of personified wisdom, together with its later expression in the personification of the Torah, has survived throughout the ages as a vital part of the ongoing Jewish tradition precisely because it represents more than a lifeless concept or fanciful flight of imagination. The portrayal of wisdom in Proverbs 1–9 as a damsel who seeks out those who love her and invites them to partake of her innermost secrets reveals a profound dimension of the Israelite people's experience of their God and his revelation in creation.[26] This portrayal is expanded and elaborated in the wisdom books of the Apocrypha and in the writings of the Alexandrian Jewish philosophers Aristobulus and Philo, culminating in the depiction found in rabbinic and kabbalistic texts of wisdom/Torah as the bride of Israel, who represents a living aspect of the divine with whom one can enter into intimate communion.

Primordial Wisdom in Later Pre-Rabbinic Texts: From Ben Sira to Philo. The reflections about the nature of wisdom in the Apocryphal wisdom books are founded on Proverbs 8.22–31. The primary contribution of the Wisdom of Ben Sira (between 198 and 175 B.C.E.) is in identifying the primordial revelation of wisdom in creation with the historical revelation of the Torah on Mount Sinai, in which primordial wisdom descends to earth as the book of the Torah and makes her abode with the people of Israel.[27] The identity between wisdom and Torah is depicted in another book of the Apocrypha, Baruch (ca. 164–116 B.C.E.), in a wisdom psalm (3.9–4.4) that draws not only on Ben Sira but also on Proverbs and Job for its language and imagery.

Wisdom of Solomon 6.12–9.18, which was composed in Greek in the first half of the first century C.E., describes the figure of personified wisdom in more vivid and elaborate imagery than any of the other wisdom writings, canonical as well as Apocryphal. Unlike Ben Sira and Baruch, the author of the Wisdom of Solomon does not explicitly identify wisdom with the Torah, but rather emphasizes the status of wisdom as a cosmic revelation and all-pervading ordering principle in creation, thus betraying the increasing influence of Hellenistic conceptions.

The influence of Hellenistic ideas is even more pronounced in the writings of two representatives of Alexandrian Jewish philosophy: Aristobulus (ca. 170 B.C.E.) and Philo Judaeus (ca. 20 B.C.E.–ca. 50 C.E.). Aristobulus stands at the opposite end of the continuum in relation to the Palestinian sage Ben Sira, who lived at about the same time. In contrast to Ben Sira's depiction of wisdom as the unique possession of the Jewish people in the form of Torah, Aristobulus focuses on the universal, cosmic dimensions of wisdom, explicitly identifying it with the Logos of Stoic philosophy without any mention of Torah.[28] Philo, on the other hand, incorporates the Jewish conceptions of wisdom and Torah within his philosophy of the Logos, which was the governing concept of his works. Harry Austryn Wolfson has emphasized the ultimate identity between Logos, wisdom, and Torah in the philosophy of Philo.[29] Through its association with the Logos, the role of wisdom/Torah in creation finds expression in Philo's philosophy in the image of an architect who first conceives the blueprint of his creation in his mind before bringing it to fruition in concrete form.[30] The dual images of architect and blueprint are also used in the rabbinic tradition to describe the cosmogonic role of the Torah, as will be discussed below.

Torah and Creation in Rabbinic Texts

Torah as Primordial Wisdom. We have briefly surveyed the development of the Israelite concept of primordial wisdom from its earliest expression in Proverbs 8.22–31 through the progressive stages of its unfoldment in the Apocryphal wisdom books—Ben Sira, Baruch, and Wisdom of Solomon—and in the writings of the Alexandrian Jewish philosophers Aristobulus and Philo. The rabbinic tradition stands at the meeting point of many streams that converge in the concept of primordial wisdom/Torah as the first of God's works, existing from "the beginning" as the instrument of creation. The streams of the Egyptian, Mesopotamian, and Canaanite wisdom traditions and creation mythologies appear to have intermingled with the stream of the indigenous Israelite wisdom tradition that gave rise to Proverbs 8.22–31. This stream gained new momentum as it flowed through Ben Sira and the Wisdom of Solomon, where it was fed by the springs of the Hellenistic tradition. The stream widened to encompass even greater currents of Hellenistic influence as it encountered Aristobulus and Philo.

It is impossible to distinguish the various streams that had become inseparably merged by the time they reached the rabbinic tradition, nor can we hope to determine definitely which streams influenced rabbinic speculations about the primordial Torah more than others. It should be pointed out, however, that it is unlikely that most rabbinic sages were even aware of Philo's writings, let alone directly influenced by them. On the other hand, rabbinic speculations about the preexistence of the Torah and its role in creation frequently invoke verses 22 and 30 of Proverbs 8.22–31 as proof texts. Underlying such speculatons is the fundamental assumption that the Torah is identical with the primordial wisdom described in Proverbs 8.22–31. Proverbs 8.22 is the primary verse cited in rabbinic literature to establish the existence of the Torah prior to creation,[31] while Proverbs 8.22 and 8.30,[32] as well as Proverbs 3.9–10,[33] are generally cited as proof of the role of the Torah in creation.

The Preexistence of the Torah. The notion of the preexistence of the Torah, which is founded upon the concept of primordial wisdom in Proverbs 8.22–31, is expressed in rabbinic literature in three basic ways: (1) The Torah is one of several things created prior to creation; (2) the Torah remained hidden for nine hundred and seventy-four generations before the world was created; and (3) the Torah preceded the creation of the universe by two thousand years.

An anonymous Midrash, which appears at least twice in the Talmud, includes the Torah as one of the seven things created prior to the world. The other six preexistent things are enumerated as: repentance, the Garden of Eden, Gehenna, the Throne of Glory, the Temple, and the name of the Messiah.[34]

A similar notion appears in an anonymous Midrash in Genesis Rabbah, which enumerates only six preexistent things: the Torah and the Throne of Glory, which were actually created, and the Patriarchs, Israel, the Temple, and the name of the Messiah, whose creation was only contemplated. The addition of a seventh preexistent entity—repentance—is ascribed to the Palestinian Amora R. Ahabah b. R. Ze'ira.[35] Finally, the Palestinian Amora R. Abba b. Kahana is said to have declared that of all these things the Torah was the first of God's works, preceding even the Throne of Glory.[36] This concept of the Torah as one of several preexistent things goes back to the Tannaitic period, where it is expressed in less elaborate form in Sip̄rê Deuteronomy.[37] The Palestinian Amora R. Levi is said to be the ultimate source of a Midrash that declares that the Torah preceded the creation of the universe by six things, listing six expressions used in Proverbs 8.22–31 to express the Torah's primordial nature.[38] All of the Midrashim mentioned above refer to Proverbs 8.22 as proof of the Torah's preexistence.

The notion that the Torah remained hidden as God's "precious treasure" (*ḥămûḏāh gᵉnûzāh*) for nine hundred and seventy-four generations before the world was created is expressed in at least two Midrashim in the Talmud, one of which is attributed to R. Joshua b. Levi, one of the most eminent Palestinian Amoraim in the first half of the third century.[39] This notion is derived from the fact that, according to Psalm 105.8, the Torah was to have been commanded to one thousand generations, but in actuality it was revealed after twenty-six generations (ten generations from Adam to Noah, ten from Noah to Abraham, and six from Abraham to Moses—Isaac, Jacob, Levi, Kohath, Amram, and Moses).[40] What happened to the other nine hundred and seventy-four generations (1000 − 26 = 974)? R. Huna is said to have declared in the name of the Tanna R. Eliezer b. R. Jose the Galilean that they were blotted out—that is, they remained uncreated.[41]

The tradition that the Torah preceded the creation of the world by two thousand years is attributed to two sages from the second generation of Palestinian Amoraim: R. Simeon b. Lakish and R. Hama b. R. Hanina. This assertion is derived from Proverbs 8.30, "Then I was beside Him as an artisan (*'āmôn*) and I was His delight day after day (*yôm yôm*)"—focusing on the repetition of *yôm*. The sages concluded from Psalm 90.4, "For a thousand years in Thy sight are but as yesterday when it is past," that each day of the Lord is a thousand years, and thus according to Proverbs 8.30 the Torah was with God for two divine days, or two thousand years, before the world was created.[42]

Closely related to the notions discussed above regarding the preexistence of the Torah are the assertions found throughout rabbinic literature that the world was created for the sake of the Torah,[43] a concept that assumes that the Torah was at least contemplated, if not actually created, by God prior to creation. Such a notion finds expression in a slightly different form in the aphorism attributed to Simeon the Just (ca. 300 B.C.E.), who is the first in the long line of rabbinic teachers whose name we know, in which he proclaims that the Torah is one of the three things upon which the world stands.[44]

The concept of a primordial Torah that precedes the creation of the universe is closely linked in rabbinic literature to the notion that the Torah itself has a central role to play in the process of creation. The rabbinic concept that the Torah is the "instrument by means of which the world was created" dates back to the Tannaitic period, where it is attributed to two leading Tannaim, R. Eleazar b. Zadoḳ (ca. 100 C.E.) and R. Akiba (ca. 110–135 C.E.)[45] This notion has been elaborated in the rabbinic tradition in a variety of ways. There appear to be three basic senses in which the role of the Torah in creation is understood in rabbinic literature: (1) The Torah is personified as the living totality of wisdom, which God employs as his architect or co-worker in creation; (2) the Torah is the blueprint or plan of God's creation; (3) the twenty-two letters of the Hebrew alphabet that compose the Torah are the basic structural elements of creation.

Torah as the Artisan of Creation. A number of images are used in rabbinic literature to express the role of the Torah as God's co-worker in creation. Several Midrashim describe how God took council with the Torah before he created the world. One tradition understands the plural "Let *us* make man" in Genesis 1.26 as referring to God and the Torah.[46] In the opening Midrash of the Tanḥuma, the Torah is described not only as God's consultant in creation, but is also depicted as assuming a more active role as the artisan of creation. Vocalizing the *'āmôn* of Proverbs 8.30 as *'ûmān*, the Midrash invokes the language and imagery of Proverbs 8.22–31 to describe how through the aid of his artisan, the Torah, God established the heaven and earth, fixed the boundaries of the deep, brought forth the sun and moon, and formed all of the works of creation.[47]

Two other Midrashim, which appear to stem from a common tradition, similarly describe the Torah as the artisan of creation. Like the Tanḥuma both Midrashim take for granted that the personified wisdom of Proverbs 8.22–31 is identical with the Torah and, in the context of describing the Torah's role in creation, vocalize *'āmôn* in verse 30 as *'ûmān*, "artisan." Moreover, both Midrashim interpret the first verse of the Torah—*b^erē'šîṯ bārā' Elohim*—in light of the *rē'šîṯ darkô* in Proverbs 8.22, understanding *b^erē'šîṯ* in Genesis 1.1 to mean *b^e-ḥoḵmāh*: "By means of wisdom/Torah God created [heaven and earth]."[48]

The shorter of the two Midrashim is attributed to the Tanna R. Judah b. Il'ai (ca. 150 C.E.).

> The Holy One, blessed be He, looked (*mabbîṭ*) into the Torah and created the world. This is what is meant by "Then I was beside Him as an artisan (*'ûmān*) (Prov. 8.30). This is what is written, "With *rē'šîṯ* God created" (Gen. 1.1), and *rē'šîṯ* means nothing other than the Torah, as it is said, "The Lord made me *rē'šîṯ* [E.V.—'as the beginning'] of His way" (Prov. 8.22). This is what is meant by "With *rē'šîṯ* [E.V.—'In the beginning'] God created."[49]

This Midrash is repeated almost verbatim in the last section of the opening proem (*p^etiḥāh*) of Genesis Rabbah, attributed to R. Hoshaiah of the first generation of Palestinian Amoraim (ca. 225 C.E.). The proem offers four possible interpretations of *'āmôn* in Proverbs 8.30, culminating in a fifth interpretation, in which *'āmôn* is understood to mean "artisan." This Midrash elaborates on the earlier tradition ascribed to R. Judah b. Il'ai, developing the image of the artisan further to encompass both the image of the architect whom the king employs to build and the blueprint that the architect consults in building.

> R. Hoshaiah opened: "Then I was beside Him as an *'āmôn*, and I was His delight day after day" (Prov. 8.30).... *'Āmôn* is an artisan (*'ûmān*). The Torah declares, "I was the working instrument of the Holy One, blessed be He." In the normal course of affairs, when a mortal king builds a palace he does not build it by his own skill, but by the skill of an architect. Moreover, the architect does not build it out of his head, but makes use of plans and tablets in order to know how to make the chambers and the wickets. Thus the Holy One, blessed be He, looked (*mabbîṭ*) into the Torah and created the world. And the Torah declares, "With *rē'šîṯ* [E.V.—'In the beginning"] God created" (Gen. 1.1), and *rē'šîṯ* means nothing other than the Torah, as it is said, "The Lord made me *rē'šîṯ* [E.V.—'as the beginning'] of His way" (Prov. 8.22).[50]

Torah as the Blueprint of Creation. In addition to the active image of the Torah as an architect or artisan, we find in rabbinic literature the more passive image of the Torah as the blueprint or plan of creation. The Midrash attributed to R. Hoshaiah (cited above) incorporates both of these images, although their interrelationship is not clarified. With respect to the image of the blueprint, in the Midrash ascribed to R. Judah b. Il'ai (cited above) God is said to have "looked" (*mabbîṭ*) into the Torah and created the world; however, this idea is not explicitly elaborated in terms of a blueprint as it is in the Midrash attributed to R. Hoshaiah.[51]

The notion that creation was first conceived as an idea or plan in the mind of God, which was then brought to fruition in the concrete forms and phenomena of the manifest world, is expressed in a number of Midrashim. One tradition records a dispute between the School of Shammai and the School of Hillel concerning whether the plan of creation was formulated during the night and executed during the day, or whether both the planning and execution took place during the day. The nature of the plan itself is not discussed, nor is any explicit mention made of the Torah in this context.[52] However, another anonymous Midrash directly links the Torah, through reference to I Chronicles 16.15 (=Psalm 105.8 mentioned earlier), to the plan of creation that had been conceived in the mind of God for a thousand years.[53] When the time of creation came the plan effortlessly—in one day—materialized as the multiple forms of creation.

> "My hand laid the foundations of the earth" (Isaiah xlviii 13)—said the Holy One, blessed be He: "For My thoughts are not your thoughts... For as the heavens are higher than the earth..." (*ibid.* lv 8–9)—a man sits and calculates, saying: This is how I shall build, this is how I shall make it; he thinks out in a little while what he does not accomplish in a decade. But the Holy One, blessed be He, is not so; for (what) he thinks out in a thousand years He builds in one day, as it is said: "Remember His covenant for ever, the word which He commanded to a thousand generations" (I Chronicles xvi 15). The heavens were created in one day, for it is said: "By the word of the Lord the heavens were made" (Psalms xxxiii 6).[54]

Hebrew Letters as the Structural Elements of Creation. In the latter part of the homily cited above, the role of the Torah in creation is described in terms of the twenty-two letters that compose it.

> And when he created the world, the Torah, as it were, gave Him light, for the world was without form and void, as it is said: "For the commandment is a lamp, and the Torah is light." Said the Holy One, blessed be He, I seek workmen. The Torah answered Him: I shall put at your service twenty-two workmen, namely the twenty-two letters of the Torah....[55]

The twenty-two letters (*'ôt*) of the Hebrew alphabet that compose the Torah are considered in certain strands of the rabbinic tradition to be the basic structural elements of creation. Rabbinic literature contains many homilies on the individual letters of the Hebrew alphabet, their form and sound and cosmic role in creation. Certain homilies explain why the Torah—and therefore the creation—begins with the letter *bêṯ*.[56] Other homilies maintain that the world was created with the letter *hē* and the future world with the letter *yôḏ*.[57] These speculations regarding the creative power of the Hebrew letters received their most elaborate expression in the *Sēp̄er Yᵉṣîrāh* (Book of Creation) (2nd or 3rd c. C.E.), the earliest extant Hebrew text of a speculative nature, which describes the process of creation as arising through different permutations and combinations of the twenty-two letters of the Hebrew alphabet.[58]

It is these "letters by which heaven and earth were created"[59] that compose the Torah. The converse of the creative power of the letters of the Torah is their potentially destructive power if the perfect structure of the Torah is tampered with in any way. Thus we find the admonition attributed to R. Ishmael when speaking to R. Meir of his work as a scribe of the Torah: "If you should perhaps omit a single letter or add a single letter, you would thereby destroy the whole world.[60] The Palestinian Amora R. Ze'ira is said to have declared that even the thin strokes of the letters of the Torah have the power to bring about the destruction of the world.[61]

The power attributed to the Hebrew letters is linked to both their form and their sound. When viewed from the perspective of their sound value the letters become intimately linked with the creative power of the divine speech. The role of the divine speech in bringing forth creation is embodied in the rabbinic epithet for God, "He who spoke and the world came into being"[62]—and what he spoke, according to the sages, was the Hebrew language. When God said "Let there be light" he spoke Hebrew, the divine language. The sounds of the Hebrew alphabet are the fundamental elements of the divine language, and as such they constitute the basic sound impulses that underlie and give rise to the manifold forms of creation.

The fact that God simply spoke and the different aspects of creation came into being is, according to a number of Midrashim, an indication of the complete effortlessness with which He creates. Psalm 33.6, "By the word (*dāḇār*) of the Lord were the heavens made," is invoked as a proof text to show that for the almighty Creator speech *is* action[63] "Blessed be He who says and does, who decrees and accomplishes."[64] God simply speaks and it is accomplished, he commands and his will is done.

> R. Berechiah opened in the name of R. Judah b. R. Simon: "By the word (*dabar*) of the Lord were the heavens made, and all their host by the breath of His mouth" (Ps. 33.6) . . . not with toil or with labor did the Holy One, blessed be He, create his world, but "by the word of the Lord" and "the heavens were *already* made." Now moreover, it is not written, "there was light" but [God said] "let there be light" (Gen. 1.2), and at once it came into being.[65]

What were the words by which God called the world into being? Ten utterances are generally enumerated in the Midrashim, a tradition which dates back to an early Mishnah: "By ten utterances was the world created."[66] Two contending enumerations of the ten utterances are found in rabbinic literature. According to an anonymous Midrash in Genesis Rabbah XVII.1, the first word of the Torah, *b^erē'šîṯ* (Gen. 1.1), together with the spirit/voice of God over the waters (Gen. 1.2) and the eight commands "And God said,"[67] constitute the ten utterances by which God created the world. According to an alternative interpretation attributed to the Palestinian Amora R. Joḥanan, the spirit of God is not included as one of the ten utterances but is replaced by the ninth command "And God said" (Gen.1.29).[68] These ten utterances will be discussed in more detail in the following section.

Stages of Manifestation. The relationship between the three aspects of the Torah's role in creation discussed in the previous sections—as God's architect or co-worker, as the blueprint, and as letters—is generally not discussed in rabbinic texts. These speculations about the Torah appear rather as isolated fragments throughout the texts and are not developed in terms of a consistent cosmology. It is only on the basis of the Midrashim concerning the ten utterances by which the world was created that we can begin to develop an interpretive scheme in which these different aspects of the Torah's cosmogonic role, as God's co-worker, blueprint, and letters, can be viewed as progressive aspects or manifestations of a single process. The Torah conceived as God's co-worker is a living, organic entity, which in its identification with primordial wisdom almost appears to take on an existence independent of God. Yet at the same time it is *God's* wisdom, the primordial thought of creation conceived in the mind of God, which contains within itself the ideal plan of the universe. This plan could in a sense be said to contain the "ideas" of all the forms in creation. These ideas are then spoken out by God, expressed by him in uttered sounds embodied in the letters of the Hebrew alphabet. These subtle impulses of sound are then precipitated to form the concrete phenomena of creation. From a single thought to differentiated thoughts to uttered words to concrete forms: this is the progressive process of creation in which the Torah participates at every stage.

The relationship between these various aspects of manifestation is expressed in the Midrashim enumerating the ten utterances by which the world was created. In both of the interpretations mentioned above, *bᵉrē'šîṯ*, the first word of the Torah, is considered to be the first utterance, which is linked by R. Joḥanan to Psalm 33.6, "By the word of the Lord were the heavens made." *Bᵉrē'šîṯ* in this context constitutes the original unspoken Word, which contains within itself the other nine utterances and the totality of creation—heaven and earth—yet undifferentiated. A word that has not been spoken out on the gross level of speech remains as an idea in the mind. The word *bᵉrē'šîṯ* can thus be understood as the unspoken idea of creation that first arose in the mind of God. As discussed earlier, this primal unspoken Word, *bᵉrē'šîṯ*, is directly linked by a number of Midrashim to the creative role of Torah as primordial wisdom.[69]

According to the enumeration in Genesis Rabbah XVII.1, the second creative utterance was the voice, yet unexpressed, that hovered as the spirit of God over the waters (Gen. 1.2). Then the voice became vocalized and burst forth onto the expressed level of speech: "And God said: 'Let there be light'" (Gen. 1.3). This is the first of eight commands[70] that progressively unfolded the details of creation from the original wholeness of the Word. With each command, "Let there be . . . ," it was so. The Lord spoke the name and the corresponding form appeared.

In this portrayal of creation we find a progressive development from unspoken thought to spoken word to concrete form. The Torah as the Word of God embraces both unspoken thought and spoken word. The unspoken thought in the mind of God is wisdom, which is the *content* of the word. The word is spoken by means of God's voice, which is the vehicle for the *expression* of the word. Wisdom and the voice/speech—both of these aspects of the word are necessary in order for the process of manifestation to be complete. On the one hand, without speech the content of the word, which is wisdom, would remain hidden, undisclosed. On the other hand, without wisdom speech would have no content to express.

Torah and Creation in Kabbalistic Texts

The Primordial Torah. The Zohar and other medieval kabbalistic texts reiterate the rabbinic notion that the Torah preceded the creation of the world by two thousand years.[71] However, the medieval Kabbalists ultimately maintain that the Torah not only precedes the world chronologically, but also ontologically.[72] The Torah is given priority not only in time but also in being, for the Torah in its primordial state participates in the reality of the *s^ep̄îrôṯ*, the hidden realm of divine emanations that underlies and gives rise to the created worlds.

The kabbalistic conception of the primordial Torah must therefore be understood in the context of the kabbalistic doctrine of the ten *s^ep̄îrôṯ*, the ten spheres of divine light through which the hidden, unmanifest God, 'Ên-Sôp̄, manifests himself: (1) Keṯer 'Elyôn (supreme crown), (2) Ḥoḵmāh (wisdom), (3) Bînāh (intelligence), (4) Ḥeseḏ (love), (5) G^ebûrāh (power), (6)Tip̄'ereṯ (beauty), (7) Neṣāḥ (lasting endurance), (8) Hôḏ (majesty), (9) Y^esôḏ (foundation), and (10) Malḵûṯ (kingdom). The ten *s^ep̄îrôṯ* function together as a single, unified organism, representing the dynamic, pulsating life of the Godhead. In their totality the *s^ep̄îrôṯ* are often depicted in the form of a man, each *s^ep̄îrāh* representing a different part of the cosmic body. Each *s^ep̄îrāh* represents a specific aspect of the Godhead and is responsible for bringing out particular aspects of creation.

The author of the *Rā'ăyā' M^ehêm^enā'* (The Faithful Shepherd) and the *Tîqqûnê Zohar*, the latest sections of the Zohar written at the end of the 13th century, distinguishes between two different aspects of the Torah: *Tôrāh d^e-'ăṣîlûṯ*, "Torah in the state of emanation," and *Tôrāh d^e-b^erî'āh*, "Torah in the state of creation." *Tôrāh d^e-'ăṣîlûṯ* is the uncreated Torah that is completely self-contained and one with God in the divine realm of the *s^ep̄îrôṯ*. This

Torah is characterized by the words, "The Torah of the Lord is perfect" (Ps. 19.8). *Tôrāh d^e-b^erî'āh*, on the other hand, is characterized by the words, "The Lord made me as the beginning of His way" (Prov. 8.22), for it is this Torah that manifests when God himself emerges from his hidden abode and reveals himself in the works of creation.[73]

Within the realm of the *s^epîrôṯ* the Torah is described by the Kabbalists as emerging in stages that recapitulate the process through which the *s^epîrôṯ* emanate from the unmanifest 'Ên- Sôp̄. In its earliest and most hidden stage of manifestation it is sometimes referred to by thirteenth-century Kabbalists as *Tôrāh k^eḏûmāh*, the primordial Torah, which is sometimes identified with Ḥoḵmāh, wisdom, the second *s^epîrāh*.[74]

Emanation of Keṯer, Ḥoḵmāh, and Bînāh. The role of the primordial Torah in the process of creation can best be understood by briefly examining the process through which the first three *s^epîrôṯ*—Keṯer, Ḥoḵmāh, and Bînāh—which are frequently associated with the primordial Torah, unfold from the unmanifest 'Ên-Sôp̄. This phase of our analysis is based on the Zohar's descriptions of this process.

In the cosmogonic scheme of the Zohar, the ultimate source of creation is 'Ên-Sôp̄ (literally, "without limit"), which is described as an unmanifest, unbounded, transcendental reality that is "hidden and removed far beyond all ken."[75] When the time of creation dawns, the unmanifest 'Ên-Sôp̄, the "Cause above all causes,"[76] emerges from its hidden abode in ten spheres of manifestation, ten spheres of divine light, or *s^epîrôṯ*. The first *s^epîrāh* is Keṯer (crown), the supernal Man on which as a chariot the unmanifest 'Ên-Sôp̄ descends into the realm of manifestation.[77] Keṯer is the supernal effulgence of the Godhead known as "brightness" (*zohar*), containing within itself all the lights of the other *s^epîrôṯ* and the totality of creation yet undifferentiated.[78] Keṯer is the supreme will that sets the process of creation in motion.[79]

The Zohar describes how with the "decision of the King" to create, the effulgence of Keṯer withdrew into itself and a hidden supernal point shone forth.[80] This primordial point is the thought of the Creator, in which he enfolds himself and the totality of the universe in potential form. From this single concentrated impulse of thought the entire creation unfolds.[81] This primordial point of divine thought is identified in the Zohar with the second *s^epîrāh*—Ḥoḵmāh, wisdom. Ḥoḵmāh is that primordial wisdom which is exalted in Proverbs 8.22–31 as existing from "the beginning (*rē'šîṯ*)" as the artisan of creation and is identified in the Zohar with the Torah.[82]

"The Lord by wisdom founded the earth; by understanding he

> established the heavens" (Prov. III,19). When God . . . created the world, He saw that it could not exist without the Torah, as this is the only source of all laws above and below, and on it alone are the upper and lower beings established. Hence, "the Lord by wisdom founded the earth; by understanding he established the heavens", inasmuch as it is through Wisdom that all things are enabled to exist in the universe, and from it all things proceed.[83]

While the Torah is generally identified with Ḥoḵmāh, wisdom, in the Zohar, it is also at times described as having its source in Ḥoḵmāh.

> There is no Torah without wisdom and no wisdom without Torah, both being in the same grade, the root of the Torah being in the supernal Wisdom by which it is sustained.[84]

The Torah in its identification with Ḥoḵmāh is hypostatized as the Father,[85] whose seed is deposited in the womb of the Mother, Bînāh (intelligence), the third *s^e^p̄îrāh*,[86] who is called the Great Voice.[87] The child that is born from the union of Ḥoḵmāh and Bînāh is identified in the Zohar with Tip̄'ereṯ (beauty), the sixth *s^e^p̄îrāh*, who as the lower Ḥoḵmāh represents the second phase of manifestation of the Father.

Unfoldment of the Divine Speech. The successive emanation of the *s^e^p̄îrôṯ* is described in several passages in the Zohar as a process through which the divine speech unfolds. The realm of the *s^e^p̄îrôṯ* is the hidden world of divine language, the ten *s^e^p̄îrôṯ* being identified with the ten primordial utterances through which the world was created.[88] The stages of unfoldment of the divine speech are ultimately correlated with the stages of manifestation of the Torah, as will be discussed in the following section.

The process through which the divine speech unfolds begins with the emergence of the primordial point of divine thought, Ḥoḵmāh, wisdom, which is the *rē'šîṯ*, "beginning," of creation. As in rabbinic literature the word *b^e^rē'šîṯ*, with which the Torah opens, is understood in the Zohar to mean "with wisdom [=Torah]"[89]—that primordial wisdom which has existed "from the beginning (*rē'šîṯ*)" (Prov. 8.22) as the instrument through which God created heaven and earth.[90]

> When God designed to create the universe, His thought compassed all worlds at once, and by means of this thought were they all created, as it says, "In wisdom hast thou made them all" (Ps. CIV,24). By this thought—which is His Wisdom—were this world and the world above created.[91]

How does this primordial point of divine thought give rise to creation? The mechanics of creation are described in a number of passages in the Zohar as the mechanics through which thought develops, for creation is viewed as simply a process of unfolding the original seed-thought of wisdom, Ḥoḵmāh, through progressive stages of development until it finds expression on the level of vocalized speech.

> When the Holy One, blessed be He, wills that His glory should be glorified, there issues from His thought a determination that it should spread forth; whereupon it spreads from the undiscoverable region of thought until it rests in *garon* (throat), a spot through which perenially [*sic*] flows the mystic force of the "spirit of life". When the thought, after its expansion, comes to rest in that place, it is called *Elohim hayyim* (living God). It then seeks to spread and disclose itself further, and there issue from that spot fire, air, and water, all compounded together. There also emerges "Jacob, the perfect man", symbolic of a certain voice that issues and becomes audible. Thus the thought that was hitherto undisclosed and withdrawn in itself is now revealed through sound. In the further extension and disclosure of the thought, the voice strikes against the lips, and thus comes forth speech which is the culmination of the whole and in which the thought is completely disclosed. It is thus clear that all is composed of that undisclosed thought which was withdrawn in itself, and that the whole is one essence.[92]

In this description the major stages in the unfoldment of the divine speech—will, thought, inaudible voice, audible voice, and vocalized speech—correspond to the five *sᵉp̄îrôṯ* Keṯer, Ḥoḵmāh, Bînāh, Tip̄'ereṯ, and Malḵûṯ, respectively. The divine will of the Holy One is Keṯer, the first *sᵉp̄îrāh*, from which issues a thought—Ḥoḵmāh, the second *sᵉp̄îrāh*. This concentrated impulse of thought, arising from that "undiscoverable region," expands and creates an abode for itself in the throat, where it is called Elohim Ḥayyîm—Bînāh, the third *sᵉp̄îrāh*. The voice of Jacob, which is *Tip̄'ereṯ*, the sixth *sᵉp̄îrāh*, then issues forth and, striking against the lips, culminates in audible speech that can be heard without—Malḵûṯ (kingdom), the tenth *sᵉp̄îrāh*, which is the Shekhinah, the divine presence.

In another passage the Zohar clearly separates these different phases into four main stages (not including the divine will, Keṯer): (1) supernal wisdom (Ḥoḵmāh), which is located in the thought and is not disclosed or heard; (2) the Great Voice (Bînāh), which is the living spirit (Elohim Ḥayyîm) that issues forth from wisdom and discloses it a little "in a whisper which cannot be heard," flowing on without ceasing in the region of the throat and forming a house for the supernal wisdom; (3) the voice of Jacob (Tip̄'eret̲), which is the audible voice that issues forth from the inaudible Great Voice; and (4) the outer, articulated speech or utterance (Malk̲ût̲) through which the voice of Jacob emerges in the open and finds expression on the vocalized level.[93]

Supernal wisdom (Ḥok̲māh) and the voice of Jacob (Tip̄'eret̲) are considered to be male, representing the upper Ḥok̲māh and lower Ḥok̲māh, or Father and Son, respectively. The Great Voice (Bînāh) and the outer, articulated speech (Malk̲ût̲) are female, representing the Mother above and the Mother below, or Mother and Daughter, respectively.[94] In both cases the male aspect provides the content, which is wisdom, and the female aspect discloses the content, giving it manifest expression through speech.

The first two stages in the unfoldment of the divine speech—supernal wisdom and the Great Voice—are said to be inaudible, taking place in silence, while the last two stages—the voice of Jacob and vocalized speech—are audible.[95] Another passage of the Zohar places these various stages in the context of the overall mechanics of creation and clarifies the distinction between the inaudible and audible phases. The first two stages—in which the primordial point of thought, Ḥok̲māh, expands and creates a "house" or "palace" for himself, implanting his seed in the womb of Bînāh, the Mother—occur in silence, and therefore "although the word *bereshith* is a creative utterance (*maamar*), the actual words 'and [God] said' are not used in connection with it."[96] The words "and God said" are used for the first time in the creation narrative of Genesis 1 at the point when the child, conceived through the union of the Father and Mother, issues forth from the womb of the Mother as a voice uttering audible speech that can be heard from without.

> Hence "and God said" means that now the above-mentioned palace generated from the holy seed with which it was pregnant. While it brought forth in silence, that which it bore was heard without. That which bore, bore in silence without making a sound, but when that issued from it which did issue, it became a voice which was heard without, to wit, "Let there be light."[97]

This voice appears to encompass both the voice of Jacob (Tip̄'eret̲), which issues forth from the Great Voice of Bînāh (the palace), and the outer speech (Malk̲ût̲) through which it is "heard without." It is this voice that is responsible for unfolding the details of creation from the original totality by means of the series of specific commands that are introduced in the first chapter of Genesis by the words "and God said."

Stages of Manifestation of the Torah. The different stages in the unfoldment of the divine speech, with their corresponding *s^e^p̄îrôṯ*, are identified in kabbalistic literature with the different stages in the manifestation of Torah. The Kabbalists generally distinguish at least three main manifestations of the Torah: (1) *Torah k^e^ḏûmāh*, the primordial Torah discussed earlier, which is generally identified with Ḥoḵmāh, the second *s^e^p̄îrāh*; (2) the Written Torah, which is identified with Tip̄'ereṯ, the sixth *s^e^p̄îrāh*; and (3) the Oral Torah, which is identified with Malḵûṯ, the Shekhinah, the tenth *s^e^p̄îrāh*.

In the Zohar all three aspects of the Torah are allotted a role in creation. The Torah as Ḥoḵmāh, the primordial point of divine thought, contains the totality of creation in potential form and is said to be the source of both the Written Torah and the Oral Torah.[98] When the wholeness of Ḥoḵmāh, wisdom, differentiates, writing issues forth in the form of the letters of the Hebrew alphabet inscribed in the Written Torah.

> Letters were imprinted on the fabric of the Whole, on the upper and on the lower fabric. Afterwards the letters were distinguished and inscribed in the Scripture.[99]

From the power of the writing that issues forth from Ḥoḵmāh, the Written Torah (Tip̄'ereṯ) is said to have produced the world, while the Oral Torah (Malḵûṯ) is said to be responsible for completing and preserving the world.[100] In the Zoharic conception the Written Torah and Oral Torah, hypostatized as Tip̄'ereṯ and Malḵûṯ, complement and support one another,[101] representing the unity of the male and female principles,[102] the unity of the upper and lower worlds,[103] and the unity of the Holy Name.[104] The Written Torah remains undisclosed, hidden on the subtler levels of creation, while the Oral Torah is revealed to human beings on earth.[105] The Written Torah on high rejoices in the Oral Torah below.[106]

The Provençal Kabbalist Isaac the Blind of Posquières, who lived in the middle of the twelfth century prior to the appearance of the Zohar, gives a detailed description of the different stages of manifestation of the Torah and their corresponding *s^e^p̄îrôṯ*, which expands and elaborates on the threefold conception of the Torah found in the Zohar and other medieval kabbalistic texts.

> In God's right hand were engraved all the engravings [innermost forms] that were destined some day to rise from potency to act. From the emanation of all [higher] *sefiroth* they were graven, scratched, and molded into the *sefirah* of Grace (*hesed*), which is also

> called God's right hand, and this was done in an inward, inconceivably subtle way. This formation is called the concentrated, not yet unfolded Torah, and also the Torah of Grace. Along with all the other engravings [principally] two engravings were made in it. The one has the form of the written Torah, the other the form of the oral Torah. The form of the written Torah is that of the colors of white fire, and the form of the oral Torah has colored forms as of black fire. And all these engravings and the not yet unfolded Torah existed potentially, perceptible neither to a spiritual nor to a sensory eye, until the will [of God] inspired the idea of activating them by means of primordial wisdom and hidden knowledge. Thus at the beginning of all acts there was pre-existentially the not yet unfolded Torah [*torah kelulah*], which is in God's right hand with all the primordial forms [literally: inscriptions and engravings] that are hidden in it, and this is what the Midrash implies when it says that God took the primordial Torah (*torah kedumah*), which stems from the quarry of "repentance" [[Bînāh]] and the source of original wisdom [[Ḥoḵmāh]], and in one spiritual act emanated the not yet unfolded Torah in order to give permanence to the foundations of all the worlds.[107]

R. Isaac goes on to discuss how from the not yet unfolded Torah, which corresponds to Ḥeseḏ, the *s^e^p̄îrāh* of grace, emerged the Written Torah, which corresponds to Tip̄'ereṯ, the *s^e^p̄îrāh* of divine compassion, and the Oral Torah, which corresponds to Malḵûṯ, the *s^e^p̄îrāh* of divine judgment, the Shekhinah.

In the above passage four different stages of manifestation of the Torah can be distinguished, each corresponding to a different *s^e^pîrāh*: (1) the primordial Torah (*Tôrāh k^e^ḏûmāh*), which stems from Ḥoḵmāh and Bînāh, the second and third *s^e^p̄îrôṯ*; (2) the not yet unfolded Torah (*Tôrāh k^e^lûlāh*), which contains all the primordial engravings and corresponds to the fourth *s^e^p̄îrāh*, Ḥeseḏ; (3) the Written Torah, which corresponds to Tip̄'ereṯ, the sixth *s^e^p̄îrāh*; and (4) the Oral Torah, which corresponds to Malḵûṯ, the last *s^e^p̄îrāh*.

R. Isaac's description adds several elements to the more common threefold conception of the Torah. (1) The primordial Torah is described as stemming not only from Ḥoḵmāh but from Bînāh as well, a conception also found in at least one passage of the Zohar in which the Torah is said to be an emanation of both Ḥoḵmāh and Bînāh.[108] (2) A fourth stage of manifestation is added to the usual threefold scheme: the not yet unfolded Torah corresponding to Ḥeseḏ. (3) The passage indicates that prior to any of the four stages of manifestation the Torah existed in an unmanifest form, in which the engravings of the Written Torah and Oral Torah, along with the other engravings of the not yet unfolded Torah, "existed potentially, perceptible neither to a spiritual nor to a sensory eye." It is only when, at the beginning of creation, the divine will (Keṯer, the first s^e^p̄îrāh) "inspired the idea of activating them" that the wholeness of the primordial Torah emerged and emanated forth the differentiated engravings of the not yet unfolded Torah, from which in turn emanated the more particular engravings of the Written Torah and Oral Torah.

Torah as the Name of God. The kabbalistic conceptions described in the above sections can be schematized in a threefold set of correspondences in which four *s^e^p̄îrôṯ* are primary.

S^e^p̄îrāh	*Stage of Divine Speech*	*Stage of Manifestation of Torah*
Ḥoḵmāh (Father)	thought	Primordial Torah
Bînāh (Mother)	inaudible voice	
Tip̄'ereṯ (Son)	audible voice	Written Torah
Malḵûṯ (Daughter)	vocalized speech	Oral Torah

While the different stages of manifestation of Torah have thus been correlated with particular *s^e^p̄îrôṯ*, the Torah is ultimately described by the Kabbalists as encompassing the influence of all the *s^e^p̄îrôṯ*.[109] In its stages of unfoldment from the unmanifest 'Ên-Sôp̄ through Ḥoḵmāh and Bînāh to Tip̄'ereṯ and Malḵûṯ, the Torah encompasses all of the *s^e^p̄îrôṯ*, all of the spheres of the Godhead. The Torah as the Word of God encompasses all of the ten words or utterances through which God brought forth creation.

The Torah as the Word of God is intimately linked in kabbalistic thought with the conception of Torah as the Name of God. The *s^e^p̄îrôṯ* are described in the Kabbalah not only as ten creative words but also as ten divine names, and the Torah is correspondingly described as that totality of divine unity which is the one Word containing all words, the one Name containing all names.

The conception that the Torah is the one great Name of God first appears among the thirteenth-century Spanish Kabbalists of Gerona, where it was elaborated by the more senior colleagues of Naḥmanides.[110] Ezra b. Solomon proclaimed, "The five books of the Torah are the Name of the Holy One, blessed be He.[111] This conception was developed by several other members of the Gerona circle.[112] A similar thesis is found in *Sēp̄er ha-Ḥayyîm*, a text that emerged independently of the Gerona Kabbalists and was printed in the first three decades of the thirteenth century in France.[113] The Zohar, the classical text of Spanish Kabbalah, expressly assumes the identity of the Torah and the Name of God, declaring that the Torah is the one supernal name of the Holy One.[114] The Zohar ultimately proclaims that God and the Torah are one, for he and his Name are one.[115]

The full significance of this declaration can only be understood on the basis of the kabbalistic conception of the creative power of language, which in turn is founded on corresponding rabbinic teachings. Implicit in the traditional rabbinic conception of the creative power of the word is the notion that an existential relationship exists between the word and what it signifies, between the name and the form that it designates. The Hebrew term *dāḇār* itself conveys the double meaning of "word" and "thing," for in the ancient conception found throughout the Near East the name participates in the reality and essence of what is named. Understood in this context the notion that the Torah is the Name of God ultimately leads to the conclusion that God and the Torah are one, for the Torah as God's Name represents the total manifestation of the divine essence and power, which are concentrated in his Name. This is the conclusion arrived at not only by the Zohar but also by Joseph Gikatilla, a prominent thirteenth-century Spanish Kabbalist who was undoubtedly influenced by the Zohar.

> His Torah is in Him, and that is what the Kabbalists say, namely, that the Holy One, blessed be He, is in His Name and His Name is in Him, and that His Name is His Torah.[116]

He further explains this statement with reference to a formula from the hymns of the Merkabah mystics.

> It is an important principle that the ancients expressed in the words: "Thy Name is in Thee and in Thee is Thy Name." For the letters of His Name are He Himself. Even though they move away from Him, they remain firmly rooted [literally, fly away and remain with Him].[117]

The letters, according to Gikatilla, are the mystical body of God, while God is the soul of the letters. The concept that God and the Torah are one was also expressed by other Kabbalists, such as Menaḥem Recanati (ca. 1300 C.E.), who maintained that "the Torah is not something outside Him, and He is not outside the Torah.[118]

According to the most abstract level of interpretation, then, the Torah as the Name of God means that the Torah participates in the essence and power of God and that ultimately the Torah and God are one. The Torah in its most complete manifestation encompasses all of the *s^e^pîrôṯ*, all aspects of the Godhead; it is the one great Name of God that encompasses all of the divine names.

How does this abstract conception of the Torah as a living manifestation of the Godhead relate to the concrete earthly form of the book of the Torah, which is composed of words and sentences that convey specific meanings? Gikatilla provides an interpretation that links the divine and earthly forms of the Torah. The Torah as it appears on the earthly plane, according to Gikatilla, is a living texture of names that is ultimately woven from the one true Name of God, the tetragrammaton YHWH. All of the names of the Torah are contained in the tetragrammaton, and the tetragrammaton is itself woven both directly and in a secret, hidden way throughout the fabric (*'ariga*) of the Torah.[119]

> The whole Torah is a fabric of appellatives, *kinnuyim*—the generic term for the epithets of God, such as compassionate, great, merciful, venerable—and these epithets in turn are woven from the various names of God [such as *El, Elohim, Shaddai*]. But all these holy names are connected with the tetragrammaton YHWH and dependent upon it. Thus the entire Torah is ultimately woven from the tetragrammaton.[120]

The conception of Torah as a fabric of names was first articulated by Moses b. Naḥman (Naḥmanides), the eminent Talmudist and most authoritative representative of the early Spanish Kabbalists. In the preface to his commentary on the Torah, Naḥmanides cites a tradition in which the Torah can simultaneously be read on two levels: in the traditional manner as historical narratives and commandments, or according to a more subtle level of interpretation as a series of divine names.

> We possess an authentic tradition showing that the entire Torah consists of the names of God and that the words we read can be divided in a very different way, so as to form [esoteric] names. . . . The statement in the Aggadah to the effect that the Torah was originally written with black fire on white fire obviously confirms our opinion that the writing was continuous, without division into words, which made it possible to read it either as a sequence of [esoteric] names [*'al derekh ha-shemoth*] or in the traditional way as history and commandments. Thus the Torah as given to Moses was divided into words in such a way as to be read as divine command-

ments. But at the same time he received the oral tradition, according to which it was to be read as a sequence of names.[121]

Naḥmanides points out that it is this subtle structure of the Torah as a sequence of divine names that accounts for the rigorous Masoretic tradition concerning the writing of a scroll of the Torah, in which a scroll is disqualified if even a single letter is added or omitted. Naḥmanides' colleagues in Gerona elaborated on this conception, emphasizing the organic unity of the Torah as the Name of God, which constitutes a perfect divine edifice (*binyān 'ĕlôhi*) in which there is not a single superfluous letter or point. The Torah, according to Ezra b. Solomon, "in its divine totality... is an edifice hewn from the Name of the Holy One, blessed be He."[122] Both Ezra and his younger contemporary Azriel b. Menaḥem of Gerona maintain that not a single letter or point can be eliminated from this organic totality without harming the entire body. Azriel writes,

> Just as in the body of a man there are limbs and joints, just as some organs of the body are more, others less, vital, so it seems to be with the Torah. To one who does not understand their hidden meaning, certain sections and verses of the Torah seem fit to be thrown into the fire; but to one who has gained insight into their true meaning they seem essential components of the Torah. Consequently, to omit so much as one letter or point from the Torah is like removing some part of a perfect edifice. Thence it also follows that in respect of its divine character no essential distinction can be drawn between the section of Genesis 36, setting forth the generations of Esau [a seemingly superfluous passage], and the Ten Commandments, for it is all *one* whole and *one* edifice.[123]

The kabbalistic conception of Torah as the Name of God thus embraces at least three levels of understanding the Torah: (1) the Torah as the one great Name of God that represents the total manifestation of God's essence and power; (2) the Torah as a sequence of divine names and appellatives; and (3) the Torah as a sequence of words and sentences with earthly referents. What is the relationship between these different levels of the Torah?

In the kabbalistic view the basic structural elements of the Torah in all its manifestations are the letters of the Hebrew alphabet, which combine in various ways to give rise to the different forms of the Torah. The scroll of the Torah, according to the Kabbalists, contains no vowels, no punctuation, and no accents precisely as an allusion to the fact that the Torah, while remaining nonchanging and inviolable in its essential nature, can be read in different ways according to the manner in which one combines and divides the letters into words.

Moses Cordovero, a leading sixteenth-century Kabbalist of the Safed school, describes four levels of manifestation of the Torah that are distinguished not only by the manner in which the letters combine but also by the degree of materialization of the letters. In its subtlest phase of manifestation, according to Cordovero, the Torah is composed of subtle letters that are different configurations of divine light. In the subsequent phase of manifestation the letters progressively materialize and combine in various ways to form, first, names of God, then appellatives and predicates referring to the divine, and finally words formed from material letters that refer to earthly events and phenomena. Cordovero uses this progressive process of materialization to explain the state of the Torah prior to the fall, after the fall, and in the Messianic Age.[124]

Torah in the Four Worlds. Cordovero's formulation of the four forms of the Torah—subtle letters, names of God, appellatives, and material words—is developed in a somewhat different manner in writings originating in the school of Israel Sarug (ca. 1600 C.E.), a Lurianic Kabbalist. In these texts each of the four forms of the Torah corresponds to one of the four worlds that are described by Kabbalists from the sixteenth century onward as existing between the unmanifest 'Ên-Sôp̄ and the gross material world: (1) *'ăṣîlûṯ*, the world of emanation, which is the abode of the ten *s^e^p̄îrôṯ*; (2) *b^e^rî'āh,* the world of creation, which is the abode of the throne, the Merkabah (throne-chariot), and the highest angels; (3) *y^e^ṣîrāh,* the world of formation, which is the main domain of the angels; and (4) *'ăśiyyāh,* the world of making or activation, which is the spiritual archetype of the material world.

The texts describe how the unmanifest 'Ên-Sôp̄, in self-rapture, begins to move within itself, generating the movement of language and weaving a texture (*malbûš*) of the twenty-two letters of the Hebrew alphabet in the substance of 'Ên-Sôp̄ itself. This constitutes the original Torah, in which the letters, in their original sequence, contain within themselves the seeds of all possibilities for further linguistic expression. In the next phase the Torah assumes different forms corresponding to the four worlds. In the highest world, the world of *'ăṣîlûṯ*, the Torah manifests, as in the original texture, as a sequence of combinations of the Hebrew consonants. In the second world, the world of *b^e^rî'āh*, the Torah appears as a sequence of holy names of God, which are formed by certain further combinations of the elements found in the world of *'ăṣîlûṯ*. As it becomes increasingly more manifest, the Torah appears as a sequence of angelic names in the third world, the world of *yᵉṣîrāh*. Finally, in the fourth world, the world of *'ăśiyyāh*, the Torah appears in its traditionally transmitted form.[125]

Combining this analysis with that of Moses Cordovero, the four different forms of the Torah can be summarized as follows: (1) *'ăṣîlûṯ*—Torah as a sequence of letters; (2) *bᵉrî'āh*—Torah as a fabric of names of God; (3) *yᵉṣîrāh*—Torah as a sequence of appellatives or angelic names; and (4) *'ăśiyyāh*—Torah as a sequence of words and sentences referring to concrete material objects and earthly events. These different forms of the Torah are ultimately encompassed in the conception of Torah as the Name of God, for in the kabbalistic perspective it is the Name of God that is the source of all language, the source of all letters, and hence the source of all possible combinations of letters that form names, appellatives, words, and sentences. All the concrete and subtle manifestations of the Torah are in the final analysis modifications of the one great Name of God.

It is interesting to note in this context that certain Kabbalists, in particular the Lurianic school, correlated the four letters of the tetragrammaton—Yôḏ-Hē-Wāw-Hē—with the four worlds—*'ăṣîlûṯ*, *bᵉrî'āh*, *yᵉṣîrāh*, and *'ăśiyyāh*, respectively—and by implication with the four forms of the Torah in the four worlds. The four letters and the four worlds are in turn correlated with the four *sᵉp̄îrôṯ*—Ḥoḵmāh, Bînāh, Tip̄'ereṯ, and Malḵûṯ, respectively—that correspond to the major stages of manifestation of the Torah discussed earlier. Our previous schema can thus be expanded to incorporate a number of new elements.

Sᵉp̄îrāh	*World*	*Letter of Tetragrammaton*	*Stage of Manifestation of Torah*	*Form of Torah*
Ḥoḵmāh	'Ăṣîlûṯ	Yôḏ	Primordial Torah	Letters
Bînāh	Bᵉrî'āh	Hē		Names of God
Tip̄'ereṯ	Yᵉṣîrāh	Wāw	Written Torah	Appellatives or Angelic Names
Malḵûṯ	'Ăśiyyāh	Hē	Oral Torah	Words with Earthly Referents

Torah as the Blueprint of Creation. The Torah as the Name of God expresses that aspect of God which is revealed in and through creation. It encompasses the totality of God's manifestations in the world of emanation, the realm of the *sᵉp̄îrôṯ*, and in the created worlds. The letters of the Hebrew alphabet that have their root and source in the Name of God are the basic structural elements that combine in various ways to give rise to the different forms of the Torah corresponding to each of the four worlds. According to the school of Israel Sarug the particular configuration of letters in each form of the Torah reflects the laws and structure of the corresponding world. Implicit in this conception is the notion that the Torah in all its manifestations constitutes the perfect and all-comprehensive blueprint of creation that reveals the laws and structure of every level of existence.

This rather sophisticated conception of the Torah as the blueprint of creation appears in a more simplified form in earlier kabbalistic texts. For example, the Zohar depicts the Torah as a blueprint in the sense of a plan composed of words that God "looks at" or contemplates in order to bring forth the manifold forms of creation.

> When the Holy One resolved to create the world, He guided Himself by the Torah as by a plan, as has been pointed out in connection with the words "Then I was by him as *amon*" (Prov. VIII,30), where the word *amon* (nursling) may also be read *uman* (architect). . . . when He [the Holy One] resolved to create the world He looked into the Torah, into its every creative word, and fashioned the world correspondingly; for all the words [*sic*] and all the actions of all the worlds are contained in the Torah. Therefore did the Holy One, blessed be He, look into it and create the world. . . . God looked at His plan in this way. It is written in the Torah: "In the beginning God created the heavens and the earth"; He looked at this expression and created heaven and earth. In the Torah it is written: "Let there be light"; He looked at these words and created light; and in this manner was the whole world created.[126]

In another passage the Holy One not only looks at the words of the Torah; he utters the words. Commenting on Job 28.27, "Then did He see it and declare it; He established it and searched it out," the Zohar explains that God first saw or contemplated the words of the Torah; then he uttered them forth and thereby established the forms of creation. Seeing, declaring, establishing, and searching out correspond to the four operations through which God brings forth creation.[127] In the Zohar's formulation of the mechanics of creation we once again find a progression from unspoken thought to spoken word to concrete form.

The Zohar maintains that in creating the world God used the Torah as the plan both of the whole and the parts of creation.[128] Through the Torah all the worlds and all beings, both above and below, were created.[129] Through the Torah human beings were created.[130] According to the Zohar the human being is a microcosm, the structure of the human body reflecting the structure of the macrocosm. The microcosm and macrocosm are in turn organized in accordance with the plan and structure of the Torah, which itself consists of different parts that combine to form a single body.

> . . . . whoever labours in the Torah upholds the world, and enables each part to perform its function. For there is not a member in the human body but has its counterpart in the world as a whole. For as man's body consists of members and parts of various ranks all acting and reacting upon each other so as to form one organism, so does the world at large consist of a hierarchy of created things, which when they properly act and react upon each other together form literally one organic body. Thus the whole is organised on the scheme of the Torah, which also consists of sections and divisions which fit into one another and, when properly arranged together, form one organic body.[131]

TORAH AND REVELATION

The rabbinic and kabbalistic conceptions of Torah can thus be seen to encompass far more than a book or scroll inscribed with letters. Although the kabbalistic conception of Torah is of course much more fully developed as part of a formal, elaborate cosmological scheme, there are nevertheless certain recurring themes that are found in both rabbinic and kabbalistic formulations. In particular, the Torah is described on at least three different levels in rabbinic and kabbalistic texts, which can be summarized as follows.

1. The Torah is personified—or, in the case of the Kabbalah, hypostatized—as a living, organic entity, a living aspect of God, which is variously described as primordial wisdom, the Word of God, and the one great Name of God. On this level the Torah constitutes that undifferentiated wholeness of divine wisdom which is the immediate source of creation.

2. The Torah is the subtle blueprint of creation, which contains the fundamental structural elements that lie at the basis of all creation. On this level the Torah has differentiated from its original state of unity into the letters of the Hebrew alphabet, which combine into names/words. The one Name differentiates into names, the one Word divides into words. On the most subtle level these names/words constitute the "ideas" of all the forms of creation conceived in the mind of God as the ideal plan of the universe. These ideas are then spoken out by God as uttered words, which are then precipitated to form the manifold phenomena of creation.

3. The Torah is a concrete written text composed of words and sentences inscribed on parchment that refer to earthly phenomena and events in the form of historical narratives and commandments. This is the transmitted Torah that is said to have been revealed to Moses and the people of Israel at Mount Sinai at a particular time in history.

What is the relationship between the finite, historical Torah of revelation and the preexistent, primordial Torah that served as the instrument of creation? These two aspects of Torah can be viewed as different levels of manifestation corresponding to different levels of creation: earthly and heavenly, gross and subtle. In rabbinic terms at the time of the revelation at Mount Sinai the primordial Torah descended from its heavenly abode onto earth, assuming the finite form of the Written Torah. In kabbalistic terms at the time of the revelation the Torah emerged from its hidden abode in the unmanifest 'Ên-Sôp̄ and progressively unfolded in stages corresponding to the different *s^e^p̄îrôṯ* and worlds until it manifested on earth as the concrete book of the Torah.

In certain strands of the rabbinic and kabbalistic traditions the process of revelation is depicted as a recapitulation of the process through which creation itself unfolded. In this view the mechanics of revelation mirror the mechanics of creation, for the Word of God revealed at Mount Sinai is the same Word of God that brought forth creation "in the beginning."

This section will briefly consider some of the most important rabbinic and kabbalistic traditions concerning the nature of the revelation at Mount Sinai, with particular emphasis on those traditions that imply an ontological conception of the Torah.

Torah and Revelation in Rabbinic Texts

Descent of the Torah to Earth. A number of Midrashim describe how at the time of the revelation at Mount Sinai the Torah, which had existed on high since "the beginning" as God's co-worker in creation, descended onto the earth and became embodied in the words of the Written Torah. With the revelation at Mount Sinai the Torah entered into creation in a new way, making its abode on earth among the people of Israel.

Several Midrashim describe Moses' ascent of Mount Sinai in terms of an ascension to the heavens, which are the natural abode of the Torah. A Talmudic Midrash ascribed to the Palestinian Amora R. Joshua b. Levi relates how when Moses ascended to heaven to receive the Torah and bring it back to earth, the angels argued with God that his glory (the Torah) should not be given to the sons of men.

> When Moses ascended on high, the ministering angels spoke before the Holy One, blessed be He, "Sovereign of the universe, what has one born of woman to do among us?" He said to them, "He has come to receive the Torah." They said to him, "That precious treasure (*ḥămûḏāh gᵉnûzāh*), which has been hidden away by Thee for nine hundred and seventy-four generations before the world was created, Thou desirest to give to one of flesh and blood? 'What is man that Thou are mindful of him, and the son of man that Thou dost care for him? O Lord our Lord, how majestic is Thy name in all the earth! Thou who hast set Thy glory [the Torah] upon the heavens.' " (Ps. 8.4, 2).[132]

In reply to the angels Moses argued that the Torah contains positive and prohibitive commandments that only concern human beings in their earthly abode and do not apply to the angels in heaven. The angels conceded and as recompense bestowed gifts upon Moses. Moses then descended to earth with the Torah.[133]

An anonymous Midrash relates that when God was about to give the Torah he decreed that "Those who are below [Moses] shall ascend to those who are on high, while those who are on high [the Lord Himself] shall descend to those who are below."[134] When Moses ascended on high, according to another Midrash, he was with God and dwelt among the angels and seraphim.[135] A Midrash declared in the name of the Tanna R. Meir explains that the reason Moses fasted for forty days and nights was in order to emulate the heavenly example while on high, where there is no eating and drinking.[136]

When Moses descended from the heavens, he brought the Torah back with him to earth. A Midrash in Pᵉsîqtā' Rabbāṯî depicts how the heavens wept and lamented while the earth rejoiced when the Torah went forth to make its abode on earth.

> When the Holy One, blessed be He, gave the Torah to Israel, the earth rejoiced but the heavens wept. . . . The Holy One, blessed be He, said to the heavens, "You who abide on high should give praise to my glory and my daughter, even more than the earth does." They said to him, "Sovereign of the universe, the earth, to whom the Torah is being given, may well offer praise, but we from whom the Torah goes forth, how can we give praise and not be grieved?"[137]

The descent of the Torah is depicted in Pᵉsîqtā' Rabbāṯî and other Midrashic texts as a marriage ceremony in which the Torah as the bride of Israel departs from the home of her father on high and makes her abode with her spouse on earth. One anonymous Midrash compares God to a king who gives his only daughter to another king in marriage and then asks if he may dwell with them since he cannot bear to leave his daughter.

> Thus the Holy One, blessed be He, said to Israel, "I have given you a Torah from whom I cannot be separated, and yet I cannot say to you, 'Do not take her.' However, in every place to which you go make for me a house wherein I may dwell."[138]

When the Torah descended to earth to become the bride of Israel, God's presence descended with it. Ultimately it is not only the Torah who is wed with Israel at Mount Sinai; it is God himself. Hence we find that the marriage symbolism is used not only to depict the union between the Torah and Israel, but also to portray the eternal covenant between the Lord and his chosen people: "Like a bridegroom (*ḥāṯān*) who goes forth to meet the bride (*kallāh*), He went forth to give them the Torah, as it is said, 'O God, when Thou wentest forth before Thy people' (Ps. 68.7)."[139] As mentioned earlier, in this version of the wedding ceremony the Torah is sometimes depicted as the marriage contract (*k*ᵉ*tûbāh*) stipulating the conditions of the union between God and Israel.[140]

Revelation as the Recapitulation of Creation. In addition to descriptions of the descent of the Torah from heaven, rabbinic literature contains numerous traditions concerning the nature of the revelation of Torah on earth. The knowledge that was revealed directly to the people of Israel at Mount Sinai is traditionally understood to have consisted of the Ten Commandments,[141] which are said to contain the entire Torah in seed form. According to an anonymous Midrash the six hundred and thirteen letters from *'ānōḵî* (I am) to *'ăšer l*ᵉ*- rē'eḵā* (which belongs to thy neighbor) symbolize the six hundred and thirteen commandments (*miṣwôṯ*) of the Torah, while the seven extra words correspond to the seven days of creation.[142]

This Midrash establishes a direct relationship between the creation and the revelation, with the Torah serving as the common link between the two.[143] A Midrash in Pᵉsîqtā' Rabbāṯî connects the Ten Words of the revelation with the ten words by which the world was created.[144] The revelation to the people of Israel at Mount Sinai represented the seed expression of the total knowledge of Torah, and it is this same knowledge that is upheld in certain strands of the rabbinic tradition as the source and basis of creation. A number of descriptions of the unfoldment of the Word in revelation recall the mechanics through which the Word unfolds in creation.

The story of revelation, like the story of creation, is described as beginning in silence—the unbounded silence of the wilderness. It is here, in the limitless expanse and freedom of the wilderness, that the knowledge of Torah was given—a universal knowledge true for all peoples, all times, and all places.[145]

> The Torah was given publicly and openly, in a free place. For if the Torah had been given in the land of Israel, the Israelites could have said to the nations of the world, "You have no portion in it." But since it was given in the wilderness, publicly and openly, in a free place, everyone desiring to accept it could come and accept it.[146]

A number of Midrashim describe how when God gave the Torah to Israel his voice (*qôl*) resounded from one end of the earth to the other and was heard by all the nations of the world.[147] But before he began to speak, the Lord first hushed the world into silence. From utter stillness the Word of God went forth.

> R. Abbahu said in the name of R. Joḥanan: When the Holy One, blessed be He, gave the Torah no bird cried out, no fowl flew, no ox lowed, the Ophanim did not spread their wings, the Seraphim did not proclaim "Holy, Holy," the sea did not roar, the creatures did not speak. The whole world became hushed and silent, and the voice went forth: "I am the Lord thy God" (Exod. 20.1).... He brought the whole world to a standstill and silenced both those on high and those below, and the whole world became waste (*tôhû*) and void (*bôhû*), as if there was no creature in the world, as it is said, "But there was no voice, nor anyone who answered, nor anyone who heeded" (I Kings 18.29).... when God spoke on Mount Sinai, the whole world became silent in order that [all] creatures might know that there is none beside Him. Then He said, "I am the Lord thy God."[148]

At the time of revelation the whole universe became "waste and void," as if returning back to the original state of unmanifest silence from which the creation arose. The revelation is depicted as a recapitulation of creation, the almighty voice of God resounding forth from out of the silence and infusing the entire universe with new life. Every particle of creation was renewed and revitalized through the power of God's Word. An anonymous Midrash describes how the earth trembled, the mountains quaked, and the pillars of heaven shook; all of Israel trembled when they received the Word of life.[149] Another anonymous Midrash vividly depicts the all-pervading power of God's voice, which spread forth in all directions, encompassing the four quarters of the universe.

> When the Holy One, blessed be He, gave the Torah on Sinai, He showed wonders upon wonders to Israel with His voice. What happened? The Holy One, blessed be He, spoke and the voice went forth and reverberated throughout the whole world. Israel heard the voice coming to them from the south, so they ran to the south to receive the voice. From the south it shifted to the north, so they ran to the north. From the north it changed to the east, so they ran to the east. From the east it changed to the west, so they ran to the west. From the west it shifted to the heavens. When they raised their eyes to the heavens, it shifted to the earth, so they looked to the earth, as it said, "Out of heaven He caused you to hear His voice, that He might instruct you, and on earth He caused you to see His great fire, and you heard His words out of the midst of the fire" (Deut. 4.36).[150]

In the analysis of the role of the Torah in creation it was seen that the Word first emerges in its wholeness and then differentiates into many words, many individualized impulses of sound, which are then precipitated to form the manifold phenomena of creation. A similar process of differentiation of the Word is described as taking place at the revelation. A tradition attributed to the Palestinian Amora R. Joḥanan relates how at the revelation the one voice of God split into seventy voices, each voice speaking one of the seventy languages of the world so that every nation could hear and understand the revelation.[151]

A number of Midrashim attempt to convey the unique experiential dimension of the revelation at Mount Sinai, emphasizing in particular the compelling power, immediacy, and holistic nature of the experience. The overpowering nature of the experience is depicted in a number of Midrashim. For example, the above mentioned Midrash ascribed to R. Joḥanan relates how when the nations of the world heard the all-powerful voice of God in their own vernaculars they could not endure the experience and their souls departed, and Israel alone survived.[152] Another tradition attributed to R. Joḥanan's pupil R. Levi relates that the souls of Israel also departed upon hearing God's all-powerful voice, but their souls were restored.[153] The Israelites were so overwhelmed upon hearing the voice of the first commandment, according to a Midrash in Pirqê de-R. Eliezer, that they fell upon their faces and died. They were revived when the voice of the second commandment went forth, but they were so terrified that they pleaded with Moses, "Our teacher! We are not able to hear [anymore of] the voice of the Holy One, blessed be He, for we shall die in the same way as we [just] died, . . . as it is written, 'You speak to us,' they said to Moses, 'and we will hear, but let not God speak to us, lest we die' (Exod. 20.19)."[154] For this reason only the first two commandments were spoken directly by God to the people of Israel; the rest of the commandments he spoke through the mouth of Moses.[155]

The immediacy of the Israelites' experience at Mount Sinai is conveyed by a number of Midrashim, which emphasize that the voice of God was apprehended by each individual Israelite in accordance with his/her own strength and level of consciousness.[156]

> Just see how the voice went forth to each Israelite, to each in accordance with his individual strength—to the old in accordance with their strength, and to the youth according to theirs; to the children, to the infants, and to the women, in accordance with their strength, and even to Moses according to his strength. . . .[157]

The voice of the Lord was heard with the power of all voices, adapting itself to the needs of each individual, and yet the voice that went forth was one.[158]

The people of Israel's experience of the revelation is described as a holistic experience that directly engaged—and at the same time transcended—the senses, involving the sense of sight as well as the sense of hearing. The revelation of Torah was not only heard by the people as the all-powerful thunderings of God's voice,[159] it was simultaneously seen as the all-consuming brilliance of God's glory.

> R. Levi said: Israel asked of the Holy One, blessed be He, two things—that they should see His glory and that they should hear His voice. And they did see His glory and hear His voice, as it is said, "And you said, 'Behold, the Lord our God has shown us His glory and His greatness, and we have heard His voice out of the midst of the fire'" (Deut. 5.24).[160]

According to one tradition at the time of the revelation the people of Israel saw the Lord himself, in all his resplendent glory, eye to eye and face to face: "Thereupon the Holy One, blessed be He, opened the seven firmaments (*rāqîʿa*) and appeared over them—eye to eye, in His beauty, in His glory, in His countenance, with His crown, and upon His throne of glory."[161] The people of Israel are said not only to have seen the glory of God; they also saw his voice blazing forth in words of fire. Exodus 20.15, "And all the people saw the thunderings (*qôlôṯ*, lit., "voices")," is interpreted by R. Akiba to mean that the people of Israel not only heard the voice of God, but "they saw a word of fire come forth from the mouth of the Almighty and hewn out upon the tablets, as it is said, 'The voice of the Lord hewed out flames of fire' (Ps. 29.7)."[162] According to a tradition ascribed to the Palestinian Amora R. Simeon b. Laḳish, the Torah was written in black fire on white fire.[163]

The revelation at Mount Sinai as described in rabbinic literature was not simply a passive experience bestowed on the recipients; it was an active call, challenging those who heard the Word of God to respond and accept it. A frequently cited rabbinic tradition maintains that although the Word of God went forth to all the nations of the world, in the end none except Israel would accept it.[164] God offered the Torah to the children of Esau, the Ammonites, the Moabites, and the Ishmaelites, but each in turn refused to undertake its observance.[165] The Lord chose Israel because Israel alone chose the Lord and his Torah.[166] Israel's acceptance of the Torah is viewed by the rabbinic sages as a crucial turning point in creation. It is through the Torah that the universe emerged from the primeval chaos in the beginning of creation. The revelation at Mount Sinai was in sense a recapitulation of creation, a renovation and reconsolidation of the universe. If Israel had not accepted the Torah then this renewal of creation would not have been brought to fruition and the world would have been reduced to its original state of chaos.[167]

> Resh Laḳish said: Why is it written, "And there was evening and there was morning, *the* sixth day" (Gen. 1.31)? Why is there an additional "the"? This teaches that the Holy One, blessed be He, stipulated with the works of creation and said to them, "If Israel accepts the Torah, you shall become established, but if not, I will turn you back into waste (*tôhû*) and void (*bôhû*)."[168]

The world is said to have become established on a firm foundation when Israel accepted the Torah.[169]

Written Torah and Oral Torah. As discussed above, the Ten Commandments that were revealed directly by God to the people of Israel are said to contain the entire Torah in seed expression. All the ramifications and fine nuances of the Torah are said to be written between every commandment,[170] and in this sense the Torah itself is simply a detailed elaboration of the meaning inherent in the Ten Commandments.

After the initial revelation of the Decalogue to all the people of Israel, Moses ascended the mountain and remained on high for forty days and nights in order to receive the fully elaborated knowledge of Torah. Certain strands of the rabbinic tradition maintain that the knowledge received by Moses included not only the Pentateuch, but also the Nevi'im, Ketuvim, Mishnah, Talmud, and Aggadah.[171] Only the Holy Scriptures, consisting of the Pentateuch, Nevi'im, and Ketuvim, were given in writing, while the Mishnah, Talmud, and Aggadah were given orally.[172] God thus gave Moses two Torahs—the Written Torah and the Oral Torah.[173] A Midrash in Pirqê d^{e}-R. Eliezer describes Moses sitting before God on the mountain for forty days, "like a disciple who sits before his teacher, reading the Written Law (*dāṯ*) in the day and repeating the Oral Law (*dāṯ*) at night." The Oral Torah that Moses learned involved expounding (*dāraš*) the meaning of the words of the Written Torah and examining (*ḥāqar*) its letters.[174]

According to a more far-reaching interpretation of the Oral Torah, Moses received not only the written text of the Torah (Pentateuch), but also all the subtle distinctions and interpretations of its laws and teachings that would be introduced by the scribes and sages in all subsequent generations as part of the oral tradition.[175]

> When God was about to give the Torah, He declared it to Moses in due order—Bible (*miqrā'*), Mishnah, Aggadah, and Talmud—as it is said, "God spoke *all* these words" (Exod. 20.1). Even the answers to questions that scholars in the future would ask their teachers did God declare to Moses, for as it is said, "God spoke *all* these things."[176]

All the teachings of the sages in every generation were ultimately "'given from one Shepherd' (Eccles. 12.11). One God gave them, one leader declared them from the mouth of the Lord of all creation, blessed be He, as it is written, 'And God spoke *all* these words' (Exod. 21.1)."[177] A tradition attributed to the Tanna R. Isaac maintains that the prophets and sages were themselves present at Mount Sinai and received the teachings that they were to expound to future generations.[178]

> R. Isaac said: Everything that the prophets were destined to prophesy they received from Mount Sinai, as it is written, God spoke "with him who stands here with us this day" (Deut. 29.14)—these are those who were already created—and also "with him who is not here with us this day" (*ibid.*)—these are those who were destined to be created.... This not only applies to the prophets, but to all the sages that were destined to arise....[179]

A Talmudic Midrash attributed to the Babylonian Amora Rab Judah in the name of his teacher Rab vividly illustrates the far-reaching implications of such an all-encompassing interpretation of the Oral Torah. The Midrash relates a story about how when Moses ascended on high to receive the Torah the Lord showed him R. Akiba, who was destined to arise as one of the greatest sages of future generations, sitting and expounding the Torah to his disciples. Moses was at first ill at ease because he could not follow their arguments. However, when they came to a certain subject and the disciples asked the master, "Whence do you know this?" R. Akiba replied, "It is a law given unto Moses at Sinai," and Moses was comforted.[180]

Torah and Revelation in Kabbalistic Texts

The rabbinic traditions concerning the revelation of the Torah at Mount Sinai are elaborated and reinterpreted in kabbalistic literature in accordance with the cosmological doctrines of the Kabbalists.

Written Torah and Oral Torah: A Reinterpretation. Moses' ascension to the heavens to receive the Torah is interpreted in kabbalistic literature as an inner ascent on the level of conciousness in which Moses was able to station his awareness "on high," on the subtler levels of creation, and directly cognize the Torah in its more subtle states of manifestation. The descent of the Torah onto earth is interpreted as a recapitulation of the original process of creation, in which the Torah emerged from its hidden abode in the unmanifest 'Ên-Sôp̄ and unfolded in progressive stages of manifestation corresponding to particular *s^ep̄îrôṯ* until it was revealed on earth.

We discussed earlier the three main stages of manifestation of the Torah: the wholeness of the primordial Torah, corresponding to Ḥoḵmāh and Bînāh, and the differentiated "engravings" of the Written Torah, corresponding to Tip̄'ereṯ, and of the Oral Torah, corresponding to Malḵûṯ. In accordance with this cosmological scheme the rabbinic conception of the Written Torah and Oral Torah is radically reinterpreted by the Kabbalists. The Written Torah is said to remain undisclosed, hidden on the subtler levels of creation, while the Oral Torah alone is revealed on earth.[181]

In interpreting the rabbinic Aggadah that the Torah was given in black fire on white fire, Isaac the Blind understands the white fire to be the Written Torah, in which the form of the letters is not yet explicit. It is only through the power of the black fire, which is the Oral Torah, that the consonants and vowel points first take form. "And so the written Torah can take on corporeal form only through the power of the oral Torah, that is to say: without the oral Torah it cannot be truly understood."[182] According to R. Isaac only Moses, the supreme prophet, was established in that supreme state of consciousness in which he was able to station his awareness "on high," on the subtler levels of creation, and enjoy "unbroken contemplation" of the white light of the Written Torah. The other prophets attained only fleeting glimpses of the Written Torah.[183] From this concept of the Written Torah and Oral Torah Gershom Scholem concludes,

> . . . strictly speaking, there is no written Torah here on earth. A far-reaching idea! What we call the written Torah has itself passed through the medium of the oral Torah, it is no longer a form concealed in white light; rather, it has emerged from the black light, which determines and limits and so denotes the attribute of divine severity and judgment. Everything that we perceive in the fixed forms of the Torah, written in ink on parchment, consists, in the last analysis, of interpretations or definitions of what is hidden. *There is only an oral Torah*: that is the esoteric meaning of these words, and the written Torah is a purely mystical concept. It is embodied in a sphere that is accessible to prophets alone. It was, to be sure, revealed to Moses, but what he gave to the world as the written Torah has acquired its present form by passing through the medium of the oral Torah. The mystical white of the letters on the parchment is the written Torah, but not the black of the letters inscribed in ink. In the mystical organism of the Torah the two spheres overlap, and there is no written Torah, free from the oral element, that can be known or conceived of by creatures who are not prophets.[184]

Revelation as the Fruition of Creation. In their descriptions of the revelation of the Torah at Mount Sinai the Kabbalists elaborate on the rabbinic notion that the revelation not only recapitulated the process of creation but also brought it to completion by firmly establishing the worlds. This section will focus on the Zohar's depiction of the revelation, which provides a number of provocative amplifications and reinterpretations of the rabbinic conceptions.

The Zohar emphasizes that even though the upper and lower worlds had been supported and maintained by the Torah since the beginning of creation,[185] they were not completely and unshakeably established until Israel received the Torah at Mount Sinai.[186] It describes how the earth shook and desired to return to chaos when it saw that God had offered the Torah to all nations and they had refused it. But when Israel accepted the Torah the earth became calm again and rested at ease.[187] One passage relates that the letters of the alphabet, which are responsible for holding together the universe, had been in inverse order since the time of Adam's transgression, and it was not until Israel stood at Mount Sinai to receive the Torah that the letters recovered their proper order as on the day when heaven and earth were created. Through the revelation the creation was once again securely established and brought to fruition.[188]

> Nor yet was the world finally completed until Israel received the Torah on Mount Sinai and the Tabernacle was set up. All worlds were then finally established and perfected, and higher and lower creatures were properly based.[189]

The worlds were firmly established when the Torah was accepted at Mount Sinai because the revelation itself is held to be a second creation. In the beginning of creation the Torah issued forth as the Word of God containing the ten utterances or words from which the universe was brought into being. At the time of revelation the Torah again issued forth from the heavens as the Word of God and split into Ten Words, represented by the Decalogue.[190] The Ten Words of revelation are directly identified in the Zohar with the Ten Words of creation, which correspond to the ten *s^e^p̄îrôṯ*, the ten spheres of the Godhead.[191] The unfoldment of the Ten Words at Mount Sinai thus represented the unfoldment of the full value of God's glory in all its aspects, encompassing all of the divine emanations—a recapitulation of the original revelation at the beginning of creation.

> Never before, since the Holy One created the world, had such a revelation of the Divine Glory taken place. . . . the glory of the Holy One was made known both above and below, and He was exalted over all.[192]

According to the Zohar the Israelites saw the splendor of the glory of the Lord face to face and eye to eye.[193] They saw the divine manifestation as clearly as one sees a light streaming through the glass of a lamp.[194] In the one light of God's glory were contained all the ten spheres of divine light.[195] All the ten *s^e^p̄îrôṯ* were revealed as one, forming the head and body of the King.[196]

As in the descriptions of the revelation found in rabbinic texts, in the Zohar the revelation of Torah is depicted both in terms of sight and in terms of sound. God's glory is simultaneously seen as the one light containing all lights and heard as the one Word containing all words, the one Name containing all names. The Ten Words (*s^e^p̄îrôṯ*) are engraved in the Name of the Holy One,[197] which as previously discussed is identified throughout the Zohar with the Torah.[198]

> For the Torah is the Name of the Holy One, blessed be He. As the Name of the Holy One is engraved in the Ten Words (creative utterances) of Creation, so is the whole Torah engraved in the Ten Words (Decalogue), and these Ten Words are the Name of the Holy One, and the whole Torah is thus one Name, the Holy Name of God Himself.[199]

The process of revelation, like the process of creation, is described as unfolding through progressive steps of differentiation. The one Word became Ten Words, and each Word became a voice. Each of the ten voices then divided into seventy voices,[200] a concept that is linked in rabbinic literature to the seventy languages spoken by the nations of the world. In the Zohar's description the langage spoken by these voices encompassed far more than human language, for it was the language of the Creator himself revealing the mysteries of creation to the people of Israel. The Zohar goes beyond the rabbinic interpretation of Exodus 20.15, "And all the people saw the thunderings," interpreting the "thunderings" or voices not simply as words of fire but as configurations of divine light that shone and sparkled before the eyes of the Israelites, illumining the hidden mysteries of creation.[201]

> Said R. Abba: "It is written: 'And all the people saw the thunderings' (Ex. XX,18). Surely it ought to be *heard* the thunderings? We have, however, been taught that the 'voices' were delineated, carved out, as it were, upon the threefold darkness, so that they could be apprehended as something visible, and they saw and heard all those wonderful things out of the darkness, cloud and cloudy darkness; and because they saw that sight they were irradiated with a supernal light, and perceived things beyond the ken of all succeeding generations, and saw face to face (Deut. V,4)." And whence did they derive the power so to see? According to R. Jose, from the light of those voices, for there was not one of them but emitted light which made perceptible all things hidden and veiled, and even all the generrations of men up to the days of King Messiah. Therefore it says: "And all the people saw the voices"; they did actually see them.[202]

The words that issued forth were thus simultaneously heard as audible voices and seen as configurations of divine light. The Zohar reiterates the rabbinic tradition that the words were inscribed on the tablets in the form of black fire on white fire.[203]

Sequential Unfoldment of Complete Knowledge. According to the Zohar the knowledge that the voices revealed encompassed all the hidden mysteries of heaven and earth.[204] The Ten Words that were perceived by the people of Israel at Mount Sinai contained in seed form the entire knowledge of Torah, including not only its concrete expression as laws and commandments, but also its subtle manifestation as the blueprint containing in potential form all of the phenomena of creation.[205]

> R. Eleazar taught that in the Ten Words (Decalogue) all the other commandments were engraved, with all decrees and punishments, all laws concerning purity and impurity, all the branches and roots, all the trees and plants, heaven and earth, seas and oceans—in fact, all things.[206]

The total knowledge of Torah is said to have been revealed in the very first word of the Decalogue: "I"(*'ānōḵî*).[207] The knowledge then progressively unfolded in different size packages. The knowledge of the first word was elaborated in the first five of the Ten Words, which contained the second five Words in potential form.[208]

> We have a dictum that the first five commandments include by implication the other five as well: in other words, in the first five the second five are engraved, five within five.[209]

According to the Zohar when the Ten Words were inscribed on the tablets, the second five Words were included in, and could be seen from within, the first five Words.[210]

The revelation is thus described as sequentially unfolding in stages —from one Word to five Words to Ten Words—each successive stage expressing the total knowledge of creation and evolution that was contained in the previous stage, but in more elaborated form. The five books of the Torah are said to represent a further elaboration of the first five Words of the Decalogue,[211] while the Torah in its totality is a detailed explication of the potentiality of all knowledge contained in the Ten Words together. Not only do the Ten Words together represent the totality of the Torah; each of the Ten Words is in itself a potent seed containing the entire tree of knowledge.

> . . . every word contained all manner of legal implications and derivations, as well as all mysteries and hidden aspects; for each word was indeed like unto a treasure-house, full of all precious things. And though when one Word was uttered it sounded but as itself, yet when it was stamped upon the stone seventy different aspects were revealed in it. . . .[212]

TORAH AND INTERPRETATION

In the previous sections we have been concerned with tracing the history of interpretations of the ontological conceptions of Torah in their progressive unfoldment through the successive layers of pre-rabbinic, rabbinic, and kabbalistic texts. These notions are not merely lifeless concepts embedded in the traditional texts; they are living, activating symbols that have directly influenced Jewish attitudes and practices with respect to the modes of preservation, transmission, and study of the Torah. The detailed laws (*hălaḵôṯ*) and highly developed scribal arts for preparing and preserving the written text of the Torah scroll, together with the other regulations and customs (*minhāgîm*) regarding the ornamentation of the Torah scroll, the public recitation of the Torah, and the proper ways of reverencing the Torah scroll in synagogue worship, point to a living awareness among the Jewish people of the sacred status of the Torah as a holy book that is more than a book, for as the living Word of God it participates in the reality of God himself and must therefore be treated accordingly. In this context study of the Torah, together with the sophisticated hermeneutical methods evolved to understand and clarify the meaning of its every jot and tittle, assumes central importance as a means whereby one fathoms the divine mysteries and, by gradually penetrating to progressively subtler levels of meaning, enters into communion with the divine reality embodied in the book of the Torah.

The rabbinic and kabbalistic conceptions of the role of the Torah in creation and revelation directly inform and shape the methods and principles of interpretation of the text of the Torah. The most fundamental starting point of both rabbinic and kabbalistic hermeneutics is the understanding that the text that is being interpreted is not a human document but a divinely revealed text—it is the Word of God, not the word of man.

On the most obvious level the Torah as the Word of God means that the entire text of the Torah was divinely revealed—indeed dictated—by God to Moses, with Moses simply acting as a scribe and recording the divine words. On a more subtle level the Torah as the Word of God points to the conception that the Torah is the blueprint of creation, its words constituting the subtle impulses of sound that God spoke in order to bring forth the forms of creation. On the subtlest level the Torah as the Word of God means that the living Word of God is itself incarnated in the book of the Torah as a soul within a body, animating the book with secret life.

Rabbinic and kabbalistic hermeneutics, founded on the perspective that the Torah is the Word of God, have evolved various methods and principles of exegesis to unfold the multilayered and ultimately infinite possibilities of meaning contained in the divine Word.

Torah and Interpretation in Rabbinic Texts

Infinite Potentiality of Meaning. As mentioned earlier Abraham Heschel has suggested that there were essentially two distinct approaches to hermeneutics in rabbinic thought: the more pragmatic school of R. Ishmael, which maintained that "the Torah speaks in the language of men,"[213] and the more mystically inclined school of R. Akiba, which found divine significance in every jot and tittle of the Torah.

In suggesting that the Torah was customary human speech, the school of R. Ishmael was not denying the divine status of the Torah as the Word of God. On the contrary, the thirteen hermeneutical principles of R. Ishmael, like the interpretive methods of the school of R. Akiba, proceed from the fundamental assumption that the Torah in its entirety is divine and therefore constitutes a perfect and complete unity in which there are no errors, no contradictions, and no superfluous words or letters.[214] R. Ishmael's awareness of the perfect structure of the Torah is vividly expressed in his admonition, cited earlier, regarding the work of a scribe of the Torah: "If you should perhaps omit a single letter or add a single letter, you would thereby destroy the whole world."[215]

The rabbis of course were aware of the contradictions, redundancies, and anomalies in the text of the Torah, and yet this awareness did not alter their conviction that the Torah constitutes a perfect unity. They used sophisticated hermeneutical principles to demonstrate that if one probes deeply enough into the subtle nuances of each expression he will discover that any contradictions and inconsistencies are only apparent and ultimately serve to illumine some aspect of the divine will that might otherwise go unnoticed.

While the hermeneutical principles of the school of R. Ishmael were based primarily on logical inference, the hermeneutics of the school of R. Akiba focused on textual scrutiny, closely examining every detail of the text for possible divine implications. R. Akiba's hermeneutics took into account every linguistic peculiarity, his interpretations extending not only to the Hebrew particles and letters, but even to the apparently ornamental "tittles" (crowns) attached to certain letters of the Torah.

The school of R. Akiba's emphasis on the significance of every jot and tittle of the Torah is elaborated in a number of Amoraic Midrashim, which emphasize the inexhaustible potentiality of meaning contained in every word and letter. According to one tradition there are seventy modes of expounding the Torah,[216] a notion that is apparently linked to the concept that every word that issued from God's mouth at Mount Sinai was heard in seventy languages. In another Midrash the words of the Torah are compared to a fig tree with an unending supply of figs or to a mother's breast whose flow of milk is inexhaustible, for the more one studies the words of Torah the more meaning (*ta'am*, literally, "relish") one finds in them.[217] According to a tradition ascribed to the Babylonian Amora R. Hamnuna, Solomon uttered three thousand proverbs for every single word of the Torah.[218] The Babylonian Amora R. Ḥisda is said to have declared in the name of another Babylonian Amora, Mar 'Uḳba, that every single stroke of the letters of the Torah requires "mounds of expositions" in order to unfold the full richness and depth of its meaning.[219]

Understood in this context the process of interpretation itself becomes a means of drawing out and unfolding the potentiality of all knowledge contained in seed form in the Written Torah. At the time of revelation at Mount Sinai the vast tree of primordial wisdom, which contained the total knowledge of creation, descended onto earth and became concentrated in the seed expressions of the Written Torah. The sages who interpret and expound the words of the Torah are thus not generating any new knowledge. They are simply transforming potentiality into actuality; they are elaborating and making explicit different aspects of the knowledge that are already implicit in the Written Torah. It is through the Oral Torah that the tree of knowledge contained in the seed expressions of the Written Torah unfolds and bears fruit.

The value of the Oral Torah in drawing out or "extracting" the meaning of the Written Torah is illustrated in a Midrash in Sēḏer 'Ēliyyāhû Zûṭā', which compares God to a king who gave his two servants each a measure of wheat and a bundle of flax. While the foolish servant did nothing at all with the wheat and flax, the wise servant baked bread from the wheat and spun a cloth from the flax. "Now when the Holy One, blessed be He, gave the Torah to Israel, he gave it to them only in the form of wheat, to extract from it fine flour, and flax, to extract from it a garment."[220]

The potentiality of knowledge contained in the Torah is ultimately held to be inexhaustible, for no matter how much one studies and interprets, no matter how much meaning one unfolds, an infinity of meaning remains yet to be fathomed. Even the greatest of the Tannaim whose knowledge of Torah was vast and unsurpassed proclaimed that they had extracted no more than a drop from the unbounded ocean of knowledge.

> R. Eliezer said: If all the seas were ink, and the reeds pens, and the heaven and earth scrolls, and all humankind scribes, they would not be sufficient to write the Torah that I have learned, and I have taken from it no more than a man would take by dipping the point of his pen into the sea. R. Joshua said: If all the seas were ink, and the reeds pens, and the heaven and earth scrolls, and all humankind

> scribes, they would not suffice to write the Torah that I have learned, and I have taken from it no more than a man would take by dipping the point of his pen into the sea. R. Akiba said: It is not possible for me to speak as my teachers spoke, for my teachers did take something from it, while I have taken no more than one who smells a citron—he who smells enjoys it, while the citron is not thereby diminished—or than one who fills a pitcher from a body of water, or one who lights a lamp from another.[221]

Torah and Interpretation in Kabbalistic Texts

Fathoming the Hidden Mysteries of Torah. The Kabbalists, like the rabbinic sages, sought to fathom the infinite potentiality of knowledge contained in the Torah. For the Kabbalists the process of interpretation was not simply a means to understand the words of Torah inscribed on parchment; it was a means to fathom the mysteries of creation and ultimately to commune with the living Word of God that pulsates within the book of Torah as its innermost soul.[222]

The Zohar upholds the rabbinic tradition that there are at least seventy different ways of expounding each word of the Torah,[223] corresponding to the seventy voices that issued forth from each of the Ten Words at Mount Sinai.[224] As discussed earlier, in its depiction of the revelation the Zohar describes these voices as configurations of divine light through which "all things hidden and veiled" were made perceptible to the people of Israel.[225] Similarly, the Zohar proclaims that every word of the Torah radiates light in many directions,[226] through which the mysteries of creation are revealed. Every single word and letter of the Torah contains "profound allusions and holy indications" of the ways and paths of wisdom.[227] All the hidden mysteries of creation that were unfolded to the people at Mount Sinai are still available to those who seek to know the Torah in its full value on all levels—gross and subtle, disclosed and undisclosed.[228]

> The Torah contains all the deepest and most recondite mysteries; all sublime doctrines, both disclosed and undisclosed; all essences both of the higher and the lower grades, of this world and of the world to come are to be found there, but there is no one to fathom its teachings.[229]

The infinite potentiality of meaning contained in the Torah is, according to Joseph Gikatilla, reflected in the way in which the text of the Torah itself is written: The scroll of the Torah is written only with consonants and no vowels in order that the infinite possibilities of meaning inherent in the consonants would not be limited by a particular method of vocalization. In accordance with this thesis, which was generally held by the Kabbalists of his time, Gikatilla concluded that the Torah is read and interpreted in a different manner in each of the worlds—for example, in the world of the *s^e^pîrôṯ*, the world of angels, and the earthly world of human beings—in accordance with the nature of the world and the power of comprehension of its inhabitants.[230]

The notion that the Torah can be read in different ways in accordance with one's power of comprehension appears to be an extension of the rabbinic tradition, mentioned earlier, that the revelation at Mount Sinai was heard by each individual Israelite according to his/her own strength and level of conciousness.[231] The sixteenth-century Kabbalists of Safed, elaborating on this conception, developed the idea that there are 600,000 aspects or modes of expounding the Torah, which correspond to the 600,000 souls who are traditionally said to have been present at Mount Sinai and who, according to the laws of transmigration, are present in every generation of Israel. Moses Cordovero of Safed (d. 1570 C.E.) proclaimed that each of these 600,000 primordial souls has its own special portion of the Torah, "and to none other than he, whose soul springs from thence, will it be given to understand it in this special and individual way that is reserved to him."[232]

Levels of Meaning. In the kabbalistic conception the many lights that shine in every word of Torah involve a hierarchy of different levels of meaning. We discussed earlier the various levels of manifestation of the Torah corresponding to the different *s^e^pîrôṯ* and worlds. According to the most developed form of this conception, as expressed in the school of Israel Sarug, the Torah appears in a different form in each of the four worlds. According to the earlier conception formulated by Joseph Gikatilla, these different levels of manifestation are in actuality different levels of interpretation, for while remaining nonchanging in its essential structure the Torah is read and interpreted differently in each world.

Underlying these various formulations is the fundamental conception that the Torah in its totality forms an organic unity that is composed of different levels, different layers. One of the analogies often used by the Kabbalists to convey the multilayered nature of the Torah is that of a nut, which was said to possess a hard outer shell, two finer inner coverings, and a kernel. In the *Midrash ha-Ne'ĕlām* to the Book of Ruth the image of a nut is used to describe the four basic levels of meaning in the Torah.

> The words of the Torah are likened to a nut. How is this to be understood? Just as a nut has an outer shell and a kernel, each word

> of the Torah contains outward fact *(ma'aseh)*, *midrash*, *haggadah*, and mystery *(sod)*, each of which is deeper in meaning than the preceding.[233]

In this passage *haggadah* apparently refers to some allegorical or tropic form of interpretation, while *midrash* refers to the hermeneutical method of biblical exegesis employed by the Talmudists.[234]

These four levels of meaning received their classical formulation in the writings of Moses de Leon, a Spanish Kabbalist (d. 1305 C.E.) who is generally held by modern scholars to be the author of the Zohar. He used the acronym PaRDeS (lit., "paradise") to refer collectively to the four levels, each consonant denoting one of the levels: (1) *pᵉšāṭ*, the literal meaning, which includes the historical and factual content of the Torah; (2) *dᵉrāšāh*, the hermeneutical meaning, which includes the halakhic and aggadic interpretations and commentaries; (3) *remez*, the allegorical meaning, which comprises the corpus of philosophical truths contained in the Torah; and (4) *sôḏ*, the mystical meaning, which includes the totality of kabbalistic commentaries, in which the words of the Torah are interpreted as references to events in the world of the *sᵉp̄îrôṯ* or to the relationship between the biblical heroes and that world.[235]

The author of the *Tîqqûnîm* calls the Shekhinah, the divine presence conceived as the last of the ten *sᵉp̄îrôṯ*, *pardēs ha-Tôrāh* (paradise of the Torah), for the Shekhinah represents the Torah in the totality of its manifestations, encompassing all of its levels of meaning.[236] The Shekhinah as the *pardēs ha-Tôrāh* is compared to the innermost kernel of a nut that is covered by the four levels of meaning.

> The Shekhinah in exile is called *pardes* [because it is clothed as it were in the four levels of meaning], but itself is the innermost kernel. Accordingly, we also call it a nut, and King Solomon said when he entered this paradise [of mystical speculation]: "I went down into the garden of nuts" (Song of Songs 6:11).[237]

According to the author of the *Tîqqûnê Zohar* and *Ra'ăyā' Mᵉhêmᵉnā'* the outer garment of the Shekhinah is the created Torah, *Tôrāh dᵉ-bᵉrî'āh*, the Torah as it appears to human beings on earth.[238] The literal (*pᵉšāṭ*) level of meaning of the Torah represents the somber garments of the Shekhinah that must be stripped away through insight and replaced by the radiant garments of the mysteries (*sôḏ*) of the Torah.[239]

The author of the main body of the Zohar also speaks of the garments of the Torah, which she dons when descending to earth. According to this conception the narrative stories constitute the outer garments of the Torah, while the commandments constitute its body and the hidden mysteries its soul. The Zohar emphasizes that in order to comprehend the totality of Torah one must penetrate beyond the outer garments, beyond the literal (*p^e^šāṭ*) level of meaning, to its innermost soul, where the hidden mysteries of *sôḏ* are eternally illumined by the light of primordial wisdom. Only the truly wise penetrate to the innermost soul, the innermost kernel of the Torah, where God and Torah are one.

> Rabbi Simeon said: Alas for the man who regards the Torah as a book of mere tales and profane matters. If this were so, we might even today write a Torah dealing in such matters and still more excellent. In regard to earthly things, the kings and princes of the world [in their chronicles?] possess more valuable materials. We could use them as a model for composing a Torah of this kind. But in reality the words of the Torah are higher words and higher mysteries. When even the angels come down into the world [to fulfil a mission] they don the garment of this world, and if they did not, they could not survive in this world and the world could not endure them. And if this is true even of the angels, how much truer it is of the Torah, with which He created them and all the worlds and through which they all subsist. When she descends into the world, how could the world endure it if she did not don earthly garments? The tales of the Torah are only her outward garments. If anyone should suppose that the Torah herself is this garment and nothing else, let him give up the ghost. Such a man will have no share in the world to come. That is why David [Ps. 119:18] said: "Open thou mine eyes, that I may behold wondrous things out of thy Torah," namely, that which is beneath the garment of the Torah. Come and behold: there are garments that everyone sees, and when fools see a man in a garment that seems beautiful to them, they do not look more closely. But more important than the garment is the body, and more important than the body is the soul. So likewise the Torah has a body, which consists of the commandments and ordinances of the Torah, which are called *gufe torah*, "bodies of the Torah." This body is cloaked in garments, which consist of worldly stories. Fools see only the garment, which is the narrative part of the Torah; they know no more and fail to see what is under the garment. Those who know more see not only the garment but also the body that is under the garment. But the truly wise, the servants of the Supreme King, those who stood at the foot of Mount Sinai, look only upon the soul, which is the true foundation of the entire Torah, and one day indeed it will be given them to behold the innermost soul of the Torah.[240]

Interpretation as Appropriation. In the rabbinic and kabbalistic traditions study and interpretation of the Torah are viewed as the primary means of appropriating the Torah. This process of appropriation through interpretation can be understood on two levels: on the exoteric level, as a process of appropriating the meaning of the Torah, and on the esoteric level, as a means through which one ultimately transcends all specific meanings and enters into communion with the divine reality embodied in the book of the Torah. Understood in the second sense, the interpretive experience ultimately culminates in mystical experience.

The Zohar contains a passage that vividly describes the stage-by-stage process through which the hermeneutical experience unfolds until it finally culminates in divine communion with the Torah. The passage depicts the Torah as a living, organic entity who *wants* to reveal her total reality to sincere seekers of wisdom. The Torah draws those who seek her ever closer to herself and progressively reveals the deeper levels of her meaning to them. The passage compares the Torah to a damsel who is hidden in a palace while her lover constantly paces back and forth outside the palace, watching to catch a glimpse of his beloved. Occasionally she reveals her face to him momentarily but then she quickly hides again, ever enflaming him with renewed passion for her.

> . . . the Torah resembles a beautiful and stately damsel, who is hidden in a secluded chamber of her palace and who has a secret lover, unknown to all others. For love of her he keeps passing the gate of her house, looking this way and that in search of her. She knows that her lover haunts the gate of her house. What does she do? She opens the door of her hidden chamber ever so little, and for a moment reveals her face to her lover, but hides it again forthwith. Were anyone with her lover, he would see nothing and perceive nothing. He alone sees it and he is drawn to her with his heart and soul and his whole being, and he knows that for love of him she disclosed herself to him for one moment, aflame with love for him. So is it with the word of the Torah, which reveals herself only to those who love her. The Torah knows that the mystic [*hakim libba*, literally, the wise of heart] haunts the gate of her house. What does she do? From within her hidden palace she discloses her face and beckons to him and returns forthwith to her place and hides. Those who are there see nothing and know nothing, only he alone, and he is drawn to her with his heart and soul and his whole being. Thus the Torah reveals herself and hides, and goes out in love to her lover and arouses love in him.[241]

In the beginning the Torah only discloses her secrets momentarily and then retreats. After some time, however, the lover of Torah is invited to enter the palace and explore its inner chambers. As he becomes more and more familiar with her the Torah gradually unveils the subtler levels of her meaning—from *p^ešāṭ* to *d^erāšāh* to *haggadah* (=*remez*) to *sôḏ*. Finally the Torah reveals herself to him face to face, and he becomes a true "bridegroom of the Torah" and a "master of the house" for all times.

> Come and see: this is the way of the Torah. At first, when she wishes to reveal herself to a man, she gives him a momentary sign. If he understands, well and good; if not, she sends to him and calls him a simpleton. To the messenger she sends to him the Torah says: tell the simpleton to come here that I may speak to him. As it is written [Prov. 9:47]: "Whoso is simple, let him turn in hither, she saith to him that wanteth understanding." When he comes to her, she begins from behind a curtain to speak words in keeping with his understanding, until very slowly insight comes to him, and this is called *derashah*. Then through a light veil she speaks allegorical words [*millin de hida*] and that is what is meant by *haggadah*. Only then, when he has become familiar with her, does she reveal herself to him face to face and speak to him of all her hidden secrets and all her hidden ways, which have been in her heart from the beginning. Such a man is then termed perfect, a "master," that is to say, a "bridegroom of the Torah" in the strictest sense, the master of the house, to whom she discloses all her secrets, concealing nothing.[242]

The above passage describes the hermeneutical process as involving a dynamic, symbiotic relationship between the Torah and the interpreter, in which on the one hand the divine reality of Torah extends herself to the interpreter and progressively reveals her meaning to him, while on the other hand the interpreter is drawn to the Torah and seeks to unfold and fathom the subtleties of her meaning. The more the interpreter understands, the more the Torah reveals. The unfoldment of each new layer of meaning results in an increasing degree of intimacy between the Torah and her interpreter: (1) When the interpreter only understands *p^ešāṭ*, the literal level of meaning (which is not explicitly mentioned in the passage), he remains outside of the palace and only catches occasional glimpses of the Torah; (2) when insight draws he becomes capable of comprehending *d^erāšāh*, the hermeneutical meaning, in which the Torah speaks to him from behind a curtain; (3) when the interpreter penetrates to *haggadah* (=*remez*), the allegorical level of meaning, the Torah speaks to him through a light veil, and (4) finally, when he begins to fathom the hidden mysteries of *sôḏ*, the Torah reveals herself to him face to face, disclosing all of her secrets and concealing nothing. Each stage in the hermeneutical process brings the Torah and interpreter into closer and closer contact until finally they are united for all times as bridegroom and bride.

BEYOND A TEXTUAL DEFINITION OF SCRIPTURE

In the above passage the marriage symbolism that portrays the Torah as the bride of Israel finds its most vivid expression. This symbolism does not simply provide a convenient metaphorical personification of the Torah; it also conveys the essential living reality of the relationship that can exist between human beings and the Torah. In this conception the Torah is not simply a book to be studied; it is a living aspect of God with which one can enter into divine communion. Not only can a person love the Torah; the Torah herself seeks for a person's love and draws him ever closer to her heart. It is this intimate love between the people of Israel and the Torah that has sustained them throughout the ages.

It is only by taking into consideration this living dimension of the Torah that we can come to a full understanding of the nature of scripture in the Jewish case. Although the Jewish people have often been preoccupied with the outer body of the Torah, with preserving and studying the written word of scripture, they have always maintained an awareness of the living soul, the living Word of God, that pulsates within the words and infuses them with eternal life. This awareness is not simply a lifeless concept that was cherished by a few mystics in the Middle Ages. As the above analysis has shown, the notion that the Torah is a living aspect of God is expressed in various forms not only in kabbalistic literature, but also in traditional rabbinic texts. We might be tempted to relegate the rabbinic speculations to mere poetical praises of the Torah if we did not discern underlying these expressions a certain experiential dimension that is still evident today in modern Jewish life and practice.

What is it that has inspired Jews, generation after generation, to spend endless hours day after day poring over every word of the Written and Oral Torah, penetrating into every subtle nuance of meaning? What is it that elevates the study of the Torah to the highest possible status so that it even takes precedence over honoring one's mother and father, earning a living, and the rescue of human life?[243] What is it that has motivated countless Jews to abandon all desire for wealth and power and, faced with persecution and martyrdom, even to risk their lives in order to study the Torah?[244] Although study of the Torah may bring certain rewards in this world and in the world to come, the prevalent view, expressed in both rabbinic and kabbalistic sources as well as by contemporary Jews, is that one studies the Torah *for its own sake.*[245] Study of the Torah is its own reward because such study is a direct means of entering into communion with the divine. Every time a group of Jews comes together to study the Torah, the Shekhinah, God's presence, is said to hover over them. Such an endeavor is viewed by pious Jews not as merely an intellectual enterprise but as a quasi-experiential technique whereby one penetrates into the divine mysteries and, by uncovering layer after layer of meaning, comes closer and closer into contact with the reality of the divine embodied in the book of the Torah.

The Jewish conception of Torah as a living aspect of God challenges us to move beyond a textual definition of scripture as 'sacred writings' or 'holy writ' to a broader definition that can also account for the ontological dimension of scripture as a living, immediate reality in people's lives. The distinction between text/reality points to a further distinction between earthly/divine, in which scripture as concrete text constitutes the earthly dimension of scripture while scripture as living reality points to its divine dimension. However, in the final analysis these distinctions collapse, for it is precisely *as text* that the divine becomes embodied on earth. In the Judaic tradition the living Word of God assumes a concrete form on earth through the medium of the Written Torah, and the Written Torah thereby serves as an intermediary between the human and the divine.

The Islamic tradition's conception of the Qur'ān presents some interesting parallels to the Judaic conception of Torah. The Qur'ān, like the Torah, is described as a cosmic reality that has both earthly and divine dimensions. In its divine dimension the Qur'ān is considered to be preexistent and uncreated and to participate in the reality of God's eternal Word inscribed on the heavenly tablet, "the Mother of the Book" (*Umm al-Kitāb*), or simply "the Book" (*al-Kitāb*). The divine reality of the heavenly Book finds its quintessential expression on earth in the Arabic text of the Qur'ān, which constitutes the embodiment of the eternal Word in history.

If we search for an equivalent conception in the Christian context, we are immediately struck by the inadequacy of attempting to draw a parallel between the Torah and Qur'ān on the one hand and the New Testament on the other. Wilfred Cantwell Smith has pointed out that God's central revelation for Christians is in the person of Christ himself and not in the New Testament, which constitutes a record of that revelation. Smith's proposition that "Qur'ān is to Muslims what Christ is to Christians"[246] can be extended to include the Jewish case: Torah is to Jews what Qur'ān is to Muslims and what Christ is to Christians. This functional parallel of course transcends the boundaries of the genus 'scripture' and rests instead on the common ground of 'revelation' as defined by each tradition. In all three cases this revelation constitutes the meeting point between the divine and earthly planes in which the eternal Word of God breaks through into history and becomes embodied in a concrete form on earth.

Smith has suggested a further analogy between the significance of memorizing the Qur'ān for a Muslim and the significance of the Eucharist for a Christian.

> By Qur'an one means, of course, not the "ink and paper", but the content of the Qur'an, its message, its words, ultimately its meaning. The *ḥafiẓ* (freely, the "memorizer"; but more literally the "apprehender") has in some sense appropriated this to himself, has interiorized it in a way that could conceivably suggest to a Christian some analogy with what happens when the Christian in the Communion Service appropriates to himself the body of Christ Who in his case is the mundane expression of God, the supernatural-natural, the embodiment of eternity in time.[247]

The functional equivalent in the Jewish case would be the study of Torah, which serves as a means for a Jew not only to appropriate the meaning of the Torah, but ultimately to penetrate beyond all localized meanings and partake of the divine reality embodied in the book of the Torah.

What are we, as scholars trained in the Western tradition of historical-critical scholarship, to make of such a notion of scripture? When most scholars think of the Torah they most likely envision the Pentateuch, which they deem to be a compilation of disparate sources dating from different periods. How are we to reconcile such a perspective with that of a pious Jew who perceives the Torah as a living, organic unity from which not even a single letter may be extracted without harming the entire body? The historical-critical scholar proceeds from the assumption that the Torah is a human document and attempts to explain the various contradictions, redundancies, and anomalies within the text by pointing to the fact that a human editor has clumsily patched together different strands of material derived from different schools of thought with decidedly different viewpoints. A Jew grounded in traditional rabbinic hermeneutics, on the other hand, proceeds from the assumption that the Torah is a divine document that constitutes a perfect unity, and he[248] thus explains, by means of sophisticated hermeneutical principles, any apparent contradictions and anomalies in the text as meaningful signposts that can serve to illumine some hidden dimension of meaning that might otherwise remain unnoticed.

Is this just some superstitious, dogmatic belief that the Jew has inherited from his forefathers, or is there something in his own experience that allows him to maintain such claims even in the face of the evidence of historical-critical scholarship? Even if he were to admit that the text of the Torah as we know it today had been tampered with and altered in some way by a human author, would he cease to believe in the divine reality of Torah? We would contend that, even if he were to acknowledge that there were imperfections in the external body of the Torah—that is, in the written text itself—he would still continue to probe its mysteries in order to commune with its innermost soul. Historical-critical scholars might analyze the Pentateuch into various sources and prove to their own satisfaction that it is a human document, and yet no amount of evidence will alter a Jew's faith in the divine reality of Torah if each time he studies the Torah he experiences the fullness of the divine presence.[249]

In refutation of the pious Jew's claim that the Torah is divine, one might point to the fact that not everyone experiences the divine presence when studying the Torah. The pious Jew must therefore be projecting his own faith into the book; the book itself has no divine reality. To such an argument he might respond that the Torah only reveals herself to those who love her. If one approaches the Torah as one does any ordinary book, without proper reverence and respect, then divine wisdom will remain hidden like the damsel in the palace and will not show her face. On the other hand, if one loves the Torah with all his heart and with all his soul and ever watches at her door, she will gradually reveal herself more and more until finally she beckons him to come into her innermost chambers where the eternal light of wisdom ever shines.

> Wisdom is radiant and unfading,
> and she is easily discerned by those who love her,
> and she is found by those who seek her.
> She hastens to make herself known to those who desire her.
> He who rises early to seek her will have no difficulty,
> for he will find her sitting at his gate.
>
> (Wisd. of Sol. 6.12–14)

NOTES

1. The term *Wirkungsgeschichte* is used by Hans-Georg Gadamer to describe the tradition of successive interpretations in the history of a text that implicitly influences each new interpretation of a text. See Hans-Georg Gadamer, *Wahrheit*

und Methode: Grunzüge einer philosophischen Hermeneutik (Tubingen: J.C.B. Mohr [Paul Siebeck], 1972), esp. pp. 283–290. In the present context the term *Wirkungsgeschichte* is being used in a broader sense to include the text's role as scripture in the ongoing life of a particular religious tradition.

2. The Torah is distinguished halakhically from the other two sections of the Hebrew Bible as having a higher degree of sanctity. This distinction is reflected in a number of regulations, such as the stipulation that whereas a Torah scroll may be placed on top of the Nevi'im and Ketuvim, the Nevi'im and Ketuvim may not be placed on top of a Torah scroll (J.T. Meg. 73d). For a discussion of the regulations concerning the classification of the books of the Hebrew Bible, see Sid Z. Leiman, *The Canonization of Hebrew Scripture: The Talmudic and Midrashic Evidence*, Transactions of the Connecticut Academy of Arts and Sciences, vol. 4 (Hamden, CT: Archon Books, 1976), esp. pp. 14–16, 56–72.

3. The theoretical ranking of the scriptures may of course not always be followed in practice. In practice the Talmud in Judaism, the works of *fiqh* in Islam, and the Dharma-Śāstras in Hinduism are the authoritative foundations of *orthopraxis*. Their authority ultimately derives from the primary scripture—Written Torah, Qur'ān, Vedas—but their scope far exceeds it.

4. For a comparative historical analysis of the ontological conceptions of scripture in the Judaic and Brahmanical Hindu traditions, one may refer to Barbara A. Holdrege, "Veda and Torah: Ontological Conceptions of Scripture in the Brahmanical and Judaic Traditions," Ph.D. Dissertation, Harvard University, 1987 (in preparation for publication). For a brief analysis of these conceptions, see Holdrege, "Veda and Torah: The Word as Embodied in Scripture," in *Between Jerusalem and Banaras: Explorations in Comparative Religion*, ed. Hananya Goodman (Albany: State University of New York Press, 1990 – forthcoming).

5. It should be noted, however, that there are a variety of opinions concerning the origin and meaning of the root *yrh*. For a discussion of the scholarly debate one may refer to Michael Fishbane's article "Torah" in *Encyclopedia Miqrā'ît.*

6. According to an alternative tradition recorded in a number of Midrashim, only the first two commandments were spoken directly by God to the people of Israel; the other eight commandments were spoken by him through the mouth of Moses. See, for example, Pirqê de-R. Eliezer §41, discussed on pp. 218–219.

7. For a discussion of relevant rabbinic sources see pp. 220–221.

8. See, for example, Tanḥ. B^{e}-mid̲bar §5, f. 242a.

9. See, for example, Exod. R. XXXIII.1, discussed on pp. 215–216 along with other relevant Midrashim.

10. See, for example, Zohar II.99a–99b, discussed on pp. 234–236.

11. Abraham Joshua Heschel, *Tôrāh min ha-Šāmayîm b^{e}-'Aspaqlaryāh šel ha-Dôrôt̲*, 2 vols. (London and New York: Soncino Press, 1962, 1965).

12. Ephraim E. Urbach, "The Written Law and the Oral Law," chapter 12 of his *The Sages: Their Concepts and Beliefs*, trans. Israel Abrahams (Jerusalem: Magnes Press, Hebrew University, 1975), vol. 1, pp. 286–314; cf. "He Who Spoke and the World Came into Being," chapter 9 of ibid., vol. 1, pp. 184–213.

13. Gershom Scholem, "The Meaning of the Torah in Jewish Mysticism," chapter 2 of his *On the Kabbalah and Its Symbolism*, trans. Ralph Manheim (New York: Schocken Books, 1965), pp. 32–86; idem, "The Name of God and the Linguistic Theory of the Kabbala," *Diogenes* no. 79: 59–80 (Part 1), *Diogenes* no. 80: 164–194 (Part 2). I am particularly indebted to Scholem's groundbreaking essay "The Meaning of the Torah in Jewish Mysticism," which provided the inspiration for my initial inquiries into the ontological conceptions of Torah in 1973. As a result of my own study of the Zohar and other kabbalistic texts, as well of Talmudic and Midrashic sources, I have evolved an interpretive framework that differs substantially from Scholem's categories.

14. Mosheh Idel, "T^{e}p̄îsāt̲ ha-Tôrāh b^{e}-Sip̄rût̲ ha-Hêk̲alôt̲ w^{e}-Gilgûlẹhā b^{e}-Qabbālāh," *Jerusalem Studies in Jewish Thought* I (1981): 23–84. Idel's article, which appeared after the bulk of my own research was already completed, presents a very different and informative perspective on the sources. See also Idel's recent article on kabbalistic hermeneutics, "Infinities of Torah in Kabbalah," in *Midrash and Literature*, eds. Geoffrey H. Hartman and Sanford Budick (New Haven and London: Yale University Press, 1986), pp. 141–157.

15. The ontological conceptions of Torah found in rabbinic texts are of central importance to the present study, since it is the rabbinic tradition that has been responsible for preserving, interpreting, and transmitting the Torah for nearly two thousand years. These conceptions were elaborated and reinterpreted by the medieval kabbalistic tradition, which, as Gershom Scholem has shown in his numerous works on Kabbalah, represents an outgrowth of currents of thought that are evident in certain mystically-oriented rabbinic circles as early as the first century C.E. I have chosen to focus in particular on the cosmogonic speculations of the Zohar, which constitutes the major text of the Kabbalah. This text did not remain confined to the intellectual elite, but was widely circulated for several centuries among the general populace and has perhaps exercised a more profound influence on Jewish thought than any other single book next to the Hebrew Bible and the Talmud.

The strands of the Judaic tradition that are the focus of my analysis do not represent only a single type of orientation or school of thought, but include both exoteric and esoteric, pragmatic and mystical, orientations. The rabbinic tradition generally represents the more exoteric strand, with its emphasis on *halakhah*, which encompasses all aspects of Jewish law—ethical, cultic, civil, and criminal—and on *aggadah*, which includes ethical and theological teachings. There were, however, certain more mystically-oriented circles within the early rabbinic tradition—among whom were such leading Tannaim as R. Joḥanan b. Zakkai (1st c. C.E.) and R. Akiba—that were concerned not only with more traditional matters of *halakhah* and *aggadah*, but also with the "secrets of the Torah" (*sitrê tôrāh, rāzê tôrāh*), in particular with the mysteries of creation (*ma'ăseh bere'šît*, lit., "works of creation") described in Genesis I and the mysteries of the throne-chariot (*ma'ăseh merkābāh*, lit., "works of the chariot") depicted in Ezekiel 1. Medieval kabbalistic speculations represent the most fully developed expression of this esoteric stream within Judaism. The Zohar itself purports to be a rabbinic Midrash derived from the Tanna R. Simeon b. Yoḥai, a famous disciple of R. Akiba, and thus claims a direct line of continuity between its own esoteric teachings and the teachings of those Tannaim who sought to fathom the secrets of the Torah.

16. For a discussion of the treatment of these questions in medieval Jewish philosophy, see Harry Austryn Wolfson, "The Pre-existent Koran and the Pre-existent Law," chapter 4 of his *Repercussions of the Kalam in Jewish Philosophy* (Cambridge and London: Harvard University Press, 1979), pp. 85–113.

17. For a more lengthy discussion of the contributions of these texts to the development of the concept of primordial wisdom/Torah, see Holdrege, "Veda and Torah: Ontological Conceptions of Scripture in the Brahmanical and Judaic Traditions," pp. 126–136.

18. For a discussion of the different stages in the development of the Israelite wisdom tradition, and of the contribution of Proverbs 1–9 to that development, see Gerhard von Rad, *Old Testament Theology*, trans. D.M.G. Stalker (New York and Evanston: Harper and Row, 1962), vol. 1, pp. 418–453, esp. pp. 441–453; Walter Eichrodt, *Theology of the Old Testament*, trans. J.A. Baker (Philadelphia: Westminster Press, 1967), vol. 2, pp. 80–92; James L. Crenshaw, *Old Testament Wisdom: An Introduction* (Atlanta: John Knox Press, 1981), pp. 91–99.

19. R.N. Whybray, *Wisdom in Proverbs: The Concept of Wisdom in Proverbs 1–9* (London: SCM Press Ltd., 1965), p. 106.

20. Martin Hengel, *Judaism and Hellenism: Studies in their Encounter in Palestine during the Early Hellenistic Period* (Philadelphia: Fortress Press, 1974), vol. 1, p. 153, with n. 289.

21. The term *'āmôn* has generally been interpreted by scholars as meaning either "artisan, craftsman" or "nursling," as will be discussed immediately below.

22. This meaning is almost certain for *'āmmān* in Song of Songs 7.2 and also makes reasonable sense for *'āmôn* in Jeremiah 52.15.

23. For the details of the scholarly debate see Gerhard von Rad, *Wisdom in Israel*, trans. James D. Martin (London: SCM Press Ltd., 1972), p. 152; Whybray, *Wisdom in Proverbs*, pp. 101–102; Hengel, *Judaism and Hellenism*, vol. 1, p. 153, with n. 291; R.B.Y. Scott, "Wisdom in Creation: The *'Amon* of Proverbs VIII 30," *Vetus Testamentum* 10 (1960): 213–223.

24. The first theory, which is espoused by R.N. Whybray, among others, maintains that wisdom in Proverbs 8.22–31 is essentially a divine attribute that has been personified to the point of hypostatization. On the basis of his analysis

of certain key words in the passage, Whybray concludes that the origin of this portrayal of wisdom is primarily metaphorical, not mythological, although there may be some evidence of mythological influence. See Whybray, *Wisdom in Proverbs*, pp. 72–104, esp. pp. 98–104.

The second theory, proposed by Gerhard von Rad, suggests that what is personified in Proverbs 8.22–31 is not an attribute of God, but an attribute of the world, immanent in nature. The "primeval order" of the universe was objectified by the Israelites as wisdom, and this objectification, von Rad asserts, "was neither a mythological residue which unconsciously accompanied the idea, nor... was it a free, poetic and didactic use of imagery.... It was much more than simply the objective realization of such a primeval order; it was, rather, a question of crystallizing specific experiences which man had had in his encounter with it. He had experienced it not only as a static organism of order, he felt himself assailed by it, he saw it concerned about man, he experienced it as a bestower of gifts." Von Rad, *Wisdom in Israel*, p. 174. See also pp. 144-176.

The third type of theory maintains that wisdom in Proverbs 8.22–31 derives from an originally independent mythological figure, and therefore its provenance must be sought in the mythologies of ancient Israel and/or its Near Eastern neighbors—Egypt, Mesopotamia, and Canaan. For references see n. 25 below.

Some scholars have proposed theories that combine elements from these three types of interpretation. For example, H. Ringgren has suggested that wisdom is fundamentally the personification of a divine attribute to which mythological characteristics taken from other traditions have been added in order to enhance the vividness of wisdom's portrayal. See Helmer Ringgren, *Word and Wisdom: Studies in the Hypostatization of Divine Qualities and Functions in the Ancient Near East* (Lund: Ohlssoms, 1947), pp. 132f, 148.

25. Some scholars have sought the provenance of personified wisdom in the Egyptian concept of Maat. See, for example, von Rad, *Wisdom in Israel*, p. 153; cf. Ernst Würthwein, "Egyptian Wisdom and the Old Testament," in *Studies in Ancient Israelite Wisdom*, ed. James L. Crenshaw (New York: Ktav Publishing House, Inc., 1976), pp. 117–118; Georg Fohrer, "Sophia," in *Studies in Ancient Israelite Wisdom*, pp. 65–67. Other scholars, such as B. Gemser and H. Ringgren, have attempted to locate a prototype for Proverbs 8.22–31 in Egyptian and Mesopotamian creation hymns. For a summary and critique of these theories see R.N. Whybray, "Proverbs VIII 22–31 and Its Supposed Prototypes," in *Studies in Ancient Israelite Wisdom*, pp. 390–400. For a discussion of possible Canaanite-Phoenician sources of the Israelite figure of wisdom, see W.F. Albright, "Some Canaanite-Phoenician Sources of Hebrew Wisdom," in *Wisdom in Israel and in the Ancient Near East*, eds. M. Noth and D. Winton Thomas, Supplements to Vetus Testamentum, vol. 3 (Leiden: E.J. Brill, 1955), pp. 1–15, esp. pp. 7–8. G. Boström argues that the figure of Astarte-Ištar, the goddess of love, lies behind the personification of wisdom in Proverbs. See Gustav Boström, *Proverbiastudien: Die Weisheit und das fremde Weib in Spr. 1–9* (Lund: C.W.K. Gleerup, 1935), pp. 156–174. However, according to this theory Astarte-Ištar did not serve the positive function

of a prototype, but rather posed as an antithetical figure over against which the Israelite figure of wisdom was established as a rival.

In addition to the above theories, which look for the origins of the figure of personified wisdom in Proverbs in Ancient Near Eastern cultures, some scholars have sought to establish Greek influence as the background for such a concept. See, for example, Eichrodt, *Theology of the Old Testament*, vol. 2, p. 85. However, M. Hengel has cautioned against such theories of Hellenistic influence on Israelite wisdom speculation, since the Greek *sophia* was personified as a divine entity relatively late. See Hengel, *Judaism and Hellenism*, vol. 1, p. 154, with n. 298.

For refutations of each of these various theories that attempt to derive the personified wisdom of Proverbs from Egyptian, Mesopotamian, Canaanite, or Greek sources, see Whybray, *Wisdom in Proverbs*, pp. 82–92; idem, "Proverbs VIII 22–31 and Its Supposed Prototypes," pp. 390–400.

26. As indicated in n. 24, von Rad has emphasized the experiential basis underlying Israel's formulation of personified wisdom, which represents an important dimension that is often ignored by modern scholars.

27. See especially the hymn to preexistent wisdom in chapter 24, which is the center and climax of Ben Sira's work. Although the Wisdom of Ben Sira is the earliest datable work that elaborates on the relationship between wisdom and Torah, the seed expression of such an identification can be located as early as Deuteronomy 4.6 and becomes even more developed in Psalms 111 and 119.97ff. While recognizing that "the complete identification of wisdom with the Torah is an accomplished fact with ben Sirach," von Rad asserts that "this was certainly no absolute innovation, for in the light of this later age's thought this equation has to be regarded as simply a theological conclusion already latent in principle in Prov. I–X and now come to maturity." Von Rad, *Old Testament Theology*, vol. 2, p. 445. George Foot Moore points out that the manner in which Ben Sira introduces this identification "makes the impression that it was a commonplace in his time, when the study of the law and the cultivation of wisdom went hand in hand, and as in his case were united in the same person." George Foot Moore, *Judaism in the First Centuries of the Christian Era, The Age of the Tannaim* (Cambridge: Harvard University Press, 1927), vol. 1, p. 265. Hengel has suggested that perhaps this identification originated in the circle of sages around Simeon the Just, the High Priest who is eulogized in the last section of Ben Sira's work along with the other great "fathers" of the Jewish tradition. Hengel, *Judaism and Hellenism*, vol. 1, pp. 161, 132. See p. 193 regarding the aphorism about the Torah attributed to Simeon the Just. See also n. 44 concerning the disputed identification of Simeon the Just with Simeon I or Simeon II.

Even if the identification of wisdom and Torah did not originate with Ben Sira, he was the first sage to glorify and expand on the notion in majestic hymns that served to link indissolubly cosmic, primordial wisdom with the historical phenomenon of Torah, bringing to light the supra-historical and heavenly dimensions of the "book of the covenant."

28. Hengel describes Aristobulus' doctrine of wisdom and creation as a

fusion of "the original Jewish-Palestinian conception of personified '*ḥokmā*' as the consort of God at the creation of the world with the biblical account of creation in Gen. 1–2.4a . . . with conceptions of Greek philosophical cosmology and epistemology, yet without giving up their specific features." Hengel, *Judaism and Hellenism*, vol. 1, p. 167.

29. Wolfson writes,

> Wisdom, then, is only another word for Logos, and it is used in all the senses of the term Logos. Both these terms mean, in the first place, a property of God, identical with His essence, and, like His essence, eternal. In the second place, they mean a real, incorporeal being, created by God before the creation of the world. Third, . . . Logos means also a Logos immanent in the world, and so, also wisdom . . . is used in that sense. Fourth, both Logos and wisdom are used by him in the sense of the Law of Moses. Finally, Logos is also used by Philo in the sense of one of its constituent ideas, such, for instance, as the idea of mind.

Harry Austryn Wolfson, *Philo: Foundations of Religious Philosophy in Judaism, Christianity, and Islam* (Cambridge: Harvard University Press, 1968), vol. 1, p. 258. See also pp. 253–261.

30. . . . [A] trained architect . . . first sketches in his own mind wellnigh all the parts of the city that is to be wrought out, temples, gymnasia, town-halls, market-places, harbours, docks, streets, walls to be built, dwelling-houses as well as public buildings to be set up. Thus after having received in his own soul, as it were in wax, the figures of these objects severally, he carries about the image of a city which is the creation of his mind. Then by his innate power of memory, he recalls the images of the various parts of this city, and imprints their types yet more distinctly in it: and like a good craftsman he begins to build the city of stones and timber, keeping his eye upon his pattern and making the visible and tangible objects correspond in each case to the incorporeal ideas.

(Op. 17-18)

Similarly, Philo writes, when God began to create the world, "He conceived beforehand the models of its parts, and . . . out of these He constituted and brought to completion a world discernible only by the mind, and then, with that for a pattern, the world which our senses can perceive" (Op. 19). This world of archetypal ideas is the blueprint of creation contained in the mind of the architect, who, according to Philo, is the Logos (wisdom)—the instrument employed by the King of all to bring forth manifest creation (Op. 20, 24-25). The Logos is identified in other passages with the Torah, which as the ideal pattern of creation is "stamped with the seals of nature" and is "the most faithful picture of the world [cosmic] polity" (II Mos. 14, 51; cf. Op. 3).

31. See, for example, Pes. 54a; Ned. 39b; Gen. R. I.4; Gen. R. I.8; Sip̄rê Deut. §37, §309, §317. Proverbs 8.30 is used as a proof text in Gen. R. VIII.2 and Lev. R. XIX.1. These texts will be discussed below.

32. See especially Gen. R. I.1; Tanḥ., ed. Buber, B^{e}rē'šîṯ §5, f. 2b; Tanḥ. B^{e}rē'šîṯ §1, f. 6a-6b; and Targ. Jer. 1, which will be discussed on pp. 194–195.

33. See, for example, Exod. R. XLVII.4; cf. Gen. R. I.4. See also Ḥag. 12a; Ber. 55a; Exod. R. XLVIII.4 regarding the role of wisdom in creation, with no explicit mention of the Torah.

34. Pes. 54a; Ned. 39b.

35. The classification of all Tannaim and Amoraim follows Hermann L. Strack, *Introduction to the Talmud and Midrash* (Philadelphia: Jewish Publication Society of America, 1959). Please note that traditions that are attributed to particular rabbinic sages may in some cases be pseudepigraphal. It is not possible to determine with certainty which traditions stem from which sages.

36. Gen. R. I.4. Note that in contrast to the Talmudic Midrash, this Midrash substitutes the Patriarchs and Israel for the Garden of Eden and Gehenna.

37. Sip̄rê Deut. §37; cf. §309; §317.

38. Gen. R. I.8.

39. Shab. 88b; Zeb. 116a.

40. Gen. R. I.4; Gen. R. I.10; Song of Songs R. V.11.4; cf. Lev. R. XXIII.3.

41. Gen. R. XXVIII.4.

42. Lev. R. XIX.1; Gen. R. VIII.2.

43. See, for example, Gen. R. I.4; Gen. R. I.10; Gen. R. XII.2; Lev. R. XXIII.3; Num. R. XIII.15,16; Song of Songs R. V.11.4.

44. 'Ab. I.2. The date given for Simeon the Just follows Strack, *Introduction to the Talmud and Midrash*, p. 107, who identifies him with the High Priest Simeon I. Other scholars, including Hengel, take Simeon the Just to be Simeon II, who according to Josephus lived at the beginning of the second century B.C.E. See Hengel, *Judaism and Hellenism*, vol. 1, p. 131.

45. Sip̄rê Deut. §48; 'Ab. III.14; cf. Exod. R. XLVII.4.

46. See, for example, Tanḥ. B^{e}rē'šîṯ §1, f. 6a; Tanḥ. P^{e}qûḏê §3.

47. Tanḥ. B^{e}rē'šîṯ §1, f. 6a–6b.

48. A similar conjunction of Genesis 1.1 and Proverbs 8.22 is found in Targum Jeremiah 1, in which *b^{e}rē'šîṯ bārā' Elohim* is interpreted as *b^{e}-ḥoḵmā' bārā'*. Cf. Targ. Neof. 1.

49. Tanḥ., ed. Buber, B^{e}rē'šîṯ §5, f. 2b.

50. Gen. R. I.1.

51. The obvious parallels between R. Hoshaiah's analogy of the Torah as

an architect and blueprint and Philo's use of the same images, in the passage cited in n. 30, have long been recognized by scholars. See Moore, *Judaism*, vol. 1, pp. 267–268; Hengel, *Judaism and Hellenism*, vol. 1, p. 171; Urbach, *The Sages*, vol. 1, pp. 198–200. Other scholars have noted the similarities between R. Hoshaiah's Midrash and Plato's *Timaeus* 27f. See, for example, Henry A. Fischel, "The Transformation of Wisdom in the World of Midrash," in *Aspects of Wisdom in Judaism and Early Christianity*, p. 80. It is interesting to note that Maimonides, in his *Guide to the Perplexed*, wondered about the expression *histakkēl* ("to look at, contemplate"), which corresponds to the expression *hibbîṭ* used in the Midrashim attributed to R. Hoshaiah and R. Judah b. Il'ai, and remarked that this very expression is used by Plato when he states that God contemplates the world of Ideas and thus produces existing beings. Moses Maimonides, *Guide for the Perplexed*, pt. 2, ch. 6. See Urbach, *The Sages*, vol. 1, p. 199, with n. 69.

Scholars are not in agreement concerning the extent to which R. Hoshaiah's depiction of the Torah as the architect and blueprint of creation reflects the doctrine of Platonic Ideas, particularly as expressed in Philo's concept of the Logos. Urbach has argued against such a hasty conclusion and has emphasized the essential differences in the language and imagery used by R. Hoshaiah and Philo to express the analogy of the architect.

> R. Hosha'ia's homily contains not the slightest reference to the world of Ideas or to the location of the Ideas. In the analogy, "the architect does not plan the building in his head, but he makes use of rolls and tablets"—a fact that Philo carefully refrained from mentioning, because it contradicted his purpose in adducing the analogy. Like the architect who looks at the rolls and tablets, so the Holy One, blessed be He, looked in the Torah, but it contains no forms and sketches of temples, gymnasia, markets and harbours, and this Torah is not a concept but the concrete Torah with its precepts and statutes, which are inscribed in letters.

Urbach goes on to assert that the analogy in R. Hoshaiah's Midrash is "only a literary embellishment." See Urbach, *The Sages*, vol. 1, p. 200.

Although Urbach is correct in pointing out the differences between Philo's depiction of the blueprint as a mental plan and Hoshaiah's imagery of "plans and tablets," he goes too far when he attempts to limit R. Hoshaiah's conception of Torah to the concrete book of the Torah. Our analysis has shown that long before the time of R. Hoshaiah, a supra-historical dimension had been superimposed on the historical phenomenon of Torah through its identification with primordial wisdom. This identification is assumed by R. Hoshaiah, and thus his analogy of the architect and blueprint must be viewed against the background of a conception of Torah that encompassed heavenly as well as earthly dimensions. This does not mean to suggest that R. Hoshaiah necessarily appropriated all of the Hellenistic elements that were incorporated into the Jewish conception of Torah/wisdom by the writers of the wisdom books of the Apocrypha and by the Alexandrian Jewish philosophers Aristobulus and Philo. In particular, it is highly unlikely that R. Hoshaiah borrowed directly from Philo in his analogy of the architect. Indeed, he was probably not even aware of Philo's writings. The similarities between their uses of the analogy can better be explained by their access to a common tradition, which intermingled traditional Jewish wisdom speculation with Greek thought categories.

52. Gen. R. XII.14.

53. The idea that the Torah served as the blueprint of creation was elaborated by Isaac Arama, Isaac Abrabanel, Moses Alshekh, Judah Loew b. Bezalel, and other late medieval writers.

54. Cited in Urbach, *The Sages*, vol. 1, pp. 200–201. (no reference given)

55. Ibid., p. 201.

56. See, for example, Gen. R. I.10; T.P. Ḥag. II.5; Sēḏer 'Ēliyyāhû R. §29 (31).

57. See, for example, Men. 29b; Gen. R. XII.10

58. For a brief discussion of the *Sēp̄er Yᵉṣîrāh*, see Gershom Scholem, "The Sefer Yezirah," in his *Kabbalah*, Library of Jewish Knowledge (Jerusalem: Keter Publishing House Jerusalem Ltd., 1974), pp. 23–30; idem, "The Name of God and the Linguistic Theory of the Kabbala," Part I, pp. 72–76. For a translation and commentary on the text, one may refer to David R. Blumenthal, *"Sefer Yetsira*: Text and Commentary," chapter 3 of his *Understanding Jewish Mysticism: A Source Reader. The Merkabah Tradition and the Zoharic Tradition*, The Library of Judaic Learning, ed. Jacob Neusner, vol. 2 (New York: Ktav Publishing House, Inc., 1978), pp. 13–44.

59. Ber. 55a.

60. 'Erub. 13a.

61. Lev. R. XIX.2.

62. 'Erub. 13b; Qid. 30b; Sanh. 19a; Meg. 13b; Gen. R. IV.4; cf. Ber. 57b.

63. Shab. 119b; Gen. R. III.2; Gen. R. IV.6; Gen. R. XII.10.

64. Ber. 57b.

65. Gen. R. III.2; cf. Gen. R. XII.10.

66. 'Ab. V.1; cf. RH 32a; Meg. 21b; Gen. R. XVII.1.

67. Gen. 1.3, 6, 9, 11, 14–15, 20, 24, 26.

68. RH 32a; Meg. 21b. Cf. the alternative interpretation attributed to the Tanna Menaḥem b. R. Jose in Gen. R.XVII.1.

69. See, for example, Gen. R. I.1 and Tanḥ., ed. Buber, Bᵉrē'šîṯ §5, f. 2b, discussed on pp. 194–195.

70. Gen. 1.3, 6, 9, 11, 14–15, 20, 24, 26.

71. See, for example, Zohar II.84b; II.161a; III.91b; III.159a.

72. The nature and meaning of the preexistence of the Torah was discussed by medieval Jewish philosophers. A number of thinkers raised the problems of time and place and ultimately concluded that the Torah's preexistence should be understood metaphorically rather than literally (e.g., Abraham ibn Ezra, Judah b. Barzillai of Barcelona). Other philosophers debated whether the Torah precedes the world in terms of chronology (Hasdai Crescas), ontology (Isaac ibn Latif), or teleology (Judah Halevi, Joseph Albo).

73. *Tîqqûnê Zohar*, Preface, 6b; no. 22, f. 64a.

74. See, for example, the letter of Ezra b. Solomon, published by Gershom Scholem in *Sēp̄er Bialik* (1934), p. 159; Azriel, *Pêrûš hā-'Ăggāḏôṯ*, ed. Tishby (Jerusalem, 1945), p. 77. Noted in Scholem, "The Meaning of the Torah in Jewish Mysticism," p. 41. See also Isaac the Blind's description, discussed on pp. 204–206, of the primordial Torah as stemming from Ḥoḵmāh and Bînāh, the second and third *sᵉp̄îrôṯ*, respectively.

75. See for example, Zohar I.103a–103b; II.42b; II.239a.

76. Zohar I.22b; II.42b.

77. Zohar II.42b.

78. Zohar I.15a.

79. Zohar I.15a; II.239a.

80. Zohar I.2a; I.3b; I.15a; I.18a.

81. Zohar II.20a; I.29a; I.3b; I.21a; III.5b; cf. III.42b–43a.

82. Zohar I.5a; I.47a; I.134a–134b; I.207a; II.161a; III.35b.

83. Zohar I.207a.

84. Zohar III.81a; cf. II.121a.

85. See for example, Zohar II.85a.

86. Zohar I.15a–15b; I.16b; III.65b; II.85a.

87. See, for example, Zohar I.50b.

88. See p. 224.

89. Zohar I.3b; I.15a–15b; I.24b; I.29b; I.30b; I.31b; I.145a; cf. I.56a; I.89a.

90. Zohar I.5a; I.47a; I.134a–134b; I.207a; II.161a; III.35b.

91. Zohar II.20a.

92. Zohar I.74a.

93. Zohar I.50b.

94. Zohar I.50b.

95. Zohar I.50b.

96. Zohar I.16b.

97. Zohar I.16b.

98. Zohar III.5b.

99. Zohar I.29b–30a; cf. I.2a.

100. Zohar I.47b.

101. Zohar I.17b; I.47b; cf. I.71b–72a.

102. Zohar II.238b; II.205b–206a.

103. Zohar II.161b; II.205b.

104. Zohar III.113a; II.161b.

105. Zohar II.200a.

106. Zohar II.205b.

107. "Rabbi Isaac the Old," MS 584/699, Enelow Memorial Collection, Jewish Theological Seminary of New York. Cited in Scholem, "The Meaning of the Torah in Jewish Mysticism," pp. 48–49.

108. Zohar II.85a.

109. See, for example, Zohar II.85a. Cf. Azriel of Gerona's interpretation: "Each single one of God's *sefiroth* is named Torah." Azriel, *Pêrûš hā-'Ăggāḏôṯ*, p. 77. Cited in Scholem, "The Meaning of the Torah in Jewish Mysticism," p. 42, n. 1.

110. The Torah is connected with the Name of God in rabbinic literature as well, although the nature of this connection is not explained. See, for example, Ber. 21a; Shab. 88b; cf. Song of Songs R. I.3.1.

111. Ezra b. Solomon, Commentary on the Talmudic 'Ăggāḏôṯ, Vatican MS Cod. Hebr. 294, f. 34a. Cited in Scholem, "The Meaning of the Torah in Jewish Mysticism," p. 39.

112. See Azriel, *Pêrûš hā-'Ăggāḏôṯ*, p. 76; Jacob b. Sheshet, *Sēp̄er hā-'Ĕmûnāh wᵉ-ha-Biṭṭāḥôn*, ch. 19 (erroneously printed under Naḥmanides' name). Noted in Scholem, "The Meaning of the Torah in Jewish Mysticism," p. 39.

113. *Sēp̄er ha-Ḥayyîm*, MS Parma de Rossi (1390), f. 135a. Noted in

Scholem, "The Name of God and the Linguistic Theory of the Kabbala," pt. 1, p. 78.

114. Zohar II.90b; II.124a; II.87a; II.161b; III.35b, 36a; III.73a; III.80b; III.113a; III.298b.

115. Zohar II.60a; II.90b; II.86a; II.87a.

116. MS Jerusalem, 8° 597, f. 21b. Cited in Scholem, "The Meaning of the Torah in Jewish Mysticism," p. 44. Gikatilla's work is contained in this manuscript under the name of Isaac b. Farḥi or Perahia.

117. Ibid., f. 228b.

118. Menaḥem Recanati, *Ṭa'ămê ha Miṣwôṯ* (Basel, 1581), f. 3a. Cited in Scholem, "The Meaning of the Torah in Jewish Mysticism," p. 44.

119. Joseph Gikatilla, *Ša'ăr[ê] 'Ôrāh* (Offenbach, 1715), f. 2b, 4b; cf. 51a. See Scholem's discussion in "The Name of God and the Linguistic Theory of the Kabbala," pt. 2, pp. 178–179, and in "The Meaning of the Torah in Jewish Mysticism," pp. 42–43.

120. Ibid., f. 2b. Cited in Scholem, "The Meaning of the Torah in Jewish Mysticism," p. 42.

121. Cited in Scholem, "The Meaning of the Torah in Jewish Mysticism," p. 38.

122. MS Leiden, Warner 32, f. 23a. Cited in Scholem, "The Meaning of the Torah in Jewish Mysticism," p. 44.

123. Azriel, *Pêrûš hā-'Ăggāḏôṯ*, p. 37. Cited in Scholem, "The Meaning of the Torah in Jewish Mysticism," p. 45.

124. Moses Cordovero, *Šî'ûr Qômāh* (Warsaw, 1883; reprint, Jerusalem, 1965/66), f. 63b. A number of Kabbalists speculated about the nature and structure of the Torah in different ages—in particular before the fall and in the Messianic Age. For a discussion of these various speculations see Scholem, "The Meaning of the Torah in Jewish Mysticism," pp. 66–86. For a survey of the pre-rabbinic and rabbinic traditions concerning the nature of the Torah in the Messianic Age see W.D. Davies, *Torah in the Messianic Age and/or the Age to Come*, Journal of Biblical Literature Monograph Series, vol. 7 (Philadelphia: Society of Biblical Literature, 1952).

125. This doctrine is first developed in *Lîmmûḏê 'Ăṣîlûṯ* (Munkacs, 1897), f. 3a, 15a–15b, 21d–22a, which is printed under the name of Ḥayyim Vital but in Gershom Scholem's view was undoubtedly written by Israel Sarug. Cf. Menaḥem Azariah Fano, *Šiḇ'îm û-Štayîm Yᵉḏî'ôṯ* (Lvov, 1867); Naphtali Bacharach, *'Ēmeq ha-Meleḵ* (Amsterdam, 1648; reprint, 1972/73), ch.1, sects. 1-61, esp. sect. 4; Moses b. Menaḥem Graf de Prague, *Wa-Yaqhēl Mošeh* (Dessau, 1699), f. 1-10. Cf. Scholem's discussion in "The Name of God and the Linguistic Theory of the

Kabbala," pt. 2, pp. 181–182, and in "The Meaning of the Torah in Jewish Mysticism," pp. 73–74.

126. Zohar II.161a.

127. Zohar I.5a.

128. Zohar I.134a.

129. Zohar I.207a; cf. III.152a; II.161a.

130. Zohar III.35b; cf. III.69b; I.134b.

131. Zohar I.134b; cf. I.186b. The correspondence between the Torah, the human body, and the universe is also recognized in rabbinic literature and is expressed in the concept that, of the 613 commandments (*miṣwôṯ*) of the Torah, the 365 negative precepts correspond to the number of the days in a year, while the 248 positive precepts correspond to the number of members (joints, or bones, covered with flesh and sinews, excluding the teeth) in the human body. See Mak. 23b; cf. Lev. R. XII.3; Zohar II.25a.

132. Shab. 88b; cf. Zeb. 116a.

133. Shab. 88b–89a.

134. Exod. R. XII.3; cf. Men. 29b; Num. R. XIX.7.

135. Sip̄rê Deut. §306.

136. Exod. R. XLVII.5.

137. Pes. R. §20, f. 95a; cf. Ber. 25b.

138. Exod. R. XXXIII.1. Cf. Pes. R. §20, f. 95a, and Exod. R. XXIX.4, in which the giving of the Torah is similarly depicted as a king giving his daughter away in marriage. Pirqê de-R. Eliezer §41 presents a slight variation on this theme, depicting Israel as the son of God who is wed to the bride Torah.

139. PRE §41. In another passage of the same chapter, Israel, the son of God, is depicted as the bridegroom to whom the Torah is wed as a bride. Pirqê de-R. Eliezer thus presents both versions of the marriage symbolism.

140. See, for example, Tanḥ. Bᵉ-miḏbar 5, f. 242a.

141. See pp. 218–219 for a discussion of an alternative tradition in which only the first two commandments are said to have been spoken directly by God to Israel.

142. Num. R. XIII.15, 16.

143. Cf. Gen. R. IV.2.

144. Pes. R. §21, f. 108a–108b.

145. Mek., eds. Horovitz-Rabin, Ba-ḥōḏeš §1, p. 205; §5, p. 222; Mek., ed. Lauterbach, Ba-ḥōḏeš §1, vol. 2, p. 198; §5, vol. 2, pp. 236–237; Num. R. XIX.26; Num. R. I.7; Pes. K. 107a.

146. Mek., ed. Lauterbach, Ba-ḥōḏeš §1, vol. 2, p. 198; cf. Mek., eds. Horovitz-Rabin, Ba-ḥōḏeš §1, p. 205.

147. See, for example, Zeb. 116a; Exod. R. V.9.

148. Exod. R. XXIX.9.

149. Exod. R. XXIX.9; cf. PRE §41.

150. Exod. R. V.9; cf. Zeb. 116a.

151. Exod. R. V.9. An alternative tradition, also ascribed to R. Joḥanan, says that the one voice split into seven voices, which then divided into seventy languages. See Exod. R. XXVIII.6; Tanḥ. Yiṯrô §11, f. 124b. Seven voices are mentioned in Psalm 29. The tradition of seventy languages is ultimately attributed in a Talmudic Midrash to the school of R. Ishmael, which is said to have declared that "every single word that went forth from the mouth of the Holy One, blessed be He, divided into seventy languages" (Shab. 88b).

152. Exod. R. V.9.

153. Exod. R. XXIX.4; cf. Exod. R. XXIX.9.

154. PRE §41.

155. PRE §41.

156. Exod. R. V.9; Exod. R. XXIX.1; Exod. R. XXXIV.1.

157. Exod. R. V.9.

158. Exod. R. XXVIII.6; Exod. R. XXIX.1.

159. Exod. R. V.9; Song of Songs R. I.2.3.

160. Exod. R. XXIX.4; cf. Exod. R. XLI.3.

161. Pes. R. §20, f. 98b.

162. Mek., ed. Lauterbach, Ba-ḥōḏeš §9, vol. 2, p. 266; cf. Mek., eds. Horovitz-Rabin, Ba-ḥōḏeš §9, p. 235. The Torah is said to have been given in fire in a number of Midrashim. See, for example, Lev. R. XVI.4; T.P. Sheq. VI.1, f. 49d; Num. R. I.7; Mek., eds. Horovitz-Rabin, Ba-ḥōḏeš §4, p. 215; Mek., ed. Lauterbach, Ba-ḥōḏeš §4, vol. 2, pp. 220–221.

163. T.P. Sheq. VI.1, f. 49d, et al. This tradition formed the basis of a number of important kabbalistic speculations. Naḥmanides' interpretation has been cited above on pp. 208–209. Isaac the Blind's speculations on this Aggadah will be discussed below.

164. Mek., eds. Horovitz-Rabin, Ba-ḥōḏeš §5, p. 221; Mek., ed. Lauterbach, Ba-ḥōḏeš §5, vol. 2, pp. 234–235; Sip̄rê Deut. §343; cf. AZ 2b; Exod. R. XXVII.9; Num. R. XIV .10; Lam. R. III.1.1.

165. Mek., eds. Horovitz-Rabin, Ba-ḥōḏeš §5, p. 221; Mek., ed. Lauterbach, Ba-ḥōḏeš §5, vol. 2, pp. 234–235; Sip̄rê Deut. §343; cf. AZ 2b; Lam. R. III.1.1.

166. Num. R. XIV.10; Exod. R. XLVII.3.

167. Shab. 88a; AZ 3a; AZ 5a; Exod. R. XLVII.4; Gen. R. LXVI.2; Tanḥ. Bᵉrē'šîṯ §1, f. 6b; cf. Deut. R. VIII.5.

168. Shab. 88a. Resh Laḳish thus interprets the verse homiletically: the continuance of morning and evening was dependent on the sixth day, i.e., of Sivan, when Israel was offered the Torah at Mount Sinai.

169. Gen. R. LXVI.2; cf. Lev. R. XXIII.3; Ab. I.2. The fact that heaven and earth could not continue to endure without the Torah is emphasized by the sages with reference to Jeremiah 33.25: "If not for my covenant by day and by night, I would not have appointed the ordinances of heaven and earth." See Pes. 68b; Ned. 32a; AZ 3a; AZ 5a; Exod. R. XLVII.4; cf. Shab. 137b; Shab. 33a.

170. Num. R. XIII.15, 16.

171. Tanḥ., ed. Buber, Kî Ṯiśśā' §17, f. 58b; Exod. R. XLVII.1; Ber. 5a; cf. Tanḥ., ed. Buber, Rᵉ'ēh §1, f. 10a; Midr. Ps. on 78.1, f. 172b.

172. Tanḥ., ed. Buber, Kî Ṯiśśā' §17, f. 58b–59a; Exod. R. XLVII.1; Exod. R. XLVII.3; Tanḥ. Wa-yērā' §5, f. 33a; Tanḥ. Kî Ṯiśśā' §34, f. 164b-165a; Pes. R. §5, f. 14a-14b; Num R. XIV.10; cf. Giṭ. 60b; Tem.14b.

173. Exod. R. XLVII.3; Num. R. XIV.10; Num. R. XIII.15, 16; Song of Songs R. I.3.2; Shab. 31a.

174. PRE §46.

175. Sip̄rā', Bᵉ-ḥuqqōṯay §8, f. 112c; Meg. 19b; Tanḥ., ed. Buber, Kî Ṯiśśā' §17, f. 58b; Exod. R. XLVII.1.

176. Tanḥ., ed. Buber, Kî Ṯiśśā' §17, f. 58; cf. Exod. R. XLVII.1.

177. Ḥag. 3b; cf. Pes. R. §3, f. 8a; Num. R. XIII.15, 16.

178. Tanḥ. Yiṯrô §11, f. 124a–124b; Exod. R. XXVIII.6; cf. Exod. R. XLII.8.

179. Tanḥ. Yiṯrô §11, f. 124a–124b.

180. Men. 29b.

181. See, for example, Zohar II.200a.

182. "Rabbi Isaac the Old," MS 584/699, Enelow Memorial Collection, Jewish Theological Seminary of New York. Cited in Scholem, "The Meaning of the Torah in Jewish Mysticism," p.49.

183. Ibid.

184. Scholem, "The Meaning of the Torah in Jewish Mysticism," p. 50.

185. Zohar I.24b; I.185a; I.207a; II.161b; II.200a; III.152a.

186. Zohar III.117a; II.94a.

187. Zohar III.193a; III.91b; I.89a; III.298b; cf. I.134b; I.77a; I.47a.

188. Zohar I.55b–56a.

189. Zohar III.117a.

190. Zohar II.83a–83b.

191. Zohar II.43a; II.93b; II.90b; II.82a.

192. Zohar II.94a.

193. Zohar II.82b; II.94a; II.146a; cf. II.83b.

194. Zohar II.82a.

195. Zohar II.146a.

196. Zohar II.82a.

197. Zohar II.90b; II.86a; cf. II.60a.

198. Zohar II.90b; II.124a; II.87a; II.161b; III.35b, 36a; III.73a; III.80b; III.113a; III.298b.

199. Zohar II.90b.

200. Zohar II.146a; cf. II.83b.

201. Zohar II.146a; II.81a–81b.

202. Zohar II.81a–81b; cf. II.93b–94a.

203. Zohar II.84a; III.154b; cf. II.83b.

204. Zohar II.93b; II.81a–81b; II.83b; cf. I.134b–135a.

205. Zohar II.90b; II.93b; II.81a–81b; II.83b; cf. I.134b–135a.

206. Zohar II.90b.

207. Zohar II.85b.

208. Zohar II.90a–90b; II.84a–84b.

209. Zohar II.90a.

210. Zohar II.84a–84b.

211. Zohar II.90b; cf. II.82a.

212. Zohar II.83b.

213. Ber. 31b, et al.

214. For a brief discussion of the thirteen principles of R. Ishmael and the hermeneutical methods of R. Akiba, see Louis Jacobs, "Hermeneutics," in *Encyclopedia Judaica*. A more detailed description of the hermeneutical principles of R. Ishmael is given in Bernard Rosensweig, "The Hermeneutic Principles and their Application," *Tradition* 13, no. 1 (1972): 49–76. For a general introduction to Midrash and Aggadah, see Barry W. Holtz, "Midrash," in *Back to the Sources: Reading the Classic Jewish Texts*, ed. Barry W. Holtz (New York: Summit Books, 1984), pp. 177–211; James Kugel, "Two Introductions to Midrash," *Prooftexts: A Journal of Jewish Literary History* 3, no. 2 (1983): 131–155; Judah Goldin, "From Text to Interpretation and from Experience to the Interpreted Text," *Prooftexts: A Journal of Jewish Literary History* 3, no. 2 (1983): 157–168; Joseph Heinemann, "The Nature of the Aggadah," in *Midrash and Literature*, pp. 41–55; Judah Goldin, "The Freedom and Restraint of Haggadah," in *Midrash and Literature*, pp. 57–76.

215. 'Erub. 13a.

216. Num. R. XIII.15, 16.

217. 'Erub. 54a–54b.

218. 'Erub. 21b.

219. 'Erub. 21b; cf. Lev. R. XIX.2.

220. Sēḏer 'Ēliyyāhû Z. §2.

221. Song of Songs R. I.3.1.

222. For a discussion of kabbalistic hermeneutics, see Moshe Idel, "Infinities of Torah in Kabbalah," in *Midrash and Literature*, pp. 141–157; Betty Roitman, "Sacred Language and Open Text," in *Midrash and Literature*, pp. 159–175; Joseph Dan, "Midrash and the Dawn of Kabbalah," in *Midrash and Literature*, pp. 127–139.

223. Zohar I.54a; I.47b; cf. II.15b.

224. Zohar II.146a; cf. II.83b.

225. Zohar II.81a–81b; II.146a; cf. II.93b–94a.

226. Zohar III.202a.

227. Zohar II.59b; I.145b; I.135a; II.12a; III.202a.

228. Zohar I.134b–135a; III.73a; II.230b; III.159a.

229. Zohar I.134b–135a.

230. Joseph Gikatilla, *Šaʿărê Ṣeḏeq*. See the conclusion of this work published in E. Gottlieb, *Tarbiz* 39 (1970): 382–383. See also Scholem's discussion in "The Name of God and the Linguistic Theory of the Kabbala," pt. 2, pp. 179–180.

231. See p. 219.

232. Moses Cordovero, *Dᵉrîšôṯ-ʿInyānê Malʾāḵîm*, ed. R. Margaliot (Jerusalem, 1945), p. 70. Cited in Scholem, "The Meaning of the Torah in Jewish Mysticism," p. 65.

233. *Zohar Ḥaḏāš* 83a. Cited in Scholem, "The Meaning of the Torah in Jewish Mysticism," p. 54.

234. Scholem, "The Meaning of the Torah in Jewish Mysticism," p. 54.

235. For a discussion of the historical development of the kabbalistic conception of the fourfold meaning of the Torah as well as of the historical antecedents of this notion in Philo, Christian and Islamic hermeneutics, and Jewish philosophy, see Scholem, "The Meaning of the Torah in Jewish Mysticism," pp. 50–62.

236. *Zohar Ḥaḏāš* (*Tîqqûnîm* section) 102d.

237. *Tîqqûnê Zohar*, no. 24, f. 68a–68b. Cited in Scholem, "The Meaning of the Torah in Jewish Mysticism," pp. 58–59.

238. Zohar I.23a–23b (*Tîqqûnê Zohar*). See pp. 199–200 regarding the distinction made in the *Tîqqûnê Zohar* between *Tôrāh dᵉ-bᵉrîʾāh* and *Tôrāh dᵉ-ʾăṣîlûṯ*.

239. See, for example, *Rāʿăyā' Mehêmnā'* III.215b. Cited in Scholem, "The Meaning of the Torah in Jewish Mysticism," p. 67.

240. Zohar III.152a. Cited in Scholem, "The Meaning of the Torah in Jewish Mysticism," pp. 63–64. Cf. Zohar III.202a, in which the different levels of meaning in the Torah are compared to the different parts of a tree.

241. Zohar II.99a. Cited in Scholem, "The Meaning of the Torah in Jewish Mysticism," p. 55.

242. Zohar II.99a–99b. Cited in Scholem, "The Meaning of the Torah in Jewish Mysticism," pp. 55–56.

243. See, for example, Meg. 16b; Pe'ah I.1.

244. See Ber. 61b for the paradigmatic story of the martyrdom of R. Akiba. See also Ber. 63b, which declares that "the words of the Torah endure only with him who would suffer death on its account."

245. 'Ab. VI.1; Sip̄rê Deut. §48; Ber. 17a; Ned. 62a; Pes. 50b, et al.

246. See Wilfred Cantwell Smith, "Scripture as Form and Concept: Their Emergence for the Western World" in this volume, pp. 29–57. See also Smith's article "Some Similarities and Differences between Christianity and Islam: An Essay in Comparative Religion" in *The World of Islam: Studies in Honour of Philip K. Hitti*, ed. James Kritzeck and R. Bayly Winder (London: Macmillan; New York: St. Martin's Press, 1959), pp. 47–59.

247. Smith, "Some Similarities and Differences between Christianity and Islam," p. 57.

248. I have used male pronouns deliberately in this section, since the rabbinic custodians of the Torah to whom I refer have been part of an exclusively male tradition. It is only in recent times that women, particularly in Reform Judaism, have begun to assume a more active role in the study of Torah.

249. A number of eminent Biblical scholars have emphasized that the Bible simultaneously has both human and divine dimensions in which its sacred status as the Word of God is ever preserved. For example, Rudolph Bultmann insists that while the Bible should be approached like any historical document, using the tools of historical-critical scholarship, at the same time it must be set apart from other historical documents in that "it claims from the outset to be God's word." "It remains his sovereign word, which we shall never master and which can only be believed as an ever-living miracle, spoken by God, and constantly renewed." See Rudolph Bultmann, "How Does God Speak to Us through the Bible?" in *Existence and Faith*, ed. Schubert Ogden (New York: Meridian Books, 1960), pp. 166–170.

TRANSLATION AND TRANSLITERATION OF HEBREW AND ARAMAIC

The translations of Hebrew passages from biblical and rabbinic texts are my own. The translations of Aramaic passages from the Zohar are cited from the translation by Harry Sperling and Maurice Simon, *The Zohar*, 5 vols. (London: Soncino Press, 1931–1934), unless otherwise indicated. With respect to the translations of passages from other medieval kabbalistic texts, I have cited Gershom Scholem's translation if the source was originally cited in his essay "The Meaning of the Torah in Jewish Mysticism," chapter 2 of his *On the Kabbalah and Its Symbolism*, trans. Ralph Manheim (New York: Schocken Books, 1965). Even in those cases in which I have not given my own translation, I have consulted the original Hebrew or Aramaic source, with the exception of a few Hebrew manuscripts that were not available to me. For editions of Hebrew and Aramaic texts cited and consulted, please refer to "Hebrew and Aramaic Editions."

The transliteration of Hebrew terms and book titles generally follows the scientific system adopted by the *Journal of Biblical Literature*, with two exceptions: (1) spirantized *b^{e}ḡaḏk^{e}p̄aṯ* letters have been marked, and (2) a hyphen has been inserted after the definite article *ha-* (with consequent loss of doubling); the prepositions *b^{e}-*, *l^{e}-*, and k^{e}-; and the conjunction *w^{e}-*, in order to facilitate reading by the nonspecialist.

In the case of well-known Hebrew terms (e.g., Shekhinah, Kabbalah) and texts (e.g., Torah, Mishnah, Talmud) the common conventional spelling has been retained. The rendering of names of rabbis (e.g., Akiba, Joḥanan) and kabbalistic scholars (e.g., Azriel of Gerona, Moses Cordovero) also follows conventional usage wherever possible, although it is sometimes difficult to determine what constitutes the most common convention with respect to proper names.

ABBREVIATIONS

Tractates of the Mishnah, Palestinian Talmud, or Babylonian Talmud

’Ab.	’Āḇôṯ
AZ	‘Ăḇôḏāh Zārāh
Ber.	B^{e}rāḵôṯ
‘Erub.	‘Êrûḇîn
Giṭ.	Giṭṭîn
Ḥag.	Ḥăḡîḡāh
Mak.	Makkôṯ
Meg.	M^{e}ḡillāh
Men.	M^{e}nāḥôṯ
Ned.	N^{e}ḏārîm
Pes.	P^{e}sāḥîm
Qid.	Qîddûšîn
RH	Ro’š ha-Šānāh
Sanh.	Sanheḏrîn
Shab.	Šabbāṯ
Sheq.	Š^{e}qālîm
Tem.	T^{e}mûrāh
Zeb.	Z^{e}bāḥîm

References to the Palestinian Talmud are prefixed by T.P.

Other Texts

Deut. R.	Deuteronomy Rabbāh
Exod. R.	Exodus Rabbāh
Gen. R.	Genesis Rabbāh
Lam. R.	Lamentations Rabbāh

Lev. R.	Leviticus Rabbāh
Mek.	M[e]k̲îltā' de-R. Ishmael
Midr. Ps.	Midrash Psalms (Midrash T[e]hillîm)
Mos.	Moses (Philo)
Num. R.	Numbers Rabbāh
Op.	Opificio Mundi (Philo)
Pes. K.	P[e]sîqtā' de-Rab Kahana
Pes. R.	P[e]sîqtā' Rabbāt̲î
PRE	Pirqê de-R. Eliezer
Sēd̲er 'Ēliyyāhû R.	Sēd̲er 'Ēliyyāhû Rabbāh
Sēd̲er 'Ēliyyāhû Z.	Sēd̲er 'Ēliyyāhû Zûṭā'
Sip̄rê Deut.	Sip̄rê Deuteronomy
Song of Songs R.	Song of Songs Rabbāh
Tanḥ.	Tanḥûmā'
Targ. Jer.	Targûm Jeremiah
Wisd. of Sol.	Wisdom of Solomon

HEBREW AND ARAMAIC EDITIONS

Bible

Hebrew Bible, ed. R. Kittel (Stuttgart, 1966–1967).

Rabbinic Texts

Babylonian Talmud, ed. I. Epstein (London, 1960–).

Deuteronomy Rabbāh, ed. Rom (Vilna, 1887); ed. S. Lieberman (Jerusalem, 1940).

Exodus Rabbāh, ed. Rom (Vilna, 1887).

Genesis Rabbāh, ed. Theodor-Albeck (Berlin, 1903-1929).

Lamentations Rabbāh, ed. S. Buber (1899).

Leviticus Rabbāh, ed. M. Margulies (Jerusalem, 1953-1960).

M[e]k̲îltā' d[e]-R. Ishmael, eds. H.S. Horovitz and I.A. Rabin (Frankfurt, 1928–1931); ed. J.Z. Lauterbach (Philadelphia, 1933-1935).

Midrash Rabbāh, ed. I. Epstein (Tel Aviv, 1956–1963).

Midrash T[e]hillîm, ed. S. Buber (Vilna, 1891).

Numbers Rabbāh, ed. Rom (Vilna, 1887).

Palestinian Talmud, ed. Krotoschin (1866).

Pesîqtā' de-Rab Kahana, ed. S. Buber (Lyck, 1868); ed. B. Mandelbaum (New York, 1962).

Pesîqtā' Rabbāṯî, ed. M. Friedmann (Vienna, 1880).

Pirqê de-R. Eliezer (Warsaw, 1879).

Sēḏer 'Ēliyyāhû Rabbāh, ed. M. Friedmann (Vienna, 1902).

Sēḏer 'Ēliyyāhû Zûṭā', ed. M. Friedmann (Vienna, 1904).

Sip̄rā', eds. I.H. Weiss and J. Schlossberg (Vienna, 1862).

Sip̄rê Deuteronomy, ed. M. Friedmann (Vienna, 1864); ed. L. Finkelstein (Berlin, 1939).

Song of Songs Rabbāh, ed. Rom (Vilna, 1887).

Tanḥûmā', ed. Stettin (1865); ed. S. Buber (Vilna, 1885).

Kabbalistic Texts

Azriel b. Menaḥem, *Pêrûš hā-'Ăggāḏôṯ*, ed. Tishby (Jerusalem, 1945).

Bacharach, Naphtali, *'Ēmeq ha-Meleḵ*, (Amsterdam, 1648; reprint, 1972/73).

Cordovero, Moses, *Derîšôṯ be-'Inyānê Mal'āḵîm*, ed. R. Margaliot (Jerusalem, 1945).

————, *Šî'ûr Qômāh* (Warsaw, 1883; reprint, Jerusalem, 1965/66).

Fano, Menaḥem Azariah, *Šiḇ'îm û-Štayîm Yeḏî'ôṯ* (Lvov, 1867).

Gikatilla, Joseph, *Ša'ăr[ê] 'Ôrāh* (Offenbach, 1715).

Naḥmanides, *Be'ûr 'al ha-Tôrāh* (1805).

Recanati, Menaḥem, *Ṭa'ămê ha-Miṣwôṯ* (Basel, 1581).

Sarug, Israel, *Lîmmûḏê 'Ăṣîlûṯ* (Munkacs, 1897) [ascribed erroneously to Ḥayyim Vital].

Sēp̄er Yeṣîrāh (Jerusalem, 1964).

Tîqqûnê Zohar, ed. R. Margaliot (Jersualem, 1948, 1978).

Zohar, ed. R. Margaliot (Jerusalem, 1964.

Zohar Ḥāḏāš, ed. R. Margaliot (Jerusalem, 1953, 1978).

Contributors

THOMAS B. COBURN received his Ph.D. in Comparative Religion from Harvard University in 1977. He has taught at St. Lawrence University since 1974, where he has chaired the Department of Religious Studies and Classical Languages and served as Associate and Acting Dean of the College. He is the author of *Devi-Mahatmya: The Crystallization of the Goddess Tradition* (1986), as well as numerous articles.

BARBARA A. HOLDREGE received her Ph.D. in Comparative Religion from Harvard University in 1987. In that year she assumed her present post as Assistant Professor of Religious Studies at the University of California at Santa Barbara. Her dissertation is a comparative study of the cosmological conceptions of Veda in the Hindu tradition and Torah in the Judaic tradition.

KENDALL W. FOLKERT received his Ph.D. in Comparative Religion from Harvard University in 1975. He taught at Central Michigan University from 1974 until his death in 1985, and was Chair of the Department of Religion, Chair of the Academic Senate, and President of the Association of Michigan Collegiate Faculties. He is the author of numerous articles on the Jaina community in India, a subject on which he was one of the leading North American authorities. At the time of his death he was engaged in pioneering field research on a community of wandering Jain ascetics under the sponsorship of the National Endowment for the Humanities.

WILLIAM A. GRAHAM received his Ph.D. in Comparative Religion from Harvard University in 1973. He has taught at Harvard University in the field of Islamic Religion since 1973, and is now Professor of the Comparative History of Religion and Near Eastern Languages and Civilizations. He is the author of *Divine Word and Prophetic Word in Early Islam* (1977) and *Beyond the Written Word: Oral Aspects of Scripture in the History of Religion* (1987), as well as numerous articles.

MIRIAM LEVERING received her Ph.D. in Comparative Religion from Harvard University in 1978. She has taught at Bates and Oberlin

Colleges, and is currently Associate Professor of Religious Studies and member of the Asian Studies Committee at the University of Tennessee in Knoxville. In 1979-80 she did field work in a Chinese Buddhist convent in Taiwan under an ACLS-Mellon grant. She is the author of numerous articles on Chinese Buddhism and native Chinese religions and philosophies, as well as *Literati Buddhism in Sung China: The Teachings of Ta-hui Tsung-kao* (forthcoming). Currently she is at work on a study of the practice of the daily office in Chinese Buddhism since 1600 as a reflection of the Chinese construction of Buddhism.

WILFRED CANTWELL SMITH is professor Emeritus of the Comparative History of Religion, and former Chair of the Committee on the Study of Religion, at Harvard University. He is the author of *On Understanding Islam* (1981), *Towards a World Theology* (1981), *Faith and Belief* (1979), *Belief and History* (1977), *Religious Diversity* (1976, 1982), *Questions of Religious Truth* (1967), *Modernization of a Traditional Society* (1965), *The Meaning and End of Religion* (1963, 1965, 1978), *The Faith of Other Men* (1962, 1963, 1967, 1972), *Islam in Modern History* (1957, 1958, 1959, 1977), *Modern Islam in India* (1943, 1947, 1964, 1972, 1979), and numerous articles on Islamics and on Comparative Religion. Translations of his writings have appeared in French, German, Swedish, Arabic, Turkish, Urdu, Indonesian, and Japanese. Among numerous honors, he has been president of a number of learned societies, including the Middle East Association of North America, the Canadian Theological Society, and the American Academy of Religion, and is a Fellow of the Royal Society of Canada and of the American Academy of Arts and Sciences.

Index

A

Abba, b. Kahana, 192
Abhidharma, 95n26
Abhidharmakośa, 93n5
Abulafia, Abraham, 187
Adad, 41
Adhiṣṭhāna, 64, 94n17
Ādi Granth (Granth Ṣāhīb), 8, 32, 52n28, 134
Aeschylus, 40
Aggadah, 183, 187, 208, 221, 232
Ahabah b. R. Ze'ira, 192
Ahura Mazda, 44
Aitareya Āraṇyaka, 104, 139, 160n67
Aiyer, Parameswara, 120
Akiba, 186, 193, 220, 222, 228, 230, 241n15, 257n244
Akkadian language, 54n41
Alcuin, 51n23
Alexandria
  role in scripturalizing process, 37, 40–41
Allah Upaniṣad, 112
Alphabet, 43, 143. *See:* Hebrew alphabet
Ambrose, 146–147
Amitābha, 67, 71, 78, 96n32
Antithesis, 38
Apocrypha, 51n21, 52n24, 186, 189–191, 247n51
Apotelesmatika, 53n35
Aquila, 189
Arabic language, 33, 237
Aramaic language, 51n21
Āraṇyakas, 104, 106, 139, 160n67
Arhats, 61
Aristobulus, 189–192, 244n28, 247n5
Aristotle, 40, 145
Aśokan inscriptions, 159n62
Ashurbanipal's library, 54n41
Assyria, 44, 56n60
Astarte-Ištar
  prototype of Israelite wisdom figure, 243–244n25
Astrology, 38–39
Aśvaghoṣa, 90
Athens, 40–41
Augustine, 146, 149
Avalokiteśvara (Kuan-yin), 77, 80–81, 84–85
Avataṃsaka Sūtra, 70, 74, 98n39
Avesta, 8, 32, 35, 47n5, 102
Awakening of Faith in the Mahāyāna, 90–91
Azriel b. Menaḥen, 209

B

Babb, Lawrence, 116–117
Babylonia
  role in scripturalizing process, 31, 36, 39, 42, 44
Babylonian Tablets of Destiny, 41
Balogh, Josef, 146–147
Baruch, 189–191
Bauer, Walter, 166n125

Bultmann, Rudolph, 27, 258n249
Bunyan, John, 151

C

Calvin, John, 151
Canaan
  influences on scripturalizing process, 31, 36, 39, 42, 190–191, 243n25
Canon
  "actual canons," 13
  as alternative term for 'scripture,' 4–5, 103, 172–179
  boundedness of, 7–9, 12, 37, 51n24, 105, 121
  Chinese Buddhist, 69, 77, 89–90, 95n26
  Christian, 37–38, 49n15, 50n21, 51nn23–24, 52n27, 149
  of Greek classics, 31–32, 40
  Hindu, 121
  Jewish, 7, 39–41, 51n21, 132
  Manichee, 36
  Muratorian, 51n23
  of Sumerian literature, 54n41
  Theravada Buddhist, 8, 61–62, 93n4, 132, 158n56
  Tibetan Buddhist, 134, 156n33
  Zarathushtrian, 47n5
Carothers, J. C., 144
Cassiodorus, 51n22
Cassirer, Ernst, 136
Cassian, 150, 167n138
Charles The Great, 51n23
Chaytor, H. J., 144, 146
Childs, Brevard, 45
Chinese classics, 9, 43, 46, 64–65, 132, 137, 182
Ching, 64, 132
Christian views of scripture, 3, 7, 23–28, 32–40, 42–43, 52, 103, 105, 141, 148–152, 161, 166, 170–173, 177–179, 181–182, 237–238
  monastic, 149–150, 166n128
  Protestant, 3–5, 10, 12, 16n6, 33–34, 68, 134–135, 150–152, 171–173, 177–178
  See: Bible
Chuang-tzu, 65. *See:* Chinese classics
Classics, 1–2, 13. *See:* Chinese classics; Greek classics
Clay tablets, 42
Codex Amiatinus, 51n22
Computer, 43, 143
Confucian views of scripture, 64, 132, 182. *See:* Chinese classics
Confucius, 64, 96n30
Corpus Hermeticum, 38
Council of Javneh, 39, 54n37
Council of Trent, 51n24
Cuneiform, 41, 43, 56n56
Curtius, Ernst, 133

D

Damasus (Pope), 51n23
Dante, 145
Darah Shikoh, 112
Darius, 44
Darśana, 111, 118, 121
Decalogue. *See:* Ten Commandments
Deuteronomy, 57n63, 244n27
Devī-Māhātmya, 116–117
Dharma (Buddhist), 61–66, 69–71, 75, 78–80, 82, 84–85, 87–90, 94n20, 100n65
  Dharmakāya, 62, 91, 100n60
Dharma (Hindu), 107

Hebrew Bible, 183, 186, 240n2, 241n15. *See:* Torah
Hekalot literature, 186
Hengel, Martin, 244nn25 and 27–28
Hephaestos of Thebes, 38
Hereaclides Ponticus, 40
Heschel, Abraham, 185–187, 228
Hesiod, 40–41
Hieroglyphics, 43, 56n56
Hillel, School of, 195
Hindu Bible, 115. *See: Bhagavad Gītā*
Hindu views of scripture, 7–9, 12, 34–35, 43, 102–122, 124n22, 125n40, 132, 136–142, 148, 162n83, 181–183.
See: Śruti and *smṛti;* Vedas
Ḥisda, 229
Homer, 40–41
Hopkins, Thomas, 109
Horsiesius, 150
Hoshaiah, 194–195, 246n51
Hsüan-tsang, 10
Hua-yen Buddhism, 65
Hua-yen Sūtra, 70, 74, 98n39
Huna, 193

I

Idel, Mosheh, 186, 241n14
Iliad, 40
Illiteracy. *See:* Literacy
Indus seals, 104, 159n62
Instrumentum, 38
Iran
- influences on scripturalizing process, 32–34, 44, 47n5, 49n14

Isaac the Blind of Posquières, 186, 204–205, 221–223
Ishmael, 186, 196, 228, 253n151
Islamic views of scripture. *See:* Muslim views of scripture
Israel
- as bridegroom of Torah, 184–185, 190, 216
- as only nation to accept Torah, 220, 223
- as preexisting creation, 192
- revelation of Torah to, 214, 216–220, 223–226, 229, 231, 240n6
- wisdom tradition of, 190ff, 242n18, 242n24, 243n25, 244nn26–27

Israel Najara, 184
Israel Sarug, 210, 212, 231, 251n125

J

Jacobi, Hermann, 175
Jain scriptures, 12, 174–176, 178–179
Jayadeva, 117
Jerome, 37, 50n21, 149
Jerusalem temple, 43
Jesus Christ, 36–37, 151, 182
- as Christian counterpart of Qur'an, 20, 30–31, 237–238

Jewish views of scripture
- Canaanite influences upon, 42
- Greek influences upon, 32, 40–41
- Hellenistic influences upon, 41, 191–192, 247n51
- kabbalistic, 182–188, 199–214, 222–227, 230–234, 236–237, 251n124
- as oral, 34–35, 38, 49n14, 105, 141, 148
- pre-rabbinic, 186, 188–191, 227
- rabbinic, 137, 182–199, 207, 213–224, 227–231, 234, 236–238, 252n131
- *See:* Torah

N

O

S

T

U

V

W

Y

Z